What People Are Sayin

Faith of a Father describes the soul-search.... ...y questions that my life and all its pain, sorrow, confusion, deliberation, attempts to compromise, decisions, and rejections could conjure up.

—**STEPHANIE AGENTIS,** secretary to the director of curriculum, Colonial Intermediate Unit #20, Easton, Pennsylvania

This is a wonderful narration, written in a delightful conversational style. . . . With every page, I empathized with Frank and saw myself more clearly. By the end of the book, the resolutions to his conflicts of faith were perfect for me as well. I felt closer than ever to God and to Jesus.

—**PEG SHAW,** head of a high school English department

In his book, Frank is writing much more than an autobiography. As an experienced and godly mentor, he's laying out a pathway to inner healing and maturity from a background of dysfunction. His book is a powerful combination of transparency, honesty, integrity, and insight. It is presented with understanding, wisdom, compassion, grace, and spirituality. Frank leaves us with the same strategy, message, and hope expressed by the apostle Paul: "What you have learned and received and heard and seen in me—practice these things, and the God of peace will be with you" (Phil. 4:9 ESV).

—**REV. JOHN AULT ("PASTOR JOHN"),** presiding pastor for New Hope Community Church (formerly Koinonia Church), Potsdam, New York; drug and alcohol addiction consultant; pastor for more than forty years

With gripping honesty, Frank explains the weave of the trauma of his youth and his quest for truth. Faith and the narrative of Christ surface as true, good, and beautiful. Rarely does someone write with such clarity and vulnerability. Tears came to my eyes many times as I read—tears of sorrow and of joy. Readers will be inspired to dive more deeply into their own story and emboldened to wrestle intelligently against fallacious and faithless theologies. Frank's vulnerability is a gift—to his family . . . and his readership.

—**REV. BETH CASE,** pastor for congregational life & care, First Presbyterian Church of Bethlehem, Bethlehem, Pennsylvania

His is a journey that challenges us to live in the tension of the brokenness in our world while embracing the power of resurrection hope. Frank allows us to experience that hope through his deeply personal journey.

—**REV. RUTH F. SANTANA-GRACE,** executive presbyter, Presbytery of Philadelphia, PCUSA

Working in men's ministry, not as a professional but as a lay person, it is often a challenge to drive home to men the core need for a personal, vibrant relationship with Christ. . . . It has been shown in many studies that if one wishes to lead families—children in particular—to faith in Christ, the dad is the way to get there. Men—read Frank's story, find your voice, and share your journey to faith as he has.

—**MIKE BATTINGER,** chartered financial consultant; principal, Andesa Financial Management, Inc., Allentown, Pennsylvania

Frank, *Faith of a Father* is a breath of fresh air in contemporary writing on faith and self-understanding. As I read your story, I found, at least in part, that I was also reading my own. And, as I found my story, I also found insight into who I am and how I think. Thank you for having the courage to write it and share it with us.

—**REV. DR. PHIL ELLMORE,** chief development officer and executive officer of the Stockton College Foundation, Richard Stockton College of New Jersey, Galloway, New Jersey

I generally have an iron-clad rule to not read any "real-life stuff" about suffering, death, or anything too heavy. I can watch the news if I want to be depressed. However, I am extremely glad that I made an exception to read *Faith of a Father*. Frank not only gave my thoughts a voice . . . he made them make sense.

—**KIM MCCALL,** teacher of the deaf and hard of hearing

Faith of a Father is a thoughtful, penetrating memoir of a reflective professional counselor who suffered traumatic childhood abuse and struggled to understand truth and God in a world that did not seem to make sense. Barbehenn skillfully brings us along step-by-step in his honest search for truth, at any cost, that will enable him to make sense of his ongoing pain. Written as a letter to his grown daughter, it illustrates how he comes to peace, joy, and hope at the end. I smiled and wept and marveled at the grace of God in Christ.

—**REV. ALLEN HARRIS,** former Inter-Varsity Christian Fellowship staff member (1968-1978); church consultant; and pastor for thirty-three years

Faith of a Father

A Father's Open Letter to His Daughter

Frank Barbehenn

Hi Al —

I am very grateful for your support, feedback, and endorsement. Thanks. Your brother in Christ,

Frank

Clovercroft Publishing

Published by Clovercroft Publishing, Franklin, Tennessee

Published in association with Larry Carpenter of Christian Book Services, LLC

www.christianbookservices.com

Cover Design by Suzanne Lawing

Interior Design by Scribe Inc.

Editing by Gail Fallen

Cover photo by Amanda Danzinger

Printed in the United States of America

978-1-940262-90-7

ABOUT THE BOOK

Using his thirty-five years in clinical practice, theological expertise, and professional self-analysis, Frank invites you on a totally unique ride. Structured as a father's open letter to his daughter Kristen, Frank's memoir explores his magnetic draw to faith . . . and the spiritual maelstrom that drew him to a profound yet deeply conflicted journey with Jesus Christ.

The highly readable story of Frank's emerging faith in Jesus is a spellbinding dance among various forces in his life. In this most personal, page-turning exposé, he courageously discloses how trauma shaped his life—nearly from the moment of his birth. Beginning in infancy, he was traumatized by an extraordinarily cold, emotionless alcoholic mother. From early childhood on, he was emotionally abused by an angry, disabled father. Later, in midlife, he was twice traumatized by disabilities—disabilities that emerged as a result of his childhood. He reveals utterly intimate details of how his mind was forged through those traumas—driving his unchosen but painstaking quest for spiritual truth. It's the story of how one man found and embraced faith—not only the circumstances that engendered it, but the forces deep inside him that shaped his hypnotic draw to it. In poignant detail, he describes how that faith *really* looks—from the inside out—from deep within his own psyche. And it all culminates in a story Frank never fully shared with his daughter . . . until now . . . in *Faith of a Father*.

Dedicated, with deep gratitude, to my brother Herb, who passed away suddenly within days of my completing this book.

This letter is addressed to my daughter, Kristen, representing all of you who are my children and grandchildren and great grandchildren . . . and beyond. I have done this for the ease of addressing all of you as well as increasing the intimacy between me and you through Kristen.

My brothers, children, grandchildren, Uncle Don and Aunt Betty, schools, stores, locations, and churches, as well as Pastor Ruth Faith, Pastor John and his wife Jane, IVCF staff Allen Harris, Dick and Mary, and Charlie are accurately identified. I do have everyone's permission to identify and include them in my story. However, Uncle Don and Aunt Betty have passed away. Dick has passed away but I have Mary's permission for herself and her support for identifying Dick. Charlie has passed away as well, but I have his wife's blessing to write about him. I also have my atheist friend's permission to include his comments about my beliefs in this letter.

While the stories are true to my recollection, the names of all others have been changed to protect their identity and privacy. All client stories are composites with details altered so that no one can be identified, nor can anyone accurately identify themselves in the stories.

With Special Thanks to
Pastor John, Dick and Mary, and the Koinonia Church;
Al Harris and Inter-Varsity Christian Fellowship; and
Father O'Reilly for their key roles in my spiritual journey

Frank@peakperformancediscipleship.com

Website: www.peakperformancediscipleship.com

Contents

Part 4 | Back to the Future: Wrapping His Royal Robe around My Past

Part 5 | Clutching His Royal Robe

Prelude

It is a cool evening in 2012. Your former bedroom is dark except for some light peeking in from the hallway. As I rock my dear grandson to sleep on the same chair your mother and I rocked you guys, I notice how warm and peaceful his tender body feels against my chest. While I gently hold him and kiss his precious head as he falls asleep, I have brief moments when I tear up in awareness that I never, ever felt such comfort as a little one. Inscrutably, I can feel the contrast between the cold and ever so slight disquiet within me—of the emotionally abandoned toddler in me—in contrast to Dylan's utterly relaxed presence. While being very grateful that our little Dylan is so passionately loved by so many—and you, Kristen, are an incredibly sensitive and caring mom—the toddler in me is momentarily but painfully aware of the difference between what is dear Dylan's place in his childhood universe . . . and what had been mine. Still, I am a fortunate man. I love your mom, you guys, your husband and my daughter-in-law, my grandchildren, and my beloved friends—as well as now having had so many years beyond my fortieth birthday to enjoy all of you . . . years I once thought I would not see. While my life is still so incredibly limited physically, I am grateful that it has been and continues to be so unlimited in its richness of meaning—even meaning in, through, around, and emerging from the nonsense I've been through. That meaning—of which you have been a part—has been how I've learned to seize my days with both joy and hope.

Why I Am Writing You This Long Letter

My Little Girl

It is December 28, 1982. Your mom is anxiously lying on a bed in a large, almost hotel-like suite at St. Luke's Hospital. She is lying on her right side with her back toward me, unable to get comfortable. From the plush leather chair next to her bed, I'm gently massaging the small of her lower back with my right hand. It is quiet as I slowly drift off into my own world, daydreaming back to the births of your brothers . . .

It was August 23, 1978. With balmy breezes and a gorgeous blue sky for our evening together, your mom had just finished a large meal at our church picnic. Now home, she was quietly resting with her head propped up on a couple of sofa pillows and her tired feet up on the arm of our couch. It was now about seven. I glanced over to catch her gently caressing her enlarged abdomen with the tips of her fingers and then staring at her watch. I nervously asked her what was happening and she said she felt these "funny sensations"—like a squeezing. With some trepidation I asked her if these sensations could be contractions. She said she didn't know, which I thought was reasonable given that this was our first child. I then asked her if the sensations were coming and going, and how far apart they were. She said yes, they were coming and going—and did so about every five minutes. A bit panicked when I heard "five minutes," I jumped up exclaiming with great nervous excitement that those sensations really could be contractions—and we needed to call the doctor immediately and hurry to the hospital! We were well prepared—we had her tote bag ready and were well practiced with Lamaze—but we had no idea how much time we actually had from the contractions to birth. But five minutes in between contractions sure made it feel close . . . and coming fast. All we knew was that we were supposed to get to the hospital immediately—and we were both mindful that she had just had a large meal.

*　*　*

That meal hadn't bothered Mom at all. I glanced at the plain circular clock above the wide doorway into the hallway; it was twenty-five after eleven. Paul had just been born. The doctor carefully placed him on Mom's flattened stomach. He was lightly covered in blood from the episiotomy, and the umbilical cord struck me as thick and dense with a kind of blue-purple hue. I don't know what I expected, but I was a bit surprised and fascinated. The doctor handed me scissors to sever the cord, then the nurse carried Paul away to clean him up.

The third shift nurse who had just come on duty was frantic for reasons unknown to us. Perhaps she felt overwhelmed with all the activity as soon as she arrived; I don't know. Mom's blood pressure was high and so the nurse tersely refused to allow us to go to the bonding room to spend time with your brother under the heat shield. "Bonding" was a new concept back then, and Mom and I were looking forward to having those few precious moments with him right after his birth. The doctor stood stately, as if he were a sentry on duty, carefully watching what was going on and calmly telling the nurse that Mom was experiencing transitional hypertension, which meant she had elevated blood pressure due to the strain of the birthing process—and wasn't in danger. He told her there was no problem having us bond for a few minutes. The nurse continued her tasks while ignoring him and wheeled Mom from the delivery room out into the busy hallway where the doctor calmly stood next to us—just observing.

It's an occupational hazard, I know, but I stood there noticing him noticing her while my mind was still back at cutting Paul's umbilical cord. I really had to give those surgical scissors a good squeeze to cut the cord. While super excited with the arrival of my first born, I did find it odd to cut the cord tying son with mother— forever breaking that most primal bond.

When the still frantic nurse crossed the doctor's path again, he asked, "Tough night, tonight?" She said, "Yeah." He told her again that he thought we could now go to the bonding room. The nurse again ignored him. He stood there for a few brief moments, and then asked in a firm and yet calm voice, "Do I have to make this request an order?" I was grateful; I thought we were going to lose our chance to be alone with Paul. This time, without saying a word or looking at the doctor, the nurse wheeled Mom to the special bonding room so we could spend those few precious moments with our newborn son.

As Mom lay on the bed with our little guy in her arms and her face beaming with pride and joy, the nurse grabbed a convex-shaped glass canopy about four feet long and two feet wide, raised up on a stand about four and a half to perhaps five feet off the floor. She carefully shifted it into place over Mom and Paul. This canopy gave off a soft heat to keep both of them warm. We spent our brief time together just touching Paul and noticing whatever we could about him. He did have a lot of dark hair sticking straight up off his head! I've never been one to think babies are cute, but my own son . . . he was cute.

* * *

It was May 30, 1980. Times change; Matt's birth was planned. The doctor proposed arranging the birth ahead of time using a new drug. We thought that'd be neat. The doctor gave Mom Pitocin to induce labor. It was in pill form which meant no control over the strength of contractions once the drug was in her—but we didn't know that at the time; the doctor never mentioned it. There was neither a heat canopy waiting for Matt nor a special delivery room with moveable bright lights shining down on Mom. The atmosphere around the birthing process was now more "relaxed." We were in a small plain room with regular florescent lighting and a window directly behind Mom's bed. A fetal monitor was on her right next to me and a little behind the head of the bed. Instead of standing next to her like I had done with Paul's birth, I had one arm around her neck and the other arm around her thigh, coaching her to breathe and push. The doctor was standing on the other side with his calm and stately manner once again.

Poor Mom. The Pitocin hit, and hit hard. I felt so sorry for her. Mom is tough; I know you know that, Kristen. She's frontier material. And she's like her dad, having incredible common sense and being very hard-working. She'd make a good soldier. Tell her to take the hill, and she'd take it, sacrificing her life if need be. And yet here she was screaming with the pain of birthing Matt, sweating profusely, as if she had been out in the heat of the midday sun for several hours shoveling hard clay dirt.

The doctor wisely directed me to look at the top of Matt's head as it was emerging, and I became excited, saying to Mom, "Hey, I can see the baby's head!" Mom was utterly exhausted but encouraged. She pushed again hard and repeatedly . . . and for a long time; Matt's head was finally birthed. But I had no idea how to react. My baby's scrunched face was a deep purple blue. Paul's hadn't been anything like that; it had been a bit bloodied from the episiotomy, but fresh looking. Matt's face looked like he couldn't breathe, like someone was suffocating him. I was pretty scared, so I stared at the doctor while not saying a word because I didn't want to frighten Mom. He stared right back at me. It seemed like forever for those few moments we read each other's gaze. He caught the panic in my face and I understood his calming look back: Matt was OK. The next moment, however, Mom eagerly leaned over to catch a look at Matt's head, and then, without any hesitation, let out a desperate cry, "Oh my God, what's wrong with my baby?" I understood the panic. The doctor calmly but firmly reassured her, "Your baby's fine. If this were an emergency, I'd be moving very fast to do what needs to be done." With that, Mom threw her head back with a deep sigh of relief to rest for a few moments. Both of us paused to take in his answer.

Matt was born weighing eight pounds, six ounces.

* * *

I'm jarred from my flashbacks by Mom's flailing arms knocking over the half-filled glass of water on the bed stand and her deep groaning with the surprise of sudden, gripping pain. I stop rubbing her back and begin coaching her: hoo, hee, hoo, hee, hoo, hee. She ignores me—acting as if we had never practiced for your arrival.

Fortunately, the doctor walks in. He slowly saunters around the foot of the bed to the other side—and slowly was indeed his style for all three of you kids. It seemed to be his metronome to pace himself and perhaps to calm his patients. It worked for Mom.

The doctor commands Mom, "Andrea, I want you to use your breathing technique now, and Frank can coach you." Unlike with

Matt, I am not bracing Mom from head to thigh. In fact, you come out easy, though I doubt Mom would use the word "easy." The doctor is so relaxed he actually lets you plop onto the bed with Mom's water pouring right into your mouth. You spontaneously breathe in the fluid, so they whisk you away to clear your lungs. My little girl is born.

Later, as I hold you in my arms, I wonder, how will my little girl's voice sound?

Legacy

It seems like just yesterday, Kid.

Like most fathers, I've had dreams and hopes for my life. Tragically, life has crushed several dreams I've had, dreams that once captivated my imagination. They will never be. Having one's hopes dashed is the way life often goes—although that truth is of little comfort. But I'm not done with my life. I have other dreams, though I am keenly aware that being deep in midlife now, I am much closer to the end, so we'll see. To my great satisfaction, I have already fulfilled certain dreams; having you three was among them. The bottom line like with most good parents was that Mom and I wanted healthy children, though, without consciously knowing why at the time, I really wanted two sons and a daughter. While sadly we lost one child by miscarriage, we were privileged to get you guys. As it is for all of us, you didn't pick the time in history, ethnicity, race, country, or family into which to be birthed. God and nature put you with us and us with you to make a life together. And so we did.

As I now reflect on my life, I wonder, how do I—how does anyone—measure a legacy? Some say that it's best measured by the people we've influenced, and my guess is that that's probably true. Legacy may include the impact we've had in our jobs or careers, and how we've loved those entrusted into our care. Some of us measure it by the fulfillment of our dreams. Others within a faith community believe the real test of a legacy is the strength and relevance of one's faith. I have to say that there are actually many aspects of my life that really matter to me: my passionate love for family; the loyalty and depth of my friendships; my servant care for my patients; my strong commitment to delivering therapeutic excellence; my dedication to a scientific basis for therapy; my determination to discern the practicality of faith in living life; and the fulfillment of certain dreams I've had since my youth. I know that that's a lot, but they all

6

grip my emotions, captivate my imagination, and motivate my days. I admit: I do want my legacy measured by them all.

But this long letter is neither about my profession nor how I have or have not loved family and friends. Those stories are for another day in another venue. I am not telling anyone else's story, including yours or Mom's or your uncle Herb's—though I cannot escape touching on your lives because you've touched mine. Instead, I am telling only my story—and it's the story of my faith journey. If there were to be only one yardstick by which to measure my life, it would be that, in the end, I would receive the affirmation from my heavenly Father, "Well done, good and faithful servant." But getting there—creating that kind of life and that legacy—has been, and still is, far from easy. While you already know me, including some about my faith, I do want to share my fuller story with you and your brothers. It's the story of how I got faith—not only the circumstances that engendered it, but the forces deep inside me that shaped the magnetic draw to it. It is the story of how that faith really looks to me—from the inside out—from deep within my own psyche. All of that is a story I've never shared with you.

Candidly, I'd like you guys to pass down the story of my journey to my grandchildren and great grandchildren. I want them to know me this way, and how it is that I believe in Jesus—whether I am alive long enough to tell them in person or not. I have thought many times before about putting my spiritual journey down on paper for all of you. But Tim Russert's book *Wisdom of our Fathers: Lessons and Letters from Daughters and Sons* crystallized my desire. He was the longest-serving moderator of NBC's *Meet the Press* on Sunday mornings. When I caught a glimpse of his stirring passion in an interview one Sunday morning about the power of a father's legacy, I decided I had to write. While I believe that the real legacy is in how one lives—not in what one says—I nevertheless wanted to tell you guys my story, and have that story be part of what I leave behind. Sadly, the man who inspired me died suddenly of a heart attack while I was writing this letter.

Beyond such fatherly narcissism, my longing for you to get to know me this way is rooted in my parents not having known me—especially my mother. That relationship felt even more lost, more bankrupt, than the one I had with my father. So, while I ached for love from them both, the longing for love from my mom felt more intense. While there is something special about a boy's relationship to his father, there is something radically unique about a boy's tie to his mother. A mom is the central female figure who influences a boy's relationships with girls. I know my longings for my mother's love strongly affected my relationship with your mother, my wife. But there is something more, something shrouded in the mystery of birth and family.

A child gets his very life from his mother. Even though I was active in the birthing process for all three of you, I felt—I knew—your mother had a privileged role as the one who was bringing you into the world. I didn't carry you guys in my body; she did. I didn't feel you move and grow within me. When Mom was carrying each of you, I'd spend time on the bed with her just staring at her abdomen looking for signs of life. I'd gently push my fingers into her skin to touch some part of you . . . or Matt . . . or Paul. But that's the closest I'd get. There was no umbilical cord tying you to me—only to Mom. However strange it may seem for a man to say this, while I didn't envy Mom's morning sickness or pains of birthing, I did ponder what it would feel like to carry my own child and give birth. I do wonder whether a mother's ability to bear life adds to the unique and powerful bond a child has to his mother—and if that deepened my longings for my own mother. Maybe I felt odd cutting your brother's umbilical cord not only because I was aware of that primal bond but also because it unconsciously reminded me of how I never really felt tied emotionally to my own mother—the very one who gave me life.

However my longings to be close to family came to be, I want to keep getting to know the three of you. And I want you guys to keep getting to know me. Just please forgive me if the motive is not pure: I am built to long for a depth of friendship with you three as well as your mother because I didn't have it growing up with my own parents, and especially so with my mother—the primal female figure in my life. But that's who I am.

In my mind, any man worth anything wants to live an honorable life, achieve something of value, give something back to people, and leave behind a legacy—a legacy of love and honor mixed with wisdom. We all want our footprints to stay in the sand for a while before the tide of time comes in to wash them away. While time will indeed wash away my footprints someday, mysteriously, it matters that they remain for a little while. To live honorably, to be remembered honorably, matters.

My footprints in the sand have never been about money or building a financial empire (not that there is anything wrong with money per se). And given that your brother Paul is now a financial expert advising people how to handle millions, how could I say otherwise? We all know that while "money can't buy happiness," it can certainly buy the opportunities within which happiness can flourish. Without it, life can be miserable. I read an interview in World Vision's magazine of a man whose family lived in the large dump outside the city limits of Cairo, Egypt. His job was to collect the trash of Cairo's residents. One of the "perks" of the job was that authorities allowed him and his family to eat the food they collected. In the interview, it was clear that this hardworking man was keenly aware of his lot in life. And his vision for the future was firm: he wanted his precious children educated by World Vision's school, and for those children to then leave that dump forever. As I read his brief but poignant story, I choked up. I didn't realize it at the time, but this man reminded me of your grandfather. Both men had been hardworking, struggled for survival, and had the vision to see to it that their children got a good education.

Still, the challenge of creating meaning in one's life is difficult in both poverty and wealth, though most people would likely choose the problems of wealth over poverty. I'm not sure that is necessarily the wiser choice. As Jesus pointed out, money is intoxicatingly powerful. It buys nearly everything in life, including social status and political power. At its face, there's nothing wrong with that. But because money is indeed power—and we all know that power corrupts—the pursuit of money can draw out the dark side of human nature, becoming an almost instinctual defense against the pursuit of truth . . . whether truth about reality around us, inner truth about self, or spiritual truth about God.

The baby-boomer generation—my generation—did lose itself in the pursuit of materialism, according to social psychologists. The focus on money, like Jesus warned, derailed us from searching for the meaning of life. We did not seek roots in traditional religion. Nor did my generation create a clear philosophy for living. We've had no philosophy of suffering except our unspoken plan to avoid it. Researchers have even labeled baby-boomer fathers "the lost boys."

And guess what we've passed on to our children: that same "lost-ness." We've offered little except the vision to pile up the happiness moments. I can't tell you how many times I've heard parents say that all they want for their children is for them to be "happy." Not to be discerning . . . or wise . . . or committed to a cause . . . or committed to God . . . or able to build character from suffering . . . or nurturing their leadership skills. Just be happy. Thus is the bent of our culture.

Over the years, in contrast to the majority of baby-boomer fathers, I have pursued the invisible things of life—ways of living that should have been there in my family but weren't: searching for truth; discovering how to love; parenting for character and leader-ship; creating and discovering life's meaning; and constructing an approach to suffering that turns lemons into lemonade. I suppose I should take some pride that I am more of the exception in my generation, but frankly, I can't take much credit for it. What hap-pened to me growing up pushed me to seek those intangible things of life. It has been more a matter of emotional survival than some grand idealistic choice. Innumerable forces had converged on me, carrying me into a spiritual maelstrom—like someone shooting the rapids, paddling to keep afloat but being unavoidably driven by the rushing water.

Whether I've liked it or not—and whether anyone else thinks it's been reasonable or not—the search for spiritual truth, and, with it, the wrestling for faith and the internal battles for its relevance to life's meaning, have been central to my journey. In fact, as you will see, it's been central to my identity. You cannot know me with-out knowing my faith journey. That journey—and the nature of my beliefs—has never been a simple thing. It has been complex and conflicted from the very beginning, long before I had a chance to choose otherwise. Those conflicts, including how I have wrestled with faith, along with some conclusions I have drawn, may offend some. I do not know. However, my sincere and honest intent is not to offend anyone, but simply to tell my own story. Strangely, most of my life has been driven by an unquenchable thirst for truth—truth about the universe and truth about God. I never planned it that way; it just happened. I take some comfort from the fact that everyone's life is a journey of having to deal with truth one way or another. And, like it or not, we all have to deal with God—though many aren't consciously aware of it or willing to admit it.

Included in my journey is what your grandparents and your uncle Herb were to me. I am aware that, to some degree, you already know your grandparents in and through me. But the fuller story of who they were or what their impact on me has been has not been told. You know my brother Herb personally, but what you don't know is how he influenced me over the years—and his pivotal role in my faith journey. How my story has played out—why and how I have searched for spiritual truth the way I have—is rooted in both my parents' and Uncle Herb's choices toward me.

You may suppose sharing like this is an occupational hazard; I know you guys believe I've discussed a lot of things during your childhood, including family conflicts, because I am a psychologist. But who I am really came first. My profession and my fathering have meaning to me because of who I am. So I talk like this, and I've fathered like this, because that's me—not because I am a psychologist . . . or because I'm theologically trained.

My adult life has been passionately dedicated to helping people build or rebuild pieces of their lives—or their core identities—in the face of suffering and trauma. This central motive has its roots in my own struggle to free myself from the ravages of trauma—and my passion to build a meaningful life. To do that, I've had to search for meaning useful enough—and large enough—to drive me from day to day through all of what life has thrown at me. But those of us who have been traumatized are not the only ones in search of identity and meaning. Across this nation, according to social psychologists, Gen Xers (the children from the loins of baby-boomer fathers), and Gen Yers following them, have sought counseling for help in answering their one burning question: *Who am I?* And with that, they long for wisdom on how they should then live. Instead of losing rapport with young people as I have grown older, which I thought was going to happen, it has strengthened. These younger generations desperately want to talk with someone who not only has life experience but also will talk transparently about it—and about whether life has any real meaning or not. Incredibly, they know intuitively that identity and meaning are two sides of the same coin.

I know some think of my profession as "listening to people's problems all day." If I thought of my work that way, I'd sell insurance instead—which I did, by the way, as a graduate student, and hated. I have little interest in babysitting people through life. Instead, I think of my work as constructing or reconstructing lives. I think of myself as a scientist, engineer, teacher, spiritual consultant, life coach, information technologist for the psyche, and mind surgeon—all wrapped in and through the artistic delivery of my personality.

My instrument is an odd one. I do not use microscopes or telescopes like my scientist friend, surgical instruments like my podiatrist friend, optometric equipment like my eye doctor friend, or pills like my family doctor friend. Instead, I use words—simply words. More specifically, the ideas those words carry. I am not a wordsmith like your brother Matt. He plays with words like an expert pianist plays the ivories. However, my expertise is with the ideas that words convey—and how to use ideas to transform lives. Ideas create lives; changing ideas re-creates lives. That's what I so deeply love to do.

My dual passion for psychology and theology makes it possible to not only tell you my story, but also interpret it. I use my expertise in both fields to get to the "hows" and "whys" of my faith—to dig into the very nuts 'n bolts that made me "me." I want you to understand how it is that I am the way I am—what I *really* stand for spiritually—and the faith choices I've made in life. Besides getting to know me better, this letter carries the hope that you might gain insight into yourself and your own spiritual quest by bearing witness to my journey. We are, after all, cut from the same human cloth. And you are your father's daughter.

I am aware that there are millions of fathers on the planet, have been millions in times past, and I am just one father among many. I have been neither a Supreme Court justice nor a Hollywood movie star. So my non-celebrity status and life may not be particularly interesting for some; in fact, it may be downright boring. Yet, I know that real people reading other real people's stories can be life changing.

As we grow up, we all have to re-invent the wheel. We all live as if the world was created just a few short years before we arrived on the planet. That's one insight that's unique to midlife. You can't see it or feel it, really, until decades have passed—until dreams have been fulfilled and dreams have been shattered. And you can't see it until you've gotten out of yourself enough to notice all the people around you struggling to make it in life just like you . . . struggling to find meaning and purpose . . . struggling to understand who they are in the scheme of things . . . struggling to be loved. Yet, when we are young—when I was young—I felt I was among the first to venture out asking what life and God were all about. I was Columbus or Neil Armstrong. Such youthful naïveté. Life had been here long before me. Others have also asked the same questions and, each in his or her own way, have wrestled for answers. Many have earned their stripes in life by living out their hard-fought wisdom. While human history is progressing, it is just like Ecclesiastes says, there really is nothing new in these struggles under the sun. Yet, paradoxically, without the struggle, there is little wisdom or identity. And, without that struggle, meaning never reaches the level of a cause worth living for—let alone ultimately risking death for. So as you join me now on this quest, please take my deliberations as the ponderings of just one father among millions across innumerable generations—though admittedly they are the ponderings of your father. And there is only one of him.

Hon, please see to it that my grandchildren and great grandchildren get to read this. I would like this story of how I came to believe in Jesus—and why—to be part of my legacy.

PART 1

The Forging of Conflicted Faith

 *My Trauma*

It Took a Village

I've borrowed the title of former First Lady and Secretary of State Hilary Clinton's book to convey how parents aren't the only ones with the power to shape us. Our neighborhoods, cities, and nation shape our identity as well.

In the first eight years of my life, from 1951 to 1959, my neighborhood "village" was Dutchtown, nestled along the fast-moving Genesee River near one of the Great Lakes—Lake Ontario. It emerged in the early 1800s as a vibrant settlement of immigrant German-Catholics. They came here to America with absolutely nothing except a dream—and the strong work ethic to achieve it. At the heart of their collective dream was the vision to build family—and, with family, community.

The name "Dutchtown" was actually taken from "Deutschtown," meaning Germantown. Over the decades, other ethnic groups that moved into the area found the word "Deutsch" difficult to pronounce. So Deutsch became "Dutch," even though few came from Holland. The vision for life, the quality of character, and the strength of religious conviction of these hard-working immigrants that became Dutchtown was the soil in which my family took root. What character you see in me is that of the immigrants of Dutchtown—including your grandparents you've never met. Their traits became my traits, passed down to you. In that way, you and Dutchtown are one.

The German Catholics who settled along the Genesee River provided the reliable manual labor for the new mills using the river's falls for power. Several generations later, I grew up with their children less than two miles from the river. At five, I stood at the falls with Nanny, my mother's mom, your great-grandmother. I think I called her "Nanny" because my older brothers called her Nanny, though I have a vague memory of someone telling me that I couldn't quite say "Grammy." For a little boy, the falls were awesome; I felt a bit uneasy looking down and out at the river. The gorge struck me as huge, with the river looking kind of greenish brown, swiftly moving as it loudly plunged over the falls. It was just this magnificence and power that drew venture capitalists to build the mills.

I grew up in my first eight years on Rugraff Street, one of many very narrow streets in the neighborhood, in a single-family dwelling built about 1880. My old home is now boarded up. (You can walk down the streets of my Dutchtown neighborhood using Google Maps Street View.) My neighborhood was so physically tight that our "front lawn" was only a few feet from house to sidewalk, and there was barely a single car width between houses where the driveway was. When I was about six or seven, your grandfather would sit on the front steps of our tiny porch while he watched me mow with our push mower. It only took a few minutes even as a young child.

Our living area was about six to seven hundred square feet, if that, not including the "cellar" (the old name for basement) and an attic with a low lying roofline—perhaps about the size of your Grampy's lower-level living room and kitchen, but much narrower. By suburban standards today, the house was tiny—but as a kid who knew no better, and an entire neighborhood of homes of similar size, I never thought anything about it.

Turning left onto Jay Street from Rugraff to go to my friend's house on Ries Street, which was close, I'd sometimes imagine walking to the river. I remember feeling that there was this invisible line shortly beyond Ries Street that I could never cross alone. When Nanny took me on the streets near the river, it always seemed so busy . . . scary busy, with lots of cars. I don't know if my parents or Nanny told me that I was never to go past Ries Street or if I just knew that the river area was too dangerous. But I never ventured beyond Ries. In whatever way I came to think that I couldn't go there, it was that area along the river that had become the industrial hub of the city.

Catholic immigrants from Ireland and Italy eventually joined the German settlers around the Genesee. Dutchtown expanded. The region grew into the mixed ethnic community of "Rochesterville," which, in time, became the City of Rochester. The neighborhood close to the river kept its name Dutchtown; I've always thought of myself as growing up "in Dutchtown." These resolute immigrant workers—now citizens—made Rochester into an industrial giant. With the invention of the automobile, and as companies around the river expanded, they branched out or moved. Many of those early historic buildings along the Genesee yet remain. Your immigrant ancestors built these industries into national and international companies, like the Genesee Brewing Company and Bausch & Lomb. Your grandfather worked at one of those giants—Eastman Kodak Company—as a "tin knocker," shaping metal parts for production-line machines. And your uncle Herb worked his entire life as a chemist there at Kodak.

Besides working at the companies that grew into large corporations, the immigrants set up small, family-owned stores. They had bakeries and butcher shops and corner stores within walking distances of one another. Along with their main jobs in these growing companies, these very small businesses became the economic backbone of our neighborhood. Neighbors relied on each other spending money at their small shops in order to survive. They also relied on each other to keep their word and pay their bills. And they did. That pattern of mutual reliance and keeping one's word continued into my childhood.

Your grandparents routinely sent your uncle Herb and me to the corner store—a kind of tiny, 1950s-style 7-Eleven. One practice of our Catholic faith was to eat something other than meat on Fridays. My parents bought fish fry for supper from the small "beer joint" on the corner of Rugraff. I've hated the smell of fish ever since I can remember, so I always had grilled cheese sandwiches instead. Your grandmother used our tiny front parlor to cut and style hair. It's unheard of today, but your grandmother used our kitchen sink to wash and rinse the hair. Even we kids kept the local economy going. At lunchtime or after school, a bunch of us grammar school kids would go to Pat Grassi's five-and-dime store right across the street from the church to buy small toys and baseball cards. Next to Grassi's was the soda fountain shop where I first combined root beer with chocolate, not vanilla, ice cream—a combination I love to this day. As small as so many of these family businesses were—including your grandmother's—they were woven into the neighborhood fabric and brought in enough money to make ends meet or supplement a spouse's income from the factories to survive. Beyond surviving, buying and selling from each other in the same neighborhood created mutual dependence and lasting friendships. That's how ethnic neighborhoods, including Dutchtown, eventually became melting pots. And that integration is how they built their village.

Over the decades, the immigrants also planted churches as the spiritual cornerstones of their neighborhoods. In the mid-1800s, the Catholic Church organized about sixty of these poor churches into the Diocese of Rochester—the diocese I grew up in. Going into the early 1900s, one visionary bishop led the way to strengthening faith in the village. He built even more churches, along with schools, charities, and seminaries. With a vision for both spiritual solidarity and the education of these immigrants' children and grandchildren, he combined schools with churches. Catholic faith and education became powerful forces among the people—with both a church *and* a school becoming the cornerstone of each neighborhood.

Dutchtown's cornerstone was Holy Family Church and School. Your grandmother saw to it that we were all very active in that parish at the corner of Jay and Ames Streets—the very heart of Dutchtown. The three of us kids went to Holy Family School—grades kindergarten through eighth. And we all went to Mass regularly; our parents and the nuns saw to it. In fact, the sisters formally walked us from school to church for Mass every school day. I would not have been able to go to college without the nuns' unwavering commitment to a no-nonsense approach to education. Their academic training was superb.

Catholic faith permeated the immigrants' lives. They exercised daily religious rituals. They kept a hold on the unquestionable belief that God existed. Catholic women, in particular, believed that Jesus' mother, Mary, performed miracles for her people. Small yard shrines to Mary dotted the neighborhood. Parents were gripped by a determination to have their children get "a good Catholic education." And faith was the foundation for values. They lived with integrity; the word "honor" meant something to them. They exercised their values in doing business with one another. And they all worked long and hard to eke out a living. It was even a matter of pride to provide for themselves and their families; it was certainly your grandfather's pride. Putting all these ingredients together:

dependence for survival on one another; common religious beliefs; common values; extraordinary hard work; and visionary Catholic leadership—and you have a potent formula for transforming a group of struggling immigrants into one strong, cohesive village.

Besides my parents, my Dutchtown neighborhood raised me—deeply shaping you through me. Your grandparents sat on the front steps evening after evening talking with good neighbors. They all shopped at the same stores. Neighbors came to your grandmother's little parlor to get their hair done. And our family went to church with neighbors. I knew neighborhood mattered. Neighbors were important to my parents and so were important to me. They were like extended family. They graciously invited me as a little boy into their homes to eat with them. I sometimes ate lunch with the neighbor directly across from us, Virginia. I also ate lunch with an elderly woman kitty-corner from our house. I was once (maybe twice!) rightly reprimanded by our next door neighbor; she was stern but gracious. I had this intuitive sense of being quietly watched by all of them, extending my parents' eyes and ears beyond my house out to the streets. One neighbor—I have no idea who—snitched on me when I threw a snowball across the street at a girl. My father sternly called me in to reprimand me for it, saying you never hit a girl—never. The nuns extended the oversight of our parents and neighbors into the classroom. The word "disobey" is not often used today; the politically correct term is "listen." But in my day, if you disobeyed Sister, it was the same as disobeying your parent. Either way, you were punished.

Admittedly, Hon, I felt the tense insecurity of spiritual doubt at a tender age. I struggled to find my way through my own parents' deep emotional instability. And I fought the horrific damage of the trauma perpetrated against me. Still, without question, my small but tight-knit neighborhood had been wrapped around my traumatized identity like a cast on a broken leg. My identity had been forged in the midst of and surrounded by Dutchtown's singular vision for living life. The collective strength of these determined families became my strength—and helped me keep my youthful sanity. Trauma or no trauma, Dutchtown's quality of character, strength of values, and depth of world view—including its rigorous work ethic—became the stuff out of which my own character and vision for life had been forged long before I had a choice. And through me, Dutchtown forged *your* character.

As I said, you and Dutchtown are one.

Shattered Dreams

In his twenties, your grandfather played center for a semipro football team. Sons do identify with their fathers, and so to this day, I love throwing the pigskin—which is how I broke my pinky—even though I never saw my dad play.

When your brothers were young, I had to make deals to throw the football. Matt wasn't thrilled to throw either the baseball or football even though he had been in Little League. Like your mom and me, he was drawn to music. And for some unknown reason, Paul loved baseball.

When I was about six, with a slight tone of condescension having been a football player, your grandfather told me America's pastime, baseball, was a slow, boring game—and you didn't even have to be an athlete to play it. He said that about golf too. I've grown up not liking either game just because he didn't. In more recent years, however, I've played golf with my good friends as well as Paul and your husband. And I've learned to enjoy the challenge. But I've had to work at enjoying it because of your grandfather's imprint. I put the game on my terms to make it my own, like figuring out something of the science of the golf swing and learning how to swing the club with my damaged body . . . not to mention the arduous and time-consuming task of just connecting with the ball.

A father's spoken word in the family is a bit like God speaking. God speaks, and whatever he utters is instantly created, like "Let there be light"—and there was light. My father spoke the word "Baseball is boring"—and it became so in my mind. He declared, "Golf is boring"—and it was so. "I don't like long sleeve shirts," he told me, because it was dangerous to wear long sleeves around machinery—and to this day I prefer short sleeves even in the wintertime. My father also told me that he didn't like jewelry on his body, especially rings on his fingers, because, as a tin-knocker, there was some risk of the ring getting caught in machinery and tearing off his finger. In fact, that

22

happened to a friend of his, and decades later, to a friend of mine. As a result, I want my hands, wrists, and neck free of any jewelry, including rings. All these things became so within me simply because my dad spoke the "word."

Needless to say, then, Paul sure didn't get his love of baseball from me. Perhaps from your mom. I'd break from work to come home in the afternoon to play with him and Matt before having to go back to the office for evening appointments, and Matt would typically want to play inside while Paul would want to go outside to throw the baseball. And me—I'd want to throw the football. I did manage to cut deals. With Matt, I'd spend time inside playing, like with Legos, and sometimes he'd go out to throw the football with me. I'd bargain with your brother Paul for fifteen minutes of throwing the pigskin in return for a half hour of throwing the baseball. At our neighborhood Turkey Bowl at Thanksgiving, Paul, now in his thirties, loves to be quarterback.

Football was big at St. Thomas Aquinas High School; we even had our own stadium. I really wanted to try out for the football team—I had a passion to play because my father played—but my mother blocked it while my father stood by saying nothing. When I was little, my father told me that he promised my mom that if he got injured again playing football, he'd stop playing. He did break his leg—and kept his word to his wife; he gave up his first love. I guess my mother didn't want me to get injured like he had, and my dad felt he couldn't stand in her way given the deal he had made with her years earlier. As a teen, I hadn't put that together; all I knew was that I wanted the choice. That's why when your brother Paul briefly explored the possibility of playing football and your mom expressed a concern about him getting hurt, I jumped in and said it was up to him whether or not he played. He finally chose not to. But the real issue there wasn't Mom's concern about Paul getting hurt—certainly a more than valid concern—but my own residual resentment that my mother blocked me from trying out. I don't know if I would've made the team. Looking back, I think it was a virtual certainty I wouldn't have. Nevertheless, I sure wanted to try. Admittedly, I was short, like my dad, and probably not fast enough, but I did have a decent pair of hands. And I was my father's son.

There's not much question that football made your grandfather feel like a man, and, I have to admit, there is something testosterone driven about the game that I love: the competition, the body banging, and the heroics of hanging onto the ball even though you know you're going to get hit. I remember neighborhood games with Uncle Herb as quarterback and me as receiver. We made a great team. I'd go out for a pass, and as I grasped the ball, I could see the opponent out of the corner of my eye coming to nail me. I felt it was my duty to hang onto the ball no matter what—and I usually did. It felt so satisfying to drop to the ground with the ball in hand.

When your brother and I play a game of Ping-Pong, which, I know, doesn't strike one as exactly high testosterone, he and I will nevertheless mentally suit up as gladiators entering the arena. Son against father, man against man—it is all so oedipal and so primal. He wants to crush me and I him. He wants to be the bigger man, shrinking his old man down to size, and I want to keep the young buck in his place. I am the patriarch, the four-star general, and he will never defeat me. At best, only match me. A well-placed shot, knocking him on his heels, is deeply satisfying. The primitive longings for dominance and the instinctual use of aggression to secure it grants deep psychic meaning to the whole encounter. All of this is your grandfather in me.

When I was seven, out of the blue my dad blurted out, "Frankie, I don't know why God took my legs. Now, I'm nothing but a d--- cripple." I recall the moment vividly. This was an extraordinary peek into your grandfather's shaken faith—even shock and desperation—as well as his loss of identity as a man. As you know, he had multiple sclerosis. What you don't know is that he had contracted this horrific disease as a young man, perhaps in his mid-to-late twenties, and not long after he stopped playing football. While I do recall him driving the car twice when I was little, I don't ever remember seeing him walk. As I got older, I saw him lose the complete use of his legs, then his arms and hands—until he became a full quadriplegic. The process was slow and torturous.

Your grandfather's self-deprecating comment about being nothing but a "cripple," which he blurted out on impulse, also revealed his lack of savvy. After all, what father declares himself virtually worthless to his seven-year-old boy? But he did. And it became another one of his "words" spoken into my mental universe—permanently imprinting my psyche. What was I to do with that? My own father felt emasculated. And he obviously felt the emotional pain of a good God, who is presumably all powerful, standing by doing nothing to help. If you think about it for a moment—which I did as a kid—how does anyone stand by watching someone else be harmed? How would any victim feel as he stared into the eyes of the person who stood by doing nothing? Though lacking savvy, my father's impulsive, self-effacing comment was much more his crying out into the universe—crying out to and through his own little boy. Like a driver stuck in a burning car screaming to those around to smash the glass and pull him out, my father was desperately screaming out to God for rescue.

This was not the first time I caught a glimpse of your grandfather's desperate fear, even terror. It was at that same age of six, when he told me what he thought about golf, that he came home from work one evening very upset. He exclaimed to my mom, "I got laid off. They told me I couldn't work anymore 'cause I was falling too much. My foreman came in and told me to clear out my locker. I didn't even get any notice. G--d--- that Bill Hansen." His terror ran through me; I just stood there staring at him. In the few moments of silence that followed, the terror between him and my mom was palpable. I froze. Your grandfather—a manual laborer like so many before him—desperately wondered how they would ever make enough money to survive.

This watershed moment crushed your grandmother's dreams. The onset of that dreadful disease and their ensuing financial crisis had broken her. But unlike your grandfather, she never blurted out anything about her emotional pain. In fact, she never discussed anything about what happened to the family . . . or its impact on her. Instead, she turned to alcohol to numb herself, driving herself into a deep depression from which she never escaped. Actually, I don't know if your grandmother began drinking because of her shattered dreams or if she had been drinking long before your grandfather's illness. And I don't know if she had been already depressed before he became ill or as a result of it. But clearly, after the dream-shattering news of his MS, your grandmother abused alcohol—horrifically abused it—and did so when I was very young. Typically, there were several cases of beer in the cellar, and she'd routinely be out cold on the living room davenport.

I don't really know, but I do wonder if my birth into my mom's world was the cause of her depression years before my father's MS. I do have a vague memory of someone telling me that she really didn't want me—that is, she hadn't wanted another son—and had gotten a doll in preparation for a daughter. Could I have fabricated that vague memory? Perhaps. But she did have a doll with a gorgeous white dress propped up on the pillows of her bed. My vivid memory of that well-dressed doll combined with the unclear memory of someone telling me she hadn't wanted me could've been my attempt at putting the pieces together of how my mother emotionally abandoned me. The fact is, Kid, I have no memory of my own mother hugging me, kissing me, reading to me at night, playing with me, or comforting me when I got hurt. It's not that I don't remember. It's that it never happened. So whether someone told me or not, this was the interpretation I had given to my earliest experiences—an interpretation that captivated my little-boy imagination: *my own mother didn't want me.*

Mother's Confusing Love

Our kitchen sink served several purposes, from washing dishes to cleaning and rinsing people's hair for my mom's business to bathing me as a toddler. I can see myself in the sink looking out into the kitchen area. I was small enough to fit into it and tall enough and strong enough to sit up without falling over. From my vantage point in the half-filled sink, I could see the circular fluorescent light in the middle of the kitchen ceiling over our supper table and the edge of the sink in front of me. Your grandmother left for a moment to get something. As I looked out, I couldn't see her, but I sure could feel myself swaying a bit. Looking down as my upper body was ever so slightly wobbling over my butt, I could see the alternating red and green squares of that now outdated vinyl-asbestos tile flooring. It felt as if I was suspended by a piece of string from the top of my head. All I knew as I sat there was that I felt like I was going to fall over the edge. Do you remember the cable cars at Hershey Park? I'd get the same feeling when I was up in one of those, with the car gently swaying from the end of a cable. That's why I was never thrilled to go up in them . . . or ride the Flower Wheel.

As a toddler, I comfortably sat on a small pink toilet seat secured onto the adults' toilet seat so that I could go potty. We didn't have a separate potty chair like parents do today. For that matter, we didn't have a refrigerator either until I was about seven; we had an "icebox." It was a brown, wooden container that was twice as high as it was wide with a shelf in the middle. It sat on our gray back porch near a small opening in the outside wall with a white access door where the milkman delivered our milk bottles. The iceman would come with huge blocks of ice on his open-bed truck—no longer horse-drawn wagons—and, with giant metal tongs, grab one and lug it into our house, gently placing it in the box. I was always amazed that the blocks of ice didn't melt sitting in the open summer sun as the driver worked his route.

We also didn't have an electric washer and dryer. Instead, your grandmother had a hand-cranked wringer washer where she manually scrubbed clothes and then twisted them good and hard to get as much water out as possible before running them through rollers to squeeze out the remaining water. She'd then put the clothes out to dry on a clothesline in our small backyard. In fact, from that little toilet seat—with the bathroom door cracked open—I could see your grandmother carefully squeezing the clothes through the rollers. When I was done, I'd call her into the bathroom to wipe my bottom. She did so dutifully, though I never saw her smile at me.

My mom saw to it that I had decent clothes for school, darned my holed socks, put patches over holes in my pants, went for conferences with the nuns about my school progress, and made my lunches, including banana sandwiches with mayonnaise and bean sandwiches with ketchup. I don't recall this, but your uncle Herb assures me that these strange sandwiches were actually his ideas—so I can blame him for a few of my eccentricities. For my birthday, my mom would make me chocolate mayonnaise cake, double layered, with bananas between the layers and chocolate frosting. It was to die for. The mayonnaise made the cake rich and moist. As you know, to this day I love having that cake for my birthday—and it continues to be one way, however small, to connect to my mother. At Christmas my mother made long rolls of butter cookies, and, as much as I like your mother's cookies, I've never tasted a Christmas cookie since that even comes close to the rich, sugar-laden taste of those butter-filled delights.

Talking about Christmas, my parents made a grand effort to celebrate it for the sake of us kids. They saw to it that we always had presents, whether before or after my dad was laid off from work. And your grandmother found creative ways to get me out of the house so that Santa could sneak in to leave them. One Christmas she had Uncle Herb take me on his paper route with him. I actually felt privileged that he thought I could help him; little did I know. When we got home after delivering the papers, there was a large box of presents—it rose to my chin—with a note from Santa. I was so disappointed to have missed him, but I wondered why his handwriting looked so much like your grandmother's.

Another year, my mom had your great grandmother Nanny walk me to the liquor store to get a bottle of wine for Santa. Nanny seemed to like spending time with me. Besides taking me to State Street along the Genesee River—the heart of Dutchtown—she would sometimes take me by bus to the broader downtown area to the Sears building for lunch. You can blame her for introducing me to ketchup on eggs, ham, and fried potatoes—a habit that has stayed with me and earned my reputation as an eccentric ketchup lover . . . as well as influencing our dear Dylan at the tender age of two who now always wants "bup bup" on his chicken nuggets, to your frustration, I know. Nanny was always kind to me, and I returned the kindness as a young adult by visiting her whenever I had a chance. I also stayed with her all night as she was dying. When we got back from the liquor store, I was again disappointed; Santa had already come with the presents.

Yet another time, your grandfather drove me around town to "charge up the car battery" while your grandmother set out the presents. This was one time I remember your grandfather being well enough to drive. I sat there on the front seat watching my dad, wondering to myself why we had to drive around to charge up the battery since the car had been driven before and the battery would've already been charged. I don't know why, but I never asked him. Once again I had missed Santa.

From these few vignettes, it's obvious that your grandparents had vision for family—and my mom in particular kept family going on the home front. But, tragically, she was devoid of affection. One afternoon I was desperate for attention. I'm not sure how old I was, but I was playing on the sidewalk and fell down. I wasn't hurt, really, and I don't even remember what I was doing. But I was unwilling to get up. I recall the moment vividly because I really wanted to see if my mother cared enough to come. I was testing her—and I knew it. George was an older boy who lived a few houses down the street from us and saw me fall. He kindly came over and asked me if I was OK. I told him that I wanted my mommy. I stayed on the sidewalk, hoping she'd come out, pick me up, and hug me, and then tell me I'd be OK. Instead, she came out, walked over, looked down at me—not even bending over to help me up—and coldly declared that I was OK. She didn't smile, but instead turned around and walked right back into the house, leaving me on the sidewalk. On her face: stone-cold disinterest. I'll never forget the look. There was no tenderness, no hug, no touch, no warmth—and no help getting up. Nothing. Hon, I know you'd never treat your Dylan that way.

Whether for something small like falling down on the sidewalk or something much bigger, your grandmother offered no comfort. Your uncle Ron, being the middle brother and four years older than me, always managed to get out the door ahead of me going to school in the morning. Typically he'd go out the back porch door scooting by the icebox while I scrambled to catch up to him. This one winter morning I came running through the kitchen to the back porch to do just that. As was my habit, I hit the storm door metal frame with my left hand and slid the hand down to the door handle to push it open while my right hand hit the glass at the same moment, opening the door. Except this time the door didn't open. My left hand slipped past the handle and my right hand smashed through the pane of glass. I found myself standing there with my right arm through the glass pane up past my elbow.

I stared at one large triangular piece sticking through my winter jacket into my right arm. Instinctively, I grabbed the dangling glass with my left hand. I could feel the urge—I just wanted it out of my arm. So I yanked it out. Now my left hand was bleeding. I didn't feel any pain, but I was scared—not because I was injured but because I had broken the window. My mother pulled my jacket off and put my arm under cold running water in the kitchen sink. She stared at my arm as the blood mixed with the water while I stared intently at her wondering if she was mad at me. Her face looked blank. I asked her, "Is Daddy going to give me a lickin'?" She said, "We'll see." She called a neighbor to ask for a ride to the hospital. The next thing I knew, I was riding in this neighbor's car. I felt scared. I could hear the question, "Did his arm get caught in the wringer?" I don't remember the answer. I do recall staring down at the blood-soaked towel around my arm; I felt mesmerized. I noticed the contrast among the colors: the bright-red blood, the white towel, and the green car seat. I was shocky. I was sitting in the back seat of the car next to my mother, but she was not holding me . . . or even bracing the towel around my arm. Neither her hands nor her arms touched me.

At the hospital a nurse told my mother that I needed to sit down, saying to her that I looked like I was going to faint. I sat on a chair by myself; my mother yet didn't touch me. The nurse then helped me lay down on a table. After a little while, the doctor came in, telling me he was going to sprinkle some powder in my wound to numb it. The nurse gently but very firmly held my left arm. She smiled at me so tenderly; she was very warm. It wasn't so much a thought as it was a feeling: "I wish I could have you as my mommy." After the doctor stitched the wound, I looked over at my right arm, thinking, "It looks like a darned sock. Mommy darns the holes in my socks. Wow, my arm looks just like that!" The doctor told me he took some pieces of glass from my arm. He then said to my mom that I was fortunate I had my thick winter jacket on—otherwise I would've lost my arm.

Your uncle Herb, who being nine years older would've been a young teen, played checkers with me after he came home from school to keep me company—his way of comforting me. However small that act of kindness may seem, it strengthened my identification with your uncle way beyond banana and bean sandwiches—an identification that grew over the years, forever changing the course of my life. Tragically, however, your grandmother had not once comforted me throughout any of this childhood ordeal. To be sure, she cared. She had taken off my glass-torn jacket. Turned on the cold water and ran it over my arm to slow the bleeding. Contacted the neighbor for a ride. And stayed with me at the hospital. She cared. No doubt about it. Yet, sadly, she hadn't once touched me to comfort me, nor smiled at me, nor reassured me. Not once. It was love—but love as duty. Duty without feeling.

Love as Feeling

My mother did what she needed to do in that emergency. She had done her duty. But, at the most basic emotional level—at the simple level of the five senses—she failed to love me. Doing her bare duty was not enough. I had no gut sense that she cared.

We now know that any caretaker doing only her duty to keep physical life going is not enough to make a child *feel* loved, let alone thrive. Years before I was born, a frightened and overwhelmed mother had left her infant at the doorstep of a large hospital. As word got out, many other frightened mothers left their unwanted infants at its doorstep. So the hospital administrators compassionately set up a ward to care for them. But staff became alarmed when some infants died for no apparent physical reason. They soon discovered that the infants who were held, hugged, and smiled at by the staff did very well. But those infants that weren't—though no one deliberately neglected them—eventually gave up the will to live and died. How those infants reacted has been called "anaclitic depression," or simply infantile depression. It is now recognized by my profession and the World Health Organization as a very serious attachment disorder. The fact is, babies need to *feel* that someone loves them. They need someone to gently touch and caress their skin. They also need sights and sounds stimulating their eyes and ears and brains. They need to see the joy of someone celebrating their existence by simply smiling at them. My dear grandchildren no doubt *feel* loved because they're touched, hugged, and smiled at by so many. The staff at that 1940s hospital accidentally but tragically discovered that not welcoming newborns into the world with such sensory love severely traumatizes them—and even, at times, destroys them.

Infants who fortuitously survive the neglect of not being adequately touched oftentimes become unable to attach to others emotionally when they become adults. Or they seek the affection for a lifetime. When these infants become teenagers or young adults, they often act out promiscuously as a way to connect with someone without facing their fears of getting close emotionally. To this day— but typically only when your mom touches me—I can sense the inner craving for physical affection. Your mom's touch sets up the contrast with the emptiness inside me. That emptiness of touch— which is an indescribable feeling—is nevertheless palpable. When your mom and I first dated, and we'd snuggle together, the warmth of her touch blew my mind. I took in her warmth like a desperately thirsty man yearning for water. I had never felt the warmth of touch except for a couple of extraordinarily brief moments in my childhood—one of them being the nurse at the hospital when she held my arm with such tender compassion. So even though I am very affectionate with you guys, and I've had years of warmth from your mom, it's still easy for me to not hug or touch. It's natural yet not to. And I usually don't even consciously miss touch because I had gotten so used to not having it as a kid . . . until your mom gently caresses me and I sense the contrast of her warm touch with the cold inner emptiness. This is why, when I am in intense emotional pain, I cannot comfort myself. There is simply nothing inside me to draw on to do so. Nothing. And that's also why, when I am in emotional pain, I am so grateful that your mom will hold me real tight—as I was grateful you stayed with me and held me tight when my brother Ron suddenly passed away.

I do not know how much your grandmother held me in the first few months of life; I do have one photo of her cradling me in her arms. No doubt she did take care of my physical needs as the hospital staff had for those abandoned infants in their care, and as she had later on when I was a little boy. But such care was without affection. However much she did or did not touch me as an infant, what I do know is that I have no memory of your grandmother ever touching me as a little boy or as I got older. And frankly, the battle for my mind as a toddler and little boy gives me the evidence that, likely even in infancy, she rarely touched me with affection.

My mother showed her love toward me by doing her duty. But that duty I could not feel—not as an infant . . . not as a child . . . not as a teen. I just couldn't. She had tightly wrapped around her a robe of emotionally ice-cold and silent indifference to my existence. Sadly, my identity formed around that terrifying emptiness.

Bedtime in the Attic

The small and otherwise sparse attic held our three beds. They were set only about two feet apart, or even less; I could reach out my right arm, and, if I stretched hard enough, touch Uncle Ron's bed from my bed. The ceiling was low and pretty severely slanted following the roofline so that my older brothers especially had to watch out for their heads. This roof space was a scary place. As a little guy, it seemed so far away from my parents; it was like being in another world. The creaky dark-brown wooden steps up to this attic abode emerged from a very small room off the kitchen where I once slept as an infant and toddler, with your uncle Ron next to me in a big-boy bed.

I don't know how long my parents let me stay in the crib in my brother's room. But, after years of therapy, I recalled many memories, including being in the crib and climbing out of it. While it is a bit unusual to have memories that far back, I do vividly recall one time sticking my foot out between the crib slats, pointing it toward your uncle Ron. My good guess is that I was around two and my brother would have been six. I don't know if I made noises or used words or was just thinking it, but he got my meaning and kissed my foot—a cutesy thing for an older brother to do. I also vividly recall one night when I got a very bad earache. I was lying on my stomach with my right ear pressed against the crib mattress trying to find relief—and crying because of the pain. From his bed next to our room, your grandfather scolded me to be quiet—so I stopped. No one came to find out what was happening to me. Decades later, it is that same ear that is now more severely damaged. The next morning I tottered out into the kitchen where your grandfather was sitting at the table eating breakfast. I pointed to my ear, and, once again, I don't know if I made noises, used words, or was thinking while making noises, but your grandfather got the message that my ear hurt. He apologized for yelling at me. I actually recall being surprised, for whatever reason. But the fact is that I never did get another apology from him for any of his failings along the way until I was in college.

As a toddler, I sometimes played with an Erector Set in my bedroom, which, by the 1950s, had become part of American folk culture. I was sitting in front of an electrical outlet—which was about at my eye level or a little higher actually—and noticed it had holes in it. I found those two holes fascinating. I also took note of the all-metal screwdriver to my left among the various metal beams, screws, and other parts of the set. The handle of the screwdriver looked huge; it was shaped in a narrow loop so that I could put all my little fingers through it to grab it. I was intrigued: Would the screwdriver fit into the hole? So I grasped the metal handle in my left hand, and momentarily pausing to pick a hole, placed it carefully into the left one. Your grandmother soon discovered what had happened, and scooped me up and away from the outlet, anxiously declaring, "We have to wait till your father gets home to take it out." I could sense she was scared for me. That evening when my father came home from work, he told me that he'd take it out with newspaper wrapped around his hand.

I was about three when my parents fixed up the attic into one large bedroom for the three of us boys. My parents thought I was ready for my own big-boy bed. The dark-brown wooden steps leading to this other world actually wound around a corner like a spiral staircase, except there was only a quarter turn. In my nightly climb up the steep steps, I'd nervously round the corner—no longer able to keep a fix on my old bedroom. It was as if my parents were a thousand miles away. Although my brothers slept up there as well, being the youngest by many years, I'd go it alone virtually every night. I normally went up with no one to take me up, tuck me in, read to me . . . or hug and kiss me goodnight. Mom just sent me up—with no ritual except that of going up alone. Not even a stuffed animal.

Besides the typical fear of the dark and separation anxiety of going to a different world by myself, I carried my fears from the day into that eerie nighttime attic. Looking back, the core fear in me—terror actually—that emerged in that attic world was my mother's day-to-day silence. She rarely talked. And her depressive indifference was shrouded in an alcoholic fog. My mother's profound emotional neglect stirred such inner turmoil that I'd lie in bed at night panicky. I'd suck my thumb and frantically rock my head back and forth desperately trying to keep that terror of my own mother from breaking into consciousness—although as a young child I didn't know that's what I was doing. All I knew was that I felt scared of the dark and terrified of the several monsters that were lurking in the shadows to get me.

Let me tell you about one such monster. I wish it were something more benign like Bill Cosby's "Chicken Heart." Your grandfather told me the story of when the military stationed him in Louisiana as a private in the army. Your grandmother had recently given birth to your uncle Herb, or as your grandfather affectionately called him, Herbie. Nanny's second husband, who, according to your uncle Herb, was a superb artist who crafted signs for businesses, made a wooden toy box with the words "Herbie's Toy Box" printed on it in large letters. Even though it was Herbie's, I got to stuff some of my toys in it too. Your grandfather told me that one chilly night in Louisiana, he noticed a black widow spider crawling in Herbie's crib headed for his infant face. Though he felt panicked, my dad said he moved quickly to whack the spider away, saving Herbie from a possible lethal bite. Beyond any willful intent, but sensing your grandfather's intense fear, I unconsciously and creatively borrowed his story to represent the terror I felt for your grandmother.

Night after night, once in bed after my long trek up the winding attic stairs alone, I imagined a black widow spider ever so slowly and gently lifting its many legs to ascend those same stairs. It stealthily ambled across the attic floor; its sole mission was to devour me. The pitch-black creature was huge—about five feet wide, with large, long, hairy legs. Reaching the bottom of my bed, it climbed up onto me with deliberate and torturously slow movements of its hairy legs, mounting itself directly over me with its mouth wide open, poised to eat me alive. I rocked my head back and forth like crazy trying to make it go away. If I rocked hard enough and fast enough, I could momentarily outrun the terror. I'd retreat under my covers, feverishly sucking my small thumb with my heart pounding in fear. The bed covers gave the illusion of some protection from the monster, magically keeping it a few inches away. I wanted to scream out in terror; I just couldn't. So I clenched my jaws as tight as I could, frantically rocking my head back and forth—fighting the valiant fight against terror until one of my brothers came up to bed.

When your uncle Ron finally came up—being younger than Uncle Herb he was usually the second up—I would typically reach my right arm out to touch his bed. I desperately wanted to reassure myself that he was there . . . that I was no longer alone. Sometimes, the fight for sanity was so nerve-wracking that I'd climb into his bed, down by his feet, curling up like a dog. He had no idea why—and I couldn't tell him. After all, no one talked about anything in my family. Not knowing, he'd shoo me away. I'd climb back under my covers but still reach out my arm to connect with his bed . . . anything to anchor myself to a reality other than the residual terror I yet had coursing through my body. By that point, fighting the turmoil had stiffened my entire body. Only after your uncle Ron came up to bed could I begin to unwind.

Such was my nightly bedtime "routine."

The drama of fighting off the monsters felt real. I didn't see the spider in the attic space like a hallucination—though my fragile mind had been on the verge of psychotic terror. I only "saw" the spider in my mind just as all children "see" the monsters of their creative imaginations. But I was fortunate. My mother was emotional quicksand. I could have lost touch with reality as I struggled not to be consumed with the terror induced by her utter silence and lack of affection. During the nightly ordeal, I'd clench my jaws so tightly holding back primal screams of terror—and did that for so many years—that, to this day, I have significant muscle damage in my jaws. I often get low-level headaches and, sometimes, intense headaches that feel almost like migraines. If it were not for my father's anger at me; if it were not for his playing with me; if it weren't for my brothers talking and playing with me, I believe I would have, as the saying goes, "lost my mind." I would have become psychotic. Their engagement of me pulled me into their reality, dragging me up and out of the dark, bottomless pit of my intrapsychic quicksand that was my mother's devastating pathology now in me.

For any child, nighttime monsters represent the threats that a child encounters during the day. The world is, after all, a scary place. Life really is threatening in various ways—and the child, like all animals, senses it. Animals in the wild know instinctively that predators lurk in the distance to get them. They poke their heads out their holes before they venture out for food or play scanning the landscape for other animals that might be stalking them. Children, like all animals, have an instinctual as well as learned fear of bad things happening to them—such as robbers breaking into the house. Like the eyes of any animal that is not a night hunter, human eyes are not made for night vision like an owl's. So the bedroom's nighttime darkness blinds the child. Since daytime vision is a human being's key primal defense, darkness leaves a child feeling defenseless and extremely vulnerable to the potential dangers she cannot see. The child feels powerless to protect herself. So the child does not really fear the dark; the child fears what might be lurking in the dark. That's why you, like most parents, wisely use nightlights.

Besides the literal fears of robbers, the young child carries emotionally charged conflicts from the family into the bedroom at night as well. Similar to the shadowy places in the bedroom she cannot quite see, the child cannot quite "see" the conflicts lurking within her own psyche. Once triggered, those underlying conflicts are projected onto the night's blackness; the bedroom becomes a darkened theatre. The child's mind plays out a movie of her own making onto the ominous shadows. She borrows images from cartoons, or even ideas and characters from family members' stories—like I did with my dad's story. Sometimes, she just uses her own creative imagination. Whatever the characters and plot, that nighttime movie symbolically captures the real drama of her daily, inner world.

In more normal families . . . with more normal challenges . . . with more normal affection, a boy like your dear Dylan is usually able to fend off nighttime fears, no matter what those fears represent. He moves beyond them and simply gets used to being alone in his big-boy bed . . . in his big-boy world. I couldn't. The sheer terror of what happened between me and my mother—with its relentless onslaught since my birth—permeated my consciousness. Trauma became my core. Like all toddlers, like all young children, in my attempt to master the terror, I created my own horror movie using your grandfather's storyline about the black widow spider. I relived the day's terror by projecting the drama out onto the curtain of darkness draping my bed night after night. Every night I was in that attic, without exception, I played out the daily turmoil between me and my mother as a virtual life and death struggle with a monster-spider. Once again, I didn't know that at the time. No child does.

In that attic, I never had a peaceful night's sleep. *Never.* Each and every night was filled with unmitigated terror. Though the attic drama continued deep in my psyche, it consciously ceased when we moved into a ranch home at age eight. After about five long years, with no distant attic room to trigger the emergence of the underlying panic, I could now actually begin to "relax" a bit. Or, at least, keep the turmoil buried better as I lay in my bed trying to go to sleep.

One Angry Young Father

No question about it, Kid. Your grandfather was a family man; he wanted to be a good father. In spite of their tough financial situation, my dad saw to it that we had a large plate full of biscuits Sunday mornings for breakfast. One morning when I was about five or six, my dad splurged—and we had three dozen stacked up like a pyramid. I remember trying to count them. Being a 1950s dad, he also made sure that we often had meat and potatoes. It was a matter of strong pride to provide in that way for us. Borrowing his pride that I sensed as a little boy, I remember telling our neighbor that my dad got us pork chops one night. So when my parents let me pick my birthday meal, with pride I chose roast beef with mashed potatoes and gravy. And now . . . well, you know what I look forward to every birthday.

Your grandfather saved his pennies in a cardboard cigar box, and every few months, he loved to treat us kids to baseball cards—in fact a cigar-box full—and divvy them up among the three of us. Uncle Ron and I would then eagerly enter the front porch arena for a challenging game of Hubbards. We'd toss our cards against the side of the house, trying to stand a card up. When one of us finally succeeded, the opponent got one shot to block: You had to toss the card so that it either landed on top of the other's card or hit the card hard enough to knock it down. The winner took all. In trying to stand my card up or knock Uncle Ron's down, I would cheat—or so Uncle Ron accused me. I would reach my hand out with the card in-between my index finger and thumb to toss it, and then crank my wrist back and forth several times to wind it up. However, each time I cranked my wrist, I'd lean a little further into it so that my arm would extend a little closer to the wall. Can't blame a little kid for trying, can you? I was anxious competing against Uncle Ron—after all, he was four years older—and, in my angst, I had trouble letting go of the card, so I'd "hunch," as Uncle

Ron called it. I loved to hunch though I never meant to cheat . . . at least not consciously.

Sometimes, my dad managed to save enough pennies for another treat. He'd gather us into the living room where he'd sit us in a circle and present us with a cigar box with a large number of pennies. We knew what that meant. He'd pitch the pennies to the four corners of the living room, under the davenport, and across to his and my mom's bedroom, and we'd scuttle to scoop up as many as we could. We got to keep what we picked up. Being older, though, my brothers always managed to amass more than me.

What pennies I managed to grab before my brothers got to them would buy some good stuff at Grassi's, where your grandfather got the cigar box full of baseball cards. I loved visiting Grassi's. Pat usually stood behind the counter saying hi with a broad smile as we strolled by to get to the back where that good stuff was. His face was rugged and pockmarked, with teeth that were yellowish to brown, and he was always warm and friendly. Sometimes on my way to the back, I'd stop to look into the mirror sitting on his counter to check out my braces or replace a broken rubber band. I still remember how my teeth ached when they first put them on. The mirror had two sides, and I thought it was pretty cool to flip it around to get a larger view of my teeth. In the back of Grassi's, one of my favorite buys was a small pack of baseball cards with a large flat slab of bubble gum. I wasn't interested in baseball, only the cards to build my reserves for Hubbards—and the slab of gum. It offered me the opportunity to practice blowing huge bubbles. We'd have competitions in the back to see who could blow the biggest before it burst and stuck to our faces.

Long before he ever used a wheelchair—and he stubbornly resisted for years because of embarrassment—your grandfather would sit on the front porch steps to get fresh air and talk with the neighbors. Harry from directly across our narrow street often came over to sit on the step and just talk with him. Sometimes, Mom, drinking her beer, sat out with my dad as they talked back and forth across the street with Harry and his wife, Virginia. Your grandfather and I would often play catch from those porch steps. I'd stand in the middle of the street and throw the ball to him as he remained sitting. Even though he had been a semipro football player, he couldn't handle the football now with his multiple sclerosis, so we threw the baseball. I had to make sure I threw it to his right side, which is where he held his glove. He almost always managed to catch the ball in the small webbing at the top, where you're supposed to, then throw it back lefty. He seemed to enjoy those times; I certainly did. I got to connect with my dad doing something normal.

Your grandfather enjoyed being a father—but harbored deep anger. I don't know if he was angry because of his shattered dreams or if he had already become an angry young man going into his twenties. When I was about seven, he told me how, as a teen, he had gotten so angry with his sister that he had her down on the floor with his hands around her throat, choking her. He said that a still small voice told him to stop—and he did. I have no idea what went on between him and his sister—or, indeed, within his family—growing up. Obviously, to have choked his own sister like that, he'd have to have been carrying a great deal of emotional pain and rage—and perhaps his now shattered dreams stirred all that up. I don't know.

Unfortunately, most men tend to express their emotional pain through anger—and my father was no exception. It is tough for men to allow the "soft" emotions of sadness and fear, or the intense emotions of terror and anguish, to emerge as tears. Men traumatized in war unwittingly keep their trauma going for years, even decades, by not allowing themselves to sob. It's a similar challenge for men who've been traumatized by their parents growing up. If you notice, women have the expression to "have a good cry," but men have no such phrase—let alone an *idea* like that. Yet the research is clear: Men need to cry to release emotional pain, just like women. But because men are testosterone driven—and have learned from the culture that big boys don't cry—they tenaciously hold onto their pain. To cry feels weak. It feels self-betraying. It feels less than manly. What men don't usually realize is that pushing pain down—fighting back tears and choosing to go forward with heads held high—only makes matters worse. The intense emotional pain comes out in other ways: depression, rage, nightmares, alcohol or drug abuse, gambling, or emotional distance. I witnessed my dad having tears twice—only twice—yet the man was in enormous emotional pain for decades, and later, in tremendous physical pain. Being my father's son, I've had to work hard to train myself to feel my tender emotions. I've had to learn to express my terror and pain as tears instead of anger—without embarrassment. If I hadn't learned this tough skill as a man, I, like my father, would've been trapped with these tough emotions buried inside.

Your grandfather often poured out his impulsive anger at us kids; he had little wisdom about how to direct it. One time when I was about five, he punished me in anger—though I don't recall for what. He actually pushed me into Herbie's bedroom, a small room off the front parlor where your grandmother did her hairdressing—turning off the light as he did so. I stood panicked. I then heard the door lock. I was so frightened that I spun in circles looking for the monsters that no doubt would attack me. I turned . . . and kept turning . . . uncontrollably spinning trying to protect myself. The fear cascaded, reaching a fever pitch. I don't recall anything beyond that point.

Your uncle Herb told me that as a young boy, he witnessed our dad putting me in the cellar, turning off the lights, and once again locking the door behind him. Herb said I screamed hysterically. Your uncle felt both angry and helpless, but, being a young boy, was himself intimidated by our father. I have no conscious memory of those terrifying moments in the cellar. No doubt, like the psychic impact of shock after a terrible car accident, those memories are forever blocked from my consciousness. The sheer panic I felt in Herbie's tiny bedroom—and the overwhelming terror in my own cellar—just added to the crushing fear of being alone in my attic prison night after night. My father's actively angry abuse, combined with my mother's profound emotional neglect, caused me to be frightened whenever I'd be isolated in any dark place.

When I was a young teen, Uncle Herb and I hiked and camped among the Saranac Lakes in the Adirondack Mountains of New York State. We were night fishing for catfish from a large boulder on the lake's edge. It was a quiet, peaceful, starlit night. In fact, the panorama of our own starlit galaxy revealed in the pitch blackness of the Adirondacks has been unparalleled for me since my youth. I loved it. But Uncle Herb forgot something. He decided to hike back to our lean-to to fetch it. The lean-to seemed like a long ways away through the woods. He took the bright Coleman lantern with him to light his path, which left me with nothing; no, I didn't have a flashlight on me. Your uncle didn't know I was still terrified of the dark and so didn't think of asking me to join him—and I didn't have the guts to tell him I was scared to be left alone. So I sat on this boulder with my fishing rod in hand watching the lantern and my lifeline to sanity disappear into the woods. When I could no longer see the lantern through the trees, I frantically pulled my hood over my head, shut my eyes tight, tightened my grip on the rod, and hung on for the ride. Waves of panic swept over me. I sat immobile, keeping that death grip on the fishing rod until he came back. In my unconscious imagination, I was locked in Herbie's tiny pitch-black bedroom and in my cellar. But the physical distance between your uncle Herb and me—along with the darkness of that night sky draped over the Saranacs—also consciously triggered the nightly drama of being in my attic bedroom all alone. Sitting isolated on that rock was an intrapsychic one-two punch that left me frozen in sheer terror.

Whenever I sleep alone in the house without your mother—like when she's at a conference or visiting Grampy with you guys—I regress. Nighttime darkness and distance from your mom work as cues for my regression, setting off my flashbacks. It is not really the darkness that I or anyone like me is afraid of. None of us is "afraid of the dark." Instead, darkness strips us of our defenses, and once stripped, the underlying terror that is always there emerges into consciousness. While never having fought in a war myself, this process is just like the Vietnam, Desert Storm, or Iraqi soldiers I've had the privilege of working with over the years who relive their war terror night after night. They are not afraid of the dark either. But darkness and sleep allow the wounded warrior's terror to rise to consciousness. In like manner, I do not—and I cannot—easily fall asleep alone in a darkened, empty house. I have to use lights to stop the flashbacks. The fact is that I can't go into any darkened, empty building alone or into my own darkened basement if the house is empty. Neither distance alone nor darkness alone sparks a flashback; they must work together. But taken together, distance and darkness will prompt whatever intensity of that infantile terror still remains deep inside me from my mother's neglect and my father's abuse— and then fear uncontrollably floods my body.

The Emerging Spiritual Maelstrom

Your Grandfather's "Just-in-Case" Faith

Your grandfather didn't immerse himself in faith like your grandmother. But he did rely on it as an anchor. I don't know if he requested the Eucharist or if Father Donovan offered it, but Father brought it to my dad once a month while we lived on Rugraff. The Eucharist would have awakened his boyhood memories—and stirred his faith deep within his psyche.

Sincere Catholics believe the priest has divine power to change a wafer into the actual, physical body of Jesus whenever he "consecrates" it. At that point, the wafer becomes the "Eucharist." During Mass, the priest declares, "This is my Body," and his words—like God's words "Let there be light" or my dad's words "Golf is boring"—create the reality. The priest's words transform both the bread and wine instantly into the actual body and blood of Jesus. The transformation is not something you can see under a microscope; the physical presence of Jesus is believed to be there by faith. It cannot be proven. The wafer, once consecrated, becomes sacred because it is now truly Jesus—and is the focal event of all Masses.

Sister rigorously prepared us second graders for our First Holy Communion. Besides learning about the Eucharist, we practiced at great length walking down the sanctuary's aisle at a slow pace, folding our hands with all our fingers pointed up to heaven, and gently kneeling at the railing in order to receive Jesus. Both Father and Sister taught us that the priests' fingers were special—anointed to touch Jesus as the wafer. No one else could touch Jesus. Sister told us that we couldn't even chew the host because we'd be chewing

45

Jesus. The wafer's appearance was not to mislead us; Jesus was actually the wafer—so don't chew him.

The day came and I was nervous. Sister required, as was the protocol, for all of us second graders to wear white, including white ties. Family and friends of each second grader eagerly came to witness our receiving Jesus. The church was packed. At the right time during the celebratory Mass, we processed out of the pews into the aisle as practiced and knelt at the railing . . . waiting. After the priest was done consecrating the "elements" of bread and wine, he came to the railing with two altar boys, one on each side. My turn came; Father carefully placed Jesus onto my tongue.

I knew the tongue was safe; it was the teeth that were the challenge. I dared not chew Jesus. Checking gently with my tongue, I made sure my teeth did not bite him on the edge. But, suddenly to my surprise—and I had not anticipated it nor had I been taught anything about what to do if this should happen—Jesus stuck to the roof of my mouth. I panicked. What was I supposed to do? What if I couldn't un-stick him? What would I do with Jesus? I couldn't stick my finger in there to get him off—only the priest's consecrated fingers could do that. It was now time to get up from the railing and slowly walk back to the pew. But he was still stuck. I could feel my anxiety rise. As I gently knelt down in the pew, I had an idea. What if I pulled Jesus off the roof of my mouth with my tongue? Not my finger, but my tongue. Could I do that? I began to knead the edge of Jesus. I wasn't biting him—just gently kneading. I figured if I could pry him off, then I could roll him up into a little ball and swallow him. My strategy worked. He began to peel off, and, as if by magic, he shriveled up, making it possible to roll him up and swallow him. I felt so relieved.

Your grandfather had the same First Holy Communion as a little boy. Now Father came to the house with the Eucharist in a special gold container around his neck—just for my dad—the wafer having already been consecrated at a Mass. Jesus had to be protected from any worldly contamination on the way over. This was, no doubt, a powerful experience for my dad: the stirrings of boyhood awe for Father's presence; unconscious flashbacks to his First Holy Communion; Jesus now coming just for him in this stunning, gold container; time alone to confess sins; and talking privately with this man of God. When Father came in, I'd have to go to the living room and sit on the davenport while he and Dad met at the kitchen table. Where the priest sat—which is where Jesus was—was now a most sacred area. My dad believed that; I could tell. As a boy, I certainly did.

I never knew what they discussed. I'd sit on the davenport pensive, then nervously get up and carefully peer around the corner into the kitchen, catching a glimpse of them talking quietly. I knew the conversations with Father were private, but I was so hoping they'd talk about what was happening to our family. I really wanted Father to make my dad talk to him—and then make him talk to us. Father would leave, but no one would ever talk—ever. Still, I kept hoping. As a boy, I knew the priest had power like God. After all, he could simply speak the "word" and turn the wafer into Jesus. Surely Father, who was holy and close to God, could tell my dad to talk with us—and my dad would have to talk. But it just never happened. Month after month, and then year after year, Father came to give my dad the Eucharist—all the while my unspoken disappointment grew. The way it felt is that God and the priest made a wafer turn into Jesus, but wouldn't—or perhaps couldn't—make my dad talk . . . let alone walk.

At the time of my First Communion, I recall your grandfather explaining to me, "Frankie, it is better to believe than not believe. If you believe—and you're wrong—you've lost nothing, because you've been a good person your entire life. If you don't believe—but you're wrong—you're in deep trouble." Your grandfather's approach to faith had a gentle, practical cynicism built into it. Faith in God might not be valid but—just in case—believe. Your grandfather's faith raised intriguing questions, like: Should one believe in God because one really believes? Or should—and *can*—one believe *just in case?*

Many years later as a teen reflecting on your grandfather's way of believing, I wondered: How does one genuinely believe something while having the attitude "just in case"? Perhaps your grandfather's approach to prayer and worship was like, "I don't know if aliens exist on other planets or not, but, *just in case*, let's send signals out into deep space to let them know we're here." Or perhaps your grandfather's morality was like, "I don't know if there is a cop around the curve, but *just in case*, I'll slow up. Besides, driving slower is safer."

How ought we to think of belief in God? That question emerged in my teens as I dealt with my father's uncertainty. His "just-in-case" faith paradoxically fed my passion to answer the question of faith definitively. It fed my dogged determination to know the truth. It wasn't enough—it has never been enough—to flip the mental coin on whether to believe God exists or not.

In his softly cynical approach to faith, your grandfather alluded to damnation as "deep trouble." To avoid it, he figured it was better to believe. But as my own youthful eyes opened, I grew much more concerned about the "damnation" playing out here and now. Our family was already in deep trouble—and we were in that trouble because we hadn't faced the truth. So finding—and then facing—the truth, whether about life or about God, mattered. Aliens may exist, or they may not. Sending signals into deep space just in case they do exist made sense to me. Slowing up on a curve just in case a cop is sitting there—that too made sense. But as a teen, I felt that if I were to believe God existed, I had to "believe" believe. Either I believed God existed—or not. I couldn't imagine believing in God—*just in case*. And given that my family had already gotten into deep trouble, what made more sense to me was that we absolutely needed to know the truth . . . about whatever, including God. *I needed to know.*

Seed of Doubt

Sister had us rigorously study the Baltimore Catechism. In fact, I had to memorize a great deal of it. One day, I flipped to the very last page and discovered a series of indulgences. Several prayers were listed: One for 120 days, another for 240, and another for 360—and yet another for "plenary." I raised my hand and asked Sister, "What does plenary mean?" She said it meant that all days were wiped out; none remained. I couldn't figure it out. It just didn't make sense to me.

You see, I was worried about going to either purgatory or hell. My father had told me I needed to believe just in case. And Sister said I should be worried as well. She said I'd go to hell if I had "mortal sin on my soul" when I died. If I didn't have any mortal sin on my soul, I'd at least have venial sin to deal with. After all, we all committed minor sins from day to day. While venial sins wouldn't send me to hell—a place of eternal fire intended to punish me forever—such sins would send me to purgatory, which was a temporary burning to both punish and purge me. Venial sins needed to be purged from my soul by the refining fires of purgatory before I could enter heaven. God would not allow me in his presence with any sin "on my soul." However—if I prayed correctly, if I prayed a prayer of indulgence, then I could wipe away some, or even all, of the punishment. That way, if I died right away, I wouldn't have to burn in purgatory . . . or not as long anyway. But, as I stared at that last page in the Catechism, I just couldn't get it. Why would I pick a prayer of indulgence to wipe away 120 days of burning in purgatory—or 240 or 360 for that matter—if I could go right to the plenary and wipe it all away all at once? I raised my hand. Sister couldn't—and didn't—answer me.

Kristen, this is my first conscious memory of my problem with religion. It was at the tender age of eleven, in sixth grade. I "caught" the Church in a contradiction. Not only did it feel odd that one brief prayer could wipe away my future torment. But I couldn't understand why the Catechism offered prayers that could clear various numbers of days off my suffering—including one that could get rid of them all. Why did they put in a prayer for 120 days, or 240 or 360, if they had already created a prayer that took care of *all* days? I also wondered: Why don't people pray the brief plenary prayer every day, or every hour, to make sure their days of intense suffering by burning with fire never accumulated? What about saying the prayer every minute—just to make sure?

The need for spiritual cleansing through intense physical suffering was of utmost importance to Sister and the church—and therefore to me as a kid. Yet here was a blatant contradiction on such an important matter. I just couldn't get it. Around and around it went in my young mind. I was actually so shaken by the striking lack of logic that I just sat there staring at the last page of my blue and white Catechism. As I faced a contradiction on a matter of such monumental importance, I knew one thing: It didn't make any sense to me—and I hated the fact that it didn't make sense.

I found out much later as an adult that indulgences, introduced in the sixth century, were also a problem for Martin Luther, who was a Catholic monk in the 1500s. He became so upset with various contradictions in the Church's teachings that he formally challenged them. This eventually led to the protesting or "Protestant" movement. Of course, I knew nothing of this movement as a young child. Sadly, the priests and nuns in grammar school told me that Protestants were destined for hell. And they warned me: If I ever dared to step foot in a Protestant church, I would be "committing a mortal sin." Should I die before "going to Confession," thereby getting absolution, I'd die with that mortal sin on my soul and go straight to hell—to burn forever.

Believe it or not, Kid, sitting at my wooden desk at that very young age pondering the contradiction of indulgences was a defining moment for me. I changed. I went from passively believing in the Catholic religion to actively searching for religious truth—and I've never stopped searching for truth since. In that way—paradoxically—it was a positive, life-changing moment. Looking back, it's incredible to think that such a pivotal moment happened at such a tender age. But it did.

In the wake of this mental shake-up—what some might call a paradigm shift—I knew intuitively I could no longer trust religious authority for clarity of truth about God. It was too easy to make stuff up. While not being the only reason, the ease with which religious leaders could fabricate spiritual "truth" became one reason—and a key motive—for my own decision years later to enter seminary. I wanted the truth; I wanted to find it for myself. To be sure, the embryonic distrust that emerged at age eleven was just a seed. After all, the religious rituals and Catholic beliefs were yet wrapped in, around, and through my psyche as a little boy. One such belief was that I dared not question my faith. Doubt could have devastating consequences. I could be damned to hell for eternity. And my dad had already warned me—better to be safe than sorry when it came to believing in God. Still, that tiny seed was real. Having been planted in the soil of my mother's deep depression, watered by my father's unshed tears of desperation, and cultivated by my own trauma, that seed germinated.

The Dawn of My Reformation

We all know most people don't usually like to discuss—let alone argue—religion. One reason is that people figure, "What's the point?" There is no basis for arguing. That is, all one has to say is, "My beliefs are by faith, not by proof." How do you argue against that? How do you get at any belief that hides behind the wall of "It's by faith, not by proof?" In fact, how do you argue *for* something— not just *against* something—that you believe "by faith?" There seems to be no way to get a handle on it. So—how, as a kid, was I to argue against the prayers of indulgence? After all, it was a matter of faith. Growing up, the problem of justifying faith in indulgences grew into the bigger issue of how in the world I was going to justify *any* faith at all in God. In sixth grade, my questioning indulgences began a process that eventually led to my asking the big questions of God.

I'm not alone. For innumerable children facing religious contradictions—contradictions created by a full range of religious officials including rabbis, priests, and ministers—the dominos of trust in their leaders, and therefore of trust in God himself, begin to slowly topple. The inconsistencies work on them deep in their psyches. By the time they become teenagers, they often feel apathetic or cynical about faith—if not outright rebellious against religion. Captivated by doubt, Christian teens may conclude, "All religion is man-made." They may cynically think, "The stories of Jesus were made up to make us believe he was God."

The word "God" is an odd word, Hon. We usually think we know what people are referring to when they use that word. But, over the years, I've discovered that we can't assume we know what someone means when he says he believes in "God." The word is too abstract. It is so abstract that it really opens the door for any of us— including religious leaders—to create virtually any spiritual picture we want and give it the label "God." "God" becomes a word we fill with our own meaning. It is like an inkblot test that psychologists use to get a picture of how someone thinks. The inkblot is just a blob of ink on a piece of cardboard with no particular form to it. The psychologist asks the person to tell them what they "see" when they look at the inkblot. What the person sees depends on their life experience. That is, they unconsciously create a picture that they then think they see in the inkblot—a picture formed by how they see reality. The picture is a "projection" of their imaginations. So what they see tells us a great deal about them—and little about the inkblot. The dark inkblot is just a cue to trigger the nonconscious intrigues of their minds—like the attic darkness triggered mine. The word "God" is like that. It is just a word, a trigger—and we project onto it whatever we want spiritual reality to be. In that way, "God" becomes an extension of our psyches; we make God into what we think makes sense to us. God becomes what we want God to be. We make God into our own image.

What people believe about God usually tells us more about them than it does about God. This is true whether we're talking about the golden calf of the Old Testament, primitive tribal gods, Greek gods and goddesses, present-day radical Islam, or New Age spirituality that believes that the invisible energy field of subatomic particles is "God." It is also true about how differently Christians picture God. Some think God is a God of harsh judgment; others think he is a God of grace only. Some Christians believe that the terrorist attacks on September 11, 2001, were God's judgment on the United States for its moral decline, while many think that's ridiculous . . . if not cruel.

Sadly, we often—and perhaps typically—believe things about God without ever questioning whether what we believe is valid or not. We rarely concern ourselves with *how* we determine the truth of what we believe. We simply believe what we want to believe. It's easier. It's narcissistic; it's kissing ourselves in the mirror. That's inkblot faith.

And that's what the Baltimore Catechism did on its last page. Church leaders created a picture of God that somehow made sense to them. I don't know how it made sense since the contradiction was blatant to even an eleven-year-old. But the man-made system of purification on that last page was a projection of their collective psyche, telling me more about their imaginations than about the God who is there. In point of fact, that last page of the Catechism became an imprint in my psyche—a mental monument to the man-made contradictions of religion. That is why, to this day, I can vividly see that last page of the Catechism in my imagination.

Besides being the first religious domino to topple, that last page—a page of stark contradiction—had also become a symbol, or metaphor, for the mind-bending paradoxes within my own family. My cynicism had actually already begun long before that catechetical lesson. I just hadn't realized it.

Losing My Dad

Your grandparents had been waiting a long time with great angst; the family's struggle for survival seemed to hang in the balance. But the Veterans Administration finally came through. They determined that your grandfather had become 100 percent disabled with multiple sclerosis through his military service. The life-changing implication was that the VA compensated him monthly for the remainder of his life for his service to his country. I've noted earlier the saying that money can't buy happiness—and it certainly didn't for my family—but it did provide some opportunities for that possibility. It allowed your grandparents to move on with life. The income made it possible for your grandparents to buy another small house, a ranch this time, in the outskirts of the city. Though I continued to go to Holy Family School until eighth grade, at age eight, I left my home on Rugraff—and the Dutchtown neighborhood that had anchored my parents and had been the cast around my broken identity.

The moving truck arrived early in the morning, parking in front of our house. I was excited. I peeked through the window, noticing that the truck was painted entirely in black, with 650 written in large white numbers on the sides. My dad called them the "650 Movers." At age eight, I had no idea what those numbers meant, but that was their name.

One item they moved was our icebox—not the old wooden box with large blocks of ice as the refrigerant—but our new electric icebox, what people now call a refrigerator. When my father got rid of our first electric icebox, he wisely took off the door, telling me that was to make sure I didn't accidentally get locked in and suffocate. With the door safely off, I thought it was great fun to climb in and peer out. I actually used the name "icebox" for "refrigerator" going into adulthood, finding it hard to change to the new name. In fact, as a teen I really did wonder why others called it a refrigerator and not an icebox since that's what I had always known it as. It was the same way for other words—like "cellar," which is now "basement," and "davenport," now meaning "sofa bed." And, as was the neighborhood practice for all fabric furniture, we covered the davenport in thick clear plastic to protect it. Getting furniture had been such a grand effort for those on such limited incomes that prolonging the life of the furniture was a top priority. Comfort was second.

In the move to Ridgeway Avenue, our new address, the two movers strained hard to lift our new electric icebox onto the small concrete stoop of our new house. One of the men lost his grip, and the refrigerator fell on his finger, slicing it open badly. He looked stunned. I stared with intense curiosity at my mother's act of kindness in bandaging the man's finger with gauze and tape. While bandaging him, she did not smile or look warmly on him at all. She just did it— like she had when I put my right arm through the back porch door.

Our new little ranch actually had a detached garage, which I thought was a big deal as a kid, set back from the house a bit. And the backyard was huge—so huge that my mother and I planted a garden where we grew corn, carrots, lettuce, potatoes, asparagus, radishes, tomatoes, peas, and beans . . . among other things. We had long rows of them—one after another after another. My father told me the property was almost as big as a football field, and, looking back, it may have been. My guess is that the garden was about fifty feet wide by about sixty feet deep to the back of our property line. Unfortunately, as you know, I never took to eating many vegetables except for peas, corn, radishes, and carrots . . . but only if the carrots were cooked with beef, like on my birthday. However, I did enjoy growing them. I especially loved picking the corn off the tall stalks, with the challenge of figuring out when they were ready to be plucked. The cobs with small, whitish kernels always cooked to a sweet, subtle savor, while the cobs with large, bright yellow kernels were chewier with a more robust taste. My father enjoyed the small kernels better. I loved them both, though I've always preferred the stronger flavor of the larger kernels. And, as you know, to this day I absolutely love corn on the cob. Even though my mom and I tended the garden together, she rarely talked to me; she was always off in her own world. At least I got to hang with her a bit while weeding and harvesting.

Sadly, your grandfather just kept getting worse. His fragile ability to enjoy the few material things we had diminished. He lost more use of his legs, then later, his hands. So he poured his time and mental energy into exercise, watching television, and chain-smoking. That's it. After decades of his disability, the city recognized your grandfather as one of the longest living MS patients in the community. I have no doubt that it was his determination. But his determination had little direction. He exercised—then lost himself in television and smoking. But the exercise had no direction. Sadly, at that time, the community offered little real help for victims of multiple sclerosis. No one advised or helped your grandfather to develop a strategic plan for his life—not the Veterans Administration, not his MS support group, and not the church. Tragically, the priest who came monthly to give your grandfather the Eucharist not only didn't coach my dad to talk to his family but also never suggested the family create a plan. No one ever asked—or answered—the absolutely central question: *Now what?* Given the MS . . . given the lost dreams . . . given the dashed hopes—now what? Obviously, my dad never thought of it himself. There was no family plan. There was no life plan. Nothing.

No doubt, holding his emotional pain inside only fueled your grandfather's depression and anger. I had always been frightened of his volatile temper, going back to when he locked me in that small room. As he got worse—as they both got worse—your grandparents argued more, especially at night. I often went to bed hearing them go at it, lying there frozen in fear about what was happening to them. Sometimes, out of the blue in the middle of the night, my dad would just yell at my mom, probably because he was so anxious and agitated—and I'd lose more sleep lying there scared . . . wondering, what's next?

It was after we moved to our ranch house that my father routinely depended on me more to take care of his basic needs. Before that, he relied more on my mother and my brother Herb. But Herb is nine years older, so, when I was ten, he was nineteen and moving on to college. I routinely had to come home after school to help my father work out on his electric Exercycle. I'd lift him on it, put his feet onto the pedals, tighten the foot straps, and then sit there in front of the cycle making sure he didn't fall off while working the on/off switch. With my dad slowly becoming quadriplegic, I'd have to turn the cycle off repeatedly in order to get up to adjust his position so he could stay on. Routinely, I'd also stand slightly next to and behind him in our narrow hallway at a wooden handrail, holding his lit cigarette so he could take puffs on command, and push his arms and legs back and forth when he chose. These were his pathetic attempts at fighting the disease—and, without ever asking, it was presumed that I was in his service to help him do so. He never asked me if I was willing to make the sacrifice to help him. Never. At suppertime, instead of my mom, I'd sometimes cut up his food and feed him.

As your grandfather became progressively worse and I grew into a teen, your grandparents built another ranch home, this time with ramps as well as hallways and doorways wide enough to accommodate a wheelchair. Yet the workload in caring for your grandfather only grew. Often I'd have to lift him out of bed in the morning. As a teen I'd weightlift, so I had the strength for a time to grab him under his armpits to raise him up. Later, as he became more paralyzed and "deadweight," I'd have to use a mechanical lift to hoist him up and over into the wheelchair. I'd wheel him into the bathroom, lift him onto the toilet, then clean him off, and shower him. If it isn't obvious, he required nursing home care—but we provided it for him instead. All these things were his unspoken demands. He never once considered going to a nursing home. I don't know how the topic came up, but one day he simply blurted out, "I'd rather be dead than go into a nursing home." Your grandmother never said a word. And that was that.

As I head into late midlife—and with your mom's and my purchase of long-term care insurance some years back—I am aware that your grandfather's "word" spoken into my mental universe once again forged an attitude within me that likely would not be there otherwise. I myself really do see nursing homes as parking lots for death. As you know, Hon, I have no interest in being a burden on you guys as your grandfather was on us. That's why I am so careful not to presume on you with my present disability, though I know it is a hassle for you to deal with sometimes. Nevertheless, I dread the possibility of going into a care facility. Like your grandfather, I'd rather be dead. I am too independent and have too many things to accomplish in life to be shuffled off to some impersonal holding ground to be put on life's shelf waiting to die. That attitude is your grandfather in me.

When I was a college student, my senior year I put together a conference where the speaker, a Christian psychologist, described to us the final days of a camp counselor. This energetic counselor went to summer camp even though he was dying—and everyone at camp knew it. Instead of being maudlin, everyone celebrated this man's last days by singing hymns with him around the campfire. That's how I'd want to go, if I had a choice. Forget all the tubes and monitors. And to heck with a nursing home. I'd want to be with my family . . . with your mom or one of you holding me in your arms or with my head on your lap . . . lying next to a fireplace—and singing hymns as I leave this life behind.

Through my tough teen years, I felt deeply ambivalent about my father. I felt so drained helping him with all his mundane tasks. Along with that, I so hated missing some after-school opportunities because of it. Yet this was my father. Still, my father was willing to use me—even use me up—in his service. My guess is that the gnawing sense of my father using me would have been very different if he had made the grand effort to love me. If he had gotten out of himself long enough to be a father; if he had talked with me; if, quadriplegic or not, he had found some way to play with me; if he had created some game plan for living life with MS; if he had become a man of wisdom who had more to offer than the burden of his own disability; if he had talked with us about what we were all going through, then—just maybe—it would have felt more like a privilege than a burden to serve him. But I didn't get much back for my efforts other than the roof over my head. Yet this was my father. What was I to think? And what was I to do? Like a good son—and just like your grandmother—I simply did my duty for my father while secretly resenting him for his presumption.

Tragically, in my father's earnest but self-absorbed struggles for survival, he had lost sight of his son. Any vision for fathering he once had when we lived in Dutchtown—reflected in buying baseball cards, tossing pennies on the floor to delight his children, and throwing the ball with his boy—had disappeared after we moved to Ridgeway. Without the engaging support of his neighbors and church, without the incredible solidarity of our Dutchtown community wrapped tight around his own terror and loss of meaning, my father spun out of control. Though he was of the "builder" generation, the generation prior to the baby boomers, he too had become a "lost boy," but for different reasons. Yes, I still had a father. But I had lost my dad.

Your Grandmother's Disillusioned Faith

Though lost in her own world of emotional isolation—and keeping a death grip on the bottle—your grandmother had nevertheless reached out to God, grasping firmly onto the lifeline of her Christian faith. Like the vast majority of immigrants before her, her faith was genuine and integrated into her daily routine. Kristen, I believe she held on the best she could. Faith kept her connected to something bigger than her turmoil—and became a source of hope in the face of her shattered dreams.

Your grandmother faithfully tied us to that larger world, seeing to it that we exercised many Catholic rituals. We mindfully wrapped holy scapulars around our bedposts for protection from bad things happening to us. We were tied to a community of invisible souls that actively watched out for us: guardian angels (I sometimes made room for mine when I sat at my school desk); a saint who found lost items; another who protected us on the highway; patron saints with whom we could have a special relationship; and Mary, Jesus' mother, who talked to Jesus on our behalf. I was proud to have St. Francis of Assisi—one of the more famous of the saints who left his father's wealth to help the poor—as my patron saint. In fact, the new pope as of this writing has adopted his name for his papacy. Given he was my patron, I knew St. Francis of all the saints would pay special attention to my life and help me along the way. Over the decades since my childhood, I've actually thought of St. Francis often. In fact, it made sense to me that Millard Fuller left his wealth—he was a self-made millionaire by the age of twenty-nine—to found Habitat for Humanity, in part because of St. Francis.

Once, I had lost some of my treasured baseball cards I used for Hubbards. My mom told me to pray to St. Anthony, the patron saint of finding lost things. I knelt at the black wrought-iron stand at the back corner of my church's sanctuary. It was directly across from the confessional booths and held all the candles lit to the saints. (Many parishioners were strongly relying on the saints.) I put a dime—which could buy a lot of baseball cards at Grassi's—into the slot of the black metal box thinking St. Anthony needed money to help me. I picked up one of the very long, thin wooden sticks, lit it from another candle, and carefully moved it to an unlit candle that would become my personal connection with St. Anthony. Now I could relax. This saint was going to find what I was looking for.

I never did find my baseball cards. I wondered, if St. Anthony had the job to find things on my behalf, why didn't he have the *power* to do it? I had the same question of St. Christopher regarding his oversight of a much more important matter: protection on the road while driving. Under my mother's eager directive, I had put a small St. Christopher statue on the dashboard of our car. I don't remember where we were, but Herb says we were all coming back from a diner at the south end of Sodus Bay. The road was very muddy. I was in the back with my brothers, and my dad was driving. (This before his MS was so crushing.) My father suddenly swerved to avoid an oncoming car, spinning out of control. Our car finally came to rest. I was in the back on the floor. (This was long before seat belts.) My mother told me to stay down, but I decided to stand up anyway to take a peak. There we were: the front of the car was perched at the very edge of this steep cliff—and there was no guardrail. Had St. Christopher protected us? I was sure that he had. But then I pondered: Why did others with statues on their dashboards get into accidents? I never understood; I was confused.

Like many devoted Catholic women of our Dutchtown neighborhood, your grandmother expressed her faith openly. She built a little shrine to Mary in our yard and had me help build it. Later, when I was a teen in high school, she arranged for us to take a pilgrimage of cathedrals in Canada with the longing hope that Jesus would heal your grandfather of his multiple sclerosis.

At one cathedral—Sainte-Anne-de-Beaupré in Canada—millions of people have come over the years seeking healing from Jesus, with about half a million seeking help each year. The cathedral was gorgeous and the grounds were magnificent. I don't know how many people were there, but it was packed, with one night's processional outside appearing as a sea of people. We joined them. All I could see were long lines of candles in a slow but singular movement against the backdrop of the night sky. It was indeed a poignant sight. All had come seeking healing from Jesus or St. Anne.

As I took in the breathtaking beauty of St. Anne's ornate ceiling and the stunning sculpture of St. Anne herself, I could feel the unspoken hope in the three of us. On the beautiful grounds, there was an open-air shrine at the top of a very long staircase of concrete steps, but I cannot recall if it was a statue of St. Anne or another personage, like Mary, Jesus' mother. Your grandmother and I slowly and prayerfully climbed it together—on our knees as was the practice there—in the hope that such show of faith would persuade Jesus to heal my dad. I begged Jesus as I climbed. It sure seemed like a very long time on my knees.

At that same cathedral, in a large room off the lobby, my dad met a woman who also had multiple sclerosis. She claimed God had healed her—but only for a time. She said she needed that time to take care of her children, and Jesus had given it to her. Then, when that need was met, the healing was reversed and she went back to the wheelchair. I momentarily wondered: What about us? And why would Jesus take her healing back?

Around the corner from us was the lobby area at the back of the church, where on the wall were literally hundreds of crutches and wheelchairs and braces of people who had been healed. I was taken aback by the sheer number of them. Healing was possible. Look at them all. For a few moments, I pondered whether the stories were true . . . while also picturing my dad's wheelchair up on that wall.

Back home, my dad just got worse. One night shortly after this spiritual pilgrimage when I was quietly sitting on the living room floor and my dad was sitting on a chair watching TV, my mother blurted out, "I will not live long. I'll be the first to go." I sat there stunned. I found myself just staring at her and wondering: what did you mean? I looked up at my father, anxiously waiting for him to say something—anything—but he just sat there in silence. The long moment passed without comment. My father and I shifted our startled gazes back to the television. I have no idea what he was thinking, but I sat there just staring at the TV—not watching it—but deep in thought about what had just happened. As I meditated on her tough words, it became clear to me that my mother's desperate hopes of her husband being cured—and with it, the hope of a different life—had been utterly dashed. My mom had become a fully broken woman. When that hit me, I was sickened with sadness. My mother's agonizing disillusionment just melded into my own. But it would be years before I caught the other meaning of her dispirited words.

 *Beyond Their Problems*

Your Grandparents' Deep Character

On one level, your grandparents were confused and lost souls. On
another level, they knew exactly what they stood for.

In order to look back and see their strong values, however, I've
had to claw my way out of the sinkhole created by their poor decisions. Having done so, it is crystal clear that their sound character
became the solid foundation for the fine character of their sons—
and through us, you guys, as well as my nieces and nephew. After
all, I chose your mom—her good, bad, and ugly—because of how I
was built by your grandparents. Your mom was on my radar screen
because of them. (And vice-versa, of course.) So your children, and
their future children, owe their character to your grandparents,
whom you've never met. Incredibly, in the ways we live as families
now—your mom and I, you and your husband, your brother Paul
and his wife, your brother Matt, and our dear grandchildren—we
all keep reaffirming the values and deep character delivered to us
by them.

Your grandparents' character was the character of Dutchtown
that had once wrapped them as a young couple. In community, they
were strong. Once they left Dutchtown, while holding onto their
core principles, they drowned. Tragically, they didn't or couldn't
apply their core values well enough to their own massive suffering to create quality family life. They lost their cherished vision
for family—and community—that they once had as young parents.
Being my parents' son, I've long understood their struggle. I've had
to work too hard for way too long to transform my own suffering

into wisdom and character—and create some decent quality of family life.

It is a maddening paradox. In a sense, your grandparents walked through life in shock. They were good people with excellent values walking about aimlessly—like accident victims wandering about with no purpose but to wander after surviving a horrific car accident. I've experienced physical shock just once, though I've lived through intense emotional shock several times—several times beyond my chronic trauma as a child. One time, as a young teen, I plugged in a toaster not realizing the insulation had been worn off the wires where they entered the plug. When I pushed the plug into the outlet, electricity instantly and intensely jolted me. I don't actually recall the jolt itself. But it threw me into the dining area, about eight feet away. I stood there frozen. I have no idea if the jolt created a popping sound, but the next thing I knew your grandmother was standing in front of me calling my name repeatedly, "Frankie, Frankie, Frankie. . . ." I could see her but barely hear her; she seemed very far away. (Though I know she called my name repeatedly, I cannot hear the quality of her voice. I do not know her voice.) I also couldn't move. But I actually had the wherewithal to think: How do I get out of this? I decided that if I cried, I might unfreeze. As the tears began to flow, I could move. But as I did, your grandmother remained frozen, offering no comfort. I stood there feeling dazed, wondering what had just happened to me. Everything around me felt surreal. Then I looked down to find that the jolt had blackened a third of my hand. I don't recall if it was the carbon remains of the burnt insulation or if the top layer of the skin itself had been fried.

My experience of physical shock—the strange sense of feeling frozen with fear wrapped in an utterly dream-like state—serves as a picture of what happened to your grandparents. Your grandfather's devastating disability shattered this couple's youthful dreams, launching them into an unreal realm of their own psychic shock from which they never returned. They wandered about aimlessly in life from that point on. Tragically, reeling from the pain, your grandmother just added to the surreal through her abusive drinking—burying the grief of her lost dreams while creating enormous emotional distance between her and her family. That's why she just stood there, frozen, calling my name but offering no comfort. At that moment, she was as far away in her own dazed world of shock as I was in mine. She never did make it back. And your grandfather calmed his nerves with nicotine, while blindly running from his terror through rote exercise and televised sports. That's one reason I do not watch hour after hour of televised sports. Give me an occasional game of football, including the Super Bowl—or golf, like the Ryder Cup, where Europe upset the United States in 2012. But rarely do I want to be the couch potato. I'd rather be living life—with my two arms and two legs.

Incredibly, in spite of all of what these two young people had gone through, they kept their solid values for a lifetime: sincerity; keeping one's word; belief in the equality of all people; compassion; and doing one's duty. Whatever else they were, your grandparents were indeed people of deep character. I want you to know that I wouldn't have what positive character I do have—and you wouldn't be the fine young person you are—without them having had the depth of character they had. They stood on a neighborhood platform of God, hard work, and integrity.

I do see the apparent paradox when I say that your grandparents modeled the character of God. Still, the whole idea that—if there were to be a God—he could be a God of sincerity, honesty, trustworthiness, love, compassion, and duty made sense to me because such core values made sense to your grandparents. Those unwavering values were modeled by your grandparents and became central to my identity. However imperfect . . . however confused . . . however pathogenic to me, your grandparents nevertheless imprinted me with their principles—Christian principles—principles which reflect the very character of Jesus Christ. Your grandparents imprinted you with those same values through me. And your grandparents imprinted you through the woman I was drawn to—inescapably drawn because she was made of the same "right stuff." That was—and remains—the power of your grandparents' deep character.

Sincerity

When your mother and I travelled back to Upstate New York for my twentieth high school reunion, Dick and his wife invited us out for ice cream. Dick was part of my inner circle in high school. Along with our mutual friend Joe, he introduced me to sailing at fourteen. As you know, I can't swim well, so that's why, besides being the smart thing to do, I always wear a life vest on our sailboats. One day at Dick's home, which was right on the rocky shoreline of Lake Ontario, he and Joe wanted to sail the Sunfish. Having been on it, you know how big a Sunfish is—not very. I had never been sailing before, and, not being a swimmer, I was intimidated. But they twisted my arm—and I caved. They reassured me that the boat would not flip. Three teens on a Sunfish . . . who were they fooling? Well, they fooled me and I went.

When we got a ways from shore, they accidentally flipped the boat, dropping me between the boom and the deck. As I made my way around to the other side, the boat then turtled, with the mast and sail pointing to the lake bottom and the boat's daggerboard pointing straight up. Instinctively, I quickly put a death grip on the daggerboard. Dick wanted my hands off so they could right the boat, of course, but I mindlessly hung on, nervously exclaiming, "I can't swim!" He retorted, "But you have a life jacket on!" "Oh," I said with great insight—and let go. They then righted the boat. We capsized so many times that I finally said to heck with it and asked to take the helm. Dick showed me how to work the tiller and sheet, and I had a blast trying to heel the boat on its edge without dropping it in the water—which I did several times—but, by that point, capsizing had become part of the fun. With the last capsize, we lost the rudder pin and had to swim the boat to shore, then carefully walk along the lakebed's rocky bottom for about a mile. The power plant nearby was constantly dumping effluent into the lake, which cushioned our walk a bit, though it made the three of us wonder what we were walking in. When we finally arrived at Dick's home, my feet were cut and very sore, not to mention having absorbed who knows what from the waste. But I had fallen in love with sailing.

The first thing Dick said when we sat down for ice cream was, "Frank, of all the people I've met since we've left high school, you are the sincerest person I've ever known." My face must've turned various shades of red—and I had no idea what to say. I certainly felt awkward. But Dick had simply seen your grandparents in me. There was no deceit or hypocrisy in them; what you saw is what you got. To be sure, I've reaffirmed that sincerity along the way as an adult, but I take no particular credit for it. Your grandparents were unpretentious—and I just happened to grow up with that same style. Sincerity makes sense to me from the inside out because it made sense to your grandparents.

In sincerity, your grandfather negotiated with the salesman, expecting him to be as transparent as he was. The salesman assured my dad that some little old lady had previously owned the car—and it had never been in an accident. So, without asking me whether I liked the car or not, he bought me the used 1968 Buick Skylark to go back and forth to college.

As I learned her abilities in the North Country snow near the Canadian border along the St. Lawrence River—snow which stayed on the ground most of the academic school year—I found myself affectionately calling her the "Tank." She was a large, heavy (over 3,200 pounds), rear-wheel-drive car with a 350-cubic-inch, V-8 engine under the hood. I grew to really like my Tank, even though she was not my choice. Being from Rochester, right on Lake Ontario, I was not only used to snow but loved it. However, the North Country snow was even more gorgeous. Being mostly farm country around the little college town of Potsdam, there was no industry to dirty the surface of the white carpet spread all around us—and the carpet was deep. Plowing it would have been foolish; instead, maintenance crews scooped it into trucks then dumped it into the river. They wisely left a layer of snow on the roads with a little sprinkling of sand for traction.

During the frigid winter, I kept a three-quarter to full tank of gas for weight in the back since it was rear-wheel drive. In my trunk, I carried sand both for extra weight over the wheels as well as to sprinkle on the snow for traction if needed, though I never did. I also kept chains to wrap onto the rear tires. When we'd get a foot of snow in the parking lot, I'd strap my chains on and—the Tank being the Tank—plow my way through. I could go almost anywhere . . . anytime. I felt invincible.

When your mom and I were engaged, we drove from college to her Mammy's farm near St. Johnsville to make wedding arrangements. We were in the backcountry of her old stomping grounds when we ran into a snowstorm at dusk. There was already a good deal of snow on the roads, so, at the intersection of two back roads, I stopped to strap my chains on. By the time I got them on, the sun had set. The road was not lit. The snow was falling heavily, giving us whiteout conditions. Turning the high beams on just made it worse, of course; the light bounced off the snowflakes right back at us, and we couldn't see. I mentioned to your mom that we should pull over to wait it out. She confidently said we didn't need to; she knew the road from memory. I said, "What?" with a bit of surprise. She said that she'd direct me from memory. I paused for a brief moment, but knowing I was in my Tank, I was game. So I rolled down my window and turned the high beams on in case we could see any treetops—my left high beam was out of line and actually pointed high and off to the left so it worked a bit to my advantage in this case. We continued on. She noted that the creek followed us on the right. We drove blind, except for an occasional treetop on my left, while your mom continued to guide us, saying, "Bear to the left . . . a little more . . . that's OK . . . now straighten up . . . now bear to the right . . ."—and so on. We must've driven that way for twenty minutes before the snowfall let up enough to see. Not once did we leave the road, or if we did, we never noticed. While your mom and I have driven an awful lot in the snow, including pushing through brief snow squalls that were just as blinding, never have I driven for such a length of time blind. Nestled in the Tank, I did feel invincible. But now that I'm thinking about it, what a testimony to the trust, however naïvely innocent, I had in your mother.

I took good care of my Tank. I taught myself how to perform oil changes and tune-ups, adjust the timing, install new mufflers and pipes, and clean and adjust the carburetor. I avoided the brakes; I don't know why, but I don't think I trusted myself with them. I also taught myself to do modest bodywork, which I wasn't half-bad at. When, after having had the car for many years and needing to repair the left rear side panel, I found out that, in fact, "the little old lady" who had supposedly owned

the car had actually crushed the entire left rear panel. The metal underneath the fiberglass repair had been massively damaged. I was angry. I
wasn't angry that the car had been damaged. I was angry because, years
before, the car salesman had insulted my father with his lie that the car
had never been in an accident. He even brazenly dishonored my dad
by using the "little old lady" line. Feeling a bit protective of my dad, I
never did tell him what I discovered.

Lying. Your grandmother hated lying. I was about six, and outside throwing around my somewhat beat-up rubber ball. I really
liked tossing the ball against this one neighbor's house. This wasn't
a toss of just a few feet against the siding of the house next door.
This was a long toss against the house sitting on our backyard. I'd
throw it into the back of that neighbor's house to see if I could get it
to bounce right back into my own yard, missing their yard and the
fence that divided our small properties. The siding was not as it is
today. Siding today is sometimes aluminum that could dent easily
by a rubber ball's impact. Or, more commonly now, it is vinyl—
where the ball makes a loud, hollow cracking sound when it hits,
and it just doesn't bounce back well. But back in the fifties, our
siding was like roofing shingles on the side of the house. When the
ball hit, it simply made a nice "thud" and bounced right back at
you. The houses behind us were close—extremely close by today's
standards—making great targets for my ball. For the record, I never
did hit a window. I was having fun throwing the ball until your uncle
Ron decided to snitch on me. Your grandmother sternly called me in
and, instead of confronting me with the truth right away, she set me
up by simply asking me if I was throwing the ball against the houses.
Like any young boy or politician with any savvy at all, I told her no.
Only after I hanged myself with the lie did she then confront me
with Ron's testimony. She brought out the jar of red pepper flakes
she used for her spaghetti sauce, then told me to open my mouth
wide, pouring the flakes in. My mouth was filled—and my tongue
burning—with those large flakes. I never did lie to her again. And,
frankly, I've hated lying ever since.

One could focus on how mean this was to do to a little boy—not
to mention risky if I had breathed those flakes in accidentally. This
is a far cry from appropriate training in truth-telling for a youngster.
But my focus here is on how your grandmother hated lying—and
now, so do I. This is not a bad thing. After all, lying destroys. It

destroys one's own mind by putting fabrication above reality. It weakens if not destroys trust in relationships. It erodes the very lifeblood of community, whether the small community of the family or the broader community of one's hometown . . . or America itself. Look at what happens when our politicians deceive us. Contrary to how so many people rationalize lying—convincing themselves it's clever and useful, just like little kids—lying, in fact, destroys. After a lie, the relationship becomes quicksand. You never know where things stand. You're playing a peekaboo game with the truth. I find lying to be dishonoring. I won't lie to you, not even little white lies (unless it's in the service of keeping a surprise, of course!), because it degrades you. And I won't lie to my clients because if they sense that I am spinelessly protecting myself from admitting a mistake, then how can I call them to have the courage to admit theirs? I'd be a hypocrite, not to mention destroying their trust in my ability to handle their damaged psyches. So I won't do it. Besides, it's just not me. I hate lying—just like your grandmother. And I hated it in that salesman.

That car salesman likely figured he could get away with the deception because he thought your grandfather wouldn't check out the car given his disability. But he had also sized up your grandfather as being just that naïvely sincere that he could get away with such an audaciously standard lie. Perhaps your grandfather secretly knew the salesman was pitching a line to him but felt so helpless with his extraordinarily limiting disability that he just made an expedient decision to cut the deal and be done with it. I don't really know. But my guess is that your grandfather really was that innocently unpretentious.

My parents' sincerity did indeed shape my character. But their naïveté laced through that sincerity also set the contours for my style of sincerity, from simple social protocols to my interpersonal style to my public speaking. My poor to lower-middle-class background shows in simple things like the way I lay out utensils around a plate. I have neither known how nor cared; I still have to double-check with your mom when I set a table. Your mom and I still use a pad under a tablecloth to protect the simple but beautiful cherry tabletop underneath—a holdover from our parents' protecting their furniture by covering it with plastic. On occasion Mom and I take the cloth and pad off to challenge ourselves and enjoy the table's modest beauty.

Interpersonally, I am like a bowling ball with lots of holes; it is easy to grab me. My down-to-earth, unpolished, and banged-around-by-life approach is just like the style of a friend of mine who is senior pastor of a large church. Over lunch one day, he shared with me how he was surprised that he had been hired by his congregation a decade earlier because he was so flawed—and showed it. He called himself the "country bumpkin" of senior pastors for large churches. Over the years, he realized that that was actually one of his strengths: Folks could identify with him. Whether he was talking to CEOs, traditional housewives, or truck drivers, his problems were their problems; his humanity was their humanity. Beyond that, the pastor and I agreed that our words would never roll off the tips of our tongues like silver dollars. Don't get me wrong; we were not being self-deprecating. We both knew we were articulate and passionate—others consider us excellent public speakers—but truly neither of us is like polished silver.

Finally, my lack of opportunities in life, due to my limited childhood and later my disabilities, contribute to a real experiential ignorance of certain aspects of life, culture, and politics. To any discerning eye and ear, it shows. It really does.

I have felt this lack in a number of ways over the years. I felt it with a good friend of mine from graduate school days with whom I once had weekly lunches. He grew up learning classical piano as well as acting at a very high level of expertise. In college, he studied an incredibly wide range of literature at a prestigious school overseas. And his family travelled throughout Europe. He was not traumatized as a child, and had his health . . . both mental and physical. Still does. His fortunate beginnings, normal childhood, and extraordinary talents stand as a stark contrast to my life. I didn't covet the money he grew up with, but I did covet the opportunities and skills that that money bought him, not to mention the inherent normalcy of his childhood that no amount of money could ever buy. Nonetheless, I have always focused on playing the hand dealt to me and maximizing what opportunities I do have—without getting too distracted by envy. Yet, since my early midlife disabilities, I've found that skill especially challenging to apply. I do covet so many simple opportunities that my friends have that I do not. It's sometimes too easy to feel sorry for myself—though it is difficult at times to tell the difference between self-pity and self-empathy.

Having said that, in my twenties, I went on a campaign to become street smart about life—to break the back of my parents' naïveté in me. I did commit myself to a two-pronged strategy for broadening my world and gaining wisdom about life. On one hand, I was naturally idealistic. That idealism fit my youth while being driven by reaching for something more than what I grew up with. Over the years, I nurtured that idealism into strength of vision. I've carried visions for my marriage, each of you, and each of my clients. Whatever my failings as a husband or a father, I do work at picturing how to love your mom and you guys. And I do actively nurture pictures of how to set my clients free from their slavery to their inner forces. Vision drives all that. Decades later now, I still am an optimist and a visionary.

On the other hand, I chose to become unwaveringly practical as well. In a television interview, Madeleine Albright, the first woman to become secretary of state, said leadership needed to be both. Leaders must have clear vision to see where they're going, she said, while being intensely practical in figuring out how to get there. In my youth, somehow I intuitively knew that. I turned my youthful strategy into a way of life. That strategy drove my professional choice to go into counseling to deal with the nuts 'n bolts of people's life challenges. I turned down two job offers in academia to teach undergraduate and graduate students. Right or wrong, I turned those jobs down because I didn't want to be experientially isolated in an "ivory tower." I wanted to "get dirty" with real life. My commitment to becoming ruthlessly realistic also fueled my passion for dealing with my issues through my own personal therapy. And my realism has driven how I've talked as a friend, husband, father, and counselor.

I've never regretted my choice to follow that two-pronged strategy.

So, I am a strange mix—as if I have to tell you that. I am street smart about the tough side of life and the human condition. But my style is clearly laced with my own creative version of my parents' naïveté. All wrapped in sincerity. Just like your grandparents.

Keeping One's Word

Unlike so many seemingly savvy politicians in Washington, DC, these days, your grandfather always stood by his word. If he forgot, and was reminded that he had given his word, he'd then stick by it. While I have not been perfect in sticking to my word, it is nevertheless a fundamental commitment of mine to do so. I can't stand it when someone breaks his or her word—or worse, when I break my own. I have no use for it. To me, one's word is a word of covenant—a binding unilateral agreement to be or do something.

I have an attorney friend who explained legal contracts and the social order this way: You can threaten jail or a lawsuit to try to get a contract fulfilled, but the reality is that a deal is only as good as the signatures at the bottom. Without keeping one's word, things just don't get done between people.

When I was getting estimates for landscaping work, I talked to one old-timer about this. He said it used to be that he'd do business with just a handshake. Customers could count on him to do an excellent job; he could always count on them to pay. However, a few years ago, someone stuck him with an unpaid balance of $20,000. His attorney told him he was nuts not to have had a contract. But who actually was nuts? A man who trusted people on a handshake? Or a man who didn't keep his word to pay? Was the landscaper sincere? Or, like your grandfather, was he sincerely naïve?

Social psychologists have noted how, in the past decade, so many people now feel free to not honor their word. They don't keep their end of a deal. They break contracts, including not paying their bills. For many, keeping their word and imputing honor to another person mean little anymore. The old-timer now has written contracts. And it's been for the past number of years now that I have had clients sign a document indicating that I can take legal action if they do not pay their bill. I also now require payment in full before I write a report to the court.

There is a marketing campaign for a local automobile dealership that states, "Reputation is everything." Besides the quality of the service or product, reputation is all about keeping one's word—and keeping one's word is indeed everything in relationships.

Yes, my attorney friend told me, you can take someone to court to hold them accountable. Still, the bottom line is that in order to make good things happen between people, people must keep their word. In fact, he elaborated on how everything we do as a society depends on all of us keeping our word—from driving on our own side of the road to not assaulting another person when we're angry. We all give our word that we won't drink and drive. Yet, about three hundred thousand drivers a day break their word to us. The price tag: about ten thousand deaths a year on our highways. The horrific killings at Sandy Hook Elementary School in Newtown, Connecticut took down twenty of our children. Yet, among the ten thousand killed on our streets every year are about two hundred of our children. Those three hundred thousand people who drink and drive daily do not keep their word to the rest of us— with tragic consequences.

When I counsel, I am trusting that people will keep implicit social contracts. So, for example, I trust that no one will bring a gun into my counseling chamber. However, the husband of a couple I was counseling was a state trooper and a former Marine who typically arrived right after work in uniform. He was a large muscular guy who had seen hand-to-hand combat in the Iraq War. In his personal relationships, however, he was what his wife and I affectionately called a "teddy bear." He still stops by the office on occasion to simply say hi, shake my hand, and let me know his gratitude for "saving his marriage." Such success and gratitude grants me deep satisfaction. However, in our first consult, he came into my consulting room with his gun holstered. As a matter of safety, I asked—and required—that he remove his gun from my office, put it in his car, and leave it there for all future appointments with me. He not only had no problem with that but also respected me for it. He knew the unspoken contract to which we were all committed.

One day, my lawyer friend painted an even bigger picture for me regarding the importance of keeping one's word. He noted how the "rule of law" means that we not only resolutely agree to stick to our word—we also agree to being punished for breaking it. We grant ourselves permission to give ourselves tickets or throw ourselves into prison if we break the rules. The rule of law makes all of society stable. It also makes our economy thrive. The only reason credit cards work, for example, is that companies agree they will only charge us for what they ask—and nothing more. The company must keep its word. The consumer in turn gives his word he will pay the charge. The whole thing works only if both sides keep their word. Punishments for breaking the rules do help motivate some people to stick to the game. For others, respect and honor yet motivate. There really is no capitalism—and no free market—without the rule of law. And the rule of law is all about holding ourselves accountable to keeping our word to one another. Frankly, I had never thought of it that way before.

But all of this makes sense to me—all of it—simply because of your grandfather's commitment to keep his word to me.

The Belief in the Equality of People

Your grandparents were indeed sincere people of impeccable integrity. And with that, they never thought of themselves as better than anyone else. After Rosa Parks dared to refuse the orders of a bus driver to give up her seat in the "colored section" to a white passenger when the white section was filled—and racial tensions escalated in this country—your grandfather imprinted my conscience forever with these words, "Frankie, I share my lunch with a colored man at work. It doesn't matter the color of your skin. It's how you treat people." Back then, your grandfather's choice of the phrase "colored man" was not disrespectful; the descriptor "African American" had not yet been used. His wise judgment was long before Martin Luther King's prophetic voice—and was another bullet between my very young eyes.

I had co-taught a discipleship training program with one of our pastors for two years. We trained congregants for thirty-three weeks for two-and-a-half hours each week for each year. It was a marathon. Without any previous discussion about the details of our theological views, we took the risk to venture out together. A bit to our mutual surprise, it went wonderfully. Our styles complemented each other well. We had no disagreements—and enjoyed playing off each other. As we walked down the hallway of our church one day, she shared a story about being at the receiving end of bigotry. I was taken aback; I had to think for a moment: oh, she's Hispanic. I rarely thought of her that way. I simply thought of her as Ruth Faith.

Perhaps that's another example of the wide-eyed, uncomplicated sincerity of my parents within me. However, I do see my attitude as a positive ability to have friendship that goes beyond ethnic differences to our common humanity. I don't usually think of your mom as having Native American blood. But I did get her Christmas gifts one year celebrating her Mohawk tribal heritage. I simply think of her as Andie—your mom, my wife. Decades ago, when your mom taught in the inner city of Philadelphia, she was among mostly African American teachers. One day, when I went to see her at work, one of the teachers told me she had been to the beach. She rolled her sleeve up and put her arm in front of me, asking me how I liked her tan. We laughed as she played off our racial differences—and through our laughter affirmed both our friendship and our shared humanity.

While so many in this country were bigoted—and raising their children to be so as well—your grandfather forged within me the then radical message that we are all created equal. Once again he spoke his "word" into my psychic universe. This time he created in me a gut-level sense that it doesn't matter what the color of your skin is or where you come from. What matters is the content of your character. I feel that truth to my core; I believe it with every fiber of my being. I have no doubt that the melting pot of our Dutchtown neighborhood was not only the backdrop for your grandparents' sincerity and integrity, but also your grandfather's disdain for bigotry. The Germans, Irish, and Italians had finally pulled together as Catholic Christians to create community . . . to work together . . . to create solidarity. Their sons and daughters went to school together. Boys and girls of differing ethnic backgrounds liked each other. With my crushes on two girls in grammar school and a definite attraction to several others, I never asked if they were German, Irish, or Italian. And we all played—and fought—together in the schoolyard, never thinking twice about the last name. Your grandfather grew up in that melting pot, as I had.

For me, Hon, the issue of character is both cross-cultural and cross-racial. Don't get me wrong. I do not believe we can be blind to the unique ways a culture expresses character. Or blind to a race's distinctive history—whether the African Americans' struggle for equality after slavery or the Mohawk tribe's forced movement from central New York into Canada (the tribe your mother's ancestors came from). Still, character is "bigger than" culture or race. It is an issue of one's moral fiber as a human being. While it is true that we are not all born into equal circumstances, God nevertheless imputes equal value to us all. And with that, I do hate bigotry. These attitudes are your grandparents—and your grandfather in particular—in me.

Compassion

At the tender age of six, I somehow knew Tiny was dying.

Your grandparents sat with Tiny outside by the front porch steps. Her demise made that front porch area feel sacred, like Father was visiting with the Eucharist. I walked out the back porch past the icebox and made my way along the side of the house to sneak a peek around the corner. My father was sitting on the steps while my mother was lying on a lounge chair with Tiny resting her pitiable face on her chest. My father told me quietly but firmly to stay inside; without saying so, he didn't want me to see her die. I was surprised—actually, I was awestruck—to see my mother gently holding Tiny, waiting . . .

I went back inside to the living room, sat on the davenport—and waited. It seemed so long. I kept thinking of her. With the way you and your husband love Baxter, you understand; it's like a family member dying. As a little boy, I kept thinking of my good times with her. We loved playing together. And one night she was of great comfort to me. Both my brothers had gone to Scout camp, so my parents took me to a drive-in movie. It was supposed to be a fun movie, with the Three Stooges. But one of the scenes had a Frankenstein monster in it. I had encountered this monster before in a horror film the family watched one night on television. My parents and brothers were gathered around the TV, and I think I had been banished to my room because it was a scary movie. But I snuck out, managing to crawl underneath the card table my father was sitting at—and watched. I have no idea if my dad noticed me but just pretended not to see, or not. But I got away with watching it. It scared the heck out of me. I used that monster at bedtime in the attic as another symbol for my daytime fears. At the drive-in, the Three Stooges movie just stirred it all up again. When we got home, I really, really, really didn't want to go up to my attic bedroom to sleep all alone. This time, somehow, I mustered up the courage to say something. So my parents let me sleep on the davenport across from their bedroom. Even though I was closer to their room, with all the lights off, I was still scared. So I anxiously waited until my parents were asleep. Then I quietly snuck into their bedroom where Tiny slept by the dresser—and curled up around her. She let me. She was my sole comfort throughout the night. I woke up early before my parents stirred and snuck back to the davenport before they awoke. They never knew otherwise. I was going to really miss Tiny. I began to cry.

Your grandmother came in from the back porch through the kitchen to the edge of the living room and stood there like a statue. Tiny was gone. She quickly told me that Tiny was in heaven with many other dogs and I'd see her there someday. This was her way of comforting me. Still, I sat there on the davenport crying by myself.

Though I cried alone, I did witness that brief moment of your grandmother's gentle compassion. And your grandmother did try comforting me with her words. Your grandfather also quietly kept the deathwatch for our family pet as he sat on the porch step next to her. Clearly, both your grandparents were compassionate, even though your grandfather's empathy had been damaged by his underlying anger, and your grandmother's had been locked away by her alcoholism and masked by her distant, blank face. Looking back, though, I can sense your grandmother's care. She had made me chocolate mayonnaise cake. She had darned my socks and pants. She had packed my lunches. And though scared, she had dutifully held my arm under the cold water after I put it through the backdoor window. Holding Tiny in her final moments was just a more salient example of a deep compassion that had been there all along.

I believe the depth of compassion in your mother—the woman I was drawn to—amplifies the compassion that was truly there in your grandparents. To be sure, both your grandparents needed rescue. And I am a rescuer because of that. Yet, however veiled in desperation their concern for others might have been, your grandparents were two deeply compassionate human beings who did help others. They modeled that. So, besides being a rescuer, I wouldn't be compassionate—and would not have married a woman of compassion—if it had not been for the deep, though veiled, compassion of your grandparents.

Your Grandmother's Duty

At a professional seminar, the speaker rhetorically asked, "Is Mother Teresa a Nobel Prize-winning, compassionate sister who helps the poor? Or is she just a sexually repressed, flaming co-dependent?" I bristled at his sarcasm. His point was that while Mother Teresa, now deceased, had done her duty, she had done so blindly. She had sacrificed her own happiness on the chopping block of religion. Instead of giving her life to others because she wanted to, she did it only to obey God, sacrificing her own happiness in doing so. If her eyes had been truly open to the high personal cost of her ministry—and if she hadn't been so trapped by blind loyalty to religion—she wouldn't have done it.

Whatever one thinks about Mother Teresa's politics, I recoiled at how this psychologist portrayed her. I understood his argument. However, he presumed that Mother Theresa hadn't really wanted to minister to the poor, but had chosen to do so only as a blind duty to God. And he presumed that she had been blind to her personal price tag for ministry. He didn't seem to understand that anyone, including Mother Theresa, could help others because one freely believed in its value and derived great personal satisfaction from his or her work—and be willing to do so at a high personal cost.

Sometimes missionary agencies ask me to evaluate a candidate's readiness for the mission field. Other times, an agency hires me to help a missionary and his family cope with the demands of the field. When we meet, we set at least this one goal: To make sure everyone's eyes—including the mission board's—are open to the costs of ministry. No one really wants to be blind. One time, I had the privilege of working with a nurse who worked with only one support staff under some very tough conditions in Haiti. Caring for hundreds daily required that he be on his feet all day. He even performed "meatball" surgery. He'd read up on the procedure the night before, then, the next day, his assistant would hold the book open during the operation. It was just the two of them serving tens of thousands—that is, until his assistant had to be sent home to the States. An indigent had attacked both of them with a machete in the middle of the night. My client escaped, but his assistant had been badly slashed. Later, my client came home on furlough to reevaluate.

The reality was that standing on his feet all day, every day, with an already painful back was damaging his spinal column, sending shooting pain down his leg. An orthopedic surgeon back here in the States told him the problem would just get worse. But there was nothing surgically to be done; the risks were too high for permanent damage to the nerve. He was in constant pain and using a narcotic to manage it. This missionary had a tough time facing what was happening to his body—let alone the implications for his ministry. While my job was to help him make a decision that made sense to him, the decision itself was his alone to make. He finally chose to leave the mission field. Rescue fantasies or not, with his eyes opened, he really didn't want to further destroy his back and the quality of his life.

Missionaries are often driven by powerful rescue fantasies forged in their growing up years. They're not alone. The same is true for medical doctors and psychologists. In counseling any of them, my job is not to change that drive to rescue unless hired to do so. After all, what's wrong with wanting to help others, as long as that desire to help is one's own free choice? Instead, my job is to make sure that the client's rescue fantasies don't play out blindly—whether missionary, paramedic, or co-dependent wife trying to "fix" an alcoholic husband. Rescue personnel ran into the World Trade Center on 9/11 with their eyes open, knowing full well they might pay the ultimate price. We do not judge these heroes by figuring out where their rescue fantasies came from. We judge them by their courageous choices. So my job is not to alter a missionary's drive to evangelize. Rather, it is to help her become aware of the price tag for doing so—and whether she really wants to pay that price or not. No wise mission board wants their missionaries oblivious to what they're getting themselves into. Board members don't want their people to go to the field because of some deep inner, arm-twisting guilt emerging from codependent patterns. Or leave their creature comforts behind to help others for fear of divine reprisal.

I don't know if Mother Theresa was blind to the personal price tag for her ministry or not. I don't know if she feared divine reprisal.

Or if she felt driven by unconscious guilt to rescue the poor. Regardless, Hon, her commitment made intuitive sense to me. It made sense
because of my mother. Like Mother Teresa, my mother had also
made a commitment. While feeling miserable—and, perhaps, in
some way, not really wanting me—my mother came to terms with
some aspects of reality. She did value me enough to do the innumerable things that any mother needs to do for her child. Perhaps she
felt driven by guilt to do them. Or perhaps she felt blindly driven by
a fearful duty to God. As with Mother Theresa, I do not know. But
I do know that she had done her motherly duties day after day after
day while feeling lousy. To me, it is possible that—buried under her
pathology and drinking—my mother loved me. Her delivery of that
love was extraordinarily limited. And extraordinarily damaging, to be
sure. Still, she may have chosen to love me while feeling trapped by
life. This is not just wishful thinking; there is evidence. As her son,
that evidence matters to me. She really wanted me to leave home
to become a success. I know, it does seem a bit odd at its face that I
would defend my mother for doing her duty toward me when I was
eviscerated by her lack of affection. Her "duty without affection" left
me a hollow man. Yet, I do defend her. I do so because, after all my
hard work to release my rage and pain in order to forgive her, I was
able—and then willing—to peek in behind her wall of silence. I could
discern her sincerity, integrity, and compassion. I believe doing her
duty was her genuine though very limited way of loving me.

   I know it may also seem odd—and even look disrespectful to
Mother Theresa—to compare your grandmother to her as I just
did. Yet, your grandmother and Mother Teresa may have had something else in common. No doubt, depression and alcoholism fogged
out your grandmother. So it is easy to believe that she did not
"feel" God's presence day-to-day. And, by her own words, Mother
Theresa did not feel God most of her life. Revealed in writings to
her spiritual directors, Mother Teresa lived over fifty years without
sensing the presence of God. This left her in inner agony. In 1979
she wrote to the Reverend Michael Van Der Peet, "[But] as for me,
the silence and the emptiness is so great that I look and do not see,
listen and do not hear."* She said the silence and emptiness had

---

   *David Van Bema, "Mother Teresa's Crisis of Faith," *Time*, August 23, 2007,
http://content.time.com/time/magazine/article/0,9171,1655720,00.html.

driven her to doubt the existence of both heaven and God. After Catholic Church leaders discovered these letters—and wisely and humbly made them public—several outspoken atheists declared that Mother Teresa's experiences proved she was really an unbeliever. Presumably, for these atheists, because God isn't "felt" by either saint or sinner, then God must not exist.

Certainly, the strongest feelings in your grandmother would've been from the alcohol flowing in her body as well as her abject depression. Except for feeling her own inner agony, the alcoholism left your grandmother an empty woman. And, like Mother Theresa, she only felt God's silence in response to her plight.

Still, both Mother Teresa and your grandmother believed God existed. He existed whether or not they felt him—whatever "feeling" the divine is supposed to feel like. They also followed God whether or not they doubted along the way.

Some people think that either you believe in God or you don't. It's that simple. And it's that clean. Black or white. But that's not true. The human mind is complex. The way we think and feel is just not simple, in spite of those who think the faith of little children should be our model. We can and do think many thoughts—even contradictory ones—at the same time. And the human heart can feel opposite feelings at the same time, like love and hate for the very same parent. You can believe in God while wondering if you are a fool for doing so. You can love God while at the same time hating him for how he manages the universe.

Over a lifetime, beliefs about God change as we change. They mature as we mature. They become more complex as we face more of life's challenges. And, over the years, our beliefs stand less on myth and more on truth the more we study the Bible and life. The strength of one's beliefs—and the strength of one's doubts—may vary because faith is in constant dialogue with life's ups and downs. All of life has mystery—and mystery makes any thinking person wonder. So faith in God is not static. And it's not necessarily black and white within the believer. We really can wonder, even outright doubt, while we yet believe. In fact, believing while doubting can give rise to duty—a duty that overrides cynicism, disillusionment, pain, and suffering. It did so for both Mother Teresa and your grandmother.

To be sure, your grandmother's alcoholism adds no credibility to her belief in God—for anyone else or for me. But that is not the point here. Both women did their duty. That is, both followed through on their priorities while being in agony with their lifelong "dark night of the soul." Mother Teresa forged on to bring love and compassion to abandoned people on the streets of Calcutta. And your grandmother forged on to bring love and compassion to me in the forms of chocolate mayonnaise cake, darned socks, Christmas presents, running my injured arm under cold water, and rushing me to the hospital.

Your Grandfather's Duty

Your grandfather was also a man of duty. He was loyal to his country. Not because God or government forced such loyalty. And not because some priest or politician said you needed to invest in a cause bigger than yourself. But because he believed in what this country stood for. When I was about seven, your grandfather told me that while he was in the military, the Japanese bombed Pearl Harbor. Though he had a broken leg and couldn't go, he wanted to fight for his country because he believed in what we stood for: freedom.

Your grandfather was also loyal to his family and friends. He carried out his duties to fulfill his commitments not because God would punish him if he didn't, but because that's who he wanted to be. He believed that a good man was a man who was true to his word and to his friends. And a good man was a provider for his family. After he got multiple sclerosis, he continued to work at Eastman Kodak Company. He didn't quit—*nor did he want to quit*. Like that man who lived in the dump outside Cairo, Egypt, your grandfather worked hard to survive . . . and to create a future for us beyond himself. He'd do anything to provide for his family. Kodak supported him in continuing to work as long as they could until he fell on the job one too many times. The last time he fell, he gashed his head, forcing his boss to call an ambulance. That's when his foreman told him he'd have to go home. Losing the ability to work took away his core sense of purpose because loyalty to family—and working on behalf of family—was a value of central importance to his identity as a man.

Your grandfather tenaciously held onto his dream of getting better. However ill-directed his obsession with getting better was, he was nevertheless loyal to himself in going after it. As the disease got worse, first taking his legs and then his arms, your grandfather developed a dogged determination to exercise. All he knew was that he had to fight—and I had to help him do so. I had to lift him up and out of his wheelchair so he could stand at the hallway railing. Once standing, he forced his legs to move back and forth. If he couldn't shuffle them himself, I had to move them. He did these every single day no matter what; his commitment to exercise was a duty to himself. Such blindly driven exercise was his pathetic sliver of self-respect in the face of an extraordinarily dehumanizing disease.

Unlike your grandmother, he did not have a pit-bull grip on the Almighty. Even so, your grandfather was loyal to Jesus Christ. Though he had not pursued his Christian faith like your grandmother, though he believed in God "just in case," and though he had strong doubts about God's love for him—he still believed. He relied on Father's monthly visits, at least in the early years of his parenting. He made the trip to Canada to tour the cathedrals, asking Jesus for help. However gently cynical and confused he may have been, he encouraged me as a boy that it was better to believe than not. And his subdued but primal cry into the universe wondering why betrayed his core belief in the existence of a Creator who could provide an answer. Beyond that, your grandfather would never have asked Jesus for healing—and he would never have kissed the saints' relics—if he hadn't in some way believed that Jesus could deliver. It was out of that belief in God and Jesus Christ that your grandfather "did his duty" in raising us kids with the values he did.

I too am a man of duty. But don't get me wrong. I struggled to free myself from *blind* duty ever since I faced the indulgences in the catechism that made no sense to me as a boy. My sense of duty is no longer blind. At least, I put the grand effort in to make sure it isn't. Nor is my duty forged from fear . . . or guilt . . . or from someone telling me I ought to do it. Whatever I do, I do because I believe in it. I do it because I rank it as a top value in my life. I do it because it is part of my vision for living life.

So, like your grandfather, I am loyal to this country. I am committed to the principles in our Constitution. Having said that, I do hate injustice in my homeland. Besides my heightened sensitivity to issues of justice because of my family history, your mom's heritage from the Mohawk tribe has deeply touched me as well. Years ago, I read how our political leaders handled Native Americans in this country's expansion driven by the vision and slogan of Manifest Destiny. Our country grew in part at the expense of Native Americans. I found our leaders' behavior appalling. The Trail of Tears is but one example. It was a forced march and relocation of Native

American nations in the southeastern part of the growing United States. Thousands lost their lives in that brutal march, not to mention the loss of *their* homeland. In fact, the Indian Removal Act of 1830 formalized the growth of the US at their expense. However ignorant I am of history—and I am not very informed—from this vantage point today, this forced march sure seems like an outrageous act of injustice.

Nevertheless, I remain loyal to this country. However poorly we implement it, our Constitution stands as an unparalleled platform for individual rights and freedom. It took another hundred years to give that freedom to blacks. But that platform made it possible. In this grand experiment called the United States, our Constitution rests on the most powerful moral premise ever declared for a nation in the entire history of the world. It is the very premise your grandfather taught me as a little boy. It is the core principle found in the Declaration of Independence: God created all people equal, with certain unalienable rights. While implemented poorly in our transitions as a nation—without due respect to Native Americans, African Americans, or women—we nevertheless are one nation on the planet that has matured into a people who are resolutely committed to a human being's unalienable right to live out his or her own life in freedom. And we stand on a piece of paper that ultimately holds our leaders accountable to that principle.

This principle makes sense to me because it made sense to your grandfather. Once again, he spoke his word into my mental universe—and it was so. He believed all men, black or white, are created equal. He believed boys, and therefore men, should never hit a woman. By implication, a man should always respect a woman. He believed that we are to judge one another only by the content of our character. Power and money were irrelevant. He believed our country's founding principles, and with them, our freedom, were worth fighting for. No, I am not naïve about the nonsense that often dribbles out of the mouths of our country's leadership. I do see Congress' self-serving, even corrupt, decisions. In contrast to your grandmother, who hated lying, many in Washington love lying. I am not saying I'd die in defense of their behavior. Still, I get to vote them in and vote them out. For that freedom, I'd "do my duty"—and die.

I am loyal to my family. Just like your grandfather, no matter what I've been through physically since age thirty-nine, I've always kept working to provide for the family. One doctor told me that, though I looked fine on the outside—no one would ever guess what happened to me—I was in worse shape on the inside than many of his patients on Social Security disability. I appreciated his affirmation, though I can't speak to his experience. All I know is that I work very hard—like your grandfather going to work with MS.

Consistent with former Secretary of State Madeleine Albright's view of leadership, Proverbs 29:18 says, "Where there is no vision, the people perish" (KJV). That's true. My parents certainly lacked vision in key ways. And sadly, they perished. Still, my father did fight against losing his legs and arms. He did work hard to provide for his family. My mom did perform her tasks as mother. And she did hope against hope for Jesus to heal her husband. Their loyalty to those causes did keep them going. Likewise, I am a man who remains loyal to his causes.

While my sincerity is laced with naïveté, I don't believe my duty is. Nor do I believe my loyalty to causes is driven by guilt. Or some co-dependent belief. Or some twisted view of altruism that others are more important than me. Nor is my duty driven by the belief that God can just use me up as your grandfather blindly did in my teens. Instead, for me, duty is driven by vision. What I am about in life drives my sense of duty as it seemed to have for your grandparents. I set my goals based upon my values—and doggedly pursue them. Like your grandparents, I keep a tenacious grip on those objectives.

Indeed, I am my parents' son. My patriotism, my work ethic, my loyalty to causes I believe in, my loyalty to Jesus Christ and the intense commitment to people I love deeply—all of these, Kid, really are your grandparents within me.

The Quiet Hero

A Lifeline

All children are like dogs or bats; they keenly sense the undercurrents in their families. In family counseling, I am mindful of the old saying, "Out of the mouths of babes." Children know when things are wrong in a family, but they are lousy interpreters of what those things are. They do not have adult information—or the necessary interpretative skills—to figure out what is going on. In point of fact, many adults can't figure out what's going on, let alone the children. So while children accurately detect that there are problems, they have little idea how to articulate them, what they mean, or what to do about them.

I was no different. All I knew was that it was all going wrong—and I had no idea how to stop it. So I threw out lifelines, though I didn't know consciously that's what I was doing. One of my lifelines was your uncle Herb. Actually, being nine years older, *he threw me* the lifeline. He drew me into Scouting, and with that, provided a strong identification with his world . . . and his character.

Your uncle Herb was a good young man, already evidenced in his midteens by his comforting me when I put my arm through the glass plate of the back porch door. Like your grandparents, he had impeccable integrity—and still does to this day. He was always hard working, whether at school, out camping, or working summers to help pay his way through college. Typical of first-born children, he was very responsible. He was on the quiet side when it came to more personal sharing but a bit more chatty about his adventures out hiking, camping, or fishing. He never lectured me about anything, but always modeled sound character while gently pulling me into his world with his quiet, unspoken knowledge that the world at home was quicksand.

The sacrament of confirmation formalized my bond with my older brother. It was the time we fifth graders were to reaffirm our commitment to Jesus Christ and the church, at which point we'd receive the "Holy Ghost" in a special way. The Catholic Church saw it as a sacrament on par with baptism where we would put our personal signature on our parents' earlier decision to have us baptized into the faith as infants. The protocol for the sacrament included picking a "sponsor"—someone I admired, who shared my faith, and would join me at the confirmation ceremony. He'd show his full support for my decision, at the same time making his own commitment to be there for me throughout life. I think this is a superb model. Though young, I was the one who chose my brother—and it wasn't by default. I had developed a strong admiration for him by age ten.

For Catholics, Hon, most religious celebrations were set in the context of a Mass and my confirmation ceremony was no different. Protestants call it a "worship service"—though there is a huge contrast between our Protestant services and the Catholic Mass I grew up with. In the "protesting movement" of the fifteenth century that became Protestantism, Christians stripped the Mass of its symbols. Protestant churches and worship services became notoriously plain—at least for one raised Catholic.

Over the first fourteen centuries as the Catholic Church expanded long before this protesting movement, church leaders developed the Mass into an elaborate ceremony. It became rich in aesthetic and spiritual symbolism. These symbols conveyed a sensory or gut "feel" for God. All religious services do, but Mass had many unique signs that carried various meanings about God. The signs subliminally taught me who God was, what he was like, and what I could expect. For Catholics who make it a point to understand the symbolism—and as a boy, I had—the artistry moves us deeply. I really grew to appreciate the symbolism in high school. Catholics consider the Mass the most sacred of rituals because its symbolism culminates in turning bread and wine into Jesus' actual body and blood—the Eucharist. The Eucharist is the central focal point of the Mass.

From medieval times to when I was a boy, the Catholic Church kept Latin as the language of choice for the Mass, making it seem like a sacred language. But Latin to this young boy was mostly, though not all, gibberish. I'd often say or sing Latin words not knowing what I was saying. And I'd hear words not knowing what I was hearing. Still, I did pick up some Latin along the way: *Agnus Dei* meaning "Lamb of God," *Ave Maria* meaning "Hail Mary," *Pater Noster* meaning "Our Father," *Salve Regina* meaning "Hail Holy Queen," and *Venite Adoremus* meaning "Come Let Us Adore Him." In high school, I studied Latin for several years—though you'd never know it by what I recall. As a young boy, I actually enjoyed some of the rich Latin hymns like "Ave Maria" . . . and still do. Recently, your mom pointed out that "Ave Maria" was playing on her CD, so I took a break, sat down, closed my eyes, and just listened. I loved it, even though I know it's celebrating Mary, not Jesus. I also really liked Gregorian chant as a child. It gave me a sense of the mystical—and I love to listen to it to this day. Before my disability, on the rare occasion when our own church choir sang it, I felt like I was at the doorstep of the numinous once again. Though I know better, it still stirs a strong aesthetic-mystical sense in me that I intuitively identify with the presence of God.

The symbols worked. They forged within me an intuitive sense of what God was like. The Mass' protocol had the priest standing at the altar with his back to us because he was standing "in between" God and us. He was the mediator. This created the feeling deep inside that I couldn't approach God directly. I would even pray to Jesus' mother, the Blessed Mother, asking her to ask him for things. I really felt I couldn't talk directly to Jesus, though his mother could. As I knelt in my pew with the priest between me and the altar, it felt like God was unapproachable. I had to go *through* someone to get to him—the priest, Mary, or the saints. In this way, God was far away. He was on the other side of the altar—and I was looking for him way over there . . . somewhere.

But God was far away in another manner. Priests often sprinkled incense as part of the Mass. It gave off a sweet-smelling smoke that added to the sense of the mystical. The smoke symbolically took the people's prayers up to the Almighty, as if he was "up there"—what theologians call "transcendent." God was not down here among his people. And it felt that way: God was way up there somewhere.

Yet, paradoxically, Jesus was also close to us—what theologians call "immanent"—in the Eucharist. Because the belief was that the Eucharist was actually Jesus himself, when I took Communion, Jesus felt oddly and uncomfortably close.

The Mass created these contradictory feelings in me—feelings that theologians would say represent both sides of God. God felt "up there." And he was. But, at the same time, he felt "down here" with us. And he was. God could come to us directly in the Eucharist once the priest spoke his words into the universe. There really is no other human event on the planet that, in one's imagination, is as inscrutably potent or intimate as a man saying words that transform bread and wine into God—*and then eating him*. None. The magnetic draw of such an authoritative—and mystical—interpretation is why many Catholics have made it a practice to "go to Mass" daily. They can count on receiving spiritual sustenance by taking in the very person of God.

So my confirmation was going to be a richly meaningful ritual wrapped in this symbolically nuanced celebration called the Mass. Jesus would be the center in the Eucharist. And the bishop of the Diocese of Rochester, who would knight us into the Lord's army, would add his prestige and presence to this ceremony's commanding awe.

A New Name

The bishop of our diocese—seen by us common folk as even more holy than the priest—came to the church in regal-looking medieval garb to confirm us children. Dutchtown packed the church. In fact, our neighbors pressed along both outside walls with barely any room to move in those aisles. Family and friends of all the fifth graders eagerly arrived not only to celebrate our confirmation but also to just be near our bishop.

I was frightened to think that I might have to personally greet the bishop; there was a special protocol for that. I'd have to kneel on the correct knee, and then slowly and gently lean over to kiss his large ring. And I could only address him as "Your Excellency." I stood in line with the rest of my anxious class along the confessional booths at the back of the church waiting for the bishop to walk by—hoping he wouldn't stop. He passed by all of us fifth graders on his way up to the altar without saying a word . . . or even looking at us. I was glad he didn't.

The bishop felt distant and cold and actually seemed stiff. Along with his vestments feeling like a barrier to me as a little boy, the bishop's manner also made it feel as if I really couldn't approach him, which just fed my growing sense that God was someone you really couldn't approach either . . . or ever really get to know. Just think: What if His Excellency had smiled at us fifth graders? What if he had stopped for a brief moment to stoop down and shake our hands? Or sit down to talk with us? What if he had engaged us ten-year-olds like Pope John Paul II, who passed away in 2005, did with young people around the world? As feeble as he was in his later years, Pope John Paul smiled and interrupted his own speeches to comment or gesture to the thousands of young people surrounding him—revealing to them the depth of his warmth and humanity. Young people loved him. And Pope John Paul loved having them love him. Not only did the bishop's vestments at my confirmation symbolically function as a barrier, but the *man* who was bishop "hid" behind them—unlike Pope John Paul.

Unfortunately, the bishop was not the only one to hide behind clothing. Women who wore black from head to toe taught me five days a week, six hours a day—for eight years. And they were all there in the church eager to greet the bishop and celebrate our confirmation. Unlike the more relaxed look of today's nuns, the garb my teachers wore included a long, black hood with white, starchy fabric on the inside surrounding their faces. Only a very small circle of a slightly scrunched face peered out from the hood. Covering their humanity further was a very wide, white, starchy board over their chests. As a boy, I actually wondered if they had breasts under what I thought of in my childish mind as "massive white chest protectors." But it wasn't just the sisters' clothing; like the bishop, it was their demeanor.

Sister Veronica, who was standing at the back of the church to make sure we were all lined up correctly for the bishop, was also my fifth-grade teacher. One day in class after she had given us an assignment, she called me to her desk in front of the class. With a stern voice, she interrogated me. She wanted to know why I had written my name in the middle of the top line of my paper rather than on the left side. She sternly queried me while the entire class silently watched. Besides not knowing why I did that, the embarrassment made me so tense I couldn't talk. As I hung my head, I could feel my face becoming red with shame and my jaw go into lockdown. I stood there frozen. Then—still in front of the class—she scolded me for not talking. But I couldn't talk; my jaw just wouldn't move.

After school—I was delayed going home, but I don't recall why—I was walking down the empty hallway when I heard footsteps in the distance. Sister Veronica was slowly marching toward me. She was short, no taller than I was. But she was a rotund looming figure to me. I was scared to have our paths cross. I went from one side of the hall to the other trying to avoid her, but she kept going from side to side as well . . . until she stood right in front of me. Of all the options available to her in how she could've treated this fearful, young boy, she chose to stare at me. She just stood there, within inches of my face—literally a few inches from nose to nose— just glaring at me. I can still see the condemning, angry frown in her cold, wrinkled face peering out from her black and white hood. The moments passed. It felt like an eternity. Fear flooded me. I just stood there, frozen once again, not knowing what to do or say. It was like being back up in the attic, rigid with fear, unable to move. The pitch blackness of Sister's clothing draped over her icy cold body was an unconscious but powerful reminder of my attic bedroom's darkness draped over my bed, shrouding within me my terror of my own mother's icy cold body. Sister was like the large, black spider slowly climbing up and over me to devour me. I felt trapped. My heart pounded while I waited to see what Sister was going to do to me next. She finally broke the silence. She unsympathetically declared that I had to apologize for my behavior earlier that day—and released me only after I nervously said, "I'm sorry." As I slowly walked away down the dark, quiet hall, I just wanted to cry. But I didn't. There was no one to cry with.

After the bishop passed us in the back of the church and made his way to the front of the steps that led to the altar, Sister Veronica nodded, which was our signal to process down the aisle as practiced, taking our seats in the pews.

After a lengthy introduction, we were called forward to the bishop—one at a time. It was now my turn. I nervously slid out the pew; I felt pretty scared. As I very slowly made my way up the aisle toward His Excellency, all eyes were on me, just as all eyes were on you when you walked down the aisle as a bride. My legs felt wobbly. This holy man who was above all our priests looked formidable and tall, made taller by a medieval hat called a miter that rose way above his head. He was dressed in richly colored vestments with many layers, the outer one having a large cross over his chest. His Excellency stood there solemn and stiff—he did not smile—with his back straight and head high, like nobility on a grave mission, with his golden staff in hand. His hand bore a large ring symbolizing his marriage to Christ and the Church—the ring I would've kissed if he had greeted me personally.

I knelt before him as required. I was so nervous my stomach was in knots, and I had no idea what he was saying. But His Excellency slowly and steadily lifted his staff up off the floor, rotating it over my head, with the end pointed toward the parishioners seated behind me. After saying some words, he resolutely tapped me on each shoulder with that staff. As he tapped, I thought back to what I had memorized. I was now a "soldier of Jesus Christ through this sacrament, given the Holy Ghost in order to make me a strong and perfect Christian." His Excellency then leaned toward me—which sent my anxiety through the roof—tapping me decisively on the cheek with his fingers. It was over. I had just been knighted as a soldier of Jesus Christ. With great relief, I stood up, went to the padded railing at the front, and knelt down—with Herb, my sponsor, standing behind me. Following protocol, your uncle extended his right arm, gently placing his hand on my shoulder, thereby confirming his lifetime commitment to me.

Protocol also required that we take our sponsor's first name as our own middle name. It was like taking on a family's last name: We were to so identify with this person that we became one in name. That day, Hon, the day the bishop of the Diocese of Rochester knighted me as a soldier in God's army, my name expanded to include Herbert.

I became: Frank William *Herbert* Barbehenn.

My New Adoptive Mother

Mother Nature

Uncle Herb was once a very powerful figure to me. Long before I took his name as mine, I had been riding in his metal basket hanging on the front handlebars of his bicycle going down Rugraff Street. My legs were crossed inside the basket—they were not dangling out—so I had to have been very small, likely younger than four. I vividly recall leaning a bit to my left, gazing down and through the bright silver metal mesh of the basket to see the macadam below moving by us real fast. It was awesomely exciting . . . which was no doubt the reason I remember it so well. I didn't feel scared. I guess I just trusted big brother implicitly—without any hesitation—though if I were three or four, he would've been only twelve or thirteen years old. I always trusted big brother—and always trusted him to have common sense. Interestingly, I have that same implicit trust in your mom's common sense, evidenced by so many things in our relationship, starting with that trek in the blinding snow.

My unquestioning trust in big brother grew, becoming stronger and more apparent in several ways during my turbulent teens. One key way was our joint camping and deep woods hiking ventures—with backpacks, maps, and a compass . . . even freeze-dried foods. Your uncle knew what he was doing; I trusted that. While we did a lot of camping with the Scouts, we did a fair amount on our own. On our hikes into the deep woods I'm not sure I could've found my way back out without him. We never took weapons to protect our-selves from bears or moose—only cameras. We just used our heads and hoped for the best. Our hiking ventures into the wilderness not only offered me a much-needed escape but also opened up my life to something a whole lot bigger than my drowning parents.

I'll never forget Camp Massawepie—Native American for "land by the marsh"—with over 3,600 acres nestled in the beautiful Adirondack Mountain Range of northern New York State. Nor will I forget Mr. Datillio. I was a senior patrol leader, the top junior leader elected by the other Scouts, at about age fifteen. Mr. Datillio, a parent of one of the Scouts who came to help, was inexperienced—but I didn't discover just how inexperienced and lacking in common sense he was until later. For our modest hike of about ten miles to a nearby mountain, your uncle, who was Scoutmaster at twenty-five, delegated closing up camp to me with the assistance of Mr. Datillio. While I didn't know just how naïve Mr. Datillio was, looking back, I think your uncle sensed it, and trusted me to guide him. But my brother hadn't picked up on this man's quiet arrogance. The rest of the troop under Herb's lead went ahead toward Mount Arab, a small mountain of little over 2,500 feet in altitude, leaving me and Mr. Datillio behind to wrap things up.

After cleaning up from the morning's breakfast and securing everyone's tent flaps—which put us about an hour behind the rest of the troop—Mr. Datillio and I took off. I carried a small map and compass, though I hadn't anticipated needing it. We hiked a dirt jeep trail until we got to a fork in the road. Just to make sure we didn't get confused, the other Scouts had carved an arrow in the dirt pointing down the left branch of the fork, with the words THIS WAY in it. Mr. Datillio cynically thought the Scouts were playing a prank on us. I told him that I didn't think they were because I thought I recalled the way—and I believed we needed to go left. Nevertheless, he thought they were spoofing us. So I pulled out the map, and after reviewing it for a few moments, it was clear that we had to take that left fork. I showed him the map. He looked at it. But I don't think he knew what he was looking at. For some unknown reason, he overruled me—declaring that we had to take the fork to the right. Didn't matter what the map showed. Nor did it matter what the senior patrol leader said; he discounted both my memory and my skills without directly saying so. He just ignored me. As a young Catholic teen who had grown up to both respect and fear authority, I didn't have the guts to challenge him any further. It was eleven in the morning.

After many hours, Mr. Datillio had managed to hike us way out of Camp Massawepie on a course for who knows where about 100 to 120 degrees off track from Mt. Arab. I patiently let the evidence build. I finally declared to Mr. Datillio the obvious: We were not going to get to Mt. Arab this way. He still didn't listen to me, though it may have begun to sink in. Only after more time passed walking aimlessly and going nowhere did he finally relent and turn around. On the way back, however, he decided to try a trail that branched off to the right, saying, "Mt. Arab must be this way." I strongly advised him that we had no idea where the trail led, and, more importantly, the trail wasn't on the map. But, once again, he never looked at the map nor deferred to me; the facts didn't matter. I dutifully followed. We hiked for about two miles, and, fortunately, the trail dead-ended at a hunting cabin. If it hadn't, he would've just kept mindlessly leading us further into the woods away from the main trail—without a map big enough to figure out where we were really going. So, with nowhere now to go except back, Mr. Datillio wisely decided to head back to the main trail and continue on our way. A little later, however, he wanted to try the next trail off to our right, only to dead-end once again at another hunting cabin. And back we went. This man was relentless. He took trail after trail to the right hoping to get to Mt. Arab before we finally ended up right back where we had started: at that fork in the road. The Scouts' arrow in the dirt was still there.

It was now seven in the evening. Except for two brief bathroom breaks, we had been at this for eight hours. I took off my backpack and sank to the ground to rest for a few minutes.

Mr. Datillio looked at me, and with a quiet, tired voice said, "We should go into town and get a motel for the night. We can clean up and really relax." In a spontaneous moment of exasperation and freedom, I exclaimed, "Mr. Datillio, don't you realize that we're considered lost? We are formally lost! We should have been to Mt. Arab by three o'clock—and that's going slow. It is now seven. It is seven! We are at least four hours overdue. They're going to be worried; my brother is going to be worried. Mr. Datillio, they're out looking for us. We can't go into town. We have to stay on the trail to Arab so that they either find us or we find them!" Mr. Datillio thought for a moment . . . and then relented. I was relieved. We cranked our tired bodies up to embark once again on what should have been our simple, straightforward ten-mile trek to Arab. But as we straightened up, the search party crossed our path. They greeted us with broad smiles and great relief, grateful we were OK—but sure wondered what the heck happened to us. I left the explaining to Mr. Datillio . . . but told my brother privately what really happened.

We finally dropped our backpacks at the base of Mt. Arab about ten thirty that night. We had hiked for over eleven hours, covering well over thirty miles. We were dog-tired. Except for our flashlights, it was pitch black. We slept at the base rather than climb the mountain at that time of night. I spread the ground cloth out, slid into the sleeping bag, and curled up for a well-deserved night's rest. I woke a few hours later to raindrops pelting my face—and a drenched sleeping bag. But I was so tired; I simply did a quick check to see if I was warm enough to avoid hypothermia. I was. So I simply wrapped the plastic ground cloth around me to protect my face—and went back to sleep. The next morning Mr. Datillio and I rose early to climb Arab to join the others.

What a glorious view!

I loved being out with nature as she revealed her splendor across the rolling mountains. On one hand, she was a tough and demanding taskmaster; you had to follow her rules—or you'd get hurt. We'd hang our backpacks over tree limbs far from our tent or lean-to so the bears would not attack us. On the other hand, she'd richly reward us for our reverence, hard work, and obedience. All the sweat poured out to humbly walk with her was returned a hundredfold with her peaceful and warming embrace as we gazed at her beauty. Looking out over the valley from atop her modest mountain, her trees were stately, pulling the canopy of the sky toward them as if they were climbing to meet the sun. And walking her trails, her flowers appeared tender and fragile yet quietly strong, arrayed in wondrous palettes of deep rich colors. Indeed, within nature's bosom lies life. But, as I've said, you must respect her.

After climbing Mt. Arab and basking in the sun and nature's beauty, the troop began the modest hike back to camp. While your uncle Herb led the way, Mr. Datillio and I were yet joined: We shared a canteen. And we had run out of water. We came upon swamp water—water that was stagnant and not freely running like a cold, clear stream. So I instructed Mr. Datillio to put a couple of Halzone tablets in the canteen before filling it to kill the bacteria.

You never drink stagnant water. We both drank the water. The next day, however, I was sicker than a dog. I couldn't figure out why until I decided I'd better ask Mr. Datillio about the Halzone tablets. No, he hadn't put them in. Once again, he ignored me. He thought he knew better. I couldn't believe it. Although those two days with Mr. Datillio are "memorable," being joined with him for that time really felt just like being back home with my parents—maddening. All three were sincere, ignorant, and blind.

Herb and I had many adventures together. No, we didn't take on "real" mountains like the Rockies. Hiking the low gentle slopes and canoeing the peaceful lakes of the Adirondacks were enough for us. We felt free to do kid stuff like sliding on our butts down long mudslides in heavy rain on Mt. Ampersand. We took on strenuous ventures like hiking and portaging a canoe, which I must say took a decent amount of endurance. Then we'd kick back in the canoe and indulge in fishing for bass. Though I was an experienced hiker, I had one moment of collapsing on the trail with utter fatigue because I foolishly hadn't taken in enough fluids. And, the Adirondacks being the Adirondacks, we had memorable moments like an unnerving instance of accidentally crossing paths with a moose.

We were way too close . . . only five to seven yards away. Our heads went to the top of its muscular shoulders; it was huge. We froze. I took my cue from Herb. I glanced at him; he wasn't moving. So neither did I. We waited to see if it would attack us or take off. The fact is, there simply was no place for us to retreat. No large trees to hide behind. Nothing. We stood like statues. I can't speak for your uncle, but my heart was pounding, just pounding . . . waiting. The moose then darted to our right, collapsing trees as he ran. Herb and I, now flooded with adrenaline, anxiously walked over to its path of retreat, crouching down to examine the felled trees. We found ourselves just staring in awe at the power of its legs. As that majestic animal pushed its way through the woods, it had crushed trees a couple inches in diameter. Have you ever tried pushing on a tree that's a couple inches thick? That moose just snapped them like twigs as he ran through. We were sure grateful it had not taken off toward us.

On another outing on another gorgeous day, we left our base site to venture out a bit. We hiked through the woods for a couple hours when the horizon broke open, revealing a stunningly pristine lake.

It was a magnificent sight . . . spectacular. Surrounding the mirror-like surface of the lake was nothing but the wondrous beauty of lush, green forest against the sparkling blue backdrop of the midday sky. The beauty of the woods and sky was doubled in its reflection back from the lake surface. I breathed it in like a man coming up for air; it filled my being. I took notice that there was no one around. It was utterly quiet. Peace filled my heart. For a few moments, it felt as if the lake had been created just for us. Just as quickly, I realized that it's been there long before we existed. Was it there for God? Or was it just there?

As your uncle and I hiked back to base after this rich and humbling encounter with nature, the skies opened and within seconds we were drenched with torrential rain. We hadn't brought rain gear for this hike, so within moments, there was no piece of clothing on us that wasn't sopped, including our hiking boots. The rain was tepid and actually felt soothing, mirroring the deeper emotional warmth and peace I felt inside. I certainly didn't interpret it consciously at the time—it was more of a feeling, really, a deeply satisfying awareness—that being in that idyllic, tranquil setting was what I could only imagine it must be like being in the presence of a nurturing mother. Without consciously knowing it, Hon, this beautiful but tough taskmaster—nature—had become my "*Mother* Nature."

An Adopted Son

In my earnest efforts to sort out what was happening to me spiritually, I wondered: When I ventured out into the deep woods encountering my new mother, nature, what did I really experience? What was it that was so powerfully—and viscerally—satisfying . . . and helped keep my youthful sanity?

Did I experience God? Many people who love being out with nature think they do. Christian tradition stands on the core belief that creation somehow reveals the invisible nature of the Creator: "There are things about him that people cannot see—his eternal power and all the things that make him God. But since the beginning of the world those things have been easy to understand by what God has made" (Rom. 1:20a, NCV). Does that mean I can "feel" God instinctively through nature? Or is God so far above nature—so beyond our human frequency—that *feeling* God is truly beyond our senses? If so, nature then becomes only a humble pointer to God, but not the vehicle through which to experience him.

Perhaps I only experienced the complex aesthetic wonders of nature itself as my imagination was captivated by the inexpressible beauty of that pristine lake; as my body was soothed and warmed by the torrential downpour; and as my heart pounded in awe in the presence of one of nature's imposing wilderness creatures, the moose. However nature got here, it's an inarguable fact that Mother Nature is ineffably gorgeous. Atheist or God-fearing, who hasn't been mesmerized by one of her magnificent red-orange sunsets?

Or could my joy in being with nature also be the species' primal longings to reunite with the good earth, common to all human beings? After all, from dust we are made and to dust we shall return—from nature to nature. We do have that expression "Mother Nature" in the vocabulary of our collective psyche, an image that is cross-culturally timeless. The Native American legend, for example, says, "Beneath the clouds [lives] the Earth-Mother from whom

105

is derived the Water of Life, who at her bosom feeds plants, animals and men."

Or could it be that what I felt was some fulfillment of my childhood longings for a warm and gracious mother projected onto the nurturing side of nature? In my young and most tender imagination, I did create a montage of the feminine—a picture, albeit vague, of a warm and caring woman—from the bits and pieces I experienced growing up.

For some reason, my mom and I were late for my first day of kindergarten—where I met young Jackie. Miss Berrigan was standing by her gray steel desk at the front of the room, gently smiling at us as we walked in. I only remember her from that first day, though I do recall my last day of kindergarten, my graduation day. On that last day, I had gotten ill. I was doubled over with nausea on our davenport and had a high fever. I really felt hot. That was once of only twice in my entire life that I have ever been so nauseous as to be doubled over. Sick or not, I really wanted to graduate with everyone else. Besides, I had my sticks to play in a song, and, already like your grandmother, I didn't want to let anyone down. So we put my white graduation gown on, with my white graduation cap and its white tassel, and walked down Rugraff and Jay Streets to my school. Once on stage in the large auditorium, I sat at the very end of my row, on the wooded chair, on my left facing the audience. Though feverish and sick, on cue, I successfully played my sticks. I managed to graduate with my class—and I was pleased.

As I nervously glanced around the room that first day of kindergarten, I noticed the colorful play horses in the back and the many wooden round tables, each with children sitting quietly around. There was only one place left to sit, and Miss Berrigan gently directed me to it. I anxiously sat down on the wooden chair, glancing around at the other children politely sitting at the table. Directly across from me, Jackie's bright, cute smile caught my eye— and warmed my heart. I immediately had a crush on her. It happened in an instant—and I carried that crush for years. When I accidentally put my arm through the back porch window a few years later and had to wear a sling, Jackie was the one who helped me get my jacket on when we went out for recess or left school for home at the end of the day. Maybe she had a crush on me too. Or maybe she was just a very kind little girl.

Then there was Sister Monica. I had her for second grade. It was lunchtime. As was the routine, Sister directed us to get our coats from the narrow coatroom and make our way back to our desks to put them on. John sat ahead of me in our row. As we were putting our coats on, just for fun, I grabbed John's hat and whacked him on the top of his head. Unfortunately, Sister caught me and called me to the front of the room. I dreaded going up knowing I would be scolded in front of my peers. As I got closer, I noticed that her face was stern but oddly warm. She looked younger than the other nuns, and seemed almost pretty through the starchy black and white hood. She held my right arm with one hand and spanked me on my bottom with the other. It didn't hurt; at least I didn't feel it. Instead, I actually felt soothing feelings of being close to a woman who exuded warmth and gentleness—a gentleness I felt even while spanking me. No other nun ever felt like her. It seems so odd to use the word "woman" for a sister, as if it is somehow sacrilegious. But, for a brief moment, Sister Monica felt like a real woman.

When I was a Cub Scout, our small den met at Raymond's house; his stepmom was den mother. I have no idea what happened to his mother. His stepmother always smiled at us Scouts and was kind to Raymond. I sure didn't have a name for what I felt as a little boy; all I knew was that she mesmerized me. She had light brown hair that flowed around her inviting face, gently curling as in softly landed on her shoulders. I was fascinated. She ran a fire drill, training us what to do in case the house ever caught on fire. I saw her warmth, kindness, and decisiveness during that drill—and I actually wished my dad would remarry like Raymond's father had so I could have a mom like her.

I'm not sure what happened to Jackie—if she left the grammar school or if my crush just evaporated, as crushes are known to do—but in seventh and eighth grades, I developed a crush on Jennifer. She too had a wonderful smile, and struck me as kind, but I was too shy to do anything about it. So I admired her from a distance. Several years later, I saw her about fifty feet away talking to a girlfriend in the lobby of my high school. Jennifer went to Cardinal Mooney High School, but extracurricular events brought her to Aquinas. She had long, flowing black hair down to her waist. I was so drawn to talk with her. I kept staring at her, debating and debating about going up to say hi, but I froze. I just couldn't muster the courage to talk, let alone ask her out on a date.

Then there was Michelle. I met her through the neighborhood clique I hung around in my early teens. I had taught myself the guitar, and a bunch of us would jam together just for fun. I have no idea how this happened, but I managed to ask her out for a date. One date—that was it. Just yesterday I found a picture of us neighborhood kids at a party I had as a high school freshman—and she was among them. At fourteen, she sure made my blood move. Shortly after this stirring encounter, your uncle and I went to a drive-in movie—some brother-to-brother time—where I nervously and somewhat incoherently tried to explore how I reacted to Michelle. I don't know what I was looking for from your uncle, but I certainly felt I needed to talk. I fumbled my way through, trying to put into words how I felt being in this young lady's presence.

I found myself describing in some detail how she moved her hands and touched her own leg. As I realized what I was saying, I felt embarrassed. It would've helped if Herb had wisely rescued me by simply noting the obvious: I had the hots for her. But I really don't think your uncle knew what to say to me. I certainly felt weird. Besides the awkward inability to articulate the process of "discovering girls," I didn't understand how I could feel such attraction for Michelle while, at the same time, feeling scared of her. To be sure, I felt scared simply because she was a girl. But I also felt scared—without knowing it at the time—because, being female, she triggered all the fears of my mother and the nuns. Michelle didn't help the situation either. She herself was aloof, unlike Jackie and Jennifer. Perhaps Michelle had her own discomfort in "discovering" boys. I do not know.

These vivid images of girls and women who were warm and caring and attractive, including the girls I took to my junior prom and senior ball who were very kind—along with moments of my mother holding Tiny and baking me Christmas cookies—became the bits and pieces I unconsciously stitched together to form the canvas of a caring mother. One image that unified this collage—an image that brought the collage to life—was June Cleaver in that time-honored series from the 1950s show *Leave It To Beaver*. However dull and cheesy such a series may seem to a twenty-first-century child, for an emotionally starved young boy of the 1950s, it became a reference point for what should have been but wasn't. If only my mother had been more of a June Cleaver.

But what has all this to do with nature?

From Jackie ... to Jennifer ... to Sister Monica ... to Michelle ... to Raymond's mother ... to the other kind girls ... to bits and pieces of my own mother ... to June Cleaver—I put together my maternal icon. Nature became the panoramic "inkblot" onto which I projected this montage. The beautiful, gentle side of nature became the beautiful, gentle side of a woman that I desperately desired in my mother. Through a creative metamorphosis in my young psyche, nature became "Mother" nature, an impersonal yet powerful extension of June Cleaver. Nature was not only the one place in the universe I could go for beauty, warmth, and gentleness. It was the only place I could go for some sense of a nurturing mother.

So—what if *all* the options I mentioned above are true? What if we can discern the Creator's power through nature? What if the Creator's grandeur blends with the unspeakable beauty of his creation? What if we, as a species, are biologically tied to the stuff of the earth in a way that creates some inexplicable sense of belonging—of being home—when we manage to get away from our own concrete and asphalt jungles and retreat to the bosom of Mother Nature? And what if I did tuck nature's powerfully feminine side deep into my bankrupt psyche as a substitute for my own mother?

What if all these are true? If they are, is it any wonder why— once Uncle Herb introduced me to her—I was so magnetically, inexorably, drawn to Nature? I was like a starving infant whose head frantically rocks back and forth searching instinctively for mother's breast, as I did as a little boy sucking my thumb and feverishly rocking my head back and forth in my attic prison desperately looking for succor. I was like the emperor penguin who waddles for seventy miles one way across tough terrain in bitter cold weather to go home—an instinct forged by the phylogenetic forces of survival and driven by inexplicable but innate pictures of "home" that captivate her entire being. I too had finally found my home. Mother Nature had become my adoptive mother—and I, her gratefully adopted son.

My Draw to Mystery

The Astronaut Kid

"If we don't have our dreams, we have nothing."

That's the tagline of a low-budget and unrealistic film called *The Astronaut Farmer*.* A NASA astronaut trainee was forced to retire many years earlier than planned. He did so to save the family farm, but he never gave up his passionate dream of space travel. Eventually, after enormous sacrifice, he built his own rocket. In the face of many seemingly insurmountable obstacles, including the federal government, he beat the overwhelming odds—and finally succeeded in launching.

As a young kid, I wanted to be an astronaut. And like that trainee, the desire has never really left me. Even though NASA tragically lost two space shuttles, I'd go in a heartbeat if I could. One could argue that that would be a bit foolish. Such a high-risk venture trades off seeing my grandchildren grow up should another shuttle explode. However, I've not heard Christa McAuliffe criticized for being selfish or shortsighted. NASA chose and trained her as a payload specialist for their Teacher in Space Project. The shuttle crew, including McAuliffe, tragically died when *Challenger* exploded seventy-three seconds after launch in 1986. She was only thirty-seven and left a husband and two children behind. It can be tough—sometimes excruciatingly painful as the film dramatizes—discerning where healthy passion for a dream ends and unhealthy self-absorption begins. Nevertheless, Kid, I'd go.

---

*"The Astronaut Farmer," IMDb.com, http://www.imdb.com/title/tt0469263/

But alas, all that is foolishly moot. A ride on the shuttle is but a pipe dream.

It was July 20, 1969; I was seventeen. I rushed home from my summer job. I even ran from the bus stop which was about a mile and a half away to make sure that I got there in time to witness astronauts Neil Armstrong and Buzz Aldrin landing on the moon. My father was avidly watching the drama unfold along with millions of others on the planet. I stood next to him, pensive, anxiously waiting for the astronauts to land in the Sea of Tranquility.

The tension mounted. When the fifteen-ton lunar module was about a mile above the moon's surface, the *Eagle's* computer sounded alarm bells—and kept on sounding those alarms as they descended. Houston determined the *Eagle* could continue its descent. But then the astronauts realized the computer, which was controlling the craft, was going to land them on unexpectedly rocky terrain.

There was no way they could land as originally planned; the module would flip over and crash. Now being only a football field above the moon's surface, Armstrong switched off the automatic landing program. He took over control. When he did, his heart rate shot up to over 150. Aldrin called out altitude and speed while Armstrong manually worked the stick. With only sixty seconds of fuel remaining, they flew across a massive boulder field desperately trying to find a flat area to touch down in. The seconds ticked off. With less than thirty seconds of fuel remaining, Armstrong thought he found a spot—and carefully worked the stick. There was absolute silence in Houston. Then the world heard, "Houston, Tranquility Base here. The *Eagle* has landed." Erupting in celebration, Mission Control replied, "Roger, Tranquility, we copy you on the ground. You got a bunch of guys about to turn blue. We're breathing again."* Like many across the globe, I actually choked up. Shivers went up my spine. Pretty sentimental for a teen. But it was indeed an historic moment for the entire watching world.

Kristen, your generation now takes venturing out into that final frontier of cosmic space for granted. It is certainly old news. But, as a kid growing up in the fifties and sixties, space was a new frontier. With the Cold War after World War II—and the proliferation of the nuclear

---

*National Aeronautics and Space Administration, "Apollo Expeditions to the Moon," www.history.nasa.gov/SP-350/ch-11–4.html.

bomb—the United States found itself desperately trying to catch up to the Soviet Union. The Soviets had made it into space ahead of us, sending up the *Sputnik* satellite in 1957 and a manned spacecraft in 1961. Their success had jarred Americans. Our leadership was stunned . . . and scared; the United States was being left behind. What if the Soviet Union developed the ability to take nuclear bombs into space—and we didn't? The entire country was scared. We were so scared that the nuns in grammar school routinely practiced air raid drills and people across the country built home bomb shelters. Just six weeks later, on May 25, 1961, when I was nine, I listened to John F. Kennedy, president of the United States, declare: "I believe that this nation should commit itself to achieving the goal, before this decade is out, of landing a man on the moon and returning him safely to the earth."

The president's bold call to shoot the moon within a decade stirred a futuristic vision in the American psyche. His vision mobilized the best talent in the nation. I don't know if he was aware of it, but he planted seeds in thousands of young minds—including mine. I began to dream about being an astronaut. Deep down, I knew that such a dream was unrealistic. After all, I was from lowly circumstances. And I was not the son of a pilot. Besides, I wore glasses; astronauts couldn't wear glasses. Yet, my simple boyhood dream persisted, fed by my implacable desire to escape the turmoil in my family. As the rocket left the launch pad, I could imagine leaving the family's troubles behind.

Boyhood fantasy or not, the president's daring challenge to put a man on the moon made space travel unquestionably realistic. So the president's seed, once planted in my psyche, grew. My unrealistic though persistent daydreams transformed into a sober pursuit of such questions as: How large is the universe? Are there other universes? How old is our universe? Did it have a beginning? And how would we ever travel long distances, like to the center of our own Milky Way galaxy? In 2008, the *Voyager* spacecraft, after completing its mission and discovering many moons never before seen orbiting other planets, left the pull of our Sun heading out into the deep space of our own Milky Way. It left at a pretty fast clip of about 36,000 miles per hour. That's ten miles every second! Still, at that incredible speed, it would actually take the craft an unbelievable 450 million years just to get to the center of our galaxy. Mind-boggling distances. NASA put a message from President Jimmy Carter on the *Voyager*—just in case extraterrestrials "run across" the craft on their way through the galaxy:

We cast this message into the cosmos. It is likely to survive a billion years into our future, when our civilization is profoundly altered and the surface of the Earth may be vastly changed. Of the 200 billion stars in the Milky Way galaxy, some—perhaps many—may have inhabited planets and space faring civilizations. If one such civilization intercepts *Voyager* and can understand these recorded contents, here is our message: We are attempting to survive our time so we may live into yours. We hope someday, having solved the problems we face, to join a community of galactic civilizations. This record represents our hope and our determination and our goodwill in a vast and awesome universe.*

I later found out that my various questions about the universe were the ponderings of fields like astrophysics, astronomy, and cosmology.

In high school, I wasn't interested in studying biology. I've never been sure why, though I recall thinking biology must be boring with all the memorizing students had to do. Today, as much as I love performing "surgery" of the mind, I would love to be a surgeon of the body as well. Go figure. In college, I loved a course that put together biology and physics, called biophysics. I found the integration of these two disciplines fascinating. Still, I didn't take to biology as a high school student. But I did have fun in chemistry class. Before the teacher would come into the classroom, several students would open the valves on the black lab tables and light the escaping gas. They made wonderful flamethrowers, with long, bright-yellow streams of fire shooting out several feet across the tabletops. Though stupid—and I wasn't about to light one myself—it sure looked awesome. During class one day, the teacher accidentally made chlorine gas, which, as you know, is poisonous—deadly poisonous. As the brilliantly yellow gas gently wafted out of her beaker, she wisely directed all of us to hang our heads out the windows, and she quickly followed. In another experiment, I was fascinated that

---

*Jimmy Carter, "Voyager Spacecraft Statement by the President," July 29, 1977. Online by Gerhard Peters and John T. Woolley, The American Presidency Project, http://www.presidency.ucsb.edu/ws/?pid=7890.

we could put two clear liquids together in a test tube and immediately create a new white substance, called a "precipitate," if you recall. In spite of these interesting experiences, I never really did take to chemistry.

My senior year I studied physics with Father Bianco. Although many of us thought of him as a bit eccentric, he was nevertheless enthusiastic about physics. He enjoyed teaching as well as setting up experiments. Perhaps his joy was contagious; I don't know. What I do know is that the invisible forces of gravity and magnetism absolutely fascinated me. Just how did gravity pull objects together? How could the moon tug on the oceans, creating tides? How could magnetic forces attract and repel objects? How could iron in the earth "grab" my compass needle in the woods and make it move? The seductive allure of these invisible forces was no doubt an extension of my burning desire to understand the invisible yet powerful forces among my family members. As a teen, I somehow sensed the parallel. Our solar system's planets and sun are in each other's orbits, forever determining one another's path. But it's the same way for family. Family members are in each other's "orbit," forever influencing one another's path in life.

Besides the symbolic parallel to my family life, I loved physics because it gave me answers—answers based on facts. It gave me answers that I could count on. After all, I couldn't get any answers for my life from the nuns, priests, Veterans Administration . . . or God. Along with your uncle, science became another lifeline.

Math is the central tool for physics—and I loved it. As a boy, math seemed so rational, clear, stable, and predictable to me. If you followed its reasoning, it would lead to rational answers.

Being an indispensable part of physics, math seemed to give me certain answers—absolutely certain answers. Two plus two equals four, and it equals four all the time. It doesn't matter whether it is Monday or Sunday, or if the year is 1951 or 2007 or ten thousand— two plus two always equals four. And the answer cannot be three or five. It just can't. So there is certainty. It also doesn't matter who you are. You can be Jewish, Christian, Muslim, New Age, Buddhist, Hindu, humanist, atheist, or theist. It just doesn't matter. Two plus two equals four—no matter who decides to look at the question and no matter who comes up with the answer. In that way, math is cross-cultural. In fact, math is cross-galactic. We will someday be able to talk with aliens through mathematical formulas. The language is universal. It is universal because it is true for everyone. Reality dictates that.

What a contrast to having no answers to my parents' dilemma. What a contrast to the way religious leaders made stuff up. What a contrast to man-made religious paradoxes, like those indulgences on the back page of my Baltimore Catechism. The search for facts, not fiction, drove science. It could give me handles when I had no handles. It could give me clarity when there had been only darkness, ambiguity, and confusion.

By the summer of '69, long after his assassination, President John F. Kennedy's vision for America had been realized. And the seed he planted within me had richly blossomed over the decade. Science now captivated my youthful imagination as it had so many young minds of that generation. I was headed into physics. Soon, in my college training, I would feel the liberating sense of meaning in getting to the bottom of things. Whether working through calculus equations in theoretical mechanics or resolving quantum mechanical dilemmas about the behavior of subatomic particles, grabbing a piece of reality by its lapels—and making that piece cough up answers as to why it was the way it was—would be viscerally satisfying. I would not be put off by the long hours of study; such hard work had already become familiar to me. Mother Nature always made me sweat to be with her . . . and get to know her. I was used to it.

America shot the moon. The price tag in money, lives lost, and damage to the astronauts' families was enormous. But we fulfilled our collective dream. Was the dream worth it? It began as an act of national survival; did it end as an act of national selfishness? For a brief mesmerizing moment—an unquestionably historic moment— the cost was eclipsed for most of us.

The historic privilege of being the very first human being to step onto the moon went to Astronaut Neil Armstrong. Astronaut Buzz Aldrin was second. Most people fixed on their televisions didn't know that Aldrin—an elder at Webster Presbyterian Church in Texas—had brought Communion with him on the Eagle. He took it privately shortly before his own moonwalk. (Webster Presbyterian keeps the chalice he used and commemorates his lunar Communion each year.) About five hours after landing, at 10:56 p.m.—with now over half a billion of us watching—Commander Armstrong slowly stepped down the ladder. Gently placing his boot onto the lunar surface, he said, "That's one small step for a man, one giant leap for mankind."* For the first time in human history—for the absolutely very first time—the human race set foot on the moon. And I got to see it.

---

*Robert Z. Pearlman, "Neil Armstrong's First Words: One Small Fib or Giant Leap By Brother?" Space.com, http://www.space.com/19119-neil -armstrong-quote-moon-controversy.html.

Good Mystery

I love mystery. Not mystery novels, but life's mysteries. To me, mystery is the cutting edge of science. Without mystery there is no motivation to do science. In fact, without mystery there is no science; there is only knowledge.

At the same time, I've always had a love-hate relationship with mystery.

Like most young boys—and like my precious grandchildren—I got excited discovering new things. I also asked a lot of questions. Still do. As I stared at the army of ants marching across our concrete back steps lugging huge pieces of food, I wondered how it was that they knew how to work together so well. And how did they do that without ever talking to each other like people do? And typical of young boys' curiosity—as well as their propensity for the cruel exercise of their power—I found it fascinating to fry some of those ants as they advanced along the sidewalk with their supplies, wondering how the others would scramble to fix the losses. I recall one moment vividly. My guess is that I recall it so well because of my own discomfort with my sadistic impulse. Still, I carefully focused the summer sun's rays with my magnifying glass onto one of their soldiers in the march—while pondering if any of them knew I was there destroying one of their own. Or even if they cared.

When I crawled around outside by the side of our garage on Ridgeway, I looked up and saw a very tall, wide blade of grass. I didn't notice anything unusual at first. And then it came into focus. I was momentarily taken aback. On that blade a very odd-looking critter came into focus—what I found out later was a praying mantis. Just a few inches from my nose, this weird looking creature just stared at me. I wondered how it was that there could be such an alien among us. I scampered into the house to get my trusty magnifying glass so I could see this creature's otherworldly features up close.

Among my other boyhood interests, I experimented with a male Siamese fighting fish. Being bred in captivity, the male was the beautiful one of the species—with long flowing fins that hung in the water like an elegant wedding gown with a long, gorgeous train trailing behind. The male had a rich palette of colors he could be born with, from ruby red to dark oceanic blue. The female's fins were shorter and her colors more pale. I attached a mirror to the side of my aquarium. The male was known to think that his reflection was another male. He'd position himself in fight mode. Squaring off with his perceived rival, he'd flare all his fins for maximum thrust and balance. Then he'd spread his gills wide open—along with some inner part of the gill as well, making him look pretty fierce—and attack. Unfortunately, the fruitless battle with his own reflection made him so charged up and frustrated that he assaulted other harmless fish in the tank who were minding their own business. By the time I got my hand in there to stop him, I lost several fish. I did manage to train him to jump for food. When I'd take the cover off the tank and move my finger into place, he'd flare his fins wide open then propel himself almost completely out of the water to grab brine shrimp off the tip of my finger. I thought that was pretty cool.

As a young teen, my best friend and I shared ownership of a large gopher snake. It was about three feet long and an inch and a half wide. We loved pulling on it to feel its incredible strength. One time, it had its head angled up under the bottom edge of the house's siding . . . just its head, mind you. We were both pulling on its body trying to break it free, and couldn't. Finally, we had to relax the tension and let it move away on its own. When it didn't like being handled—and it sure didn't that time—it hissed just like a rattlesnake. It wasn't venomous, but it was still unnerving to have it get upset at us. It was amazing how wide it could open its jaws to devour an egg that was huge compared to its head. And fascinating to see that egg slowly travel down its narrow body—whole.

The alien appearance of odd creatures like the gopher snake and praying mantis actually accounts for why so many reasonable adults have unreasonable phobic reactions to insects and snakes. Primal instinct reacts to such radically different life forms as possible threats to survival. Interestingly, our instincts haven't caught up with modern civilization, at least not yet. Our genetic makeup as a species simply hasn't changed to create phobic reactions to SUVs that kill more people than snakes or insects. I felt that primal threat as a kid. I especially felt it with our snake—as do most people. But I directed my nervousness into excitement.

From insects and snakes to dealing with trauma, that propensity of mine to transform threats—even primal threats—into excitement has been part of my idiosyncratic style across most years of my life. I learned to take fear—and pain—and transform them into a meaningful engagement of life. I had to. I'm not sure where that propensity comes from. Perhaps it's my creative twist on your grandparents' determination to survive; I'm not sure. But I do use my fears. And I go to great lengths to use them wisely. I do have this simple-headed attitude that you either let life crush you—and what's the point in that—or make the most of what you got.

My brother Ron went to Thomas Edison High for students interested in the trades. Sadly, your uncle had suffered significant brain damage by a doctor's forceps at birth. That damage affected him in a number of ways. He was socially awkward, didn't make eye contact well, and had an odd gait. I enjoyed my brother. When I was about six or seven and your uncle about eleven, he ventured out into the field of chemistry. He gave me the privileged position as his assistant. Your uncle enjoyed mixing chemicals—just to see what would happen. He created some concoction with such corrosive power that the chemical mix ate a hole through the vinyl of one of our kitchen chairs. That mix then ate deep into the chair's padding—many inches, in fact—leaving charred collateral damage along the way. I don't recall what the original experiment was all about. But I do remember thinking we were in big trouble—and being very glad your uncle Ron was the older brother in charge of that experiment.

As you can see from these brief vignettes, long before the president of the United States stirred my interest in space science, the simple, boyish desire to learn thrived. It thrived in spite of my trauma. In fact, my family problems fed my passion for learning. I did seem to have had a keen appreciation for the idea that "information is power" decades before that expression came into use in the eighties. In grammar school, we had a drawing contest for the Pope Pius reading guild. We were to depict the power of reading. I drew the major stages of a caterpillar becoming a butterfly. I divided my paper into three sections, one for each phase of this tiny creature's transmutation. The first stage on the left was as a caterpillar. The second in the middle was the cocoon. And the third on the right was the butterfly struggling to leave its cocoon. The utter transformation of this alien creature captivated my imagination. How could a fuzzy, many-legged critter wrap itself up in a miniature sleeping bag only to emerge as what seemed to be an entirely new creation?

In my young imagination, this picture of "caterpillar-becoming-butterfly" captured the transforming power of knowledge. The dramatic symbolism of my art didn't escape adult attention. Along with other student artwork, it won an award—and a place in a display at some public building in downtown Rochester. My artwork reflected how I was unconsciously grappling with my trauma. It was my latent hope that somehow, someday, I'd be able to enter some "cocoon" state and, with enough information—with the right kind of power—come out the other end utterly transformed. In that new state, I'd be free. I'd finally be free from the turmoil of my family. I find it amazing that my psyche created this powerful metaphor at such a tender age. But I find it even more incredible that it became my inner template for later being magnetically drawn to what the apostle Paul called "the new creation."

I had this determined desire to learn even though learning was so difficult for me. An optometrist internationally known for his work on my eye condition diagnosed the problem in my midthirties. My eyeballs are large. Actually, they're huge. You'd never know it by looking at me; my eye sockets hide their size. The doctor told me candidly that looking into my eyeball was like looking into the ocean. The muscles around the eyeballs are so strained in moving my huge eyes back and forth that the energy used to move them actually interferes with processing the information entering my eyes. For most of my life, all I knew was that reading was both very slow and very difficult. My SRA tests in grammar school, which tested reading comprehension under the pressure of time, were never good. I'd read a paragraph but not know what I just read. And later in high school I tried speed reading to no avail. Nowadays in schools, such visual difficulties are still typically missed—and misdiagnosed as learning disabilities. My case, among others, was used in Harrisburg to secure state legislation mandating better visual screening in Pennsylvania schools for just that reason. Because it was never diagnosed for me as a kid, I thought I had some brain problem, that I just wasn't smart. I hated reading fiction because reading was just so slow and grueling. In both high school and college, in order to survive, I had to take notes of everything I read. Then, I had to take notes of my notes. Then—once again—I took notes of those notes. That's how I got the information through what I thought was my "thick skull."

I worked hard in high school because my parents wanted us to go to college. I worked hard because I needed scholarship money to get there. I also worked hard because of the unconscious caterpillar-becoming-butterfly hope that knowledge would set me free. Beyond that, I worked hard to prove myself—to prove myself to myself, not to anyone else. I did achieve my goal: the St. Thomas Club award for all four years. It was the highest honor in the school, earning me a permanent place on a plaque in the school's lobby. I was proud of that. But not because I thought it proved I was intelligent. It didn't prove that to me. What it did prove was that if I worked hard enough and long enough I could achieve something. So I've always worked hard. I've always worked long. And I've always believed I had to. I didn't know my reading difficulties had nothing to do with intelligence until my thirties, long after my formal studies. This reading disability, however, did fuel my growing interest in math and science. You simply don't have to "read" numbers and formulas fast.

The expert who diagnosed my eye condition showed me how else this problem shaped my daily behavior. You may jokingly think this is typical male behavior, but when I look for something in a drawer, I won't "see" it—even if it's on top. That is, it doesn't even register in my brain to be processed. When I drive, talking with a passenger and watching highway signs at the same time is very frustrating. The eyes are so busy trying to "see" that I cannot listen well. When information quickly changes on the television screen, I simply can't process it. To this day, I can read an article in *Reader's Digest* but not be able to tell you what I just read. At a store, when I swipe my credit card through the machine to pay, the instructions do not register in my brain. I have to slow myself up to say one word at a time to have it click. I am so slow that the cashier will typically point to what I have to do next.

I am aware that my eye limitations blend with my sincere, yet somewhat innocent, even naïve, style, making me look as if I'm not "with it" or lacking common sense—or just plain dense. Certainly, you wouldn't want me as a pilot in the air force—although, somehow, I compensate well enough to play a mean game of Ping-Pong.

Visual limitations or not, and family trauma or not, I do love solving nature's mysteries. Whether it's the little boy's curiosity for planet Earth's odd-looking creatures or the big boy's multi-billion dollar search for alien life forms on Mars or Europa, mysteries get my blood moving. One reason I'll never burn out with my profession is that I so love the mystery of the human mind. My list of spellbinding mysteries is endless. I know many judge that such mysteries are useless for day-to-day living. But, in spite of what life throws at us, many of us are still very curious. Over 500 million people watched the fascinating series by astrophysicist Carl Sagan, *Cosmos: A Personal Voyage*. The Discovery Channel is dedicated to satisfying our innumerable curiosities. *The Blue Planet*, *The Planet Earth*, and *Life* series were incredible explorations of our world with some never before seen photography. Millions bought the book *A Brief History of Time* by the most renowned theoretical physicist living, Stephen Hawking. (Sadly, for decades, Lou Gehrig's disease has trapped this man's brilliant mind in a mangled body.) And I am presently making my way through *The Elegant Universe*. Without such incredible mysteries to tease us—or even seduce us—all we would have is what Ecclesiastes declares as the boring, even depressing, cycle of life. We get up, work, eat, sleep—in order to get up and do it all over again. I have to say, whatever else my life has been—and it has indeed been many things—it has never been boring.

Bad Mystery

While I've loved the intriguing mysteries of our universe, I've nevertheless always hated the dual mysteries of suffering and death.
Right or wrong, I've taken suffering and death personally. But I'm
not alone. The research—and common sense—reveal that those
traumatized by intense suffering do wonder, why me?

When traumas hit, victims call everything into question. They
doubt the core beliefs and formulas they've lived life by. Some say,
"I've played by the rules and where has it gotten me?" Or "What's the
point?" Or "Nice guys do finish last." And they wonder whether life
has any real meaning or not. I've done the same. I've not only taken
my suffering personally and wondered, *why me*? But I've pondered
the more central question, *why*? Why does such nonsense exist at all?
What purpose does it serve? For your grandparents who suffered so
much—for anybody who suffers badly—of what practical use are the
glorious wonders of this magnificent universe when you don't know
where your next meal is coming from? Who cares about the "good"
mysteries of life when, like your grandfather, you're fighting the "bad"
mystery of an incipient disease that then slowly and tortuously decon-
structs your physical identity while simultaneously tormenting you
emotionally?

I said I've hated the dual mystery of suffering and death—and I
do. Yet, I am inextricably tied to suffering in a way where, as a moth
is drawn to the flame that ultimately consumes it, I cannot escape
being inexorably drawn to dealing with these mysteries. And this is
so even though I am keenly aware that questioning life's dark side
has been driven by my need to penetrate the mystery of the dark side
of my own mother. I've tried to discover—actually, if I'm honest,
I've viscerally demanded—answers as to why my no-name family
would have suffered so much.

In my demanding pursuit for an answer, I've wrestled with the
one key question: Just what is suffering and death all about anyway?

124

When your older brother Paul was just a tot, your mom and I went to see *Bambi* at a drive-in theatre. I had never seen it. I thought it was going to be bunny rabbits and deer and lots of fluff. Our little guy was standing on the center console between us when we heard a gunshot. Bambi's mother was killed. Paul looked down at me with big saucer eyes and asked, "Do mommies die?" That question floored me as a young parent. With great hesitation and a momentary glance at your mom, I said, "Yes, Paul, mommies die." I wasn't going to lie to him; I hate lying. Besides, what if something were to happen. How would that impact him . . . as well as his feelings toward me? But I whispered to your mom sarcastically, "Thank you, Walt Disney." I really hadn't expected to introduce your brother to death, let alone our deaths, at such a tender age or in that way.

To be sure, death doesn't only come from the end of a gun. It is built into the order of things. Evolutionary biologists and the producers of *The Lion King* see suffering and death as a natural part of life. "Mother Nature," it seems, not only showers all creatures with rain that fosters life but also tortures those same creatures with diseases—like multiple sclerosis that turned your grandfather into a quadriplegic. Or cancer that your brother Paul fought at twenty-three. In the end, Mother Nature destroys us. In fact, she destroys every living organism she births into this universe. Movies like *The Lion King*—and some professionals who claim expertise on death and dying—not only encourage us to accept death, but even to embrace it. Death, after all, is a necessary part of life. One theme that I gleaned from the *The Lion King* was that as I age, I need to face my imminent demise and pass the torch on to you. You are the next generation who must grasp that torch firmly, letting go of the past—and me. So, you and I must not view death as an enemy to fight, but rather as an inevitable part of the never-ending cycle of life that we must embrace, thus making your future possible.

Mother Nature not only delivers suffering and death, but does so with exquisitely orchestrated violence. Look at the war-like behavior among some insects. Thirty Japanese hornets can kill and behead thirty thousand honeybees in just three hours in order to steal their food. If I did the arithmetic right, that's about one beheading every eleven seconds for each hornet. Such is the militant aggression built into the instinctual fabric of these little creatures. Set to music, such aggression makes for even more powerful battle scenes than those found in the movie *Braveheart*. Mother Nature's choreographies of violence are simply unparalleled. Note the elegant dance between the wolf and fawn: the wolf's dog-eat-dog, unrelenting pursuit is matched by the fawn's graceful but terrified retreat—until, five miles later, she collapses in utter exhaustion and the wolf crushes her throat with its powerful jaws. Then add to Mother Nature's repertoire worldwide earthquakes, volcanic eruptions, and tsunamis that have killed millions of human beings over the millennia. It's all part of her game of life—the survival of the stronger, survival of the smarter . . . survival of the fittest.

Whether any of us like it or not, all living creatures suffer. My second dog Tiny that I had since age four had severe arthritis in her hind legs, which she painfully dragged behind her until we mercifully put her to sleep. After sixteen years of having known her, like so many dog owners, I was deeply attached to Tiny. And Tiny loved us.

Research on dogs, dolphins, chimps and parrots is revealing just how complicated animals are. In fact, some researchers believe that animals have a wide array of mental and emotional functions that are similar to ours—common building blocks of consciousness so to speak. It makes sense to me because I believe I saw such building blocks in Tiny. When she slept, I'd notice times when Tiny would rapidly move her eyes back and forth and growl. I've always presumed she was dreaming—just like us. But, of course, I never knew what she was seeing in her dreams. It's an incredible challenge discovering what an animal sees when the creature cannot talk. As part of my experimental training in psychology, we put tiny electrodes into a frog's brain to find out what it actually saw when a bug flew by. As best as we can tell, a frog doesn't see an insect as an insect; all it sees is a dark blob of a certain size against the much lighter background of the sky. Likely, the hungry frog doesn't need to be able to discern if the blob is an insect or not because most blobs in its world are indeed its next meal. And that's all it needs to know.

One time, when I was about twelve, I filled Tiny's dish with a certain canned dog food she absolutely loved for dinner. But I decided to test her. My Siamese fighting fish wasn't the only pet I trained; I had previously trained Tiny not to eat dog treats I placed on her nose. She'd even drool big, long gobs of saliva onto the floor instead of taking the treat—until told to do so. I decided to see if I could take her dinner dish without her reacting. Fortunately, I had enough wisdom to move slowly as I reached down to grab her dish. Tiny froze. She then peeled back both rows of teeth and gave me a soft, slow, intense growl. I froze. I had never seen Tiny do that before. She had given me a "shot across my bow." She was eating, and I was threatening to take her food away, stirring her primal instinct for survival. The message was clear: back off—or else. We all can feel the remnant of that instinct if someone were to reach for our plate as we're moving the fork to our mouth. Waiters and waitresses wisely ask us if we are done with our meal before taking our plates. Such cultural courtesy is unconsciously driven by the knowledge that taking a plate without permission stirs up primitive aggression. But even though I threatened Tiny's innate need for food—and she was clearly upset—she chose not to hurt me. She controlled her aggression as if she knew she ought not to hurt me—perhaps a kind of dog morality. Tiny did much better, in fact, than many people with road rage.

The fact is that there are researchers who believe that some animals may use a phylogenetically primitive form of moral behavior—and have evidence to support it. Certain primates show moral behavior like sharing tools and raising orphaned children as their own. One primate stood between a poisonous snake and her friend at the risk of her own life. And many people do think dogs have a kind of "dog morality" that is like a young child's morality. When Tiny did something "wrong"—and as the alpha "dog" I'd scold her—she'd put her head down and tuck her tail between her legs, looking shamed, like little boys and girls do when scolded for something wrong . . . just like I felt when my dad or the nuns scolded me. Did Tiny put her head down because she didn't want to be scolded? Did she do that because she actually *felt* some shame or guilt? The final chapter on that scientific mystery has not been written. But I've always believed Tiny reacted to me with some sense of her own morality. I've never asked you, but do wonder now if you've ever thought that of your Baxter.

As a young man of twenty, I held Tiny firmly in my arms on the way to the veterinarian as your mom drove. Tiny knew where we were headed—as she always knew—and was scared. She was shaking like a leaf. I gently handed her to the doctor on the other side of the counter. He asked if I wanted to stay to hold her while she "went to sleep." Perhaps, in my ignorance, I hadn't even thought of that possibility. Or perhaps I was so upset I had blocked the question on the way. Either way, the question took me aback. I just shook my head no. As a young man who had lived and played with her for fifteen years, I couldn't bring myself to hold her while she died. I couldn't do what my mother had done with our first Tiny. I'll never forget the look on Tiny's face as I left, and I have since deeply regretted not holding my childhood companion while she passed away. I've always wondered whether Tiny felt abandoned by me in her own dog way.

While all creatures suffer and die, we just happen to be the ones who can sit back and write about it. No other animal writes books about suffering and death. No animal builds libraries. And no animal builds courtrooms. But we do. In a sense, the universe became conscious of itself through us. We are the only animal that craves answers to life's deep mysteries. And we're the only animal that demands justice in the face of suffering. Hebrews 2:7 does say we were made just a little lower than the angels. And so we were. But that wonderful ability to ask the tough questions and contemplate the nuances of our own pain—and do so in exquisite detail—just adds to our agony. Not having answers is part of our human misery. Beyond that, it does really look like suffering and death are simply part of the never-ending cycle of life. Nevertheless, I hate it.

Then again, who really likes it?

Faith and Bad Mystery

Some with staunch faith in God believe we are more than our bodies. They picture us as ethereal "souls" trapped in physical casings that mysteriously become liberated upon death. In the meantime, they believe suffering teaches us soulful lessons such as having to depend on God for our emotional sustenance. Believing that God is teaching us some specific life lesson through suffering is supposed to provide both meaning and comfort.

But when suffering is so intense—and for so long—one wonders about one's own stupidity for not yet getting the divine object lesson. Besides, what's the point of suffering in this life—heck, what's the point of life itself?—if one is simply waiting for the liberation of one's soul into the next?

For others who fervently believe the Creator is in ultimate charge of reality, all suffering becomes personal—really personal—one way or another. Some believe God intentionally sends them suffering. They find reassuring solace in the belief that their enigmatic suffering must have some profound meaning—even if they can't discern it—because God sent it. All that matters to them is that God knows the meaning; they don't need to know if he knows. The traumatized may even see their suffering as a personal act of divine love, causing them to be refined by the Refiner's fire of suffering—a kind of purgatory on earth. They may even count it a privilege to suffer for the Almighty, trusting he has some inscrutable purpose for it all.

But many others of good faith who also believe God has power over all reality wonder: Why did God *perpetrate* this against me? Or, like your grandfather, why did God *allow* this to happen to me? That is, why did he stand by—how could he have stood by—and do nothing? They passionately carry the flag of justice, wondering where and how they can ever find it. They viscerally declare to the Almighty, "I don't deserve this!" That declaration of innocence—and with it, the demand for justice—is as old as the book of Job

129

in the Old Testament. Job suffered through several traumas while vehemently denying culpability for them. He repeatedly declared to his friends that he didn't earn his suffering. He actually experienced post-traumatic stress disorder, which included depression with suicidal longings. Those longings revealed Job was at his breaking point. He demanded answers, and had intense inner debates with God over why he suffered so. He obsessed over how he should picture God. Since Job believed God is in charge of all reality, it came naturally to Job to feel as if God was intentionally and repeatedly traumatizing him.

The dramatic impact of trauma on Job is actually similar to that of rape trauma on a woman. When a woman is brutally raped, she not only asks why but demands justice—even vengeance. So, when you believe the Creator has all power in the universe and the final say in your life, trauma can feel like a divine rape. It provokes gut-wrenching rage at God. It even provokes a scary desire to get even with him. In his journal writings published under the title *A Grief Observed*, the renowned C. S. Lewis grappled with his own faith when he lost his dear wife to cancer. Feeling like God had done this to him—whether sending the cancer or allowing it to happen— Lewis wondered if God was indeed a cosmic sadist. He secretly pondered this in the privacy of his own journal.

All of us trauma victims—like Job and Lewis—realize that the infinite Creator God of this elegant but cruel universe can't be brought to justice. He just can't. After all, isn't *he* the final judge himself? Who's bigger than God to go to? And he is the one who defines what is "just." Nevertheless, we'd like to question him. Actually, we'd like to vigorously interrogate him. As the title of one book goes, however, how does one put "God on the witness stand"? How do we get our say face-to-face with the Almighty? How do we grab him by his lapels and shake him . . . no, throttle him, and make him talk? How do we get him to repent of his mismanagement of the universe?

Atheism—defined as not believing that God exists—often, though not always, is a form of vengeance toward the Almighty. Since we cannot interrogate him or hold him accountable in any way for his alleged brutality, believing God does not exist becomes a passive-aggressive way to get even with him in one's imagination. It's a deep inner declaration to the Almighty: *I can't stand what you have done to me—so I am done with you.* It is fantasized capital punishment: *God is dead to me.* Many leave the church and synagogue after that intrapsychic execution.

Regardless of our beliefs, Hon, in this growingly shallow culture we simply don't talk much about suffering and death. We figure death is death, and there's not much you can do or say about it, except at funerals when those who are religious hope for an afterlife. How many of us sit around the dining room table discussing the dual mystery of suffering and death—and its meaning in our lives? Thinking ourselves wise, we consider such conversation at best morbid, or at worst, a ridiculous waste of time. If this seems overstated, note that our head-in-the-sand approach is why when someone we care about suffers or is dying, we have no idea what to say or what to do to really help. We may provide hot dinners or needed transportation, but we delegate the uncomfortable job of discussing suffering and death to chaplains, rabbis, ministers, and priests. Sometimes psychologists. Sometimes hospice. Or we nervously visit our friend in the hospital, not knowing what to say, and hoping our friend doesn't get too maudlin.

We use various ways to insulate ourselves from death so we don't have to deal with it. Even though there are huge practical problems with this in an urban society, it would help us deal with death if we carried our dead into some backfield, dug a hole, and, with heartrending tears, lowered them into it with our own two hands. Instead, we hire others to handle our deceased. We let them paint our loved ones with cosmetics to make them look less dead so we don't have to face their decay—or at least not as much. And we let them put their rotting bodies into expensive, attractive boxes. After a tragic accident, one well-meaning coroner repeatedly refused to let a friend of mine see his dead son before the undertaker handled the stiffened corpse. My friend simply wanted to say good-bye to his boy; the coroner refused. The coroner decided, on his behalf, that he shouldn't see his dear son with the frozen look of terror that emerged right before he crashed into a tree. The coroner judged his son had to be cosmetically transformed first—to protect the parent. While the coroner may have meant well, my friend felt patronized . . . and furious.

When we grieve the loss of a loved one, we typically don't "listen" to our pangs of grief to learn what we can learn. In this culture, our mourning ritual is both subdued and brief. We gather round for a few moments at the ceremonial burial hoping to provide some needed comfort for those left behind. But rarely do we thoughtfully provide the bereaved the necessary long-term support or in-depth discussions of death. We do not give the mourner enough time to process her emotions. Nor do we give her enough time for discerning the pieces of the puzzle needed to move on—let alone working her way through those pieces. Friends move on too quickly, without realizing that we will need them even more *later*—often much later—after the shock has worn off. Family doctors and psychiatrists even drug the bereaved if they cry too long or too hard. We simply want to be done with it.

To be sure, we all know we have no choice in this game of life; we're on for the ride. But we secretly white-knuckle that ride hoping to dodge the bullets of suffering as long as we can. We pursue happiness, buy life and disability insurance, and go to doctors. While we don't know how and when, we do know where the ride ends. But we don't want to discuss it.

Kristen, I've had to discuss it. After all, my father did hand me that justice flag of "Why me?" In carrying his flag, somewhere along the way it dawned on me that not only had I hiked Mother Nature's marvelous forests filled with incredible wildlife and climbed her gently rolling mountains, feeling her tender arms embracing me. But I also had borne witness to her slowly and tortuously crushing my own father with multiple sclerosis. Mother Nature not only held my dad's life in her bosom, but she also carried the power of his suffering and death as well. I wondered how it was that she could be so gently nurturing toward me while yet being so cruel to him. But how foolish of me. Nature is not a real person, so "it" is not cruel; "it" just is. Nature neither thinks nor feels—except through us. With flag in hand, I realized what Job and Lewis came to see: that God is really the one behind it all. He thinks. He plans. And he feels. So it was with him I had to deal.

While not having all these pieces of the puzzle in my waking consciousness as a teenager, I did have many of them—and began to ponder: If a personal Creator really exists, does the struggle for survival reveal his plan for life? Do the accidents, diseases, and every creature's final demise in death reveal the deep workings of his mind? Did Tiny's arthritic pain matter to him? Does the wolf's relentless pursuit of the sweet little fawn and the fawn's primal terror reveal God's heart? Did my mother's tragic demise reveal God's ultimate purposes for her life? If so, then just who the heck is this God? And if not—then what in the world has happened to this planet . . . to the universe?

A Watershed Time

A Kairos Moment

From about seventh grade to my junior year in high school, my best friend Sam—he's the one I owned the gopher snake with—and I hung around a lot together. And commiserated together. Sam was not raised Catholic, nor did religion seem to matter to him. He went to Thomas Edison High, the same school your uncle Ron went to. Like my dad, his father had multiple sclerosis and his family was struggling to cope with it just like mine. Both fathers were badly disabled and wheelchair bound. Sam's mother was likely an alcoholic, though I am not sure. At the very least, she liked her beer, but even more so her Calvert's whiskey—and, like your grandmother, used alcohol to deal with the stress of her husband's disease. As your grandmother's alcoholism advanced, she turned to Sam's mother's choice of Calvert's whiskey.

Sam and I ventured to make our own wine from grapes we took from a small vineyard that bordered my backyard. We secretly stored the fermenting grape juice in his basement, letting it age for months before we imbibed. We joined Boy Scouts and lifted weights together. We'd compete against each other, testing who could press more weight, and even measuring our biceps and chests to see whose were the larger. His muscles were always a bit bigger, although in fairness to me, he was taller, had a larger build, and was about fifteen months older, which mattered a lot at that age.

Sam was a very angry young man—not that I wasn't, but my anger was much more suppressed. He decided to "rebel" by abusing alcohol like his mother, indulging in sexual promiscuity, and joining a gang near Thomas Edison. Because of the authoritarian and emotionally repressive environment I grew up in with my dad and the Catholic Church, I was scared to rebel. Don't get me wrong; I wanted to. Yet there was this invisible barrier, kind of like the barrier I didn't dare go through on the other side of Ries Street in my Dutchtown neighborhood. Sam, however, wasn't scared—or at least he never showed it—so I began to borrow his "courage" thinking he'd show me the way through. Besides, I did have my own propensity to transform fear into adventure. Still, Sam was older, and I have to admit I looked up to him.

Sam tried drawing me into drinking. On one campout with the Scouts, he brought a soda bottle filled with his own mother's Calvert's whiskey, which we drank together by a stream under a moonlit night. When I got back to my tent, which I shared with my brother, Herb quietly pointed out that I smelled of alcohol. That's all he said.

Sam also wanted me to join his gang. Back then, gangs wore leather jackets and carried several weapons: razor blades; switchblades; sometimes, scissors; as well as brass knuckles. Most high school gangs in my city kept their violence within limits. The object was not to penetrate organs and kill someone; that would land you in big legal trouble. No, this was about creating fear by slicing someone superficially but badly enough to make them back down, thereby proving your manhood. Believe it or not, there was a strong sense of fair play among gangs.

Sam and I pulled a prank on Uncle Herb at a Scout meeting, but I don't recall why. We were outside in the parking lot filling his metal hubcaps with dried macaroni and the inside of his car with balled-up sheets of newspapers. Out of nowhere someone from a gang in the Holy Family neighborhood where we held our Scout meetings walked right up to us. Holy Family parish actually had a finished basement beneath the school classrooms in a building separate from both the church and convent where the nuns lived. This basement held two bowling lanes, billiard tables, pinball, a long meeting room where we met for Scouts, and a large bar area. Creating such an appealing recreation center for both youth and adults had been part of our church's vision for building neighborhood unity. Sam and I were just outside that building in the parking lot. Sam slowly rose from putting macaroni in the hubcap and met this guy eye-to-eye. I stood next to him. Sam's opponent then pulled out scissors from the pocket of his leather jacket, waiting for Sam to make the next move. Sam stood his ground, staring back at him without flinching, no doubt debating his next move. But Sam didn't have a blade. There was a very long pause; neither of them moved. I stepped in to break the deadlock, declaring that this was an unfair match because Sam didn't have a weapon. We discussed meeting at Lake Ontario's beach for the two of them to fight it out in swim trunks and no blades. They both agreed. Sam was grateful for the help. Uncle Herb drove us the next day, but the guy never showed.

At another Scout meeting, that same gang member, this time with an entourage of ten, waltzed downstairs to our storage room where we had all our camping equipment just to harass the young Scouts getting supplies. One of the Scouts scurried back to get Uncle Herb. I followed right behind. Your uncle stormed the narrow storage room, grabbed this guy by the pants' belt and the back of his shirt, and pushed him out of the storage room and up the stairs. I momentarily felt proud of your uncle. The gang took off. But we knew they'd be back.

Your uncle and I have slightly different memories of what happened next that led to another confrontation. But we both agree that shortly after your uncle threw the guy out, we found ourselves in a face-to-face with the entire gang. With the adrenalin pouring through me along with the keen but anxious awareness that I had not yet learned to street fight, I nailed the leader square in the face and quickly grabbed him by his leather jacket. I really wanted to make sure he had little chance to draw a blade on me. If he drew it, buffed or not, I knew I'd just have to back down. As I grabbed him, I realized he was an old nemesis from grammar school.

Back in the early years of grammar school, my parents told me I wasn't allowed to fight 'cause I'd rip my good school pants. My dad wasn't working due to his MS, and money was very tight. I was frightened of my father's anger, so I hadn't fought back against anyone when I was younger. However, as I entered seventh grade, I had had it with being known for not fighting back and my image—my self-respect really—became a bigger concern than my parent's reprisal. I also thought my father would secretly understand my urge to fight back, being both an athlete and an army soldier. So I began a campaign of self-respect to correct my image. I never looked for a fight—my father had taught me not to. But I wasn't going to avoid one any longer. One day, Harold pushed me aside at the school's double-door entranceway as he had done other times. This time, I reflexively reached for the knot of his tie, pushed him up against the wall, and pressed the knot against his throat. He looked stunned— and scared. I then let him go. I sure valued my new drumbeat. I had several other small confrontations like that, causing my peers to adjust their attitude.

My self-respect rolled on through high school, bolstered by my pumping weights with my friend Sam. In homeroom, one boy stole money from the rest of us every time he collected for missions. He had a reputation as a tough guy and bully and was not shy about throwing his weight around—including drawing a blade on you. As he strode down my aisle to collect our money, he'd routinely pull the knife without opening it and poke it into our ribs. Everyone in my homeroom, but especially those in my aisle, was understandably scared to stand up to him, including me. But, one day, I just had had it. Right before lunch, knowing he was stealing again, I refused to give to the collection. As was his routine, he gently poked the unopened knife into my ribs threatening to use it if I didn't cough up some money. With the adrenalin flowing and my hands shaking, I bolted up out of my seat, threw my lunch bag across the room, and declared, "I've had it"—and told him to "bring it on." I waited. Everyone in the class froze. To my surprise, he backed down. That was the last time he hassled me.

As I had my former nemesis in my two hands, I realized that this was one relationship where I had yet to balance the scale. It was now time. The rest of the gang, Uncle Herb, and the Scouts all spread out around us to watch the fight. The gang left your uncle alone. Like I said, gangs did have a sense of fair play, and let their leader and me duke it out one-on-one.

I didn't know if he had a blade on him or not, but I gave him no opportunity to pull it. He was trying to orient himself and recover from my punch to the face when, with both hands on his leather jacket, I wrestled him to the macadam and locked him in a choke-hold. He just wasn't strong enough nor clever enough to wrestle free from my grip. I'd succeeded in cutting off his air and he was panicked. He froze. I momentarily felt the deep satisfaction of having succeeded in one last corrective to the imposed timidity of my early childhood . . . laced with a hint of the sweet fruit of revenge. I kept the chokehold on, but loosened it just a bit so he could get air. I didn't want to injure him, just scare him and win the fight. As I slowly released my hold so he could breathe a bit as well as test his reaction, he didn't try to break free. Knowing the fight was over and that his buddy was deeply frightened, one of the gang grabbed my hair and yanked my head back, demanding I let go or he'd kick my face in. Once again fair play; he gave me warning. Like a good soldier, I declared that I would let go only if my brother told me to. Uncle Herb gave the word and I let go. Just as I did the police arrived, and the gang scattered.

Sam invited me to a gang fight coming up near Edison; he really wanted me to join him. On the bus ride home the day before the fight, I sat alone in the back just staring out the window, debating. Do I or do I not go? To join the gang would have trained me in street fighting and given me status. As I said, I admired Sam in ways. He was older, bigger, stronger, and rebelled when I didn't yet have the guts to. Even so, I had little use for the way he did it: drinking until puking, sex with girl after girl without real friendship, and slicing one another up as if that really proved something. While I was sorely tempted because I was so fed up with my home life, Sam's world didn't make sense to me. What was the point? Sex without friendship made no sense. Violence to establish one's masculinity didn't make sense either—even though I had enjoyed the feeling of my own testosterone with an old rival. Beyond that, violence struck me as stupid. Besides, coward that I was, I really didn't want to get sliced up if I saw no real point to it. It's not as if I'd be getting injured for some sober cause.

On another campout Sam and I got into a bad argument, the last one in a long series about the direction of our lives . . . and friendship. But this time, Sam coldcocked me. I was dazed, no doubt as my old nemesis had felt when I had hit him. Besides being shocked that my best friend just nailed me without any warning, I knew I couldn't take him. Besides being stronger, he was skilled at street fighting. Looking back, I believe he struck out at me because he knew what I was saying was the truth, but he didn't want to deal with it. Hurt, embarrassed, and bleeding, I sat down on a long log next to the small campfire to lick my wounds while Sam took off with a friend. Your uncle Herb was perched on another log across from me. He peered over the flames, quietly declaring, "You were becoming just like him." That's all he said. That's all he needed to say. That simple confrontation mirrored what I had already known, and it sealed what I had already decided: Sam's path was a dead end.

Hon, I didn't know this consciously at the time of my confirmation—it only revealed itself here in this pivotal moment— but deep in my heart on that special day, my firm pledge of loyalty as a knight was less to the God whom I did not know and more to the brother whom I did. Sitting on that log wiping the blood off my face, I knew where I did not want to go with my life.

And I now knew where I did. After all, I was a "Herbert." With sadness, for he and I had been the best of friends, Sam and I forever parted ways.

Too Late

Randy came up with a bold idea—and he eagerly wanted us to persuade the Basilian Fathers to do it. It would be a great step forward. To our amazement, they enthusiastically granted our little band of spiritual innovators—Randy, Dick, Joe (it was Dick and Joe who introduced me to sailing), John, and myself—full permission to revamp the chapel. We first removed all the wooden pews. Then we set up a small, simple altar where we could gather 'round in a semicircle on one side of the altar with Father facing us from the other side. It was revolutionary. We asked our beloved Father O'Reilly to "say Mass" for us early in the morning shortly before school began. He was thoroughly delighted. Sometimes, Dick and I would bring our instruments.

We didn't just play for those early mornings in the chapel. Under the direction of Fr. Cassidy, Randy, Dick and I actually started a folk band at school about the time the Kingston Trio had emerged from San Francisco's North Beach club scene. At that time, the Trio was making American folk music popular, with top of the chart hits like "Tom Dooley." Along with giving us official standing in the school community, Father sang and played whatever instruments we didn't. Dick played banjo usually. I strummed guitar, and sometimes, banjo . . . if I "cheated" and tuned it like a guitar. Randy thumped the bass and was our lead singer; he had a great voice. And Father, well, he played tambourine or maracas and sometimes, bass. Believe it or not, Kid—and, I know, given my singing voice nowadays it's hard to believe—Dick, Father, and I sang backup for Randy. Father was game, so we ventured out into the growing coffeehouse venue.

I don't know what you know of the history of the coffeehouse. But it had its roots in the Italian-American immigrant communities like Greenwich Village and San Francisco's North Beach. My youth culture of the 1960s copied these coffeehouses. A coffeehouse, as you know, was easy to set up. The entertainers didn't really need

141

much floor space, and folks who came to listen just needed small tables and chairs. Coffeehouses combined several functions. They were safe places to hang out with friends—but doing so without the problems of alcohol. They also became opportunities for folk singers to perform, eventually growing into political springboards for singers like Joan Baez and Bob Dylan. Baez and Dylan, in fact, began their careers in coffeehouses, integrating their then controversial political messages with their fine musical talent.

Catholic groups throughout the country wisely began using coffeehouses for youth outreach. That's why Father not only eagerly supported our venture but also joined in it himself. We really liked the growing informality of our faith; it all felt more alive. Along with the small folk band at school, I also joined a large folk group at my new church, Holy Name. We traveled around in a bus singing at churches, nursing homes, Rotary Clubs, and other organizations. Touring gave us a chance to hang around other teens who shared similar values. Being a bunch of straight-laced, good Catholic teens, we all concluded we didn't need alcohol to have fun with one another. Nor did we believe promiscuity was wise. Both beliefs—which, in my youth, were deeply rooted in the character and modeling of your uncle Herb—I've held to this day.

The Catholic Church does not easily change—and doesn't without leadership from the pope. Shortly after he became the Church's new pontiff in the early sixties, Pope John XXIII convened the Second Vatican Council. That Council radically updated the Church. Over two thousand bishops and theologians worked together for three years. The pope not only invited Protestant and Orthodox observers, he also welcomed government officials from all over the world. What a change from grammar school—inviting Protestants to help them update the Church's image. Such openness had been unheard of before that. There was a new drumbeat in the Catholic Church.

This radically innovative council was the backbone behind the changes in our churches and schools—and those changes were numerous. The Council instructed priests to switch from saying the Mass in Latin to saying it in the people's language, which, for the United States, was English. Both children and adults would no longer hear portions of the Mass as medieval gibberish. In addition, the priest could now say Mass facing the people. God was "with us" in community like never before, to be seen and felt among his people, no longer way "over there" or "up there"—somewhere remote. The Council allowed contemporary musical instruments, like guitars and banjos, as a regular part of worship. The musical aesthetic that was meaningful for young people would now be tied to their experience of God. It was Pope John XXIII—and this Second Vatican Council—that not only made possible our grand innovations at Aquinas, but also gave new life to the Church throughout America . . . and the rest of the world.

I welcomed the many changes in the Catholic Church, making the Mass more relevant to us young people. Like Randy, I was enthusiastic about the radical changes to our school's chapel—and how those changes gave us a sense of ownership of the Mass as well as really enriching its meaning to us. I have some very fond memories of our intimate moments together with Father as we stood around our small altar, sharing the Eucharist together in our little community. Still—I had already been conditioned for years as a kid to worship in a certain way. So, as much as I welcomed the innovations, I actually felt more spiritual during the traditional Mass. Whatever "spiritual" means and whatever it's supposed to feel like, the old ways felt more spiritual. I ran into this challenge also when, in wholehearted response to the Council, Holy Name parish, where I played in the large folk group while going to Aquinas, built a contemporary church building. It had a low concrete dome as its roof, lots of lighting, and floor to ceiling glass windows—not stained glass—making it very bright inside. On one hand, it felt strangely liberating. On the other, it felt like going into just any other building. This plain sanctuary along with its updated worship style did nothing for me to create a sense of the spiritual or transcendent.

To this day, the conditioning of my emotions to the traditional Mass said within medieval architecture makes the plain services of most Protestant churches, including our own, feel "blah" to me. The *Kyrie Eleison*—which means "Lord have mercy"—actually does feel sacred to me; I don't experience the *Kyrie's* Latin as gibberish. Gregorian chant, which was part of a medieval monk's life, actually induces a feeling of other-worldliness. That conditioning has never left me. Put me in a darkened Gothic or ornate sanctuary with stained glass windows and the sweet smell of burning incense, singing the *Kyrie Eleison* and Gregorian chant, with lit candles, bells ringing, and priestly vestments, and I'll "feel" like I've entered some spiritual portal that transports me into another realm. It *feels* like I am in the presence of an out-of-this-world deity.

My spiritual reaction to modern architecture and updated symbols is not intended as a criticism at all; it's just how I felt in high school . . . and yet today. As a young man, I reminded myself that neither the building nor the style of worship is sacred. God is not found in special boxes anymore. And there is no special aesthetic that uniquely conveys the Spirit of God. The Spirit is not tied to symbols. The whole universe is his temple. So I am aware that how I *feel* is a matter of how I became accustomed to the integration of aesthetics and religion—and has nothing to do with true spirituality.

While I really valued the reforms sweeping the Catholic Church, the seeds of my own radical reformation had already grown. I had key questions lurking in the background of my turbulent mind while I faithfully continued to meet early mornings for Mass with my close friends. To be sure, I liked the informal yet sober worship times we young men shared with Father. And I had a great time playing in the folk bands at school and at church. But I really had too many questions and not enough answers. And, right or wrong, what "answers" I had from the Church I doubted or outright rejected. As memorable, as poignant, and as meaningful as those early morning chapel services were with my dear friends and Father, and as unifying as sharing the Eucharist was with them, I nevertheless found it unbelievable that the wafer became Jesus. At the same time, I strongly doubted the Pope's infallible authority on matters of faith. And the saints seemed impotent and irrelevant. Beyond all that, I grappled with whether it really made any sense at all that God became a human being. All this, and more, I freely discussed and debated with my fellow innovators in the hallways of my school where we all honored "iron sharpening iron," a style of back-and-forth dialogue that Proverbs tell us sharpens a person—and a way of talking I so strongly value to this day (27:17, NIV).

Along with tough questions without answers, my faith continued to collapse under the cascade of events I witnessed at home: the bankruptcy of my parents' marriage; the emptiness of my relationship with them; climbing concrete steps begging Jesus for healing; being used up tending to my father's needs; and cleaning him after he went to the bathroom. My spirit took a beating. I watched my own dad slip away bit by bit no matter what we did—pray, climb steps, or exercise. I witnessed his body becoming stiffer and stiffer, with his fingers and hands becoming more and more gnarled. And the older I got, the more I "woke up" to your grandmother's drunken stupors.

One night in my senior year, she hit the Calvert's whiskey so hard that she fell hard to the floor as she tried feeding our pet bird before heading to bed. When I heard the loud thud and the birdcage rattle, I ran out to find my own mother lying prostrate on the floor in an alcoholic daze, unable to get up. I was terribly shaken. I knew she was drunk. I knew. Yet I momentarily doubted myself because my father denied the obvious. He made up some self-deceptive excuse about her being on diet pills. I picked my mother up off the carpet, stared into her glazed eyes, and, though physically buffed from weight lifting, struggled to carry her deadweight into their bedroom. I gently laid her down on the bed next to my father, pulling the covers up over her. All the while my dad remained conspicuously silent.

It all churned within me, sometimes consciously, all the time unconsciously. I couldn't take it anymore. Faith seemed so impotent and—the Church's new drumbeat notwithstanding—irrelevant. My home life had become the hard evidence proving that there really wasn't a God . . . or at least a god worth bowing the knee to. Deep in my troubled psyche, I now knew: religion was useless. Absolutely useless.

In our own iron-sharpening-iron councils in the hallways of Aquinas, Randy and I wrestled the most with our faith. Randy's sober debate, however, led him to seriously consider going to a Catholic seminary, which he eventually did. He later left, however—disillusioned. Dick and Joe dabbled in the tough questions we raised, but they came from what seemed to be "normal" Catholic families. I got to talk with my friends' parents a few times; they were delightful. Though my times with these gracious parents were brief, they did give me reference points for what I didn't experience at home. For my good friends, the deeper spiritual questions were simply not pressing as they were for Randy and me, although Randy's family seemed much healthier than mine as well.

The night of our high school graduation, the four of us went out to Dick's place on the lake and stayed overnight on his father's boat, playing poker and talking about our futures. As our evening wound down, we took our places in the spacious cabin to sleep. Resting in my sleeping bag on the berth, my mind raced. So I made my way to the foredeck—and just sat, staring into the night sky. I found myself going over and over again in my head: I can't do this anymore. I just can't.

Randy joined me on the foredeck. He must've sensed I was pensive because he asked me what I was thinking.

I said, "I just can't do this anymore. I don't believe Christianity. I can't believe it."

Randy asked me to explain.

"It seems ridiculous to me . . . God becoming a human being. Who can believe such things from so long ago? Angels . . . saints . . . rituals. So much mumbo jumbo."

Randy noted that it was indeed challenging.

I said, "We all create beliefs to live by, and this was the one delivered to us—to you and me—by well-meaning but ignorant people. What if we had been brought up Jewish?"

Randy simply nodded with understanding.

We talked for a while further. Before heading back to his berth, Randy graciously affirmed, "You have to do what makes sense to you. We all do."

His parting comment was very supportive, surprisingly so since he had decided to go to a Catholic seminary. However, as I said, Randy had his own troubling questions.

I continued my inner debate for a while longer. I thought: Look at your parents. Ignorant and pathetic. Look at the nuns. Hiding from real life. And the priests. Some are cool, but . . . they're all depriving themselves of women. Look at how we go through all those incantations at Mass—for what? We're like primitive tribes. We dance around, sing, and mumble words into the universe, only to have life go on the same. Nothing changes for having believed. Nothing. And none of it makes any sense. "God" must simply be our word for the good things that happen to us. Or God is the all-perfect, all-knowing parent, just like what we believed about our parents when we were toddlers—when we were so young, so dependent . . . so naïve.

Sitting there quietly but pensively debating within myself, the tension just kept mounting. It mounted until it reached some intrapsychic crescendo and I finally had the guts to declare to myself: *That's it, there is no God.*

My psyche shook like a leaf. For a good Catholic kid to think that thought—to actually think that God does not exist and mean it—was scary stuff. Real scary. What if I was wrong? What if hell were real? Still, it felt like something snapped inside me. As it snapped, there was a cascade of thoughts and feelings. It felt as if I had cut an umbilical cord . . . to what, I wasn't sure. Or had taken a straightjacket off my mind. The maddening grip of religious mysteries and contradictions momentarily released. I could feel the liberation.

The thoughts and feelings continued. I felt the chokehold of confusion about my family's suffering give way. Not sure to what. But it gave. Perhaps to resignation. Finally—there was some peace. It seemed like I didn't have to figure it out anymore because it couldn't be figured out. Things were the way they were just because they were. For some people—like my friends Dick and Randy and their parents—life went well. For others, like me and my parents, it just didn't. That's the way it was. Survival of the fittest. Like the fawn running in terror from the wolf, my parents had been running in terror from life—only to be unavoidably brought down by the jaws of life crushing them. They were not among the fittest to survive. They were among the weak, the poor, and the oppressed. They did not survive. That was life. And that . . . well, that was simply the way it was.

The cascade subsided.

For a few moments, I just took it all in. I basked in the peace. It was soothing . . . not unlike the soothing warmth of that mid-afternoon downpour on my hike with your uncle. Then, for some reason, I committed myself to a new search for the hard truth. I had no idea where that impulse came from nor any idea where it would lead me, except that, unlike my good friend Randy who continued to put his hope in religion, I had chosen to put my hope in science.

I made my way back to my berth. I climbed onto my open sleeping bag once again, grabbed the top half of the bag that had been dangling to the floor of the boat, and pulled it up over me. The bag was sopped; the boat was taking on water. Stunned, I quickly woke the other guys so we could bail and find the leak. As we scrambled, I jokingly pondered to Randy, "I wonder if the boat going down is a sign." Randy laughed.

And so we left Aquinas, Randy for seminary and I for Clarkson College of Technology. Clarkson was a private school of engineering and science located in the college town of Potsdam, New York, just a bit southwest across the Saint Lawrence River from Cornwall, Canada, where your mom and I went for dinners when we dated. I have to admit—I liked the phrase "of Technology." The name itself gave the college a sense of credibility. I was now going to study and discover things that could be proven. I would not believe by faith anymore, but by sight. I would believe in something, whatever that something was, for which we now had hard evidence. I would believe *because* of the evidence. What a contrast to all those years—almost eighteen of them—of training in myths about an invisible world for which there was not a lick of evidence.

PART 2

Discovering the Real Jesus

 *Leaving Home*

Toward Independence

I had just graduated Aquinas at seventeen in the summer of '69, the same memorable summer Neil Armstrong stepped onto the lunar surface. Like Uncle Herb, I had worked hard in high school to achieve my good grades. I knew I was college bound—it was our parents' goal for us—so I also worked hard in order to earn scholarship money to help pay my way. I earned a New York State Regents scholarship, certain merit scholarships, and received a scholarship from the Veterans Administration. I also worked several summers at Eastman Kodak Company to pay for books and other living expenses. Upon entering college, within a few brief months from September to December of that fall my freshman year, I soared to great joy, only to end that semester at Christmastime gripped by deep sadness.

For several summers I worked in the dental X-ray department at Kodak where we made the X-ray packets dentists put in your mouth to take pictures of your teeth. Along with substituting on the production line machines, I was a "handler," which meant I delivered and then stacked large palettes of supplies in the dark rooms for the workers. I rotated shifts weekly, so every third week I worked the night shift, from eleven in the evening to seven in the morning. I never got used to swinging from one shift to the next. By the time my body adjusted to one shift, I was into the next. Without adequate sleep, the night shift was tough, especially working in the dark room. They used low-watt red bulbs to light the areas just enough to see what you were doing, but never enough to keep me awake. I worked one machine in the dark room that cut black paper into large rectangles. The thin but precisely cut paper would be placed in the larger dental packets to protect the film from light exposure. The machine automatically cut the paper, but I had to shut it off when the shallow receiving tray was loaded. Then I had to unload that tray and put on a new roll of black paper. Simple enough, but I often fell asleep at my post. More than once the foreman walked by and barked, "Wake up!" By then, the overflowing tray would have been filled, and the dutiful machine jammed.

As part of quality control, I also had to sort the good packets from the damaged ones in the lighted main room, and then bind them together, making them ready for packaging and shipping. Believe it or not, back then, even though these packets would go into people's mouths, I never wore gloves, nor was I required to wash my hands before handling the packets. I'd sit on a stool, and, as I collected the good packets together, I'd count them, putting fifty into the stacker. I'd wrap a plastic band around them, then heat seal the band. As my arm reached up to the stacker to put the packets in, however, I'd often fall asleep, and the packets would tumble out of my hands. Without regard for sanitation, I'd pick them up off the floor to try again. I was so desperate to stay awake I used No-Doz, but even that was not successful enough. I just got the jitters.

There was a wide range of ages and attitudes among the men working on the production line. One old-timer who had been there for nearly thirty years on the same machine—on the same machine . . . incredible!—would actually work through breaks and often shorten his lunchtime to see if he could beat his own production record. The other workers saw him as quirky, and no one understood why he'd push himself like that. My guess is that it was his only way of creating some modicum of interest in a job that was incredibly mundane—and dehumanizing. Though it did pay his bills. I often operated the machines, substituting for men out sick or on vacations. The machine rapidly pumped out dental packets onto a slow-moving conveyor belt, lining up twenty-five at a time, skipping a few inches, then pumping out the next set of twenty-five. I'd sit at the end of the conveyor belt, grabbing two sets of twenty-five packets each, then placing them into the stacker. Once I filled the stacker with fifty packets, I wrapped and heat-sealed a band of plastic around them. Once packaged, I'd lift them out of the stacker and place them in large trays. The machines were designed so the operator had time to do all this as other packets were making their way down the belt. My guess is that the procedure for grabbing, stacking, banding, and sealing took about five to seven seconds. When I operated it, I didn't feel rushed, but sure did have to keep it moving.

Unlike that old-timer, one young man couldn't imagine doing this almost mindless task every seven seconds or so for the entire day, every day, for thirty more years. Neither could I. At least your grandfather's job as a tin-knocker was creative where he got to solve problems and design parts for the production-line machines. But the production line itself with its virtually infinite repetition of simple tasks was a real loss of meaning for most of these men. This young man was among them—and he felt trapped by his lack of education. One time, he got so upset telling me about his lot in life that he picked up a fifteen pound roll of lead foil, held it over my foot, and dropped it. My guess was that he wasn't really angry at me but at the fact that I was in college and he wasn't—though tell my foot that. Fortunately, my job required steel-tipped shoes; the roll missed my arch and bounced off the metal tip. Needless to say, perhaps, that was the last conversation about work I had with him.

At that moment, however, I understood. From the old-timer breaking his own records to that young man's fifteen pounds of dropped lead, I knew I was grateful that your grandparents had the unwavering vision for me to go to college. The fact is, they fully supported me heading off to the North Country. Heck, it was their dream to see me off.

In the summer transition between Aquinas and Clarkson, I did not work in the dental X-ray department but in your grandfather's department where they machined parts. But I was no tin-knocker. I didn't have your grandfather's skills for that. It's interesting to note how in our American education system—unless you've gone to trade school like your uncle Ron—an eighteen-year-old is a well-educated do-nothing. I knew nothing about making a real living. As the expression goes, it was all "book learning." That summer gave me some practical appreciation for your grandfather's ability to make enough money with his hands to have a family at such a young age.

In your grandfather's former department, because I knew nothing about making a real living, I simply assisted anyone who did. I often worked with an electrician some twenty-five to thirty feet up in a Langley repairing or running wiring in the warehouse ceiling. The Langley was a small metal platform, about three feet by four feet with a tubular metal railing around it to protect the worker from easily falling off. Huge scissor-like folding metal arms hydraulically pushed the platform up to those heights. The platform was just large enough to hold two men. On one occasion when I came in to work overtime on a Saturday, I was told we needed to change the long fluorescent light bulbs in the fixtures hanging from another warehouse ceiling. This ceiling was even taller than the one I usually worked on—and the Langley couldn't go quite high enough to reach the lights. In order to reach the bulbs, one man stood with his feet on the small tubular railing—with nothing to secure him. He held the light for stability. Obviously, the Langley simply wasn't designed for such acrobatics. The two men standing on the warehouse floor watching the drama asked me to assist. It was an incredibly awkward moment for a seventeen-year-old who was intimidated by authority. I managed to decline, noting that I could assist from inside the Langley but was too afraid to stand on the railings—with nothing to grab but the light fixture itself and no harness. But, I thought to myself, fear or no fear, this was just a really dumb thing to do. And I momentarily wondered, *Is this what you normally do to change light bulbs?* Of course, looking back, it was foolish of them to do it. But I think they knew that, and they neither tried to force me to go up nor made fun of my fear. Neither of them offered to assist.

Work at times was slow, but the men scrounged up jobs for me. One, which I thought was odd, was to clean the warehouse ducts for the heating and air conditioning. The metal ducts were some twenty-five to thirty feet up, hanging from the ceiling. I wondered why they wanted me to do that, but who was I to question them. I was being paid.

The metal ducts branched off from a large central exhaust plenum. Climbing a very long but narrow metal ladder straight up the wall about twenty feet to the plenum, I entered the ducts. With rags in hand, I began on my knees, but the ducts quickly narrowed, so I had to crawl, as if I were spelunking. I managed to slither my way out to the very end of one duct, shoulders scrunched, hanging out about two-thirds of the way across the warehouse ceiling. Along the way, it had become so tight I had moments where I wondered if I'd get stuck. Amazingly, I had no fear. However, decades later, when I had an MRI, I did have a claustrophobic reaction. Go figure. Peering out the last vent at the end of that now narrowed duct, I saw and overheard the men talking. Several were concerned that the braces were not designed to hold a man; they were made to hold only the light metal duct. All of them were afraid the braces would snap—and I'd be thrown to the concrete floor some twenty-five feet below. At that moment, I realized they had never done this job before, didn't really need to, had made the work up just to keep me busy—and I needed to get the heck out of there immediately. With my shoulders in tight, I scooted backwards as quickly but as carefully as I could without rocking the duct back and forth. When I came out at the large plenum where I had started, I found my supervisor lying on the plenum floor, fast asleep. Lazy, but I didn't care; I was just grateful to be back. I was not assigned to that job again.

After that summer job, I headed off to Clarkson. I was excited to go for many reasons—the main one being to get away from home. I desperately wanted my world to blow open. Working at Eastman Kodak that first summer after high school was a great opportunity for me to be away from the house during the day. It was so satisfying to have responsibilities that had nothing to do with shuffling my dad's feet back and forth. And it was so refreshing. It just further whetted my appetite for the full freedom of college. However tragic their situation, Hon, and however uncaring it may seem, I wanted to let my parents go. I really, really wanted my own life.*

*For my thoughts on how my independence emerged from my passion to talk, go to the website www.peakperformancediscipleship.com, and look for the topic "Independence and Talking."

A New Primal Woman

A good friend of mine from the hallowed halls of Aquinas had chosen Clarkson as well, so we decided to room together to make the transition easier for both of us. It gave me more emotional security to know I'd have a familiar face on campus. Both my parents came up with me. It was part of their unspoken dream to send me off to college. By that time, your grandfather was significantly less embarrassed using a wheelchair, so I pushed him around the hilly campus to see some of the sights. My dorm room was small and simple. A plain light-blue counter ran across the length of the outer wall which was to be our desks. On either side were our beds, and next to our beds were small, built-in dressers. That was it. It was home for a year. I said good-bye to my parents in front of Cubley-Reynolds, my new dorm. They showed no emotion. My mother didn't hug me or touch me—which fit the pattern; she never hugged me. My dad, being quadriplegic, couldn't hug, of course. But I didn't feel free to hug either of them. I did wonder how they felt with their youngest and last leaving home.

As you yourself experienced, all freshmen scramble trying to figure out how and where they will fit in with the campus culture. As I geared up for a tough semester of physics, the fraternities let no grass grow under their feet. The frat brothers swarmed the dorms with sorority gals to make their pitch. I soon learned that the popular theme among fraternities and sororities was, what *they* called, the three "Bs": booze, beds, and broads. But I had already fought those peer battles and made my strategic decisions regarding the three "Bs" back in high school when my best friend and I parted ways. I was still a "Herbert."

After innumerable visits by the ubiquitous frats with the sorority sisters—and just as many nos to their invitations—two sorority sisters came knocking on my door. When I opened it, they brazenly sashayed right in and invited me to a party, eagerly promising "plenty of beer, a drunken good time, and lots of girls." By this time, I had had it with the pitch. I told them politely that I was not interested. They arrogantly scolded me. Looking around, they declared I was as boring as my room. Maybe so . . . for them. I told them they had to leave.

Peter showed up at my door shortly after those two unabashed sorority girls. I was sitting on my bed, right next to the door—and I remained seated when he knocked. A little paranoid now, I gently cracked the door just a bit so we could talk, blocking it from opening further with my left foot. He was alone. I was in no mood to invite him in. Pete said he wanted to invite me to a picnic. Not a party, mind you, a picnic. He had my attention. He handed me the ticket, which I reviewed carefully . . . looking for beer. I said, "I don't see beer listed. Will there be beer there?" Pete's face turned beet red as he sheepishly said no. I affirmed, "Good, I'll come. By the way, what organization do you represent?" With a wide-eyed look and tone of surprise, he said, "Uh . . . uh, Inter-Varsity Christian Fellowship." I didn't ask Pete anything about the organization, just where and when to be there.

One of the first people I met at this Inter-Varsity (IV) picnic was Marie. IV was actually a joint chapter between Clarkson and the state university on the other side of town. At that time, Clarkson was nearly all young men, so Marie was from the state university. She walked up to me with a warm smile, introduced herself, and began asking me about myself. If Marie hadn't been a junior—and frankly out of my league—I would've asked her to marry me immediately. She was engaging, intelligent, mature, and gorgeous as well. And, as I discovered, great fun. Her charming personality was a powerful contrast to my mother's flat, distant, and cold presence. At the same time, Marie had incredible depth of Christian character, holding the same strong values that your uncle Herb modeled for me—another powerful contrast to the sorority girls who pitched sex and alcohol as the way to a good time.

Marie quickly became the embodiment of that inner collage I had put together as a child of what a woman should be. She was the warmth, beauty, charm, gentleness, intelligence and sensuality of Mother Nature combined with the care and sweet smile of the ever-so-young Jackie, wrapped in the principled steadiness of a June Cleaver. Without question, Marie became the new primal female imprinting my psyche forever. Little did I realize that that imprint would become the reason why the apostle Paul's teaching on Jesus as the new Adam—what he calls the "last Adam"—would later make deeply intuitive sense to me. From that point on, I knew Marie was the kind of woman I'd want to marry. When I met your mom a year and a half later, I was magnetically drawn to her for the same reasons—and have been ever since. I don't need to tell you—but I'll say it anyway—your mom is warm, charming, delightful, intelligent, beautiful, and sensual, with a great sense of humor. She is principled and a loyal Jesus follower. Given that you are now in your thirties, I do feel free to add that, along with her strong values and strength of personality, your mom also had long flowing hair down to her curvaceous waist that any man worth anything would die to lose himself in.

There certainly was wisdom in the frat boys bringing the sorority girls to solicit interest—because Marie became the draw to IV meetings for me. I went back to IV functions for several reasons, but one was just to be with her. We young people would lie around on the lounge floor at the state university talking and massaging each other's backs. Sometimes, I got the privilege to massage hers. Other times, we'd all just sit in a circle and talk. Marie often led the way in discussing our spiritual journeys. She was always gracious and incredibly friendly to all of us without ever being flirtatious. Candidly, she didn't have to be.

As for me, blowing open my horizons on campus, not feeling the albatross of my parents' pathology around my neck, making many new friends fast, and discovering a young woman who gave me a reference point for everything I ever imagined a woman could be made me feel like a million bucks. I felt like a new man . . . a freed man. Right or wrong, that sense of becoming new as well as being set free later fed my intuitive draw to the apostle Paul's vision of being a new creation in Jesus Christ, where he wrote, "The old has gone, the new is here!" (2 Cor. 5:17, NIV).

Losing My Mother

No doubt Alpha Phi Omega extended the spirit of the high school folk group I had been in through my local parish—a spirit of helping others and having fun doing it. We created many campus projects in the four years I was a member of this service fraternity—and I made great friends doing so. I also made great friends through Inter-Varsity, where I met Marie. IV was a joint chapter of the state university and Clarkson where friends extended out my iron-sharpening-iron hallway dialogues from Aquinas. Not only did we IV students discuss the challenges of faith on our campuses, but we had a seminary-trained IV staff person, Al Harris, assigned to us who helped us analyze our broader culture. Al and IV staff across the country were committed to training students to think for themselves and dialogue about tough cultural issues, so Al would take us students to Ingmar Bergman movies to discuss their messages and our reactions to them. So you can blame Al for our family practice of having to discuss movies.

Even though my study schedule quickly became intense, that was OK. This was my profession—physics. The intensity was expected. And we physics majors actually enjoyed the material . . . most of the time. During the grueling week, we'd go from seven in the morning to midnight or one in the morning, either in class or doing homework. On weekends, it was not unusual to be up until 3:00 or 4:00 a.m. Friday and Saturday nights working on calculus or physics homework. Sometimes, we'd actually have extra classes during the week at night with the physics prof to help us figure out homework problems. The classroom was usually filled with us students, reflecting our dedication as well as the difficulty of the material. The professor was very gracious and eager to help us. Mathematically analyzing river water flowing around a rock was extraordinarily challenging. But even the professor found it a bit perplexing how to approach relatively "simple" problems like how to mathematically analyze Snoopy's motion when he was walking on a raft as that raft was being taken down river by the current. Yes, I actually enjoyed dissecting such problems while knowing it was preparing me for eventually analyzing the motion of sub-atomic particles.

My roommate and I, along with two new friends down the hall— one of whom has continued to be a friend over the decades—began our four-year tradition. We'd blow off steam by playing floor hockey in the dorm basement—and the fact is, we really had to blow off steam a lot. From within my skin today, it is beyond my comprehension how my young though buffed body endured banging into stone walls and falling on the concrete floor over and over again, year after year. Adjacent to the main room we used as our arena was a laundry room, a long but very narrow room of stone walls with openings at both ends into the main room. To make our matches even more interesting, we decided to add this room to our arena. The one with the ball would typically make a break for it down this one-person alley between the machines and the wall. At the other end, we'd crush one another against the machines or the wall as we tried to make our exit. Needless to say, one shot now, and it'd be over for me. Somewhere under the many layers of paint on one basement wall you'll find our names and year of graduation.

After a grand semester, I went home for a well-deserved Christmas vacation. As was my routine, I walked through the garage into the kitchen. But this time, I immediately became transfixed. I gazed in horror at your grandmother. Her skin was yellow. Besides the more typical glassy-eyed look, her eyes were also yellowish and bloodshot. Her legs and abdomen were huge, filled with fluid. She wasn't just drunk; she was seriously ill. I called Herb right away. He had married and moved out by that time. I told him Mom needed help right away, and he supported my decision to take her to the family doctor immediately. Your grandfather was useless; he was so lost, so blind, so self-absorbed, he hadn't even noticed the change.

My mom was so stiff and bloated, there was no way she could get into the front of my car. I had to lift her into the back seat. After examining her, the doctor rushed out to the waiting room with his own horrified look on his face. He told me I must take my mother to the hospital immediately. I'll never forget his stunning words, "Your mother is in a walking coma." I was scared. Was my mother dying? Nervous and spinning a bit, I didn't think to ask the doctor . . . but

I think I knew. I drove with a sense of panic. I kept looking in the rearview mirror wondering if she was still alive.

While I have a most vivid memory of seeing her in the back seat in my rearview mirror, I have no memory of driving into the hospital, taking my mother in, or sitting next to her in her room.

While driving your grandfather to the hospital to see her, I gently told him that Mom needed to stop drinking. He ignored me—and blamed some doctor who prescribed her diet pills. Later, Uncle Herb led the way with opening up the Calvert's whiskey and pouring it all down the kitchen sink in the hopes of our mother coming back home.

Five days after admitting her, however, I got the phone call from the hospital. My mom was gone. She had died alone. At that moment, I felt so sad—and so defeated. Whatever she hadn't been to me, she was still my mother. I desperately wanted her to live. I was hoping—I was naïvely hoping against hope—we could have a fresh start. It was not to be. Now I had to tell my dad. I walked out from the bedroom, down the hallway, and into the kitchen where your grandfather sat, with his elbows on the table and his fingers curled inward, gnarled from the disease. I looked at him . . . and he looked at me. He knew, but I said it aloud anyway, "Mom's gone." He looked quietly terrified. I honestly don't know if he felt sad. I only sensed his unspoken fear: *who is going to take care of me now?*

No one—not a single soul—mentioned your grandmother's diagnosis. No one said anything about her real condition—not the doctors, not my father, not a priest . . . no one. But I knew. She had drunk herself to death. Only years later, after I faced more of my own history, did I realize that she had died of cirrhosis of the liver— profound damage to that vital organ due to drinking.

I slowly climbed the steps into the funeral parlor and tentatively walked into the viewing room. I couldn't go up to her right away . . . I just couldn't. I nervously sat on a chair, staring at her from a distance. For a moment, I actually thought I saw her chest move. I just stared; I swore I had seen her breathe. I was unnerved. It seemed so surreal. I said something to Herb about her breathing. He gently put his arm on my left shoulder, and, in a soft tone, assured me that he saw it too, but that it was just an illusion. I felt his big brother tenderness at that moment and drew great comfort from it.

Sitting there mesmerized by her dead body as she lay quietly in the casket, I flashed back to my mother blurting out she'd be the first to go. It became clear to me. When she had announced that she'd go first, it really was her way of quietly declaring, "It is finished." Together we had climbed the concrete steps at the cathedral on our knees earnestly begging Jesus for healing for your grandfather. Unlike the apostle Paul, she didn't hear "My grace is sufficient for you." Instead, she simply heard "I will not heal your husband." That painfully disappointing divine lack of response killed whatever lingering hope my mother may have had. So she decided her maternal duty toward me would soon be over. She determined to survive until she sent me off to college—when and where she had hoped I'd somehow be OK venturing out on my own. I'd be free. Once there at Clarkson, she could relax and let go; she could die. However much she did her solemn duty out of guilt or a sense of blind obedience to the Almighty, and however much she resented me being a boy instead of a girl, it was clear to me that she wanted to live long enough to see me off. Little did I know at the time that *why* she died when she did—regardless of *how*—would become another imprint in my psyche.

Maybe I'm fooling myself, Kid. I may be. But I believe that however wrapped in pathology and poor choices, and however pathetically limited in making those choices, my mother's choice to hang on so she could see me off to Clarkson was clear evidence of her underlying genuine care for me. That mattered to me. Always has.

Shrinking My Dad

My uncle Don was a strapping ex-Marine and a great storyteller. In fact, with his deep bass voice, broad shoulders, and measured cadence, he was spellbinding. His winsome narratives typically climaxed in great humor, with your mom and I laughing so hard we'd end up bent over crying tears with our sides hurting. I have rarely laughed like that since. But Uncle Don never did discuss his life or personal relationships. Nor did he ever ask any questions about my college, my family, or me. He did, however, make it a point to give me some pithy advice one day about six months after my graduation from Clarkson. We were standing in our two-car garage at the black iron railing on the concrete wheelchair ramp into the house. I don't know why we were standing there. And I don't know what, if anything, we were talking about that prompted it. But as we both grasped that railing and gazed unfocused into the garage, he gently said, "Frankie, don't let the a—holes of the world walk all over you." That's all he said. Like your uncle Herb, when it came to advice, he was a man of few words. Having come from the West Coast with my aunt Betty, he lived with us for many months while looking for an engineering job. My uncle got to see my father's demeanor first-hand—so I knew what he was referring to. Given my uncle's stature in my youthful eyes, his words stuck with me. What my uncle didn't know was that I had already begun to stand up to my dad shortly after your grandmother passed away.

I had felt threatened to disagree with, let alone confront, my father—even though he was physically impotent. I did try to respectfully disagree with him in high school . . . to no avail. Still, growing up, his explosive anger was never far from the surface. So we usually couldn't challenge his pronouncements about us without provoking some frustrated outburst. Using that unbridled anger, he'd control us from his chair—and had done so from when I was very young. Locking me in a tiny darkened room and again in the pitch blackness of our cellar when I was just a little guy were clear examples of his impulsive anger and his need to irrationally control me, making a powerful impact on my already fragile psyche. I carried that fear of authority with me into young adulthood—as evidenced by my nervous deference to that incredibly "green" parent Mr. Datillio in our trek to Mt. Arab when I was sixteen. Now, at eighteen, with my mom gone, I still feared my father.

One sunny morning while home on vacation from Clarkson, as was our routine, I prepared the mechanical lift to get your grandfather out of bed. I needed that lift to move his deadweight to the small bathroom and then clothe him. Your grandfather was usually edgy in the morning and often snapped at me with an irritated tone. This morning was no different. No doubt, he was even more depressed, lonely, and frightened after my mom passed away—and, underneath those emotions, he likely felt that his miserable existence was now even more meaningless. Nevertheless, like with that bully in my high school homeroom, I had had enough. I firmly but respectfully scolded him, "You are now going to lie there in that bed until you decide to apologize to me for the way you talked to me." I walked out. After a bit, he sheepishly called me in. With a soft tone, he said, "Frankie, I'm sorry. I just feel so lousy." That was only the second time I recall that that man apologized to me. The first, as noted earlier, was after he scolded me to be quiet when I had had an earache while lying in the crib. This time, to my utter surprise, he had a tear streaming down his cheek. I don't recall ever seeing him have tears before that moment—not even with his own wife's passing. I sat down on the edge of the bed, leaned over, and gently hugged his face for a few brief moments. I kissed his cheek. Nothing further was said.

I had done what I needed to do. However small it may seem to an outside observer, however brief the poignant exchange may have been, the man who once so easily intimidated me from his wheelchair was, for the first time, my equal. It was a pivotal moment. I now could be my own man. No, I wasn't done individuating from my father; I would spend years doing that. But that moment was what it was—as well as being transitional. That sincere but lost man's cruel reign had come to an end. I pulled the lift over to the side of his bed, wrapping the cloth around his stiff, motionless body . . . and continued our early morning routine.

It wasn't the last time we'd have words. A couple years later, sitting at the kitchen table, your grandfather blew up at me when I confronted him with his disrespect toward me once again. This time, there was no apology. Instead, on impulse, he declared: "Get the h--- out . . . leave." I did. I drove off, finding a place on a nearby street to park. That evening, I settled into my Tank, making it my home for the night. The next day, I came back to pick up a few things. I took a small collage from my bedroom that had been meaningful to me and taped it on the interior of the car's roof over the back seat. That back seat became home. After a couple weeks, your uncle compassionately took me in until I went back to school. From Herb's, I called my girlfriend, your mom, seeking comfort.

Whether I've liked it or not, my father forged much of my identity. But, like what all children need to do, I worked at separating out from him, sorting what to keep and what to toss. I kept his sound character—like sincerity and standing on one's word—while tossing his naïveté and his unwillingness to dialogue about life. Unlike my dad, I've also worked hard to discover and express my more tender emotions. Given how he had disrespected me for years growing up, he left me no choice but to muster the courage to push him back as a young adult—requiring him to finally show me some respect. It was only in pushing back that I could begin to respect myself.

Along with vigorously supporting you guys to say what you mean and mean what you say to me, I have intentionally allowed myself to shrink in your eyes. I've fervently believed I had to become less powerful in your eyes so that you could become more powerful in your own—power to create your own destiny and power to change the world as you see fit. To exercise power—whether the power of the personal or the power of leadership—you cannot feel like you're forever contending with a father's meddling influence in your life. Besides, the fact is that by the time you guys had grown into young adults, I had already "done my damage." For better or worse, who I was as a man and father had already forged a great deal of who you guys had become. I frankly find that fact of life unnerving; we parents just shouldn't have such immeasurable power to shape another's identity from the inside out like that. But we do—a fact that, as a parent now yourself, you no doubt appreciate.

So, while I will always be your father, I see myself as your father-friend, not father–authority. As far as I'm concerned, I have no say in your life, except as you invite me in or as it impacts directly on the quality of my life with you. To be your own woman—for your brothers to be their own men—I've needed to become small . . . very small. By the independence of all three of you, as well as by our conversations around the dinner table—including some of the shots taken at me!—I'd say I've succeeded.

The Seduction

Read It for Yourself

Charlie loved to talk. I was never sure if or when he ever studied. And Charlie loved to sing. He had an incredible voice that sounded exactly like Bing Crosby's. I know Crosby was long before your time. He had huge record sales and motion picture fame in the 1930s going into the early fifties. In fact, he sold over four hundred singles, the largest number ever. You probably are acquainted with his smooth as silk voice through the Academy-Award-winning song "White Christmas." In the living room of his home where he lived off campus with his father, Charlie played us a record of Crosby—and sang along with it. There was no noticeable difference between Charlie's voice and Crosby's—none—though you'd never guess such a voice would emerge from his lanky body and his unsophisticated style. He presented like Susan Boyle, whose voice stunned the audience and the judges on *Britain's Got Talent* in 2009. We loved his voice so much, your mom and I had him sing at our wedding. If Charlie had gone to some amateur competition—and though we encouraged him to do so, he never did—he could have made it big.

Charlie was a grad student at the State University of New York at Potsdam and a senior member in our IV chapter—and seemed to know a great deal about religion. And he was a careful thinker. But because of my many years of Catholic training, including four years of theology at Aquinas, I believed I knew more than anyone in IV about religion. I really had a bit of a chip on my shoulder. Catholic kids growing up through the rigorous parochial school system tended to view public school kids—and Protestants in general—as much less informed about faith. I guess I carried that attitude with me. But Charlie knew a lot.

I told Charlie how I saw things. God likely did not exist—though I offered I didn't really know. Like the saint himself, Thomas Aquinas, Charlie thought the universe needed a personal Creator. I told him that if we needed a Creator for the gorgeous sunsets, then didn't we need one for human suffering and death as well. However, don't we all feel like C. S. Lewis? No one really wants to believe that the Creator of the universe would be cruel, designing ways to torment his creatures before he utterly destroys them in death. That's too horrifying a prospect. But, I asserted with Charlie, if there really was only one God—and he was all-powerful—then he would have had to have created everything, including suffering and death. If he didn't, then who did? And wouldn't there then be two gods, not one?

I didn't know it at the time, but for just this reason, many discerning people are atheists. The philosopher Bertrand Russell, renowned in his day for his bold, even outrageous, atheism, wrote *Why I Am Not a Christian*. I read that book with great interest some years later. Even though he presented his views early in this century, his arguments are timeless. His book speaks for many people yet today. Commenting on the same perplexing question Charlie and I wrestled with, Russell said, "When you come to look into this argument from design, it is a most astonishing thing that people can believe that this world, with all the things that are in it, with all its defects, should be the best that omnipotence and omniscience have been able to produce in millions of years. I really cannot believe it."* Though incredibly ignorant of philosophy at the time of my late-night talks with Charlie, I likewise thought we were better off not believing in a God—for the same reason. Except that "all the defects" for me included the maddening nightmare of my own family trauma.

I also asked Charlie rhetorically, if not a bit sarcastically, that if we say there is a God, aren't we saying that God "just is?" Then who made God? Nobody? So why can't we also say the universe just is? Why does the universe need a maker?

---

*Bertrand Russell, "Why I am Not a Christian," http://users.drew.edu/~jlenz/whynot.html.

Years later, I recall seeing Carl Sagan in a television interview. He rhetorically asked the same thing: why couldn't the universe really "just be." Sagan was a renowned astrophysicist who gained worldwide fame for *Cosmos: A Personal Voyage*. He received the John F. Kennedy Astronautics Award for promoting America's space program. And later, he briefed Apollo astronauts for their moon landings. In a 1981 interview with *U.S. Catholic*, Sagan candidly shared, "I have some discomfort with both believers and with nonbelievers when their opinions are not based on facts . . . . If we don't know the answer, why are we under so much pressure to make up our minds, to declare our allegiance to one hypothesis or the other?" And in another interview in 1996, Sagan asked this key question: "Where's the evidence?"*

As a young man, I found myself asking Charlie the same question: Where *is* the evidence?

One night we were sitting on the cafeteria steps of Cubley-Reynolds. I was momentarily staring straight ahead. Charlie issued me a challenge: "Have you ever read the Gospel, the story of Jesus, for yourself?" The question took me aback. I thought for a few brief moments. Then I turned my head toward Charlie with a look of surprise in my eyes and my jaw half-opened. His simple question had just knocked the chip off my shoulder. After a few thoughtful moments, I humbly admitted to my friend that in spite of all the Catholic training, I had never read the story of Jesus for myself.

The well-intentioned priests and nuns had always fed the story to us in tiny bits and pieces, with the fragments tied to various rituals and symbols, like the stations of the cross or the Mass. But those bits and pieces didn't add up to much of a storyline—at least not for me. In fact, I sat there on the steps dumbfounded because I didn't know the entire story. All I knew was that Jesus was supposed to be the God who died for my sins. And someday, if I were good enough, I'd go to heaven—after God purged me of my venial sins through intense torment by fire in purgatory. When it was all said and done, that was all I really knew. Yet what little I knew of the story had been well integrated with symbols that embedded those bits and pieces into my psyche.

---

*Quoted in "Carl Sagan," Celebrity Atheist List, www.celebatheists.com/wiki/Carl_Sagan.

Hon, integrating a strong message with rich symbolism is a strategic way to express as well as shape the human mind. That's why nations have flags, national anthems, and military songs for soldiers to march by. And it's why churches, whether Protestant or Catholic, as well as synagogues and mosques, have rituals, special clothing, special buildings, and special faith songs. In these ways, the message and the medium become one, etching the message deep into the psyche through the five senses. So the bits and pieces of the Jesus story tied to the elaborate rituals became an integral part of me. That's why moving toward disbelief in God—and disbelief in Jesus—was so torturously slow. It was like pulling out a brain tumor . . . without damaging the brain.

Even so, as I made my way to college, I soberly rejected both the medium and its message. Or so I thought. I wanted my passionate search for truth to be based on evidence. So Charlie's gentle confrontation had embarrassed me. I thought I knew so much about Christianity. In the wake of his incisive question, I thought back to how the priests and nuns had taught me. They pictured the Bible as so sacred that they thought it was best *for them* to interpret it to us. Instead of studying the Bible for myself, I had to memorize portions of the Baltimore Catechism. Even in theology classes at Aquinas, I was not required to read much of the Bible. Given my choice to stand on evidence, I now thought that having a final judgment about the faith without my own firsthand knowledge was just too weak a position. Given that Catholicism was my history, it just didn't seem fair—to the faith or to myself—not to review the facts for myself. And then I could be done with it, once and for all.

In that way, my Catholic upbringing did have a hold on me. I just couldn't walk away. I had to look at the evidence now for myself. If I hadn't been raised Catholic, thinking I had to be fair wouldn't even have been an issue. Fairness wouldn't have been on my radar screen at all. But it was. I had to look at the evidence for myself before I threw Christianity away.

I knew most of us hold opinions—even strong opinions—for which we have little evidence. So I was aware that I was not alone in having such a strong reaction to my training without firsthand knowledge. People have opinions about all kinds of things—including, and maybe especially, religion—for which they have little real evidence. Sometimes, they haven't even a clue what they're really talking about. They don't study the topic for themselves. I know that even now I hold opinions about some matters for which I have little knowledge or evidence. For example, I hold the opinion that it is more than likely—actually, I believe it is a virtual certainty—that life exists on other planets in the universe. And I think it is likely that certain life forms are as advanced or more advanced than us. Yet I have not one shred of real evidence. In fact, one could argue the contrary. If extraterrestrial civilizations are more advanced than us, then where are they? Why haven't they discovered us? All I really know is that we exist. We're here. Still, given there are billions of galaxies with trillions of stars with trillions upon trillions of planets orbiting them, I strongly tend to believe that ET exists. I do try to hang on to such opinions a bit loosely, knowing I am indeed ignorant. After all, what sense does it make to believe something—or go down on the sword for something—for which one has little evidence? Yet, I believe it enough that it drives my hope—along with that little-boy curiosity in me—to live long enough to witness a robot landing on Jupiter's moon Europa to drill beneath its ice into its oceans below looking for life. (Check out the movie *Europa Report* for a sci-fi version of just this venture.)

Even my own emerging profession—which is *supposed* to offer judgments based on science—has way too many opinions with little or no basis in fact.

The speaker at one of my professional seminars was internationally known for his work. He blatantly noted that he did not have tissues in his office; he believed crying was useless. He believed in a "stiff upper lip." His clients were to deal with reality head-on . . . with no tears. What ignorant arrogance. From trauma research, we know that, whether male or female, we must release inner pain to set the psyche free. We must cry. Crying is not the only thing that needs to occur. But it is one necessary thing. Unshed tears are like intrapsychic superglue—keeping painful memories stuck in the psyche, unconsciously controlling how we feel and behave. Based on science—not myth—we need to allow ourselves to cry as long, as intensely, and as often as we need to cry until our hearts are done crying. When we cry, we "make room" for other healthy experiences and emotions. This is true whether we are a traumatized soldier, rape victim, or a grieving spouse. We need to cry. Yet here was a prominent figure whose cavalier opinion influenced young, malleable minds—a fine example of the self-importance of one's own opinion-without-evidence. A psychological mythmaker selling his snake oil. The proverbial fool.

The world is full of opinions. That's why I went to Clarkson, a school of *technology*—not a school of mythmaking. So I owed it to myself to look at the original evidence for the faith given to me. Contrary to Carl Sagan, however, I did feel pressured to make a decision. Not pressure from anyone else—just myself. The pressure was to make sure my final judgment was solid. I wanted it to be an informed decision, one with integrity. On one hand, I felt I had to nail down the truth because I had so much untruth in my family growing up. On the other, while I desperately wanted to be free from magic and myth, I didn't want ignorance and hatred to drive my anti-religion stance—as they seem to have for self-proclaimed atheist Bill Maher, the host of *Real Time* and former host of *Politically Incorrect*.

Maher, a comedian known for his irascible political satire, often takes on the Catholic religion with a vengeance. He accused Pope Benedict XVI of being a former Nazi. Having lived a life of promiscuity and drugs by his own admission, Maher vigorously rejected his Catholic faith like his father before him. But he never set himself free from bitterness. His virulent rage yet drives his mocking cynicism and irrepressible desire to get even with the Church. Maher's trapped—but doesn't even know it. I didn't want my disillusionment, cynicism, and anger to trap me. Besides, as I said, this would be the first time I actually read the full story of Jesus. And, as you know, I always love to learn. So I took Charlie's challenge.

The Story I Never Heard

I carefully read *The Passover Plot* to give me another take on the whole Jesus story. Like I noted earlier, I value dialogue and the risk that dialogue brings. I read that book and studied the Bible story in my "spare time." Here's the very brief storyline I put together that I had just never heard growing up.

John the Baptist was the last of the Old Testament prophets and considered the greatest. He had the privileged position of baptizing Jesus as the Messiah right before Jesus went off into the desert for over a month. During that time alone, it seems that Jesus pondered becoming a revolutionary leader. The times were ripe for a rebellion. The Roman Empire occupied the Jewish land of Palestine; they had military and political control over the Jews. The taxes were outrageously high, made higher by corrupt Jewish tax collectors who pocketed a lot of the money before it got to Rome. The taxes were so burdensome that they stirred intense anger among the Jews. During Jesus' month-long inner debate, Satan took him to a mountaintop, offering him the earthly empires before him. It seems that Jesus was sorely tempted to use his power and charisma to mobilize an uprising against Rome. In its wake, he could build a geopolitical empire where he'd be king. But in that desert drama, Jesus chose not to pursue political power. Instead, he affirmed his Father's radical vision for his destiny.

After Jesus began his ministry, the Roman tetrarch Herod imprisoned John the Baptist for publicly condemning him for an illicit marriage to his former sister-in-law. After hearing about Jesus' healings—and fearing for his own life—John sent two messengers to Jesus asking if he really was the Messiah:

> When the men came to Jesus, they said, "John the Baptist sent us to you with this question: 'Are you the One who is to come, or should we wait for someone else?'" (Luke 7:20, NCV)

John knew the Old Testament prophesies about how the Messiah would come as the new king. John likely thought Jesus would usher in a new geopolitical empire by overthrowing the Romans—a vision that Jesus himself had been tempted with. John was not only scared, but confused. Jesus sent the messenger back explaining to John:

> "Go tell John what you saw and heard here. The blind can see, the crippled can walk, and people with skin diseases are healed. The deaf can hear, the dead are raised to life, and the Good News is preached to the poor. Those who do not stumble in their faith because of me are blessed!" (Luke 7:22–23, NCV)

That was the tough though reassuring message back to John. Tough because Jesus wasn't going to rescue John from his beheading.

John wasn't the only one wondering about Jesus. Jesus intrigued—and confused—innumerable Jews who were grinding their jaws under Roman rule, including those scheming to mount a bloody insurrection. As Jesus' extraordinary reputation as a miracle worker and teacher spread, his potential role in rallying the masses excited the revolutionaries.

Jesus' growing influence deeply concerned the Jewish religious leaders. After all, *they* were the ordained priests and ministers. They were the real guardians of the faith. Besides, the religious leaders became fed up with Jesus' public criticisms of them. And given that they had been given power by the Romans, the religious leaders didn't want Jesus to provoke a revolution. So they tried to trap him. Sometimes, they'd send their cronies to trip Jesus up in public. One time, after trying to draw Jesus into their trap with some ingratiating comments, they asked, "Is it right to pay taxes to Caesar or not?" (Matt. 22:17, NCV). This was a very politically charged question—and they knew it. They were setting Jesus up. Those who wanted revolution in Jesus' hearing were likely hoping he'd use the issue of taxation to start an uprising. If Jesus answered that the people should *not* pay the high tax, then Jesus would feed the cause of revolution. He might even spark an immediate rebellion. Open rebellion or not, with that answer, the Romans would likely arrest Jesus for trying to incite one. That would play directly into the corrupt religious leaders' hand. If Jesus backed off, however, and told the people to pay the high taxes, then he'd risk disappointing the revolutionaries as well as many others—and hurting his ministry. The trap was set. Jesus took a coin and asked whose picture was on it. The people answered, "Caesar's." Jesus said, "Give to Caesar the things that are Caesar's, and give to God the things that are God's" (Matt. 22:21, NCV). With that answer, Jesus escaped Roman arrest—though likely he strongly disappointed many Jews.

Jesus did nothing to take on Rome. He even called Jews to a love-the-enemy tactic. Roman soldiers could legally require a male Jew to carry his pack for one mile, if so ordered. That ill-intended law just rubbed salt in the wound of the Jews under Roman occupation. But Jesus taught that if the Roman soldier ordered that one mile, then offer to go the second (Matt. 5:41). With such hatred for the Romans brewing among the Jews, Jesus' teaching to walk that second mile was one tough pill to swallow. Jesus' seemingly naïve, nonviolent approach ran directly against the cause of violent revolution. His position on taxes and his stand against violence disappointed more and more Jews. Negative feelings toward Jesus among the revolutionaries, and likely among many other Jews as well, escalated.

But then there was Lazarus.

Lazarus had been dead for four days. Jesus loved Lazarus dearly, along with his two sisters, Martha and Mary. When Jesus came to visit Lazarus' gravesite, Martha was pretty upset, wondering why he hadn't come earlier to heal him. In point of fact, Jesus had deliberately not come when asked. He had told his disciples that he wasn't going back to heal Lazarus so that they could actually see for themselves "God's glory"—and believe. So when Martha asked Jesus why he hadn't come, Jesus told her that Lazarus "will rise again." Martha said she knew he would at the end of the world. But Jesus then asserted, "I *am* the resurrection and the life. Those who believe in me will have life even if they die." Then Mary came. She fell at Jesus' feet sobbing, "Lord, if you had been here, my brother would not have died." This time, as Jesus saw her tears flow down her cheeks, instead of confronting her as he had Martha, he himself wept. Then he made his way to the tomb. Those who had gathered to comfort the sisters as well as greet Jesus went along. Jesus asked for the large stone to be rolled aside. Surprised by his request, Martha warned Jesus that it had been four days and there'd be a terrible odor. Jesus challenged her again, "Didn't I tell you that if you believed you would see the glory of God?" The stone was rolled back. Then Jesus commanded, "Lazarus, come out!" (John 11:25–44, NCV).

The dead man came out.

The shock waves of a dead man coming back to life spread quickly in the region. In its wake, the groundswell of excitement about Jesus grew rapidly. With such fervor spreading among the masses, the unsettled religious leaders now feared Jesus even more. They knew if the political unrest continued, Rome would likely crack down not only on the masses *but also on them*. They'd lose their positions of power and the creature comforts that came along with them. So they plotted to take Jesus out.

It was festival time—and people knew Jesus was headed to town. With great excitement on the arrival of this incredible miracle worker and hoped-for King, the people spread branches out as Jesus entered town—believing he would become the new king. Christians now call that day Palm Sunday. The revolutionaries sensed that this was a huge opportunity for Jesus to rally the masses. Once again, they got their hopes up. But, to their utter disappointment, Jesus failed them once again. He did nothing—absolutely nothing—to stir the people against the Romans. Instead, he once again publicly took on the religious leaders, only earning more of their fury against him. With Judas' help, they hatched a simple plot to get the Romans to arrest him.

When Pilate, the Roman governor of the region, interrogated Jesus, Jesus persuaded Pilate that he thought of his kingdom as not of this world. That's the key reason why Pilate found Jesus innocent of insurrection—and wanted to drop the charges. Jesus was no threat to him as governor. Nor was he any threat to Caesar as King; Jesus was politically and militarily irrelevant. But, instead of declaring Jesus innocent and letting him go, Pilate decided to quiet the Jews down by offering Jesus to them to do with as they chose. Pilate asked the people present—though we don't know who they were— what they wanted. They shouted they wanted Jesus crucified. Jesus had backed himself into a corner with no way out. He'd have to die.

That's the story line I put together as a college kid; I had not known it before. My religion had been focused on ritual, symbols, and incantations—not on the story.

It seemed that none of Jesus' disciples understood what was happening. Nor why. Who really was this Jesus? He held such promise. He had charisma, wisdom way beyond that of the ministers of his day, and extraordinary powers. Yet he had become impotent and irrelevant to what the people really wanted. His strategic plan, if he had one, made no sense. In fairness to the revolutionaries, Jesus' own twelve confidants hadn't understood his mission of liberation either. When the Romans arrested Jesus, his disciples scattered and went into hiding. Peter, a leader of the band of disciples, tried to make his way through the crowd to safety. Someone spotted him— and confronted him with being a follower of Jesus. Terrified, Peter vehemently denied it. The disciples must have wondered, just like John the Baptist, was Jesus really the King? Was he the divine liberator we'd been looking for? If he was, then just what was he liberating us from? Jesus deliberately chose not to overthrow Rome to build his own earthly empire; his kingdom was not political. He himself made that crystal clear to Pilate.

That left the disciples, and me, with the question: just what was his kingdom?

Drawn Against My Will

When Jesus spoke, he healed people. He put mud on blind eyes, which, when washed off, allowed people to see. His touch cured lepers. He told a dead man named Lazarus to come alive, and the man came hobbling out of the tomb. Jesus even multiplied a few loaves and some fish into the thousands. All of it on command. If I had thought the rituals and incantations of the Catholic Church were medieval magic, then Jesus was both the Harry Houdini and the David Copperfield of biblical times.

It all did seem like magic, Kid . . . childlike magic . . . more magic than the Church ever threw at me. Yet, the story drew me in. Perhaps the off-handed but inexorable power of my father's words about golf, baseball, short-sleeve shirts, jewelry, and bigotry spoken into my mental world made subliminal sense of the alleged power of Jesus' words. They both spoke—my dad and Jesus—and it was so. Being drawn, however, was honestly frustrating. I had wanted to be done with religion.

One could reasonably argue that the Church had already trained me to believe in magic—from holy water to the saints. So Jesus' outlandish miracles were no giant leap. Clearly, that was—and still is—a distinct possibility. But I don't think so. After all, I had irrevocably rejected the belief that a wafer could become the literal body of Jesus—and that belief was central to my Catholic faith . . . *central*. And I carried my nonnegotiable commitment to stand on evidence into my reading of the Jesus story. Still, I knew it was possible that such grand myths could yet unconsciously draw me in because the Church had already thoroughly saturated my mind in myth.

Did I desperately want to believe in miracles? Perhaps the display of crutches and wheelchairs I saw on the cathedral walls had set up the irrational hope for miracles. Besides, having witnessed your grandparents' torturous demise, did I want to believe in some miraculous relief from it all? On the cathedral grounds, I had prayerfully crawled up those concrete steps on my knees in the hopes of one. But no miracle happened. So I got solid confirmation that, once again, God was useless—impotent and irrelevant, just like Jesus felt to the revolutionaries. I actually felt better off not believing in miracles.

The miracle stories turned me off; frankly, in a way, they still do. Yet, as a young man, they intrigued me. The fascination came in wrestling with the question: just what was Jesus' "kingdom?"

Some would argue that the story would never have grabbed my interest apart from the Spirit of God working in me. After all, Jesus did say his Father revealed who he was to the apostle Peter. While that is true, to say the Spirit was mysteriously opening my eyes begs the question. How would I know if it was the Spirit of God enticing me ... or my own foolishness? Besides, right or wrong, I was—and still am—too committed to finding evidence for what I believe. So I needed a more nuts-'n-bolts explanation of why this story pulled me in.

One reason came out in my rich dialogues with Charlie. Charlie pointed out that there really isn't that much teaching in the Jesus story. And, upon reflection, that's true. There are great challenges, like the tough teaching to love your enemy, and pithy perspectives like the Beatitudes. But Jesus' teachings are not lengthy ... or many. They come in brief summaries, likely passed down through oral tradition and then later written down. The writers didn't focus on his teachings as much as they did on his numerous miracles—using them to show that Jesus was God. In fact, the apostle John's gospel starts out with exactly that bold declaration: "In the beginning there was the Word. The Word was with God, and the Word was God" (John 1:1, NCV). The "Word" is Jesus. John's imagination is absolutely fixated on Jesus being God. Perhaps the apostle believed Jesus was God precisely because he created things out of nothing by simply speaking words— just as God had done in Genesis in creating the world out of nothing when he said, "Let there be light"—and it was so (Gen. 1:3, NCV).

The apostles' laser-like focus on Jesus being God was news to me however. I hadn't known that before. During high school, I thought the Catholic Church had foolishly made that up. After all, I had the stark imprint from the Baltimore Catechism where the Church had made up indulgences. Over the years, I've discovered that I was not alone in doubting the Church's integrity. Many people have thought that the Church made this stuff up. Like Karl Marx, they think that a few people made up religion to be an opiate for the ignorant masses.

A few years ago, one colleague of mine sarcastically told me that. He said that not only do churches offer people drugs, but that my own Presbyterian church—being a large church—offered the more expensive prescription version. So, as a freshman in college, when I came to grips with what the writers themselves said about Jesus, I was taken aback.

Jesus' audacious claim to be God has drawn attention from around the globe. Many have tried to prove him a fraud, including the author of *The Passover Plot*, written in 1965, when I was just beginning my high school training. As I noted earlier, that's one book I read my first year in college. The author's cynical challenge was interesting. He claimed that the apostle John and a wealthy member of the Sanhedrin, Joseph of Arimathea (who deeply respected Jesus), conspired together to make it look like Jesus died. They surreptitiously colluded to give Jesus a drug during his horrific crucifixion to make him unconscious—with the uneasy hope that they'd get him down before he actually died of suffocation. Without telling the other disciples, the apostle John and Joseph made sure they got him down in time. One big problem with his view is that the gospel writers—who were not in on the conspiracy—apparently lied about the miracle stories. So a key unanswered question would be: Why would *they* lie? This is not to mention that the dutiful Roman soldier made sure Jesus was dead by driving his spear into his side—unless that too was a lie.

Perhaps the apostle John and the other enthusiastic writers made up the miracle stories to make Jesus look like God in order to persuade us. Or perhaps the writers foolishly used the myths that were handed down to construct their own storyline—thinking they were true. Whether the stories were made up or not, what became clear to me at eighteen was that the Catholic Church hadn't made them up. Church leaders did not contrive the outrageous idea of Jesus being God. The writers of the Jesus story—not the Church—had already done that. In clear conscience, I no longer could blame Church leaders for fabricating Jesus' divinity. Nor could I blame them for making up miracle stories. The religious leaders had simply reacted to the narrative that others had already created. So I began to separate the story from the institution. Doing so was huge for me . . . huge. After all, the Church and the story—what little I knew of it—had been one. Now, I no longer needed to deal with my Catholic Church leaders; I had to deal with the storytellers themselves.

But Still . . .

Isn't it possible that I unconsciously needed religion to keep my sense of identity? Isn't it possible that I sought to rediscover my faith in order to secure my fragile ego? Couldn't my sincere but naïve parents and the well-meaning but misguided Church leaders have so enmeshed my growing identity with the symbols of faith, including the uniforms, aesthetics, architecture, and rituals, that to let go of faith would have been to let go of the internal scaffolding of my psyche—to let go of "me"—leaving me an empty young man? My mom, after all, had kept herself "propped up" by faith until she finally and fully came to terms with the fact that Jesus was never going to heal your grandfather. So, was it "like mother, like son?" Did I prop myself up like she had? Did I pick up my mother's flag after she set it down in utter despair at the end?

To the last question, I have no doubt, Hon, that I picked up my mother's flag. I had already picked up my dad's. It's patently obvious. My entire life—and this entire letter—is about carrying their flags. Whether the flag came in the form of my mother's last moments of utter hopelessness or my father's inconsolable cry into the universe, the flag was the same: *Does God exist?* And, if he does: *Does he care?* I've carried that flag for a lifetime—and been in life's sweat tank way too long struggling to find answers.

To the other questions: I did have my own core emptiness. And the painful fact of life is that my troubled parents did traumatize me. So, in a way, I was fragile—very fragile. Still, I don't think the Jesus story drew me because I felt empty or brittle—though I am aware I could be wrong. I could. But I don't think so. Here's why.

Yes, your grandmother drowned in despair with no hope for her future, dying emotionally bankrupt. But, in contrast, I was looking forward to my future. *My* future. *My* life more on my terms, not my parents'. And getting institutional religion off my back felt freeing. In fact, it's been off my back since. Beyond that, though traumatized,

I did have a strong sense of self. Moral values had shaped my core—through the modeling of my parents; the training of the Church; the incredible solidarity of values among the Dutchtown neighbors; and finally, the modeling of the young man with whom I had my most profound identification, your uncle Herb. Over the decades, I've never left those values nor could I ever overturn them. Whether I would be an atheist or Christian theist, I could never betray those values—never—because I thoroughly believe in them. "Me" and my values were—and are—one. My values were and are the scaffolding of my identity; they permeate every fiber of my being. Sincerity, keeping one's word, duty emerging from love, compassion, and the equality of all people, make me "me." The values delivered to me by your grandparents and sealed into my character by your uncle Herb had become my identity. So, in spite of trauma, I had a clear sense of "me." In that way, I did not have a fragile ego. I was a Herbert. God or no God, I knew who I was. Still do.

So, if I'm right, and I wasn't drawn primarily to fill some core emptiness of identity, then just what was it that kept pulling me in—and doing so in spite of my youthful cynicism?

Ghostbusters

In my reading, it seemed that it didn't come together for the disciples until Pentecost. That's when, in a single moment of time, the Spirit of Jesus caused them to have an ecstatic experience of his love. Beyond that, he emboldened them to tell the world what they had seen:

> People of Israel, listen to these words: Jesus from Nazareth was a very special man. God clearly showed this to you by the miracles, wonders, and signs he did through Jesus. You all know this, because it happened right here among you. Jesus was given to you, and with the help of those who don't know the law, you put him to death by nailing him to a cross. But this was God's plan which he had made long ago; he knew all this would happen. God raised Jesus from the dead and set him free from the pain of death, because death could not hold him . . . .
> Brothers and sisters, I can tell you truly that David, our ancestor, died and was buried. His grave is still here with us today. He was a prophet and knew God had promised him that he would make a person from David's family a king just as he was. Knowing this before it happened, David talked about the Christ rising from the dead. He said:
> He was not left in the grave.
> His body did not rot.
> So Jesus is the One whom God raised from the dead. And we are all witnesses to this. (Acts 2:22–24, 29–32, NCV)

It became clearer. I noted already that Charlie had pointed out how there just weren't that many teachings in the gospels.

Apparently, the disciples hadn't come to be so excited about Jesus simply because they loved his teachings. That's why there just weren't that many in the story. They grew impassioned—and emerged radically loyal to the point of death—because they were witnesses of Jesus being alive after having been dead. That's the final reason why they believed he was God.

I think it's as easy to believe in ghosts today as it was back then. Perhaps easier. There are now television programs dedicated to exploring the paranormal realm—including both human and animal spirits. As a friend of mine mused, "Well, the energy has to go somewhere after we die." So when the disciples encountered Jesus after he was dead, they were taken aback, thinking they were seeing a ghost:

> While the two followers were telling this, Jesus himself stood right in the middle of them and said, "Peace be with you."
>
> They were fearful and terrified and thought they were seeing a ghost. But Jesus said, "Why are you troubled? Why do you doubt what you see? Look at my hands and my feet. It is I myself! Touch me and see, because a ghost does not have a living body as you see I have."
>
> After Jesus said this, he showed them his hands and feet. While they still could not believe it because they were amazed and happy, Jesus said to them, "Do you have any food here?" They gave him a piece of broiled fish. While the followers watched, Jesus took the fish and ate it.
>
> He said to them, "Remember when I was with you before? I said that everything written about me must happen—everything in the Law of Moses, the books of the prophets, and the Psalms."
>
> Then Jesus opened their minds so they could understand the Scriptures. He said to them, "It is written that the Christ would suffer and rise from the dead on the third day and that a change of hearts and lives and forgiveness of sins would be preached in his name to all nations, starting at Jerusalem. You are witnesses of these things. . . ." (Luke 24:36–48, NCV)

The straightforward but commanding assertion that Jesus was not a ghost but a living body entranced me. The storytellers couldn't have been more gutsy. They boldly offered their own anecdotal "proof" that the risen Jesus was no ghost: He ate fish and let the disciples touch him. Incredible, isn't it? Of course, such an audacious claim could be like Hitler's big lie. Hitler used the idea that if you're going to lie, lie real big—bigger than anyone would ever imagine—because, "white lies" notwithstanding, the ignorant masses would never think someone would be so brazen as to lie so outrageously. You know Hitler's big lie. *Did the gospel writers brazenly lie?* I wondered.

In his 1994 book *Resurrection: Myth or Reality*, which I read years later, the Episcopal Bishop Spong does sincerely believe the disciples made up the miracle stories, including the one of Jesus eating fish after having been dead. Jesus was simply a fond memory—albeit a powerfully precious memory—stirring within the loyal disciples a deep inner sense that he lived on. It's similar to how many people today think of their loved ones who have passed on. Many believe they can *feel* their loved one with them. Some even believe that they can feel their loved one's presence so strongly that they can talk with him or her—and that the deceased loved one looks down on them with compassion, offers comfort, even nudges them with ideas or thoughts . . . much like the Catholic practice of praying to the saints. John Edwards, from the early 2000s TV series *Crossing Over*, made his living off people who believe that way. Using literary license, according to Bishop Spong, the disciples carefully fabricated fantastic stories—which, in their day, would have been a reasonable and ethical thing to do—to convince others that Jesus was important and his spirit was still with us. They weren't conspiring to tell a "big lie" about Jesus; they were simply and sincerely trying to persuade. So they fictionalized Jesus.

The bishop hadn't written his controversial book until a couple decades after my own inner debate as a young man. But like him, I did wonder if the disciples had simply made up the stories—though perhaps not maliciously so. Here's a really bizarre vignette—as if the various miracle stories aren't already strange enough—that especially fueled my ongoing cynicism as a freshman in college. The Gospel of Matthew notes that precisely at the moment when Jesus died, several weird things happened, including:

> The graves opened, and many of God's people who had died were raised from the dead. They came out of the graves after Jesus was raised from the dead and went into the holy city, where they appeared to many people. (Matt. 27:52–53, NCV)

When I read this, I spontaneously flashed to the 1950s black-and-white horror movies I had seen as a kid that portrayed zombies coming up and out of their graves. It sure seemed that the storytellers made up such fanciful anecdotes to make the story even grander. After all, it's easy to be grand when you're writing fiction.

I didn't know it at the time—I was just eighteen and had no idea what was happening in seminaries—but theologians across the globe were thinking the same thing. They likewise earnestly thought that such stories were just too far-fetched. They still do, as do many lay people. I taught a discipleship class where this particular zombie story came up. One woman asked, "Are we really supposed to believe this happened?" But many lay people also wonder about these doubting theologians: Why would you spend your entire professional life studying the Bible if you didn't believe it?

I think I understand. Like me, many theologians eagerly entered seminary when they were young and idealistic. Some took the Bible literally; some didn't. Those who did became more disillusioned and cynical the older they got. Life's evidence piled up against the Bible. There were too many unanswered questions. And they just couldn't believe the childlike miracle stories anymore. But—and this is a huge but for these sincere men and women—they still wanted to keep their faith. They had been imprinted with faith as a child or young adult—like I had. It was still important to them. And as one theologian told me, "It's comfortable." So in order to keep the faith of their youth, they became creative. One prominent theologian made up the idea that the miracle stories were not true stories, but "truth stories." For example, the story about Jesus multiplying loaves and fishes simply cannot be true. It can't. It is just too much of a reach to believe that someone could create something from nothing. Back in Jesus' time, if someone had had a video camera to record the memorable event, we'd only see Jesus teaching the people. We wouldn't see any instantaneous creation of bread. In that way, the story is not a "true story."

Nevertheless, these theologians genuinely believe such a poignant story is rich in symbolic meaning. It points us to a "spiritual" truth: God is our spiritual nourishment. He is our psychological and spiritual "bread of life." So, these theologians believe that the writers made up the story of multiplying bread to make that point. Another is that zombie story of dead people waking and going into town—with the spiritual lesson that God is the wellspring of all life.

For such "modern" theologians in the twentieth and twenty-first centuries, the multiplication of loaves of bread and dead people popping out of graves like a 1950s horror movie are "truth stories." They are not actually *true* stories. In capturing our imaginations with their simplistic grandeur, such bold stories convey deep psychic meaning both spiritually and emotionally. Today, we wrongly—and naïvely—take the outlandish and childlike miracle stories literally.

In my own much simpler way as a freshman, I did wonder like a modern theologian: Were all the miracle stories only fiction whose purpose was to teach spiritual lessons? Still, I kept on reading the story. On one hand, I did so to fulfill my duty to myself to read the original source. On the other, I have to admit that the story fascinated me. Yet, I was deeply skeptical. I wondered if I was a fool for even considering the possibility that the stories might be true. After all, I felt I had already been fooled growing up with so many intricate Catholic myths—though, in fairness to myself, how is a child supposed to know better? As a young man, like Bishop Spong, I really didn't want to naïvely believe the gospel writers—not right after having naïvely believed my Church leaders as a kid. I had had enough of sincere naïveté . . . from my parents to Church leaders to Mr. Datillio. That's why I was at Clarkson, a school of technology—a school of evidence, not myth.

Mesmerized

Obviously, the story of Jesus coming back to life physically—along with the entire package of bizarre miracles wrapped around him—was, and continues to be, a very tough sell. Yet, we have seminaries across the globe still studying that very same Jesus story. The story changed Western civilization; it is now in the process of transforming the Third World.

Still, that two-thousand-year-old story ending dramatically with a dead man coming back to life gets tougher and tougher to swallow in this twenty-first century. We live in a high-tech world with a vast universe before us. That technological world conditioned me as a teen. Combined with President Kennedy's hypnotic vision for shooting the moon, it shaped my future studies. I poured myself into physics. And physics poured itself into me, shaping my thinking.

The grand effort to "box in" and analyze just a tiny, tiny piece of reality—like a hydrogen atom—shaped certain beliefs within me. It also trained my expectations. For one, it taught me that I could never change reality; I could only manipulate it if I "obeyed" it. I have since always expected to obey reality if I wanted to get anywhere in life. That was similar to my childhood lessons with nature. I needed to respect Mother Nature—I needed to obey her while hiking and camping—if I were to enjoy her.

Physics also taught me that truth was rarely easy to come by. I have since always expected that from life. If truth comes by easily and cheaply, then rarely is it true. You have to work hard for truth. Sometimes, you have to fight for it. I tasted that firsthand in grappling with tough questions in science. I learned the difference between hard-fought truth and baseless opinion. One has to be careful, however. Even in science, when you think you have the truth, you oftentimes don't. I had to spend a great deal of time and energy in the attempt to get answers out of Mother Nature. I spent hundreds of hours setting up equipment and thousands of hours doing complex mathematical calculations to that end. Grappling with reality like that was frankly humbling—very humbling. Years later, as a psychologist, I realized that such rigorous work in physics was actually my better training for "boxing in" the human psyche.

As a young man, I was in reverential awe of the universe before me. Still am. The humility learned from physics fed my sense of just how grand and mysterious this universe is. I brought that humble awe to the Jesus story.

I was somewhat aware of how large the universe is—and how small we are. For example, I knew that light travels very fast, about 186,000 miles per second. It takes under two seconds—just two—for the moon's light to hit our eyes, though the moon is over a quarter of a million miles away from the earth. Still, at that mind-boggling speed, it takes light about 100,000 years just to go from one side of our own Milky Way galaxy to the other. And it was only in this century that we discovered there is a universe out there beyond our galaxy—a universe filled with billions of other galaxies. It is impossible to fathom.

I also was in awe at how everything that lives eventually dies. All living things eventually fall apart into the basic molecules from which they came. From dust to dust. I was keenly aware of this tough fact of life as a boy celebrating Ash Wednesday. The priest put ashes on my young forehead as a firm, undeniable reminder that I would indeed die someday . . . and then decay into ashes.

Decaying is actually a very active process. A lot happens to decay something into mere dust. And that dismantling process extends throughout the entire universe. Scientists used to think the universe was static . . . unchanging. That it has been—and will always be—the same. Many people still do. But the universe is far from stable; it's constantly changing. In as little as eight billion years from now our expanding sun will destroy the earth—though the heat of the sun will burn up all life on our planet billions of years before that. Beyond that—and this sends shivers up the spines of some—certain evidence suggests that trillions upon trillions upon trillions of years from now, the universe may become dead and cold. At this point, though, no one really knows the universe's fate. But the prospects aren't pretty.

I know that to many, all this may seem both boring and irrelevant to faith. But having an informed awe of the universe deeply affected me—and fed into how I reacted to the Jesus story. It really bothered me how small the disciples' universe was. Really bothered me. It still does. Their world was very small. Extraordinarily small. In fact, it was just plain tiny. I don't think they even knew North and South America existed, let alone that we live on a speck of dust in a virtually infinite universe.

To get an updated feel for just how small our speck really is, go on YouTube to "Pale Blue Dot" (the original, by astrophysicist Carl Sagan). In 1990, Sagan persuaded NASA to command *Voyager 1* to take a picture of planet Earth gently hanging in the emptiness of cosmic space shortly before leaving our solar system. At that point, *Voyager 1* had travelled about 3.7 billion miles from Earth. While revealing his skepticism about God, Sagan's brief but poignant description of that pale blue dot—a speck the size of one-tenth of one pixel—is worth listening to. The *Pale Blue Dot* is one incredible photograph. And it is one incredible perspective—which is exactly why NASA took the unprecedented photograph.

I wondered: To pull off living forever with a new body, wouldn't God—if he existed—have to rescue the whole universe from decay? He'd have to transform it, wouldn't he? But, in his tiny, tiny world, did the apostle Peter realize this? Had he even asked the question? I discovered that the apostle Paul had:

The creation itself will be liberated from its bondage to decay.... (Rom. 8:21, NIV)

There it was. The apostle Paul had asked and answered that grand question. Creation would have to be changed. The universe would have to be miraculously transformed into a place where there was no decay. But in my twentieth century, could I really take his belief for *his* tiny world and wrap it around *my* now unimaginably huge cosmic world? Could I take his comments seriously? Would my entire universe—could *my* universe, not his—actually be liberated from decay? I stared long and hard at our grand universe through my youthful eyes. Then I stared long and hard at what Peter said about Jesus coming back to life. It was truly unbelievable. Incredulously so.

Years later, I discovered that innumerable theologians worldwide—though not all—had already decided that it is indeed incredulous to believe the apostles' view of creation's liberation from decay given what we now know about our universe. In our century, it is a fool's vision. That's why so many theologians and ministers liked the idea of a "truth" story in contrast to a "true" story. In my youth, I wrestled with the very same issue.

Inevitably, as science and technology advance, our universe is just going to get even more complex. As a young man, I couldn't help but wonder about the future of faith. I thought: It's already been over two millennia since Jesus. How will people fifty millennia from now react? Or one hundred millennia? Or one million years? Or—how about three billion years from now when humans will have to leave Earth permanently because the heat from the expanding sun will burn up the planet? How will those people find it reasonable to rely on such an "old, old story"? By then, the story would be absurdly ancient. As we master space travel—and get farther from our own planet Earth—won't such an antiquated document become even more bizarre? More and more unbelievably foolish? And therefore more and more irrelevant? Even today, the majority of Europeans have abandoned faith in Jesus. Fast forward to one billion years from now: Who will be left standing believing a billion-year-old story about a dead man coming back to life?

Or, would our discovery of other dimensions to the space-time continuum make the Jesus story more palatable? More believable?

Hon, the panorama—swinging from Jesus coming back to life to my now virtually infinite universe—involuntarily gripped my imagination. I found myself utterly mesmerized.

In the Eye of the Beholder

In my long talks with Charlie wrestling with whether to believe the story about Jesus coming back to life, I found myself repeatedly asking: Does it make any sense at all to imagine that life—at least, human life—could ever be put back together after being utterly and completely destroyed? After all, decaying crumbles all flesh—the blood, brain, and even bone—into a bunch of carbon molecules. That's obvious when we sprinkle someone's ashes somewhere. So, in order to "come back to life," life would have to be recreated. How was I to make sense of Jesus being recreated—with a body of flesh? Flesh that ate fish. Flesh that lives forever. And, in an age of hi-tech astrophysics where we know space and time are integrally tied together, what does "forever" even mean?

Then I had other odd—very odd—but valid questions buried within this tough one. Questions for which, of course, no one has any answers, like: Where is Jesus now? If he has a body, does he have to eat? Does he have to go to the bathroom? Is he in another universe, waiting? I know, Hon. Such questions just seem so ridiculous; they seemed absurd to me at the time as well. But, I thought, if such questions were indeed silly—if they really were that absurd—then Jesus never did come back to life. If Jesus really, actually, came back to life, then it was reasonable to ask: Where the heck is he? Jesus being at the "right hand of the Father"—like our creed affirms—told me nothing about the state or location of his "forever body." Just what does Jesus now "do"?

In the age of modern science, how could I unashamedly wonder about such weird questions?

Once again, I wasn't alone. As I've already noted, innumerable religious leaders were—and still are today—desperately trying to keep the faith of their youth. But they can't and don't believe the miracle stories . . . or that a dead man came back to life . . . let alone that God would rescue our cosmic universe from decay. Such claims are so extreme that the modern mind feels embarrassed entertaining them. That embarrassment drives a vast number of theologians across the world—and the students they instruct who later become our pastors—to not only view the miracles as "truth stories," as symbolic, but to "spiritualize" most of what we think about Jesus. They wanted to fictionalize him. To fictionalize Jesus became the least embarrassing way for theologians to save their faith. And, in this day and age, the most intelligent. It made it possible for them to keep the faith of their youth while remaining respectable to their scientific peers . . . as well as intellectually sane.

Many lay people think like these theologians. They too fictionalize Jesus. Yet, they want to have their cake and eat it too. While spiritualizing Jesus, they hang onto the idea of an afterlife; they still want to be eternal. They don't want to think that death is like before conception—nothingness. So they dump the afterlife into some ghost-like, ethereal realm that we float around in after death. Our spirits remain alive. Many think their near-death experiences—hovering above the operating table or seeing bright lights—are their spirits floating away from their bodies, only to get sucked back in at the very last moment. *Heaven is for Real* is a recently released movie depicting just that. This is likely what the disciples thought when they first saw Jesus—that he was a spirit or ghost. It's easier to believe this way . . . much easier. Nothing outrageous with *this* physical world ever needs to happen then—like liberating the billions of galaxies in the universe from decay. A ghost-like Jesus—or simply a remembered Jesus—is much more palatable than a risen Jesus who ate fish.

As a young man, I didn't know anything about this worldwide effort to fictionalize the Jesus story. So, without knowing it, Kid, this is where I parted company with them. I had no use for spiritualizing the miracle stories, let alone debunking the entire story. None. It's not that I wanted to defend the stories. Far from it. It's that I didn't want to turn the stories into psychological metaphors to make them tolerable—let alone acceptable. For me, the stories were either historically true or useless fabrication. I didn't care at all whether they had any psychological meaning or not.

That's because I already had had my fill of symbolism and myth-making from the Church. I had had enough of the Church's spiritual lessons that were irrelevant to the stuff of real life. New metaphors and new fictions would just have been more of the same. All hollow. The symbols and rituals of the Catholic Church; the fictional scenarios about purgatory; the contrived power of St. Christopher to protect me on the highway; the fable of St. Anthony finding lost objects; praying the rosary hoping Mary would intercede; the voodoolike practice of wrapping the Holy Scapular around my bedpost to protect me; and the childlike hope of climbing concrete steps at a shrine in desperate search of a miracle—all of these "spiritual things" seemed irrelevant to the tragic but real stuff of my family life. All these practices were absolutely impotent. There was no real power to deal with the sin perpetrated against me. No concrete power to heal my dad's gnarled body. No inner psychic power whatsoever to set free my mother's intoxicated mind. It was all fiction. And it was all irrelevant. I really had no use for more metaphorical, pie-in-the-sky fictionalized "truths." Why in the world would I want more hollow metaphors? Why?

I wanted reality. I wanted some real meat. Add to that the fact that I've never had any use for some ethereal afterlife—whether floating around in some other universe or hanging around in this one, in hotel rooms and basements. In my youthful search, either the miracles were real—you actually could take a video of them—or I would remain a seeker or atheist. Unlike so many theologians— though I didn't know it at the time—there was nothing in between. There was no other way through. But then again, I didn't have a professional career to salvage; these theologians did. If they became atheists, what would they then do with their careers? What would a theologian-turned-atheist do to make a living? Sell insurance? Besides, letting go of the faith of one's youth takes guts. Real guts. After spending most of your professional life trying to understand Jesus, how do you just walk away? Thus the compromises.

In grappling with whether these stories were real history or not, I pondered the question: If indeed the storytellers had made up their tales to convince us that Jesus lived on, then why did they take those tales all the way to the bitter end? It just didn't make sense to me. Why would they have spent their entire lives telling stories they themselves had made up? Why would they die for those stories? Especially if they had no other social or political axe to grind—and they clearly didn't. They certainly seemed convinced that Jesus had come back to life physically.

Once again, I thought like a modern theologian without knowing it: Maybe the apostles made up the stories because they really, really believed he was God—and thought their stories were necessary to convince others. But I kept asking myself: How did they themselves become convinced Jesus was God in the first place? Something had to persuade them.

Was it miracle after miracle?

Then again—how does anyone become convinced that someone else has the pipeline to God, let alone be God . . . whether witch doctor, Mohammed, Confucius, Buddha, the pope, minister, priest, bishop, rabbi, or New Age humanist on public television?

All I knew as a young man was that truth, like beauty, is in the eye—and mind—of the beholder. What is one man's folly is another man's wisdom. What makes sense to one person makes no sense to another. Though it might not make sense to me for the apostles to die for made-up tales, it might have made sense to them. People have died for all kinds of causes—some causes being much crazier than others.

The Outsider

Besides never having been a disciple before Jesus' death, he was a Pharisee, the class of religious leaders Jesus publicly attacked—the reason for which he had been murdered. As a devout and highly educated Pharisee, the apostle Paul persecuted Christians after Jesus' death, functioning as a marshal going house-to-house arresting both men and women to be tried and executed for their belief in Jesus. Notoriously, he gave his consent to Stephen's stoning. Clearly, Paul had no fond memories of Jesus *because he hadn't followed him.* Paul was no disciple. Instead, Paul saw the Jesus followers as heretics and a significant threat to the Jewish faith.

So, I found myself really wrestling with this question: Why would Paul have made up his story of encountering the risen Jesus?

The Romans had arrested Paul. Paul himself was a loyal Roman citizen, but after he encountered the risen Jesus, the Jews had trumped up charges against him because they wanted to stop him from spreading the story that Jesus was alive. After a preliminary investigation, the Romans found no evidence of illegal activity. Still, they decided to take Paul to the king. The king had been debriefed—and knew the charges were false. However, he also knew that the problem was a religious dispute among the Jews regarding Paul's story—that a dead man named Jesus was now alive. As king, he needed to quiet things down. Besides, the king himself was intrigued. He apparently had studied the Jewish prophets—studies that fed his fascination with Paul's story. So he decided to hear Paul's testimony. As a young man, I found Paul's story spellbinding . . . as had the king:

Agrippa said to Paul, "You may now speak to defend yourself."

Then Paul raised his hand and began to speak. He said, "King Agrippa, I am very blessed to stand before you and will answer all the charges the evil people make against me.

You know so much about all the customs and the things they argue about, so please listen to me patiently.

"All my people know about my whole life, how I lived from the beginning in my own country and later in Jerusalem. They have known me for a long time. If they want to, they can tell you that I was a good Pharisee. And the Pharisees obey the laws of my tradition more carefully than any other group. Now I am on trial because I hope for the promise that God made to our ancestors. This is the promise that the twelve tribes of our people hope to receive as they serve God day and night. My king, they have accused me because I hope for this same promise! Why do any of you people think it is impossible for God to raise people from the dead?

"I, too, thought I ought to do many things against Jesus from Nazareth. And that is what I did in Jerusalem. The leading priests gave me the power to put many of God's people in jail, and when they were being killed, I agreed it was a good thing. In every synagogue, I often punished them and tried to make them speak against Jesus. I was so angry against them I even went to other cities to find them and punish them.

"One time the leading priests gave me permission and the power to go to Damascus. On the way there, at noon, I saw a light from heaven. It was brighter than the sun and flashed all around me and those who were traveling with me. We all fell to the ground. Then I heard a voice speaking to me in the Hebrew language, saying, 'Saul, Saul, why are you persecuting me? You are only hurting yourself by fighting me.' I said, 'Who are you, Lord?' The Lord said, 'I am Jesus, the one you are persecuting. Stand up! I have chosen you to be my servant and my witness—you will tell people the things that you have seen and the things that I will show you. This is why I have come to you today. I will keep you safe from your own people and also from the others. I am sending you to them to open their eyes so that they may turn away from darkness to the light, away from the power of Satan and to God. Then their sins can be forgiven, and they can have a place with those people who have been made holy by believing in me.'

"King Agrippa, after I had this vision from heaven, I obeyed it. I began telling people that they should change their hearts and lives and turn to God and do things to show they really had changed. I told this first to those in Damascus, then in Jerusalem, and in every part of Judea, and also to the other people. This is why the Jews took me and were trying to kill me in the Temple. But God has helped me, and so I stand here today, telling all people, small and great, what I have seen. But I am saying only what Moses and the prophets said would happen—that the Christ would die, and as the first to rise from the dead, he would bring light to all people."

While Paul was saying these things to defend himself, Festus said loudly, "Paul, you are out of your mind! Too much study has driven you crazy!"

Paul said, "Most excellent Festus, I am not crazy. My words are true and sensible. King Agrippa knows about these things, and I can speak freely to him. I know he has heard about all of these things, because they did not happen off in a corner. King Agrippa, do you believe what the prophets wrote? I know you believe."

King Agrippa said to Paul, "Do you think you can persuade me to become a Christian in such a short time?"

Paul said, "Whether it is a short or a long time, I pray to God that not only you but every person listening to me today would be saved and be like me—except for these chains I have."

Then King Agrippa, Governor Festus, Bernice, and all the people sitting with them stood up and left the room. Talking to each other, they said, "There is no reason why this man should die or be put in jail." And Agrippa said to Festus, "We could let this man go free, but he has asked Caesar to hear his case." (Acts 26, NCV)

Maybe the other apostles had made up their stories. After all, they had been disciples of Jesus for three years and became devoted followers . . . for whatever reasons, crazy or not. But the apostle Paul? Did he make up his story as well? What in the world would be the point of doing that? He had no history with either Jesus or the other apostles. Maybe he misinterpreted his experience. Maybe. But making it all up?

The Hook

Hon, as I disentangled the Jesus story from the myths, magic, symbols, rituals, uniforms, ornate architecture, incense, Gregorian chants, Latin, contradictions, as well as the demeanor of the religious leaders—as I was doing all that—the story became more and more de-institutionalized. The Catholic Church and the story were no longer one. With that, the story became real.

To say perhaps the obvious, at the heart of this real story were eyewitnesses. But that obvious fact became my platform. It also emerged as the platform for the followers of Jesus. In fact, what made a "disciple" into an "apostle"—like the "apostle" Paul or the "apostle" John—was that the disciple had been an eyewitness to the risen Jesus. They had seen Jesus alive after having been dead—and had seen him with their own eyes.

Any child of an alcoholic family determined to get to the truth fights upstream against the invisible forces that insidiously blind the family—and himself. And then that determined child struggles to get the family to wake up to the tough truth he has witnessed. I was no different. I had seen with my own eyes how my mother abused alcohol. I saw her drink the beer. I saw her drink the Calvert's whiskey. I saw her bump the hallway walls as she staggered to her bedroom. I saw her on the floor in a stupor. I am the one who picked her up off that floor and carried her to her bed. I saw it all. In spite of my father's massive denial and conspicuous silence, I not only saw it but knew I saw it. I viscerally knew she was an alcoholic. I knew because I had witnessed it. But I had to fight my father's insipient blindness—and fight his blindness blinding me. At those times when my father's denial put an unseen veil over my own eyes, I became confused, anxiously struggling to figure out just what was the truth.

Still, I knew.

Like all children, I didn't know how to interpret things well as a boy. As I was waking up to what was happening, one moment I'd interpret the truth correctly . . . and the next I wouldn't. Still, at some level inside me, I had a sense of the truth—and figured the details out along the way. Similarly, as the apostles slowly woke up to who Jesus was, they'd see the shocking truth one minute but lose it the next. One time during Jesus' ministry, Peter did affirm that Jesus was the Messiah. Yet, right after Jesus' arrest, Peter vehemently denied knowing him. Did he deny Jesus just to protect himself? Or did he also deny him because, like John the Baptist, he now fearfully wondered if he really was the Messiah? Or both? I certainly understood this peekaboo game with the truth. Later at Pentecost, however, Peter finally and fully woke up. I understood that too. I had to do my own waking up to the fact that my mother had been an alcoholic.

However confused, however ignorant, and however frightened I was in that peekaboo game with the truth about my mother—I knew. I knew what I had seen.

Just like the apostles.

I know what the apostles had witnessed was radically different from what I had witnessed growing up. Still, the pattern of waking up to an unbelievable truth was similar. I identified with them. It was that identification that became the hook in me—and it hooked me involuntarily. It penetrated my core. *I knew the apostles knew that what they had seen was real—because I knew what I had seen was real.* No matter where I stood in my mental universe to get the leverage I needed to break the hold of that identification, I couldn't. I just couldn't write the apostles off.

The hook was set.

Eyewitnesses

I know that genuinely empathizing with the apostles as eyewitnesses does not make their reports either valid or accurate. I am simply connecting my own intrapsychic dots. It's why these storytellers became believable—*to me*. In fact, I so felt what they felt that—besides your mom and I simply liking the names—we named your brothers "Paul" and "Matthew" after the eyewitnesses to the risen Jesus.

I am also aware—painfully aware—that the evidence for Jesus' coming back to life has nothing to do with science. Instead, we have eyewitness testimonies—reports that could never be repeated in a laboratory.

The difference—the huge gap—between eyewitness testimonies and the hard evidence of repeatable experiments has haunted me over the decades. Still does. Although, having said that, innumerable advances in astronomy stand on the eyewitness reports of scientists peering through telescopes—scientists who do not do experiments. They can't put a planet or star into a lab. While I realize science is just one tool for discovering truth, the gap between scientific experiments and people's testimonies has really mattered to me. And it has mattered to many others. After all, people see things differently. People recall things differently. People interpret things differently. Because of that, those who appreciate science have the propensity to dump such ancient tales of a dead man coming back to life into the trash bin, like so many unproven reports of UFO sightings. And many have.

Yet, I have to admit that the corroborating testimony for Jesus coming back to life is actually strong. The real problem doesn't seem to be the question of witnesses; we have plenty of witnesses. The problem is *what* they claimed to have witnessed. The apostle Paul was very sensitive to precisely this issue saying,

> And if Christ has not been raised, then our preaching is worth nothing, and your faith is worth nothing. And also,

we are guilty of lying about God, because we testified of
him that he raised Christ from the dead. But if people are
not raised from the dead, then God never raised Christ.
(1 Cor. 15:14–15, NCV)

Likely many reading my open letter have no doubt as to the
truthfulness of my report regarding my mother's drinking. Yet,
I cannot do a single scientific experiment to now prove she was
an alcoholic. I can only *testify* to what I have witnessed. However,
though your uncle Ron has passed away, I did have corroborating
testimony in both my brothers. The details of their reports may vary
from mine; they did experience our family universe differently. But
the bottom line has been the same: We all bore witness to the fact
that our own mother was an alcoholic. While not an experiment,
such corroborating testimony is still evidence. It is the kind of evidence our court system uses to adjudicate matters.

Whether I've liked it or not—and I haven't—and whether anyone else might think it's foolish of me or not (and many might),
identifying with the eyewitnesses was, and still is, the most powerful intrapsychic force within me that makes the stories believable.
It was not the only force within me that fueled my faith. But—it
was *the* singularly compelling factor that moved me from magic
to miracle. I certainly didn't believe because it was more rational
to believe. And, as best as I can tell about myself, I didn't believe
because I had already been conditioned by my Catholic training to
believe. However, I could be wrong. I was young. The fact is, I had
little time to individuate from my upbringing, though I did spend
years of my childhood and early adulthood trying to do so. Still, it
really may be that I was unconsciously drawn back into essentially
the same magic I grew up with—with just a new twist to it all. If
so, I can neither discern that nor feel that. Consciously, what I do
know is that I believed because the apostles knew what they had
seen—*and so had I*. My mother drank herself to death; their Jesus
had come back to life. I knew what I saw; they knew what they saw.
That's it. That was, and still is, the hook. The faith of my youth
rested squarely and fully on the eyewitness reports that Jesus came
back to life. And it still does.

Belief in the existence of God—for me—has never rested on any
argument about intelligent design. Kristen, you already know how

beautiful, how majestic, and how complex I believe nature is. And you know how drawn I am to her. Still, as I've noted before, if some god so intelligently designed this universe, then why did he weave enormous violence and tragedy into its very fabric? What was, and still is, wrong with the character—*character*, not intelligence—of this designer? Diseases and accidents as well as violent aggression are not only integral to the animal kingdom but also the human condition as well. Joining that atheistic philosopher, Bertrand Russell, I ask once again: is this really the best a god could do?

Nor has my faith ever rested on some New Age idea that I am one with the energy of the universe. I could care less about being one wave form among zillions in a vast universe of mindless energy. In a recent conversation with a colleague, she told me that she thinks all people have some "spark" within them—but that spark has nothing to do with a divine person. Just some universal energy. She then asked me: "Why do you think of God as a person? Have you always thought that way?" I told her that, given my Catholic upbringing, I've always thought of God as a person, but along the way, wrestled with whether or not he existed. For me, I said, if god is an energy wave form, then that god is no God. "It" would be just energy. Regarding the big issues of life, why would I care about such energy, apart from some low-level scientific curiosity?

Instead, my belief in God rests solely on one thing and one thing only: that Jesus came back to life. So my faith rests on eyewitnesses. It cannot rest on some argument about intelligent design, for the character of that designer comes into question.

To my surprise—and comfort—as a young man, I discovered that that's precisely how the apostle Paul thought:

> And if Christ has not been raised, then your faith has nothing to it . . . . If our hope in Christ is for this life only, we should be pitied more than anyone else in the world. (1 Cor. 15:17–19, NCV)

To seal his discussion about how faith in God stands on only one thing, Paul says:

> If the dead are not raised, "Let us eat and drink, because tomorrow we will die." (1 Cor. 15:32b, NCV)

Paul couldn't have made it any clearer or plainer than that. Either Jesus came back to life or there's nothing else. And that is exactly where my heart has been since my youth. Exactly. Either Jesus is alive—or I am an atheist. There is no other option for me.

Since my midnight discussions with Charlie, this hook—believing the apostles knew what they had seen because I knew what I had seen—has been more powerful than all my informed skepticism. It overshadowed my youthful rebellion against the mythmaking of the Catholic Church. Over the decades, it has outweighed all my doubt. It has even overpowered my informed sense of just how crazy the cosmic implications are of a dead man coming back to life. This hook has done all that—though, admittedly, it has barely done so. Still, it has. And I've never been able to take that hook out. Right or wrong, I've tried. But I can't. My own witness to what happened in my life is such a part of me that I cannot shake my trust in the apostles' witness to what happened in their lives. Both then and now, my gut has told me: *They knew what they saw.*

Blind Faith

Once the hook was set, Hon, everything else followed. It had to. If Jesus had come back to life, then he must've multiplied the loaves of bread. Lazarus must've come hobbling out of the tomb. The dead must've woken up from their graves and gone into town. And, someday, God would free our universe from decay. Once my psyche latched onto the eyewitness reports that Jesus had come back to life, then the other reports had to be trustworthy as well. If the apostles knew what they had seen *after* Jesus died, then they knew what they had seen *before* he died. I decided if I could trust one story, I could trust them all.

Trust one story, trust them all. Was that really reasonable? As a young man, I thought so. I had unnerving moments, however, especially in seminary, when I anxiously questioned: Just how blind was I to trust the eyewitnesses? Had the hook in me blinded me?

Many people are comfortable with blind faith. For them, passionately believing in God is—by definition—"blind." Faith is blind precisely *because* there is no evidence. But it never could be so for me. I grew up with too much blindness: the pathological blindness of my parents and the obviously sincere, but for me, misguided blindness of Church leaders that stirred confusion and cynicism. Given that, how could I ever be content with *blind* faith? Besides, I never saw the point in believing in something blindly.

Some people wear "blind faith" as a badge of honor, as if they were more courageous or more spiritual than others. But, as I've noted before, faith is the perfect inkblot. With *blind* faith, you can project anything you want to believe onto the world around you— and who can challenge it? After all, it is "by faith" that you believe, not by sight. But so many people make up so many things. There has been and continues to be no dearth of mythmaking out there—with an equal amount of blind faith to receive it. To what end? So we can create any and all manner of myths—idols really—that make us feel comfortable with our universe?*

In medieval times, for example, Catholic Church leaders held on to the myth too long that the earth was the center of the universe, not the sun. Church leaders did so believing that the idea of the sun at the center was contrary to Scripture. In the end, they put Galileo under house arrest for the rest of his life because he taught that the sun was the center. But in 1992, Pope John Paul II, in humility, admitted that those leaders were not only wrong but also were wrong in not allowing the growing scientific evidence to influence how they interpreted Scripture. Quoting Saint Augustine, Pope John Paul further declared that the true meaning of Scripture is never opposed to the hard evidence. In fact, he said, it is not the meaning of Scripture itself which is opposed to truth but the meaning people want to give it.**

Blind faith. We can wear it as a badge of honor all we want, but it is still blind—based on nothing . . . absolutely nothing. I mentioned earlier in this letter that believing by faith blindly makes it impossible to challenge the content of that faith. Where does one go with the conversation? There is no evidence—and no logic—to appeal to. It's a dead end. Blind faith is at best an emotional crutch. At worst, it can be dangerous—leading to an idolatry of one's own imagined truth, thereby exchanging the truths of God—and life—for lies.

Hon, I've never wanted my faith to be blind. If faith were to be blind, wouldn't we be stuck? For how do we discern the difference between divine inspiration and human inane imagination? Between today's inspired prophets of the God who is actually there and our modern delusional "witch doctors" of the gods who are not there?

Unfortunately, religion and politics are among the top "ink-blots" out there. Whether church leader or laity; whether priest, minister, theologian, or New Age spiritualist; whether Catholic

---

*If interested in my other thoughts about modern idolatry and blind faith, please go to the topic entitled "Blind Faith" at my website www.peakperformance discipleship.com.

**Pope John Paul II, "Faith Can Never Conflict with Reason." Address to the Pontifical Academy of Sciences, October 31, 1992. *L'Osservatore Romano*, no. 44 (1264), November 4, 1992.

or Protestant; whether liberal or conservative, you can easily project whatever you want to believe into these two arenas. Physics taught me to not be easily impressed with opinion—whether *my own* or someone else's—especially opinion without any real evidence. And I'm certainly not impressed with opinions without evidence about the very God of the universe. So right or wrong, both as a young man and now, I cannot live my life in blind faith. I just can't.

Seeing Is Believing

Moving into my sophomore year at Clarkson, besides nervously hoping that my newfound faith in Jesus wasn't blind, I was also banking on my earnest commitment to science not being blind either. Interestingly, through physics, I was learning that rigorous science stands on eyewitness accounts—just like my faith stood on eyewitness accounts.

Whether repeating arduous experiments or making meticulous observations, like in astronomy, we have to use witnesses in science. With enough good training, anyone can be a witness. That's the power of science. For example, anyone can drop a ball to the ground and measure its acceleration—a fundamental experiment in the physics of motion—and get more or less the same results as anyone else. I did that in my high school physics lab. Or again, with training, anyone can track the paths of the stars revolving around the Milky Way's black hole in the center of our galaxy—and compare the results to what others saw. In science, witnesses cross-check witnesses. In doing so, they hold one another accountable. They have to.

I knew the obvious as a young man however. The story of Jesus—including his murder and coming back to life—could not be repeated in a lab. Nor could we repeat an event like the assassination of Abraham Lincoln in order to analyze it. Jesus' death and resurrection, and Lincoln's killing, happened once and only once. That's always bothered me about the study of history. You can never repeat events to analyze them. Still, to get the story about Jesus or Lincoln, we rely on various eyewitness reports like we do in astronomy. We then collect and cross-check them. If they agree enough, we tend to believe we have the truth. We then craft a narrative that best tells that story, like the book *Killing Lincoln* or one of the Gospels.

For me, since college, my faith stands on various eyewitness accounts—accounts which more or less agree with one another on

what happened to Jesus. You can certainly call into question my judgment to *trust* their testimony; I myself call my judgment into question.
But eyewitnesses I have. My trust in Jesus arises from my trust in
them. In fact, my trust in those eyewitnesses *is* my trust in Jesus—
because there is no Jesus apart from their story. In that way, Jesus
and the apostles are one. I know of no other Jesus than the one they
wrote about.

The idea that Jesus and the apostles are one is not as odd as it
may first seem.

As much as I've longed for such an experience, I've never been to the
moon. And obviously have no hope of ever getting there. Yet, what I do
know about our moon—that is, the detailed story I believe about it—is
from what the astronauts have told us as well as what the scientists have
learned from the rocks they brought back. That story is *their* eyewitness
testimony. My trust in these people *is* my trust in what I believe about the
moon; I have little knowledge of the moon apart from their story. I've
never studied the moon's surface or the rocks brought back home by the
astronauts. So I know of no other moon than the one they've told us about.
Their "moon story" is *my* moon story.

The same is true for Abraham Lincoln. The story any of us
believe about Lincoln is the story put together from the eyewitness
reports. Their "Lincoln story" is our Lincoln story.

The same thing is true for Jesus. The story I believe about Jesus
is the story put together in the Gospels from eyewitness reports.
The difference is that in the twenty-first century, it is easy to believe
the eyewitness accounts of Lincoln's murder. And, for most people—
though interestingly, not all—it's easy to believe the astronauts' story
about the moon. It is quite another thing to believe the story about
a dead man coming back to life.

That's why, as already noted, innumerable modern theologians
do not believe the Jesus story. Coming back from the dead is a bridge
too far. *So they no longer trust the eyewitnesses.* The apostles' story is
no longer their story. Not anymore. I mention modern theologians
again because I've learned that trusting the eyewitnesses has been so
controversial among church leaders that denominations have split
over it. Understandably, theologians didn't want to give up their
faith—faith they've held near and dear for most of their lives—
though giving it up would be reasonable if they no longer believed
the story.

After declaring all miracles mythical—and the eyewitnesses as not trustworthy—many theologians chose to search for the "real Jesus." The real Jesus, they thought, was "hidden" behind the myth. No one who studies history questions that Jesus was a real historical figure. He did indeed live. People can read the popular book *Killing Jesus* to get some sense of the evidence. The question is: Who was he, really? Who was he behind the Gospels made up to convince us he was God?

This worldwide effort has been called "The Quest for the Historical Jesus." In fact, there was a book written with just that title. This gives you another glimpse at just how much the controversial eyewitness reports repulsed theologians, while at the same time, revealing how much Jesus intrigued them. It shows how far they were willing to go to try to create a more palatable Jesus they could hang on to. Many thoughtful theologians have been upset with this movement, however. One noted that the real Jesus they ended up "discovering" was, not surprisingly, a Jesus who looked just like them.*

Why? Because they had little evidence for the Jesus they were making up.

Like the wayward Israelites, in their quest for the real Jesus, these theologians ended up creating their own golden calf. A theological golden calf. A "golden-calf" Jesus. They crafted it from their own creative imaginations—a projected Jesus—a made-up Jesus not based on evidence. While debunking the gospel writers' Jesus as mythical, they created their own mythical Jesus. Then, they imposed their "idol" back onto the Gospels.

It would have been more honest—to themselves as well as others—if they had just admitted that because they no longer trusted the eyewitness reports, for them the Christian God simply did not exist. Instead, they made stuff up and taught young seminarians the stuff they made up as if it were truth. Those seminarians became pastors who then passed those fabrications on to their congregants. One pastor I know, who is a good friend, has done just that. He told me Jesus died as an example of love, but that's it. Of course, none of the miracles happened. And Jesus never came back to life—though

---

*Dr. Luke Timothy Johnson, "Introduction," *Jesus and the Gospels* (Chantilly, Virginia: The Teaching Company, 2004), DVD.

the story is a touching and commanding narrative. One time, he noted to me: "Nobody knows what really happened back then." In the end, for him, and for so many church leaders across the world, Jesus became a kind of spiritual social worker—not the Son of God who came back from the dead.

You and I have never talked about it, so I don't really know how aware you are of this worldwide effort to turn the Jesus story into fiction. I certainly knew nothing of it at Clarkson at age nineteen. Nor did I have any training to articulate any of this. I was so young and uninformed. Still, I did wrestle with the very same issue in my own way: Were the miracle stories all fabricated, intended to be only spiritual metaphors? Like I said already, however, I had no use for metaphors. A psychologized Jesus—a Jesus who really could do nothing about the tough realities of what I grew up with—would have been a useless Jesus.

So I trusted the Jesus story. But I trusted it as I trusted the Lincoln story and the moon story: seeing through the eyes of the witnesses. For me, Hon, biblical faith has never been blind. Not then. Not now. It hasn't been precisely because the risen Jesus was not what the apostles *believed* by faith. And it's not what they believed by *blind* faith. Rather, the risen Jesus is what they *saw* with their own eyes. Right or wrong, I ended up trusting their eyes. Their Jesus story became my Jesus story.

Rediscovering Church

Living Water

This small band of spiritual innovators were two down-to-earth university professors and their gracious wives who were university administrators; a dedicated family doctor and his family; a large blended family whose parents were high school teachers; a good-humored truck mechanic and his family; and a young, vivacious elementary school teacher whose husband was a graduate student of engineering at Clarkson. Several of us eager undergraduate students joined them in the spiritual venture—and they were more than happy to have us.

So started Koinonia church—*koinonia* being a Greek word meaning "fellowship." Like my tiny band of invigorated spiritual innovators at Aquinas, these half a dozen "townie" families were deeply concerned with what they called the "deadness" of their local churches. They had brought their sober concerns to their leadership—to no avail. In their words, the leadership "just didn't get it." These visionary families believed that community—somehow—had to become deeper, richer . . . more alive. And given that Potsdam was a very small college town in the most northern part of New York, with Clarkson on one side and the state university on the other, they couldn't understand why the institutional churches were not enthusiastically reaching out to the students. They were not befriending them. Nor did they talk to them about the Jesus story. But, these families thought, what better time to reach out than when young adults are trying to find their way as they leave home—your mom and I among them. So they met for prayer and Bible study while making it a point to connect with us students, even graciously inviting us into their homes. Dick and Mary, the high school teachers with the large blended family, embraced me and several others.

I loved working on Dick and Mary's small farm about ten miles outside Potsdam—and to this day I love the physical labor of working the land. I love to sweat. I love to get dirty. I love the immediate reward of physically working with my hands. When you move a large, stubborn rock—it's moved. When you feed the ornery pigs—they're fed. When you plow the mostly clay field, every foot of dirt the tractor turns is now turned. I simply love being close to the earth. My guess is that it is an extension of my early, deep bond with Mother Nature. But that love of working the land was no doubt fed by my identification with your grandfather's love of manual labor and tending to our family garden with your grandmother. Whatever the reasons, I have always loved to work with my hands and nature's rich soil.

And you know your mom. She's frontier material. Growing up in the Mohawk Valley of New York on Mammy's farm, she would have loved a farmette. We seriously toyed with buying one when we were looking for our first house. If we could have afforded it at the time, we might have, though there were other factors that influenced our decision, like being close to both our jobs so we could have more time with you guys growing up. Over the years, I've had fantasies of combining depth therapy with farm labor to help troubled teens— teens who could use manual labor and structured discipline as well as rich dialogue about who they are in order to build character. But, needless to say, given my disabilities, that hasn't—and won't— ever happen. But that fantasy no doubt played off my transformative experiences working on Dick and Mary's land.

I got acquainted with these two midlife teachers through Koinonia's Bible study, though I really got to know them by helping them strip down their old rustic farmhouse. We gutted the interior, making way for the reconstruction. They slept in tents—including through the harsh North Country winter—until the house was far enough along to move into. While both were dedicated high school teachers, they really looked forward to farming the land to supply some of their family's needs. Several of us students routinely showed up to help pull down old walls and put up new ones.

Once Dick and Mary moved in, we'd sit around the dinner table together after a hard day's labor, talking and laughing and getting to know one another. Dick asked probing questions of us—questions that people don't normally ask in polite company. But then he'd turn the scope on himself, talking about his own difficult childhood; his and Mary's previously failed marriages; the growing pangs of their new marriage together; how they became such self-consciously intentional Christians; and their present struggles in growing in maturity. While Charlie and I did indeed have rich conversations, I was, in the words of C. S. Lewis, "surprised by joy" at the quality and range of soul-baring conversations of this vibrant midlife couple. I never knew people could—or actually did—talk that way.

I was always more than welcome in their home, as were so many others. It was the North Country; they never locked their doors. We were always free to just walk in, work in the field, or join them for dinner. Sometimes, I'd help Mary prepare dinner—something I never recall doing with my own mother. In stark contrast to my mother, it was a rich encounter with this late thirtysomething woman. We'd always gab while preparing dinner, and, having a great sense of humor, Mary was delightful to talk with. Given the times back then, she and Dick wrestled with their roles as husband and wife. Mary told me all about it, not breaking any sanctity of privacy between her and her new husband, but with his full support that I might simply learn from her. Besides, for them, such ruthlessly honest conversations were a way of sharing "truth in love" in getting to know one another. They simply called it "fellowship."

At that period of our cultural history, the feminist movement, titled women's liberation or "women's lib," had moved into its second wave in the sixties and seventies. This wave bluntly addressed women's roles in the home and workplace, as well as their sexuality. This movement challenged Mary's views of men and women. It made her soberly question her role as a wife. At the time, I was writing a paper on feminism for a Psychology of the Sexes class—and Mary agreed to let me interview her, which gave me further insight into her struggles as a woman.

Since that college course, I have wondered if the physical differences between the sexes made any psychological differences. Still, I've also always believed that men and women should treat each other equally—while embracing differences. Certainly, the culture your mom and I grew up in during the fifties and sixties formed our psychology and the general direction of our lives. It molded the professional career options for your mom, which was key in her choice of becoming a teacher. It also shaped our roles together in your mom being a stay-at-home mom for the early years of parenting. Yet, within those cultural contours, we chose our roles mostly based on our abilities and interests—not on gender. With your mom having grown up on Mammy's farm and her father having been a truck driver, she is quite comfortable driving a tractor or a truck—roles that in our generation, were considered more "male." When we moved, she drove the U-Haul truck. Not only did I not care, but such skills and interests were simply part of my attraction to her. So we've always had an egalitarian relationship. We've pooled our wisdom—and ignorance. We've shared whatever skills we had to make joint decisions and create a life together. This was for me, I think, an extension of your grandfather's belief that all people are created equal.

But poor Mary. She was in transition with two sides of her in conflict. One side was a traditionalist, believing that the man should be the "head of the house" and the final decision-maker. Her other side, however . . . One evening while preparing dinner, Mary was pulling the innards out of the bird we had killed earlier. She mumbled, "I wonder if this is a chicken or rooster." When she realized she had two egg-shaped organs in her hand, the broadest smile burst onto her face as she declared, "I guess it's a rooster. Here's one for women's lib!" That's what Mary *really* thought.

Benny—whom you met a few years ago, and your mom and I were thrilled to see after so many—would often join me in my ten-mile drive to the farm under the pretext of getting away to study. Inevitably, we'd end up around the stone fireplace chatting for hours with Dick and Mary. Other times, Dick and Mary would just go to bed, leaving Benny and me to our books. The fact is, we'd just lie in front of the fireplace, books piled up to one side, yakking away about life—our shared faith in Jesus, bowling, girls, and cars. Or lie in silence, mesmerized by the dancing flames.

Ben and I had strong mutual respect and earned each other's trust along the way—from cars to girls. Our junior year, Benny's father bought him a car—a new Mercury Cougar, I believe. Benny was an only child and tended to be spoiled that way. (And yes, I was a bit envious.) The day he got it, he let me open her up on the back roads in the North Country's near pitch blackness of her starlit night sky.

Loved the moment. We were both careful drivers. But we both did like some modest speed, and driving together was a fun alchemy. On our way to an Inter-Varsity Christian Fellowship conference held at Middlebury College in Vermont—where I met your mom—Benny and I raced some good friends. On one long straight stretch—it may have been Route 87, but I'm not sure—we easily reached a speed of about a 115 miles per hour, which I barely noticed until we navigated a slight curve. Of course, that was nothing compared to your mom's recent experience of entering the curve on the Pocono Raceway at about a 155 miles per hour. Still, we "won" our brief race—only because the other driver didn't feel comfortable pushing the needle beyond that point. He was wise. I am keenly aware that careful or not, skilled or not, youth is indeed wasted on the young.

Benny's father had also gotten him a motorboat—also new— which certainly wasn't wasted on Ben. Like his car, Benny "wore" his boat like a glove. He'd work that throttle doing tight figure eights among other maneuvers that made it feel like we were on an amusement park ride. He knew how to take that boat to its edge— but never foolishly further. And he was an excellent skier, having competed in tournament slalom skiing, another reason for the new boat. It was Ben who introduced me to skiing. The first time out, he took me back over his wake without having instructed me how to maneuver. I flexed my knees trying to keep my balance, but foolishly found myself trying to steer by turning the rope I had in my hands. Needless to say, I fell in, but then found myself wondering why I wasn't coming back up to the surface. I had forgotten to let go of the rope . . . duh.

Around the flickering flames, Ben and I navigated life, including our relationships with your mom. Your mom and I met in a Bible study at that conference, and after the study, found ourselves skipping down a dirt road with our arms around each other's waist. After we stopped skipping, we didn't drop our arms. And so it began. Once I started going out with her, with a bit of a smirk on his face, Ben expressed a genuine, albeit competitive, interest in dating her as well. I made it clear to him that I had begun dating her first—and he'd have to wait. And he did. He had already gone out with my previous girlfriend after we had broken up, so maybe he thought he had a good shot waiting for me and Mom to break up. I don't know. Nevertheless, he genuinely respected my "request." We remained good friends, and, as they say, the rest is history. I have missed Benny and the dancing flames a great deal.

Time after time, like an insatiably thirsty man having found an oasis with cool, quenching waters, I'd eagerly drive out to the farmette. This dynamic midlife couple—and their pastoral setting—became home for several years. Whether around their long dinner table or their rustic stone fireplace, talking with them fed my longings to connect with others . . . my longings for family. Their simple country place carried the ineffably satisfying mix of being snuggled in Mother Nature's bosom combined with emotionally nourishing conversations "in the name of Jesus." Faith, intimacy, and nature were all rolled into one. Being there gave me an unforgettable reference point for the quality of conversations and ambiance that I'd value for a lifetime.

The sweet fellowship of this most engaging couple was always laced with humble self-analysis. Dick's reflections were even ruthless. Looking squarely at themselves was a central part of their persistent discipleship. In spite of their fears—and they had many—they chose to look into life's mirror. While facing themselves was not easy, and, at times, a most fearful prospect, they nevertheless considered it part of life's adventure. They never said that; they always modeled it. They showed me the difference between "fun" and "adventure." For Dick especially, dealing with life always created an "edge." Life carried risk. To live, you had to risk. You had to go to the edge. Doing so, however, stirred fear. But fear was part of the adventure. Their modeling of life "in Christ" as an adventure—an adventure to be lived with passion—fed into my already existing style of using fear to my advantage. Whether rocking my head back and forth as a little guy in my attic prison in my struggle to remain sane; or managing the low-level primal nervousness of handling a gopher snake in my early teens; or standing up to an abusive father; or leaving the Catholic Church; or grappling with the Jesus story; or creating a bit of an edge with my good friend Ben; or facing my trauma in my twenties and beyond; or building a life with your mom when intimacy still frightened me—life was an adventure. Fear made it so. For this dear couple, like most of the great saints of the church over the centuries, taking the risk to look at themselves was central to that venture.

I bought in, Kid. Both personally and professionally, I turned their discipleship into my way of life.

Living Organism

Dick and Mary, as well as the others who founded Koinonia, regularly searched Scripture to rediscover "church."* They had stepped out of the institutional church. Now they wanted to get a fresh take on it all. This venture just added to my excitement. Under the "townies'" leadership, we were learning the sharp distinction between the church as an organization—an institution—and the church as a living organism. We researched what it meant to follow Jesus in community—what "church" could be. In that effort, we studied the early church in the book of Acts as well as a few of the letters written by the apostles to help guide us.

Several of us thought of Pastor John as a Paul Bunyan. It wasn't his modest stature. It was in the way he trimmed his beard, in the strength of his lower jaw, along with his down-to-earth manner and his willingness to do physical labor. John worked part-time cleaning the furnaces of folks in the North Country to add to his modest income that the few families under his leadership were able to scrape together to hire him. He and his wife didn't mind the harsh winters. Later, when they got their own little ranch home, John would chop wood for the stove. If I was there at the right time, I'd help load it for the tough winter months ahead—winters with temperatures down to seventy below zero with the wind chill. When it was that bitter cold, I would lift my Tank's hood, take off the air filter, and spray ether into her carburetor—knowing I had only one shot to start her. John and Jane were tough young people who quickly grew to love the North Country. And we all loved John and Jane. They were young people of impeccable integrity and hard work, reminding me of your uncle Herb—which was part of my draw to this visionary young minister.

---

*I am referring to the church universal, not the Catholic Church as an institution.

In his midtwenties, John came to lead us. He had graduated from Trinity Evangelical Seminary, which both then and now is nationally known and well respected. Like Trinity, he was solidly biblical in his thinking; he himself had come to trust the eyewitness reports. He was gently humble, always shaping his beliefs by a careful study of Scripture. Whenever he preached, he explained the Bible passage clearly rather than using it as a springboard for whatever he wanted to believe and promulgate. Without question, every time he preached, we learned about Jesus. Or how we could build community. Or how we could grow in character.

While at Clarkson, Koinonia moved from a movie theatre to a local church to a house. Once again, I helped tear down old walls to build new ones. The graduate student of engineering and I often worked together tearing the walls down, and foolishly, never wore masks. We'd end up hanging our heads out the window heaving up the thick black dust we inhaled and momentarily gasping for fresh air. It was all part of the fun.

Though himself young, Pastor John carried a passionate and specific vision for this tiny church. He strengthened the home Bible studies. He trained his lay leadership, mobilizing them to be decision makers. He even trained his leadership to hold him accountable to them. What humility. Under his leadership, this small band of spiritual innovators grew into a large community—large for the North Country. We experienced what church was really meant to be. He modeled how to use our gifts to love one another through thick and thin. In this little community, I came to understand what the apostle Paul declared, "Together you are the body of Christ, and each one of you is a part of that body" (1 Cor. 12:27, NCV). The tender intimacy among us stirred great joy in me. This band of visionaries modeled for me what "church"—whether Catholic or Protestant—was, or should be, all about.

Pastor John also carried a vision for several of us students. He set up a training program to help us study the Bible. He equipped us to think through our faith and how to dialogue with our campus culture. As we sat around his breakfast table, we'd freely discuss our reactions and challenges to campus life. We got to ask any and all questions we needed to ask. Pastor John didn't preach at us. He helped us talk about ourselves and the challenges of faith as students.

Talking—and learning to be independent thinkers of our faith—
were tied together around that early morning breakfast table.

This twentysomething man also carried a vision for me
personally—though being young and naïve, I hadn't realized it at the
time. He believed in me long before I did. Pastor John nurtured my
leadership potential before I was self-aware enough to even think of
myself that way. Beyond that discipleship training program, he set up
preaching opportunities for me that set the drumbeat for life in my
own teaching in the church. I found out later that he had greased the
skids for my leadership in Inter-Varsity Christian Fellowship. Our
IV chapter was a joint chapter of the State University and Clarkson
that had grown to well over a hundred. Pastor John's discipleship
through dialogue and the superb training offered by the IV staff
equipped me well. I was voted in as president of the joint chapter of
IV my senior year. By year's end, I was honored by my peers from
Clarkson's Phalanx Honor Society with an award for "outstanding
leadership in extracurricular activities as president of Inter-Varsity
Christian Fellowship"—all because of this passionate pastor's vision,
belief, and investment in me. Frankly, I was too young, dumb, and
lost otherwise. Those experiences emerging from this young pastor's
vision paved the way for my future leadership in the church.

If it isn't obvious, Kristen, I am immeasurably indebted to and
very grateful for Dick and Mary, for the Koinonia fellowship, and
for Pastor John and his most gentle wife, Jane.

Thrown into the New Age

Pastor John asked me if I wanted to be baptized.

I was only an infant when the priest baptized me into the Catholic faith. Right or wrong, I no longer believed that infant baptism "cleansed mortal sin from my soul." That's the phrase I recall being taught about infant baptism as a kid. I didn't know what it really meant until seminary. I had long rejected it anyway as a high school kid. Given that the "hook" had been set—and I now chose to believe the Jesus story—I wanted to be baptized. Unlike my infancy, I liked the idea of my being aware of my own baptism. It would symbolize that following Jesus was *my* decision and nobody else's. One could say that this was like a confirmation ceremony. It was a come-of-age, self-conscious affirmation of the Christian faith already delivered to me through my Catholic upbringing. And in a sense, it was. After all, I hadn't overturned belief in the central storyline. Still, as a college kid, it didn't feel like a reaffirmation of the faith my parents delivered to me. It felt like a new affirmation of a newfound faith in a newly discovered Jesus. So I wanted to be baptized.

Pastor wanted to make sure I was prepared. So he met with me to go over how I now really thought of my faith, just like we do in our Presbyterian church as part of the Inquirer's process. He then explained that instead of sprinkling water on my head like they did to me as an infant, he'd baptize me by dunking me in the Racquette River—which I thought would be pretty cool. He also gave me a little booklet on how the Holy Spirit worked. This booklet explained that, from what the Bible said, the Spirit could empower someone for living a life of faith by "baptizing" or "filling" him. As was his style, the pastor casually suggested I read it over, and that it might be something I'd like to pray about. After our meeting, I read the booklet, but really didn't understand it. According to the author, the Spirit could "fill" a person, even giving him or her the "gift of tongues." This gift could be the skill of speaking a foreign language or just making strange sounds. Bizarre. How could you speak a foreign language you never learned? Either way, it was supposed to be something that helped one's faith. I really had no idea what this little booklet was talking about since I had never seen this baptism with the Spirit or the gift of tongues. I was clueless.

The Koinonia community gathered around us students at the edge of the Racquette River. Karen, a bright and engaging first year student from SUNY, and Ed, a freshman engineering student from Clarkson who was also my fraternity brother, were to be baptized too. Pete, a "non-techie" freshman from SUNY, still wasn't sure what he believed. But he joined us to celebrate our baptisms; I was glad he did. Pastor John waded out into the waist-high, quietly moving water. Turning to us, he briefly explained the meaning of baptism. Pastor then invited me out to join him. He put one hand on my chest and the other under my back while I held onto his arm. Right before he dunked me under, he cited the apostle Paul's words that I was now being buried with Jesus by baptism into his death—represented by going under water—so that I could be joined with him in his coming back to life—rising up out of the water. Given that I now believed for myself that Jesus had come back to life, my adult baptism really felt meaningful. After Pastor John baptized us, we hugged one another, and the Koinonia families hugged us as well with a genuine sense of joy that we had chosen to follow Jesus. They really cared about us young people. Karen, Tom, and Pete later met up with John, Jane, and me at the pastor's home to pray.

Tom, the engineering grad student with whom I tore down many a wall, had quickly become an older brother to me. Like your uncle Herb, he was a sincere young man with a strong work ethic. He had a deep bass voice and tended to speak with a careful conviction that seemed to go beyond his years. Later, when I dated your mom, she got to know Tom and his wife as well. We had such respect for these two fine people that your mom and I asked them—and they agreed—to be your legal guardians should she and I die at the same time. We knew they'd bring you up in the faith we had come to hold dear. And we trusted that their solid character would become yours. Because Tom was like an older brother to me, I was grateful that he had eagerly come to witness my baptism.

The six of us knelt quietly in a circle on the pastor's living room floor. Pastor John was next to me on my left, his wife Jane and Karen next to him, and Pete to my right, with Tom directly across from me. After a short time of prayerful silence, Pastor John began to pray out loud. But it sounded like gibberish; it was all nonsense to me. I opened my eyes to watch him for a moment, thinking this was pretty weird. I first wondered, and then figured, that John must be "speaking in tongues" like the booklet had mentioned. I closed my eyes again, thinking I'd ask him about it later. As soon as I closed my eyes, out of the blue—and in an instant—an invisible force threw me to the floor. It was sudden and without warning. It was as if a jolt of electricity had hit me—like the jolt I got as a teen when my hand touched the bare wire of the kitchen appliance. I have no memory of the trip to the dining area after the electrical jolt and I have no memory of the trip to the floor after being hit by this spiritual jolt. In that moment, an intense surge of love coursed through me. It was focused and strong—not some gently sweeping diffuse sense of being cared for. Forgive the analogy, Hon, but it's the only one that will do: This moment was like the most intense sexual encounter I could have ever had with your mom multiplied a hundred fold—several hundred fold, actually—without the physical desire. It was literally an orgasmic surge of love that shook my entire body. I was thoroughly flooded with joy. The intensity of these emotions requires me to use the word "ecstatic."

In the wake of this surge, I actually wept with the overpowering feeling of God's love. Imagine weeping because you feel loved. Incredible. It stood in stark contrast to my entire childhood experience of my mother's love as duty—absolutely devoid of any positive feeling. Needless to say, this experience imprinted me for life. I remember it like it was yesterday. It didn't scare me at all. You'd think it would. After all, it was a profound mind-altering experience. Instead, it filled me with joy. It was joy beyond anything I could ever have imagined—and it simply cascaded for the remaining hours of the afternoon and evening.

As Tom picked me up from the floor, the electric charge of God's love continued to course through my body. With tears streaming down my cheeks, Tom hugged me as we knelt there. I just kept saying over and over, "God loves me . . . God loves me . . . God loves me." And Tom kept saying, "Yes, he does . . . yes, he does . . . yes, he does."

Still reeling from the overwhelmingly visceral sense of God's presence, and filled with joy beyond words, I pulled back from Tom's hug to find that Karen had experienced the exact same thing. Pastor John and the others said that she and I had hit the floor at the same time. Yet no one had touched us. In fact, Karen had been kneeling across from me in our little circle, so we had not touched each other in any way and had not even been looking at each other. Karen also wept with the ecstatic feeling of the love of God. Pete, however, who hadn't been sure about Jesus, did not experience this energy-force. He knelt there as a bystander, like the others. I felt bad for him. But for me, that moment of being literally thrown into the new age of God's love was unparalleled by any other experience in my life— before or since. Had I really encountered the Spirit of God? If not, then what the heck had happened to me . . . and Karen?

At the time, it was without question that we had just encountered the Spirit of Jesus. Pastor John told me that he and Jane and Tom had previously experienced the same thing. I hadn't known that. He said his guess was that this is why the disciples were so energized, so bold, and so transformed after the Spirit came to them on Pentecost. I now could see why. It was as if Karen and I were intoxicated, but intoxicated with the love of God—just like the disciples after the Spirit filled them on Pentecost. In fact, those gathered around the disciples at Pentecost actually murmured that they were drunk. The disciples retorted that they weren't intoxicated, but filled with the Spirit. I now understood Pentecost.

If all the symbols and Gothic architecture wrapped around the Mass once felt like a spiritual portal into some transcendent realm, then the pastor's living room had become a hole ripped into the universe's space-time continuum transporting us into the glorious presence of God. It reminded me of Moses' divine encounter where he was so charged up he had to cover his face with a veil to hide the "glow." Karen and I glowed as if we were lovers in love—not with each other but with God. Tom said they could've hooked wires up to our hands to light up New York City.

If this intense experience was really a taste of what the disciples experienced at Pentecost—right after having spent over a month with the risen Jesus!—no wonder they transformed the world with the message that Jesus was alive. To have talked with him at length after having been crucified, then to have experienced the energy-force of this new age at Pentecost, would have been a double whammy to seal their faith. How could they not have trusted their own five senses? How could they ever have contained themselves? They couldn't . . . and didn't. That's why they went everywhere they could proclaiming that this Jesus whom the Romans had crucified had come back to life—and they were witnesses of it. That is why they could go out with such boldness, even dying for the story. At the tender age of eighteen, I understood.

Obviously, I've never seen the risen Jesus. So over the decades, as one who so deeply values evidence, I've tried to discern some other explanation for what happened to Karen and me. But to this day, I cannot write off what we experienced as some group-generated, hyperemotional experience or self-induced trance state. It just never happened that way. So, if not that, then what? Nevertheless, that day I knew. I knew I had encountered the Spirit of the living God. I knew that Jesus was alive . . . somewhere.

The Kingdom of God

As Karen and I were settling down a bit—though admittedly not much—Pastor John asked if we had received the gift of tongues. I had no idea; neither did Karen. But, believe it or not, in our brief pauses between sentences, our tongues were flapping around as if driven by some inner energy trying to find its way out our mouths. Once again, it wasn't unnerving. It didn't feel like we were being controlled by some alien force. The tongue simply felt very oddly energized, and we could stop its movement voluntarily. This energy poured through us as we continued to feel the cascading joy. We felt beyond safe through it all—though admittedly, the whole thing was bizarre . . . to say the least. After asking his question and then seeing our mouths, John said with a smile, "I guess you did!"

That night, Karen and I went with John and Jane and a few others to one of the larger churches in the North Country to share what had happened to us. That entire night Karen and I were lit up like Christmas trees at Rockefeller Center—and could barely contain our excitement. As important as having your uncle Herb as my confirmation sponsor was to me—and it was—this encounter with the Spirit of God became my real "confirmation." No ritual, no pomp and ceremony, no medieval garb, but a dynamic encounter with the Spirit of the living Jesus. While the eyewitness reports were *the* singular hook that moved me from magic to miracle, that dramatic encounter with the Spirit of Jesus drove those reports deep into my psyche and sealed them in emotionally—and permanently. In its wake, I had even more drive to study the Jesus story—and that is one understatement.

Our little church community knew very well what the apostle Peter had said on Pentecost: the miracles were signs that Jesus was from God. But we all sensed that there was something more to those miracles.

For us, the new age ushered in by the Spirit had become real. Really real. Under Pastor John's leadership, the story of the early church—the story beyond Jesus coming back to life and "ascending into heaven"—came alive. Our journey seemed to parallel the early disciples' journey; some of the things that had happened in the early church seemed to be happening to us. So our new age community pondered one key question: What really could we expect God to do among us? Could we expect *all* the same things that had happened in the book of Acts and seemed to have happened in the church communities at Corinth and Galatia—including what we thought were miracles of healing? And just why had such miracles happened? After all, not everyone got healed of everything.

I reread the miracle stories in the Gospels. Given my longings to see your grandfather walk—let alone throw the football—one miracle especially captured my attention:

> A few days later, when Jesus came back to Capernaum, the news spread that he was at home. Many people gathered together so that there was no room in the house, not even outside the door. And Jesus was teaching them God's message. Four people came, carrying a paralyzed man. Since they could not get to Jesus because of the crowd, they dug a hole in the roof right above where he was speaking. When they got through, they lowered the mat with the paralyzed man on it. When Jesus saw the faith of these people, he said to the paralyzed man, "Young man, your sins are forgiven."
>
> Some of the teachers of the law were sitting there, thinking to themselves, "Why does this man say things like that? He is speaking as if he were God. Only God can forgive sins."
>
> Jesus knew immediately what these teachers of the law were thinking. So he said to them, "Why are you thinking these things? Which is easier: to tell this paralyzed man, 'Your sins are forgiven,' or to tell him, 'Stand up. Take your mat and walk'? But I will prove to you that the Son of Man has authority on earth to forgive sins." So Jesus said to the paralyzed man, "I tell you, stand up, take your mat, and go home." Immediately the paralyzed man stood up, took his mat, and walked out while everyone was watching him. (Mark 2:1–12a, NCV)

Rereading this eyewitness report of the paralyzed man's liberation, I choked up—and I still get choked up reading it.

It's loaded with meaning for me. As I sat in my dorm room meditating on this vignette, I hoped for that man's story to become my dad's story. Jesus' setting that man free stirred memories of all the wheelchairs and crutches I had seen hanging on St. Anne's Cathedral wall. No matter what my father had been to me, I longed for his liberation from disability—and was deeply saddened that Jesus had not chosen to set him free.

Jesus confronted the teachers of the law: "Why are you thinking these things? Which is easier: to tell this paralyzed man, 'Your sins are forgiven,' or to tell him, 'Stand up. Take your mat and walk'?" Then Jesus simply told the paralytic to get up and walk. No incantations. No frenzy. Just get up and walk. And he did. That put real muscle behind saying, "I forgive you." It didn't matter to Jesus which one he did; he had the power to do both. Seemed to me that if Jesus were God, then he'd be able to do just that—say anything he wanted to and have it be so. But I doubted myself. I thought again that maybe my conditioning set me up to believe that kind of magic. After all, I had an entire childhood of witnessing a priest speak his words and turning bread into Jesus' body—and witnessing it almost daily. Beyond that, though I didn't think of it at the time, my father spoke his words into my psychic universe—like jewelry is uncomfortable and golf is boring—and they were so.

As a young man continuing to find his way with his emerging faith, it sank in further that Jesus speaking his words was not the same as the priest speaking his. The priest's words transformed the wafer into the literal body of Jesus. Yet one could never see—*physically see*—the body of Jesus in that host. You could only believe in that transformation by utterly blind faith. But, right or wrong, my deep passion was to have any and all of my beliefs stand on evidence—not blindness. When Jesus spoke his words, you could see and hear the results. Your five senses told you this was real. Jesus spoke and this man got up and walked around for the whole town to see. For that town—and for me—seeing was believing.

So now I doubted myself less. If God were God (if Jesus were God), then he should be able to say anything he wanted, like "Let there be light!" or "Stand up—take your mat and walk" and have it be so. And he did. They all saw it. The apostles saw it.

I found I wasn't alone in thinking this way. Jesus' authority to speak and have it be so made sense even to a Roman soldier, a

non-Jew (a Gentile), and a centurion with his own authority over a
hundred men:

> There was an army officer who had a servant who was very
> important to him. The servant was so sick he was nearly dead.
> When the officer heard about Jesus, he sent some Jewish
> elders to him to ask Jesus to come and heal his servant. The
> men went to Jesus and begged him, saying, "This officer is
> worthy of your help. He loves our people, and he built us a
> synagogue."
>
> So Jesus went with the men. He was getting near the offi-
> cer's house when the officer sent friends to say, "Lord, don't
> trouble yourself, because I am not worthy to have you come
> into my house. That is why I did not come to you myself. But
> you only need to command it, and my servant will be healed. I,
> too, am a man under the authority of others, and I have soldiers
> under my command. I tell one soldier, 'Go,' and he goes. I tell
> another soldier, 'Come,' and he comes. I say to my servant, 'Do
> this,' and my servant does it."
>
> When Jesus heard this, he was amazed. Turning to the
> crowd that was following him, he said, "I tell you, this is the
> greatest faith I have found anywhere, even in Israel."
>
> Those who had been sent to Jesus went back to the
> house where they found the servant in good health. (Luke
> 7:2–10, NCV)

This Roman soldier followed Caesar's orders, keeping the Jews
oppressed. Yet he was kind, and he also knew of Jesus' reputation
as a healer. Though Jesus was a Jew and not a Roman, this soldier
humbly chose to cross lines and ask for his help. As a soldier both
under authority and as one who had authority over others, he knew
how orders worked. All he had to do as a commanding officer was
speak—and it was so. That was his personal experience. That's how
he bridged his world to Jesus' world. The soldier knew intuitively—
deep in his own psyche—that all Jesus had to do was speak, and it
would be so. Why? Because that's the way it was for him. That was
his hook. And so, he trusted Jesus.

But it wasn't just that Jesus spoke and made things happen that
drew me. It was his attitude doing it.

Lazarus died shortly before Jesus went to Jerusalem at festival time, what we now call Palm Sunday. After Jesus first wept, perhaps over the pain the women felt, Jesus raised his head and then gently commanded the others to roll back the large stone. As the stone rolled aside, he ordered Lazarus to come out. Jesus' tears—integrated with his strong command to Lazarus—cued me into his deep motive: *Jesus hated death.*

Jesus seemed to hate many things. He hated corruption. He hated sin. And, along with death, he hated suffering. At every turn, Jesus fought back at an out-of-control world. He fought people's suffering—whether from blindness, paralysis, or hunger. He fought sin and corruption, publicly scolding religious leaders for their hypocrisy. He fought death—and ultimately beat it. It began to click. Miracles were not just signs. They were his works of liberation—the liberation of people from the ravages of sin, suffering, and death. Jesus' ministry was a campaign against human misery. It was an anti-sin, anti-suffering, anti-disease, and anti-death revolution.

The panoramic unfolded. Jesus' mission had nothing to do with conquering Rome—but with conquering sin and death. Jesus' mission had nothing to do with building a geopolitical empire—but with rebuilding his Father's empire of the universe. The story line was indeed one of liberation—not political, but *cosmic* liberation. In the wake of my personal Pentecost, I was getting it. It sank in.

Jesus emerged into my youthful consciousness as the leader of a revolution ushering in his Father's kingdom—the kingdom of God—beating back the powers of sin and death. His passion to set the paralyzed man free, to heal the Roman soldier's servant, and to raise Lazarus back to life—that passion to fight life's nonsense—was my passion. He absolutely hated what I hated. And he fought for what I have always fought for. His ministry was a radically pro-life movement. Wherever there was death, no matter the form, he spoke his word of life. He fought the fight with us—except, as the apostle Paul noted, he was the One with the power to win (1 Cor. 15:24).

I loved it.

The New Age Experience

We were all taken by surprise with the dramatic encounters with the Spirit of Jesus. While many of us had such an experience, not all did. Your mother didn't—although she had been raised a Christian and never really questioned her faith. I don't recall such encounters ever happening during worship services. And, to my knowledge, no one even had a repeat of the encounter. I hadn't. Just once in my lifetime—that was it. Frankly, that's another reason I don't think Karen and I contrived it. If we had, likely we would have unconsciously reproduced it. But we couldn't . . . and didn't.

During prayer meetings, many of us did use the "gift of tongues" to pray out loud. One would speak in tongues and another would "interpret," that is, offer its meaning to the group. Still others would have what some called "a word of instruction," from the Spirit. On one hand, these kinds of intuitive practices made some sense after having been "filled with the Spirit." Yet, on the other hand, given my commitment to hard evidence, these practices were very "squishy" to say the least—with no grounding in anything verifiable. An "interpretation" or "word of instruction," for example, was simply a spontaneous thought that entered my or someone else's mind. Then we'd share it with the group. Not exactly sound evidence for God at work. At the time, I wondered: How do I tell the difference between a thought "from the Spirit" versus my own thoughts—good, bad, or indifferent? As a young man, I didn't have an answer—nor did anyone else. And I still don't. But, at that time, we all believed we had the Spirit within us actively giving us ideas, and our experiences seemed to match that of the church at Corinth:

> So, brothers and sisters, what should you do? When you meet together, one person has a song, and another has a teaching. Another has a new truth from God. Another speaks

in a different language, and another person interprets that language. The purpose of all these things should be to help the church grow strong. (1 Cor. 14:26, NCV)

So we stayed with the practice. Having meetings where we looked to the Spirit to give us interpretations or words of instruction made this new age experience relevant to our daily lives. We were part of the Spirit working in this world—and it was happening right here among us.

But—what about healings? What about our growing liberation from the nonsense of life? Could our little band of followers expect, on occasion, miraculous freedom from diseases or liberation from other problems as well?

Miracles of healing certainly happened in the book of Acts—and those miracles strongly encouraged us. In the earliest expansion of the church chronicled in that book, two apostles, Peter and John, were going to the temple to pray. A man disabled since birth was at the temple gate, begging for money. Peter and John looked at the man—then told him to look at them—and Peter said,

I don't have any silver or gold, but I do have something else I can give you. By the power of Jesus Christ from Nazareth, stand up and walk! (Acts 3:6, NCV)

Instantly, the man's feet and ankles strengthened, and he jumped to his feet and began to walk.

Like Jesus, it seemed that the apostles Peter and John could simply speak a word of liberation into our universe and have it be so. This man then went into the temple with Peter and John, thanking God. The people in the temple who knew this man's history of disability were floored. The apostle Peter wisely used the opportunity. He said to the crowd that had now gathered,

You handed him [Jesus] over to be killed. Pilate decided to let him go free, but you told Pilate you did not want Jesus. You did not want the One who is holy and good but asked Pilate to give you a murderer instead. And so you killed the One who gives life, but God raised him from the dead. We are witnesses to this. (Acts 3:13b-15, NCV; brackets mine)

In his public teaching, Peter over and over hammered home that they were witnesses of Jesus' coming back to life. This was exactly the same case offered by the apostle Paul, the "outsider." And it was the same for the apostle John:

> We write you now about what has always existed, which we have heard, we have seen with our own eyes, we have looked at, and we have touched with our hands. We write to you about the Word that gives life. (1 John 1:1, NCV)

Their experience wasn't spiritual or "mystical"; it was with all five senses. They were eyewitnesses.

With cautious anticipation, our little band of twentieth-century disciples kept wondering: Were such gifts of healing meant for us as well? At nineteen, with my father still alive—and having tasted of this new age—I got my hopes up that Jesus still might heal him. The Koinonia community joined me in fervently praying for him. Yet, once again, Jesus did nothing. I was heartbroken.

Still, I kept on reading the book of Acts. Everywhere the apostles went, healings followed. People brought the sick into the streets, laying them on beds and mats so that the apostle Peter's shadow might fall on some of them as he passed. His shadow!

The apostle Paul had similar liberating power in Jesus' name:

> Some people took handkerchiefs and clothes that Paul had used and put them on the sick. When they did this, the sick were healed and evil spirits left them. (Acts 19:12, NCV)

Incredible. In our eager anticipation in reading Acts as well as the apostles' intriguing letters to the growing churches, these implausible signs of the liberation of the human condition persisted. So, we wondered further: Did the Spirit only work through the apostles in the early church? Or did healings come about through others as well?

The apostle Paul noted many years later to the church at Corinth that the gifts of miracles and healing were two gifts among many in the church. Perhaps, we thought, these gifts were not limited to the apostles:

> Together you are the body of Christ, and each one of you is a part of that body. In the church God has given a place first

to apostles, second to prophets, and third to teachers. Then God has given a place to those who do miracles, those who have *gifts of healing*, those who can help others, those who are able to govern, and those who can speak in different languages. Not all are apostles. Not all are prophets. Not all are teachers. Not all do miracles. Not all have gifts of healing. Not all speak in different languages. Not all interpret those languages. (1 Cor. 12:27–30, NCV; italics mine)

While not everyone had every gift—that's why we needed community—it sure seemed like healings happened in the church at Corinth *without* the apostles being there. And the same thing seemed to be true for the church at Galatia:

Were all your experiences wasted? I hope not! Does God give you the Spirit and work miracles among you because you follow the law? No, he does these things because you heard the Good News and believed it. (Gal. 3:4–5, NCV)

I didn't understand it. No one did. Unlike the churches at Corinth and Galatia, the Spirit brought no miracles to our little church like we had hoped. We prayed for them, but they just didn't happen. Not like then.

Did we misunderstand the Scriptures? Were we trying to create our own golden calf? Don't get me wrong. Many judged, myself included, that they had gotten "answered prayers," where things happened in the natural course of events that they believed—right or wrong—the Lord had something to do with. Admittedly, since all of life is a series of good things and bad things, it's easy to think that good things are answered prayers. Still, when good things happened, we all gave the Lord credit. And there were some good things that we thought might be "miracles of timing."

Right before one of my trips back home to see my dad, I had a mechanic put air shocks on my Tank to deal with the extra weight we were going to pack into the car. The shocks were designed to be wider than normal shocks. Coincidentally, I unwisely had not replaced the cable to my emergency footbrake that had badly rusted and hung by a thread. Entering Rochester, your mom and I had just pulled off the highway onto Dewey Avenue and turned into a gas station. As I coasted in and pressed the brake pedal to come to a complete stop, the brakes failed. I found myself pushing the pedal to the floor with no response. Fortunately, we were moving so slowly we coasted to a complete stop within moments. I got under my Tank to discover that the mechanic had not moved the brake line to accommodate the wider shock. The outer metal covering of the shock had rubbed the brake line up and down the entire trip—and had worn a hole in it. It was at that precise moment when we had coasted to a stop that the final layer of metal broke free, and the brake line dumped the fluid. I shudder to think of what would have happened just one minute earlier on the highway with no emergency brake.

Perhaps that was indeed a miracle of timing; I'll never know. But whether it was or wasn't, Jesus' revolution—and that of the apostles Peter, John, and Paul—was one of obvious miracles, not guesswork. They simply spoke the word, and someone would be instantly healed. Yet, just like during my childhood, I never saw a single healing among us. To their credit, the pastor and elders never used hype or theatrics or promoted emotionalism in the group. Our little church asked the Lord for miracles—strongly and repeatedly— but then whatever happened was whatever happened. No one intentionally contrived anything; the pastor and elders were people of integrity.

For me and many others, our cautious anticipation eventually gave way to disappointment. If we were the new age community . . . if we already had some of the signs of that new age, then why didn't we experience healings like the early church? That question lurked in the background. Along with picturing the crutches and wheelchairs up on the cathedral wall, I recalled my father dutifully kissing one of the saint's many relics housed in a small glass case—as was the Catholic practice—just like those desperately sick people touching the apostle Paul's clothing or handkerchief. On one hand, I understood that Jesus did not heal everyone in his time or in the early church. That was a given. Yet, on the other hand, I wondered why we couldn't see just one obvious healing among us—one clear sign or down payment on our full liberation yet to come. Have to tell you, Kid, it was disheartening. Even disillusioning . . . again.

Being a New Age Disciple

Discouraged or not, I kept standing on what evidence I had—the eyewitness accounts. Still, my disappointment as a young man in not seeing a miracle of healing, especially for your grandfather, just fed my residual cynicism.

Though a bit jaded, my encounter with the Spirit of Jesus had nevertheless energized my faith. How could it not? Having said that, over the decades I've become aware—painfully aware—that there is a full range of unfounded, mystical "God stories" out there, including Christian and New Age. And now mine is among them. But I've made it a point to never use this mystical experience to decide my faith. I rely on evidence too much to allow such an ill-defined experience to make my final decision for something of such importance. Still, I know my ecstatic encounter fits the Jesus story, and, like I said, the encounter sealed my faith.

Miracles or not, and answered prayers or not, we all believed that the Spirit was ushering in the new age among us. Under our young pastor's leadership, we learned that whether we received healings or not, the cosmic drama was still the same:

> Not only the world, but we also have been waiting with pain inside us. We have the Spirit as the first part of God's promise. So *we are waiting* for God to finish making us his own children, which means our bodies will be made free.
>
> (Rom. 8:23, NCV; italics mine)

My dad would have to wait—and I with him. It wasn't the first time I had to wait. And it certainly wouldn't be the last.

So what were we to do while waiting? What were we to do between now and the time we'd die? Our pastor wisely focused our attention on one central purpose of the Spirit in this new age—building character:

And all of us, with unveiled faces, seeing the glory of the
Lord as though reflected in a mirror, are being transformed
into the same image from one degree of glory to another; for
this comes from the Lord, the Spirit. (2 Cor. 3:18, NRSV)

Pastor John taught us that the Spirit is working in us to transform us into the character of Jesus. To do this, we had to cooperate
with the Spirit. We were to put off our "old self" and put on our
"new self" (Eph. 4:21–24). Putting on the new self was considered
the very "fruit of the Spirit":

But the Spirit produces the fruit of love, joy, peace, patience,
kindness, goodness, faithfulness, gentleness, self-control. . . .
Those who belong to Christ Jesus have crucified their own
sinful selves. They have given up their old selfish feelings
and the evil things they wanted to do. We get our new life
from the Spirit, so we should follow the Spirit. (Gal. 5:22–
25, NCV)

Our pastor called us to grow up in character. But in so doing,
I realized that your grandparents' deep character of sincerity and
compassion; the ever-present value system of my ethnically mixed
neighborhood; the strict moral requirements of the Catholic
Church; and the unwavering modeling of your uncle Herb had all
come together to condition me to think this way already. *It wasn't
new.* In high school, I had already decided not to follow my best
friend into sexual impurity, drunkenness, violence, and embittered
anger, sins the apostle Paul listed elsewhere in this letter. Instead,
I followed the example of your uncle Herb. Later in college, I
didn't follow the fraternities into the three "Bs"—booze, beds, and
broads—continuing my choice to follow my brother. I knew the
path of sin was foolish. It was your uncle who had shown me the
way—the way of the Spirit—whether he knew it or not. And I had
chosen to follow the Spirit by following my own brother—whether
I knew it or not.

Character mattered. I already knew that. So what the apostle
Paul said about the active work of the Spirit in this new age—of
helping us in the struggle to put off the old self and put on the
new—made immediate gut-level sense to me. The Spirit of this new

age had already shaped the entire culture I had grown up with. My Dutchtown neighbors, my Catholic leaders, my parents, and your uncle Herb were all part of a world order shaped by the Jesus story. And through all of them, the Spirit had already forged my core identity.

I don't know how strange it sounds or how oddly obsessed it appears to you, Hon. But every single day of my life since my baptism in the Racquette River and the encounter with the Spirit, I have intentionally worked at continuing to build the sound character already delivered to me by your grandparents and Uncle Herb. Pastor John (who reminded me of Herb), his wife Jane, Dick, and Mary—they all lived it. I borrowed that vision from them. While in certain ways I have failed in being the loving father and husband I've wanted to be—and I continue to fail at times—I have always capitalized on my failures. Using a sober version of the hilarious bathroom scene in the movie *Liar, Liar*, when I fail, I grab myself by my intrapsychic lapels and throw myself up against the metaphorical bathroom wall to make myself wake up—in order to "crucify" my sin. I use failure to fight for wisdom. Failure and wisdom are, after all, two sides of the same coin. I've worked very hard to learn the skills to better love those entrusted to my care. It is my hope that I have been a "loving-enough" husband and parent—and now grandparent. Each of you will be the final judge of that. However much I have or have not succeeded in loving each of you, my discipleship has always meant working hard to do just that. My daily goal since my youth has been to grow up into mature character as measured by the law of love and the fruits of the Spirit.

I feared God as a boy. After my encounter with the Spirit, however, fear of God has never driven my discipleship. I've not avoided "the near occasion of sin" for fear of purgatory. And I've not built character for fear of going to hell or desperately trying to "work my way to heaven." It wasn't because I was arrogant or cavalier. It was because I had caught the vision. This was who I now was:

> Think only about the things in heaven, not the things on earth. Your old sinful self has died, and your new life is kept with Christ in God. Christ is your life, and when he comes again, you will share in his glory. (Col. 3:2–4, NCV)

Without consciously knowing it, that vision of a new life captivated my imagination as a little boy. It became evident with that grammar school drawing of the caterpillar-becoming-butterfly. Perhaps it was the Spirit already working in me. I'll never know. What I do know is that at some level in my mind, I dreamed of going from the caterpillar's body—representing my being trapped in my family's sin—to the butterfly's, symbolizing a wondrously new identity, free from it all. I longed to die to my family's pathology, only to emerge as a new creation. That creation would bring me the freedom I so desperately sought. A freedom where I could fly like the butterfly rather than crawl like some slow and lowly caterpillar. Little did I realize that this simple drawing had foreshadowed my passionate and irrevocable draw to the central dynamic of the new age—a metamorphosis of putting off the old self and putting on the new.

Whether miracles of healings were meant for us today—or not—I had become a new age disciple.

Father O'Reilly's Blessing

Father O'Reilly was one of my engaging high school teachers—and a football coach—from St. Thomas Aquinas. He enthusiastically agreed to witness my marriage to your mom. Father had been the one who eagerly joined our little band of innovators in saying Mass before school started. Though from two different generations, when he and I got together to discuss my upcoming marriage, we also talked about our faith journeys. Father was exceptionally—and refreshingly—transparent. He shared his own story at some length.

Father almost left the priesthood. Like me, he was "baptized in the Spirit," but his happened at a gathering of Catholics at a conference at Notre Dame. The Catholic church was in revival. A "back-to-the-Bible" movement grew within the Church across the country as part of what became known as the Catholic Charismatic Renewal. This affected millions. Father's excitement was so contagious that the bishop gave him charge of the Bible movement in our home diocese. In the wake of our talk, Father invited me to speak at my alma mater. He really wanted this earnest young man to talk to his students about faith in Jesus. Trusting me, he just set me loose to say whatever I wanted to say. I felt honored. I considered it both a privilege and an opportunity. After I talked with the students, Father and I spoke further about our faith.

He now questioned the Catholic belief in "working your way to heaven"—meaning heaven had to be earned. Like the protesting movement centuries before, he was discovering that the apostle Paul taught we were saved by grace. That is, we were saved only by Jesus' dying for our human condition and coming back to life. Not by being "good." Being good didn't earn God's love; being good emerged in response to God's love. Yet, questions or not, it was clear Father had already concluded something both extreme and far-reaching: whether Protestant or Catholic, those who accept Jesus were Christians. Father's changing beliefs stood within the context of

Vatican II, when many beliefs I had grown up with were reversed—
including no longer condemning Catholics for going to a Protestant
church or reading a Protestant Bible. The Church now stood on
the belief that Catholic and Protestant bibles tell us the same Jesus
story. And Catholics and Protestants believe in the same Jesus. So
we are brothers and sisters together in the same faith. In my day,
Kid, Father's belief was one very radical—and gutsy—conclusion
for a Catholic priest.

Father O'Reilly and Pastor John travelled to St. Johnsville on
a cold winter day. Along with your mom's local Methodist minister, they witnessed our vows. Each man had an active part in our
service. It was an interesting integration of faith journeys woven
together for an hour on our behalf. From my need to feel yet tied to
Mother Church; to the memories of early morning Masses with my
dear friends and Father; to my new age discipleship through Pastor
John; to marrying a woman who fit the new imprint of a new primal
woman, the ceremony was rich in meaning for me.

When Father was ready to leave the reception, he came over
to our table to say goodbye. Being young and as yet deferential to
a priest—along with my deep respect for Father—I asked Father
what he thought about my going to seminary . . . a Protestant seminary. Without any hesitation, Father graciously—and with great
discernment—smiled at me. He then put his arm around my neck
and onto my shoulder, saying, "Frank, there is something a whole
lot bigger than the Catholic Church happening."

Father believed the Spirit of God was moving within us—he in
midlife and me as a young buck. However, he also knew what was
happening across the country. It was a grass roots, counter-cultural,
back-to-the-Bible, and, for many, "Spirit-filled" movement. In 1971,
Look magazine called it "The Jesus movement."

The Jesus movement grew in the late sixties and early seventies,
when I was in high school and college. It stood alongside the Black
Panthers, hippies, Yippies (politically radical hippies), and women's
liberationists. I saw rock music put together with the gospel—called
"Jesus music." I witnessed the spread of Christian coffeehouses; I
played in some. We even saw the start of Christian radio. Campus
Crusade organized Explo '72 in the Cotton Bowl in Dallas, Texas,
drawing about eighty thousand young people. Many of the movement's top performers sang there, including Johnny Cash and Kris

Kristofferson. Billy Graham closed the week. I went by bus to Fort Lauderdale, Florida, with Inter-Varsity Christian Fellowship for a week of evangelism. A few hundred of us young people ventured there from all over the country. After some solid training, I talked with others on the beaches and in coffeehouses about Jesus. Back then, the separation of church and state was not the issue it has become today. Government officials of Fort Lauderdale opened their arms for us, giving us their full support for the citywide effort. They believed we were a positive force. They even issued us white wristbands identifying us as members of this evangelistic group—in case police found us ministering to someone using illegal drugs.

Those of us in the Jesus movement felt we had somehow entered the biblical narrative. I say "we" as if I was part of this movement. But I never thought of this movement as a "movement." Nor did I ever consider myself a part of it. I was simply a member of IV and the Koinonia community. And one of several of Pastor John's understudies.

It never ceases to amaze me—the power of words. I cannot describe the quiet joy mixed with peace Father O'Reilly's words gave me. For the first time—and without holy water—I felt truly "blessed" by a priest. Unlike the bishop at my confirmation, Father did not hide behind his uniform. He was open, transparent, and genuine. All of our conversations came together in that moment of his arm around my shoulders—conversations which wrapped me with his rich and struggling humanity.

Father courageously reached beyond Catholicism. In doing so, he endorsed my youthful vision. He was truly ecumenical. His enthusiasm for my faith was an incredible shot in my arm. At that watershed moment, whether he intended it or not, Father had become a transitional figure. He became my bridge from Catholicism to Protestantism. Father set me free to finally cut the cord to Mother Church. Still, like any son whose cord tying him to mother has been cut, I was yet the son of Mother Church. Mother Church's Jesus story had become mine. But it was now mine on my terms. Father didn't think poorly of me or consider me damned to hell for that. Instead, he believed I was a genuinely passionate son finding his own way. He believed that as the Spirit of God was leading him, the Spirit of God was leading me, even to a Protestant seminary. He affirmed the panoramic that there was something a whole lot bigger than the Catholic church happening—and believed this young man was an integral part of it.

Kristen, in reaching beyond his vestments and the institutional rules, Father's humanity deeply touched me. To borrow from an old Simon and Garfunkel song released while I was in college, he really became a "Bridge over Troubled Water."

PART 3

In Mad Pursuit of Jesus

The Basement Wall:
A Place to Ask Why?

Strange Bedfellows

It actually began one typical day my junior year, about a year before I married your mom. Out of the blue, one of my beloved professors had a heart-to-heart talk with our small but dedicated class of physicists-in-training. He said that the market for physicists was glutted; there were no jobs out there for us. Physicists were driving taxis in New York City to make ends meet while actively waiting for job openings in their field. We were speechless.

Now what?

I loved physics. Still do. But as much as I loved it, I took our young midlife professor's words as sober counsel, as did many others. I began to look at the options.

At Clarkson, I found myself eagerly investing in people—in my fraternity brothers, my hallway friends, my classmates, my many IV friends, my new family of Dick and Mary and their children, and the many other families of the Koinonia community. I enjoyed people, and people enjoyed me. I was becoming what I tongue-in-cheek call a "rehabilitated introvert." Other students valued me enough to come to my dorm room for counsel. I never "noticed" it; it just happened. But the college staff noticed. My junior year, they asked me to seriously consider being a resident advisor for my senior year. I felt honored. At the same time, I was approached by the student leadership of Inter-Varsity Christian Fellowship to consider being nominated for president. After Koinonia's and IV's training, I felt ready and eager to lead the joint chapter as president—a role which fit me much more like a glove than being a resident advisor in a dorm.

My increasing interest in people was one powerful factor that drew me to psychology. Beyond that, the intricate workings of the human mind intrigued me. After all, I've always loved the "good mysteries" of life. I didn't know it at the time, but my underlying wrestling with the powerful but "dark" forces deep in my own damaged psyche drew me to the "bad mystery" of the human mind as well. I wanted to solve the mystery of those dark forces. Beyond solving, I unconsciously wanted to master my own.

In the wake of my newfound faith in Jesus, my drive to deal with life's "bad mysteries" actually intensified. My passion grew *because* of the Jesus story; it did not lessen. Jesus hated the dark side of life . . . like I did. The apostles courageously bore witness to how Jesus hit the mystery of evil, suffering, and death head on, even spending the rest of their lives spreading the good news that he had "solved" the problem of the human dilemma. Words could never capture how I longed to learn more.

So, shortly after our professor talked to us, I began to picture the human psyche as the meeting place for both my passions. Good mystery and bad mystery seemed to come together in the human mind—whether in a Stalin, my parents, or my own heart. So I thought about putting together the strange bedfellows of psychology and the Bible. I wondered about going to seminary. After all, the Bible was the only place to find evidence for God; there simply was nowhere else to go. Not if one wanted something concrete—and utterly practical—like a dead man coming back to life as evidence for God. Seminary would give me the tools to analyze the Bible; physics, obviously, would not. While both disciplines deal with eyewitness reports, the tools and the objects of study are different—very different. One set of tools is for "seeing" physical reality clearly. The other is for "seeing" Jesus as the revelation of God clearly.

It wasn't only the avid scientist in me that drove the seven-year marathon in my pursuit of understanding. But I hadn't come to terms with it until my third year in seminary. The fact is that I had already been imprinted with my mom's intense pursuit of Jesus. In her own way, she had been loyal to Jesus her entire life. She had been passionate about the Church's rituals. She had been driven by the vision to have us kids get a good Catholic Christian education. She had desperately grabbed Jesus' robe seeking healing for your grandfather's MS. And I have no doubt that besides the alcohol, faith in God had propped her up from day to day—with pictures, statues, the holy scapulars, a shrine, and going to Mass—to do her duty as wife and mother. So, besides borrowing my father's pit-bull determination, I had also borrowed my mother's spiritual obsession. I turned her mad pursuit of Jesus into my own. Of all the other things I could have been doing with my time and effort after college—whether trying to build financial wealth or forging another career—I ended up passionately pursuing Jesus instead. Just like my mother.

Your mom had secured a teaching job with the public school district in Philadelphia. Or so we thought. So we headed to Westminster Theological Seminary. With the U-Haul trailer behind us, we slowly made our way down a steep winding hill near the seminary. I recall the moment vividly as we made our way down: I felt frightened. Koinonia was over a year behind us. My mother had been gone for four years. My father was lost in his own world with his own struggle for emotional survival. My brothers had moved on. And your mom and I were far away in a large city, knowing absolutely no one.

We pulled into Westminster's parking lot to register. Out the front door of the main building walked an IV staff person we had gotten to know at a month-long training conference just the summer before. I can't tell you the relief we both felt; we now knew someone in this big city. He had left IV to become a pastor of a small church here and readily invited us to join him. We eagerly accepted his offer. Your mom and I both thought it was another sign God wanted us at this seminary. Or he was at least taking care of us, given our choice. We went . . . and stayed with that church community for the next three years of my studies. That was our introduction to "Presbyterianism."

Shortly after arriving, your mom casually called the city to confirm arrangements for her job. She was told that they had made a mistake: *there was no job*. Now what? We already had an apartment lease, little money in the bank, and now, no job—with your mom's career adrift. And more fear.

That Sunday, at our first worship service, a tall, slender man with a most charming and disarming smile sitting behind us introduced himself. He was quite engaging. As we talked, he asked what we were about. When we told him, he eagerly invited your mom to call him for an interview; he was the principal of an inner-city elementary school. She called, interviewed, and immediately got hired for a position. It was a golden opportunity for your mom. It became a way to put together her missionary interest with teaching. While the money was significantly less, we managed to survive. Once again, your mom and I believed God was taking care of us.

Thus began your mom's long-standing teaching career—and my hard-driving marathon in the pursuit of Jesus.

His Bottom Line

My journey at seminary wasn't just "book learning." Far from it. I wrestled for truth. And I grew as a man.

Mom and I developed friendships with elders and ministers, peers at seminary, church friends in suburban and central Philadelphia, as well as colleagues of your mom's at her school. We lived alone in suburban Philadelphia for a year and then with a family in the city proper for two years. We became members of that church in Oreland and then helped launch its daughter church in the city. And this is not to mention nurturing our young marriage. It was a rich time.

Having said this, my book learning at seminary was different from my studies at Clarkson. In my physics training, there was no massive amount of reading. It was a huge amount of math. But you don't have to—in fact, you can't—speed read math. You *study* math; you don't "read" it. Physics also brought the delightful challenge of trying to picture reality through that math, like what the inside of an atom really looked like—which, by the way, is impossible to picture. Still, I didn't have to read fast. Now, however, I had to. I had to read thousands upon thousands of pages each semester. One course alone in church history required studying five books—over sixteen hundred pages. And I typically had five courses. It was all way too much for my eye condition—though, like I noted before, at that young age, I didn't know the problem was my eyes. In the back of my mind, I continued to think that I just wasn't that bright. I barely hung on. I learned to read smart, figuring out what to focus on and what to let go. I bought CliffsNotes and organized study groups where we'd divvy up the material and give each other reports. Feeling embarrassed, I did not go to the professors for advice in narrowing the material down. Besides, I didn't think they either could or would.

As was my style from high school and the style of many young men at seminary, I engaged in iron-sharpening-iron dialogues with my peers. Most of our invigorating talks were in the service of trying to

251

grasp what the Bible was saying. When I began that first challenging semester, I quickly learned that I didn't know much about the Bible compared to most of my peers there; they had already been steeped in the Bible from their growing up years. I felt like I was on one long entrance ramp having to push the "pedal to the metal" to enter the flow. Conversations were often way over my head. But as strangers became friends, they were willing to help bring me along.

To blow off steam from this academic pressure cooker, I took a martial art called Tae Kwon Do, originating in Korea. The art form focuses more on the legs for kicking than on the arms. Later, during my training as a psychologist, I also studied Tai Chi. It uses very slow movements to mobilize "chi" or energy within the body and the earth. Whether that energy exists or not has yet to be proven. I did manage to accidentally change my body temperature, giving myself fevers; my instructor found that evidence of my growing "mind-body" skill. I've always needed to connect with my body as a way to balance myself after using my mind so intensely—whether hiking and camping, floor hockey at Clarkson, these martial art forms, rousing games of Ping-Pong, or later in life, gardening, sailing, golf . . . and yes, still Ping-Pong. Back at seminary, we played a creative version of Ping-Pong where we'd let the ball hit the floor before we returned it. We'd work up quite a sweat. In my youth, that was actually doable. Since I played a mean game of Ping-Pong, others were having to step on the gas to catch up to me.

My lack of knowledge of the Bible showed in the classroom as well. Like a good student, I'd raise my hand often, asking question after question about what the professor was talking about. I was used to asking a lot of questions in physics; you dared not let anything go by that you didn't understand. Besides, if one of us didn't understand something, likely most of us didn't understand it. So I wasn't embarrassed asking questions. However, one seminary professor took me aside in the hallway after class, graciously asking me to not raise my hand so often. He said it slowed up his lectures too much. Perhaps he figured I was the only one who wasn't informed enough for his class. I don't know; maybe I was. Still, I had never had a professor ask me that before. Not asking questions just put me further behind however. Later, I took a course from him called Atheism, which given my divided mind, was intriguing. He seemed much more relaxed and very willing to answer any and all questions—even venturing to share a bit personally. He told us that when he had gone through a surgical procedure, many young men eager to see "God at work" in everything asked him what he had learned spiritually from his suffering. His reply, "Nothing!" I loved it. Such candor from several professors made our studies more down-to-earth and relevant.

As with any institution that gathers young men together, the testosterone flowed—not only across the Ping-Pong table but also in our iron-sharpening-iron debates. Fluffing one's feathers was not uncommon. In my first year there, I had a chance to talk with one third-year student (the third year was the last year for the Masters of Divinity degree) about my Catholic upbringing. Out of the blue he declared in no uncertain terms that "Catholics cannot be saved." I looked at him dumbfounded, exclaiming "What?" I recoiled in disgust at his arrogant assertion. I told him that such an attitude was outrageous. I pushed back saying Catholics can and do believe in Jesus like Protestants can and do. Regardless of my own journey in leaving the Catholic Church, I never doubted that the pope and my parents were followers of Jesus, just like the pope and leaders in Vatican II never doubted that Protestants were Jesus followers. I further told him that no one needs to have all of one's ideas correct to have faith in Jesus. I said, Catholic or Protestant, we all have untested, foolish, or just plain stupid beliefs we cling to. The only questions are how many and what are they. He unfluffed his feathers, and I walked away.

I'd also stay up late with other students studying Hebrew, the language of the Old Testament. Actually, I think I complained as much as I studied. Talking about fluffing one's feathers: On the first day of class, this newly hired young professor of Hebrew set the drumbeat—a drumbeat that struck me as self-centered and foolishly demanding, both then and now. He said he wanted to take the best students in the class, move them to the edge of the cliff, tip them out over that edge—and whoever hung on, hung on. Except to prove something to himself, I never understood the point of that. We'd complain because we'd be up to two and three in the morning trying to master the material. Then we'd have to get up a few hours later for an early class. I was used to long hours at Clarkson, but pushing it for Hebrew didn't make sense. We were only learning the basics so we could use our tools, like a theological dictionary. We weren't trying to become experts in Hebrew—nor could we ever in one year. I found out that the previous senior professor who stepped down because of his fight with cancer had just that attitude. Perhaps this new young instructor was trying to prove this old but revered professor wrong.

Up to that point, I had never flunked a class. But one day, my pastor of my Presbyterian church had been invited to give a sermon at chapel. I vividly recall the one moment when he held his hands up and out saying that over the years, he had seen many seminarians graduate with their diploma in one hand and divorce papers in the other. I was struck by his warning. Weeks later, standing by the stacks of books in the basement library, and beginning an even more grueling semester of Hebrew, I decided to draw a rare line in the sand. I chose to "flag" that second semester Hebrew; it was too late to drop. It just wasn't worth the cost of my time or my relationship with your mother. When I read my instructor's obituary a couple decades later and found out he died suddenly of a heart attack in midlife, I did wonder if his body paid a dear price for his blinding, demanding pace.

Besides the massive amount of reading, my journey at seminary was different in another way. While I went there to get the tools to study the Bible, I also went with a singular question from which all my other questions flowed: Just what did God have to say about evil, suffering, and death? What? Obviously, no experiment could ever tell me the answer. Science never asks or answers the question: What does God think? Nor can science answer why questions like just why does anything exist? Or why do evil, suffering, and death exist? Only the Bible offered me the hope of an answer. What I already knew was that Jesus fought it all. But what I didn't know was how it got there in the first place. In my youthful zeal, driven by my parents' unspoken pain, disillusionment, and questions, I wanted—no, I secretly demanded—an answer to the question of why it was that my no-name family was allowed to suffer so much. Little did I realize how strong that demand was until decades later. Still, in my youth at seminary, I wanted to know how God felt about all those people on the cathedral grounds begging him for healing—healings that for most never came. I wanted to know how he felt about what my parents had done to me. I wanted to know his bottom line on all this.

The Basement Wall

My "why" question was the same exasperating question Job had asked thousands of years prior. As I noted at the beginning of this letter, there really is nothing new under the sun. And, in a sense, that's true. But it was now *my* turn to ask why. And, over many, many centuries after Job, Jesus had come—and he had come back from the dead. *Job never saw Jesus.* He did not have the privileged position in the flow of human history to be aware of a dead man coming back to life. So while his question was my question, my answer was not his answer. I now had the answer to the why question from Jesus and the apostles. But it was one tough answer. That answer brought me to the brink of unbelief once again—and nearly bolting from seminary. In fact, I almost left twice.

I was told that the Bible was the "Word of God." Mysteriously, all the books in the Bible—written over centuries if not a couple of millennia—were supposedly the words of God. And you know how I am with mystery. I was used to the hard work of getting to know Mother Nature, so I was ready to do the hard work of getting to know nature's Creator. I began to study his many words to get to know him and how he really thought about his universe. But I quickly discovered that his words were as clear as mud to me. You'd think God being God, he could have come up with a better, more coherent, and simpler way of talking to us. But the Bible is what it is. Like it or not, it's all I had.

I sat my butt down in a hard, unpadded chair . . . at a desk . . . in the library's basement. It became the routine place where God and I met for our sober talks—and for my inner wrestling matches with what he had to say. I often stared at the basement wall—too often actually . . . way too often for any sane man—meditating on his words. I am keenly aware that many good people could care less about such an obsessive effort to thoroughly understand what God has to say about the human condition. They rightly content

themselves with the attitude that "bad things happen to good people," "the rain falls on the just and unjust," "life happens"—and,
beyond that, "beats me." While most people suffer some in life,
those who suffer intensely—those who have been traumatized—
rarely can or do content themselves that way. They simply can't.

When those who suffer intensely go to church, all too often
their own leaders encourage a "Don't Ask, Don't Tell" approach to
faith. I've had many clients over the years come to me frustrated that
they could not really talk with their own minister. When they tried
talking about their spiritual struggles—asking their tough questions
and even honestly, though nervously, sharing their sober doubts—
the pastor would downplay or dismiss the questions. Or even gently
scold them for not having enough faith.

I've had other clients tell me that their pastors don't really believe
the miracle stories, let alone a dead man coming back to life. These
pastors allow their parishioners to flounder in spiritual uncertainty
because they don't offer clear biblical teaching. In contrast, I've had
clients whose pastors will actually support a congregant's spiritual
quest—encouraging questions and honoring the sacred but tormenting doubt—while offering sound biblical teaching to guide the struggling sojourner. Much like Pastor John.

Beyond that, I have a guess—it's a good guess but still a guess—
that many church leaders rarely preach from the pulpit or teach in
adult education classes what the Bible's bottom line is about evil,
suffering, and death.* That's because the Bible's view is so extreme.
Even shocking. It is so outrageous that many priests, ministers,
and theologians simply do not believe it. In contrast, some leaders
do believe it. But they judge that the average pew-sitter would be
turned off to God rather than turned on if they really knew what
the Bible said about it. That's why one highly esteemed television
pastor would not preach on such matters—and said so publicly in
an interview. These leaders believe they need to preach "positive
Christianity." They focus on what God will do for us today—if
we have faith. For such preachers, teaching what the Bible says

---

*I value evidence but do not have statistical data to support my guess. I do
have anecdotal knowledge, however, of how innumerable seminary instructors
and pastors do not believe the miracle stories nor the Bible's interpretation of
the human condition.

about the human condition is way too morbid, too deep, and too provocative for who they think are the shallow masses looking for a spiritual fix.

But the traumatized—myself included—are not looking for a spiritual fix. Like Job in the Old Testament, the traumatized always ask why: Why me? Why my suffering? They ask it of life. And they ask it of God. Further, like Job, the traumatized protest, "I don't deserve it!" For them, intense dialogues on the tough questions of life are never too morbid or too deep—or too provocative. After all, the traumatized have already been provoked by life—which is one incredible understatement. Trauma victims typically scramble to try to pick up the pieces of their now-fragmented identities. And they feel burdened by the heavy morbidity of their depressive suffering. So questions can never get too dark. Viscerally, they demand answers. The demand usually feels like a matter of emotional survival. Many look to religion for answers. Some to the synagogue. Some to the church. Some to the mosque. I was no exception. That demand drove me to seminary.

Innumerable inquiring minds, however—not only the traumatized—want to know the answer to why. Why is the game of life like it is? Just why are we the way we are? The Jewish author of the epic story of our human beginnings in the book of Genesis created a picture of why his people—and all of us—suffer so much . . . and then die. Innumerable people over millennia have wondered the same. Popes and theologians over centuries have been driven to understand Jesus' rescue of us from that dilemma. Beyond them, the great saints of the church bravely faced their own inner demons in their struggle to understand human evil. For example, the courageously self-disclosing Catholic Saint Augustine, whom Protestants also highly respect, penned his own inner debates. You can read them in his book *Confessions*. While written over sixteen hundred years ago, his wrestlings are timeless. My patron saint, Saint Francis of Assisi, left his father's wealth in his struggle to live out his faith—and live it with some real integrity.

And the list of inquiring minds goes on. Martin Luther: he struggled in his faith, rediscovering that we are indeed saved by faith in Jesus—and cannot simply work our way to heaven. Isaiah: before being sawn in half, this great prophet predicted the Messiah's murder centuries before. He would have given anything to see what we have seen in Jesus. John Calvin: this theologian and lawyer obsessively struggled trying to put together a singular picture of God. Stephen Hawking and Carl Sagan: these atheistic physicists stared at the basic questions of life through the lens of science.* Bertrand Russell: this renowned philosopher struggled with how a smart and loving God could ever have built such a wonderfully intricate universe filled with so much suffering and death. All of these people and millions more on this planet have wanted to know: Why? *Just like your grandparents.*

Over the decades, I've had the privilege of working with clients in all walks of life who have wrestled similarly—whether of Jewish, Muslim, or Christian faith; or holding to Westernized versions of Eastern philosophy; or grasping at straws not knowing what to believe; or strongly committed to the belief that there really is no Creator God. I do think any human being that honestly wrestles with the big picture and hasn't buried the issues of suffering and death deep in their psyche has asked the why question in one creative form or another.

Sadly, my parents' inquiring minds had been buried under their pathology. But they certainly wanted to know. I know this because they passed their flag onto me. I've carried *their* flag—and I carried it right into the library's basement with me. I *became* my parents' inquiring minds. When I sat to talk with God, my internalized parents sat with me. They sat with me reading God's words . . . the three of us wrestling with what the heck he meant. Time after time, we found ourselves just staring at that basement wall, struggling to understand how God saw things.

So, both the traumatized and the non-traumatized ask the tough questions of life. But in our culture today, talking with the traumatized about such questions has too often become an awkward matter left only for private discussions behind closed doors with a chaplain or psychologist—or been buried under a hefty dose of Zoloft or Xanax.

Hon, you have not been traumatized by me or your mother. But like the great saints of the church, you nevertheless have an inquiring mind. You do have a genuine interest in the tougher

---

*Carl Sagan could be classed as an agnostic, that is, as one who didn't really know whether God existed or not.

matters of life. So, please feel free to pull up a chair next to me—and next to your grandparents. I invite you to read some of God's challenging words along with us and to join your bewildered grandparents and me in our hypnotic stare at the basement wall in the grand effort to get to God's bottom line in how he really thinks about the human condition.

 *Here We Go*

Death for Evil

Catholic leaders had more or less the right idea when they said that infants are born with "mortal sin on their souls"—but they unfortunately said it in a very simplistic and misleading way. What I believe they intended to say is that we are born trapped. And they're right.

The author of Genesis, perhaps Moses, painted one extreme picture of that human trap.* Unbelievably extreme. He used simple symbols similar to other pagan myths on human beginnings, like a tree, garden, and snake, to tell his story. The meaning of that story was also simple . . . but powerful. For anyone taking this epic seriously—like a young seminarian looking for truth—its meaning made the drama between God and the human race look incomprehensibly violent.

As the story goes, there was a tree in the middle of the garden: the tree of knowledge of good and evil. God told Adam and Eve—the name "Adam" meaning "mankind" or "humanity"—to not eat its fruit or even touch it. If they did, they'd die. But this couple chose to believe the lie that they would never die.

---

*I was taught in seminary that Moses wrote it. But we don't really know.

Standing on the platform of that lie—not willing to face reality—they chose to engage evil. In doing so, they entered the universal drama of good versus evil. The race's engagement of evil—our first choice to sin so to speak—became the "original" sin. Thus our "fall" into evil.

I noted earlier that your grandmother had taught me that straight-out lying to someone was evil. And I had learned in my family that the ploy of self-lying—self-deception—indeed destroys. Those truths were evident here. Believing the big lie that we'd never die, the race chose to engage evil. And God chose to follow through on his threat. But I was floored with his punishment. God's reaction was not to scold Adam and Eve. Instead, he delivered what he had promised—death. As its prelude, however, they'd have to suffer. For the woman, suffering came in the form of childbearing pain. And for the man, as hard labor in the struggle for survival (Gen. 3:16–19). These examples of suffering no doubt represented all the struggles—and all the suffering—that life would throw at us. So the idea was that God was "punishing" us by having us suffer through our existence—an existence now made miserably short. We'd have to die. The leader of the Jewish people made all this very clear:

Then God said to the woman:

> I will cause you to have much trouble
> 　When you are pregnant,
> And when you give birth to children,
> 　You will have great pain.

　　Then God said to the man, "You listened to what your wife said, and you ate fruit from the tree from which I commanded you not to eat.

> "So I will put a *curse* on the ground,
> 　and you will have to work very hard for your food.
> In *pain* you will eat its food
> 　all the days of your life.
> The ground will produce thorns and weeds for you,
> 　and you will eat the plants of the field.
> You will sweat and work hard for your food.

Later you will return to the ground,
because you were taken from it.
You are dust,
and when you die, you will return to the dust."
(Gen. 3:16–19, NCV; italics mine)

Before I entered seminary, Pastor John had already taught me that once Adam had sinned, the dominos began to fall throughout human history. Coming from Adam, we somehow had all become slaves to sin. Hon, the idea that we were slaves was intuitively reasonable to me because it fit my reality. I not only witnessed but also was at the receiving end of my parents' slavery to their inner forces. I knew intimately my own struggles to free myself from the stranglehold of their pathology—pathology that wrapped itself in and around the depths of my psyche much like a brain tumor wrapping itself in and around the neurons of one's brain. Besides, like the apostle Paul, I knew—and felt—the struggles with the more "normal neurotic" conflicts of choosing between good and evil within us. So believing we were slaves to dark forces within us was easy; I was already a slave. So were my parents. Moses was right: The consequences of that slavery were devastating. But I hadn't anticipated the fuller meaning given to our slavery to evil. God required us to suffer and die in this life *because* we sinned. I was taken aback; actually, I was shocked. I hadn't put evil and death together before . . . not like that. But Moses had. In Moses' mind, we suffer and die *because* we chose to indulge in evil.

So there it was: My answer to the question why. All those who joined the night processional on the cathedral grounds—thousands of strangers from all over the country, including me and my parents— all of us mysteriously earned the nonsense life threw at us. *We earned it.* We earned it because we were all sinners birthed into a race of sinners who—one way or another—engage evil. We all partake of the tree of knowledge of good and evil.

Right or wrong, I reacted to this story—and reacted strongly. Don't get me wrong. I didn't want to; it just happened. And I didn't like how I reacted. I had come to seminary with an eager expectation of answers along with my ubiquitous excitement to learn. But I involuntarily recoiled from Moses' epic. I found myself pondering with great angst: In order for God to be God, he not only created the world but also the rules of the game of life that came with it. So—why? Why had he decided that our choosing to sin would earn suffering and death? I found no explanation. None. It was frustrating. All I had was this extraordinarily brief and ancient cryptic depiction.

I also learned to my surprise that both Catholics and Protestants stood on this ancient story. Both sides believe that the first couple's original choice to enter into the drama of good and evil brought an original "condemnation" of intense suffering and death that has held the human race in its unalterable grip from the beginning. That's the universal church's belief in "Original Sin." Since that original or first act, we are all born with sin that kills. We are all birthed into that spiritual maelstrom. So this epic drama, for both Catholics and Protestants, is the tale of our race's primal fall into evil . . . and the horrific devastation in its wake.

I had the privilege of counseling one Catholic Christian client struggling with the sudden loss of her son to a dreadful car accident. She had a great deal of knowledge of the Bible. But it wasn't simply "head knowledge." The fact is, she had a deep sensitivity to the issues of life. With her eyes slowly welling up as she reflected on her son's sudden demise, she noted in a quiet voice, "The cemetery is full of condemnation." Incredibly, in a poignant moment of feeling her deep pain, she reached back to this epic. She understood exactly what Moses depicted—and saw his truth in her son's untimely death.

To be sure, modern medicine throws billions of dollars at suffering and death. Since the Industrial Revolution, we live longer—over twice as long as we did in the early 1800s. Someday soon, we will rebuild body parts through biogenetics. We're already doing that in the laboratory. In the science of cryonics, we can preserve our brains—the one organ that carries most of the information that makes us "us"—in ultracold temperatures for a thousand years until technology can put that brain into a newly engineered body. So far, a couple hundred people have done so. And candidly, without modern medicine, I would've been dead at forty. To be sure, the contours of the human condition have changed and will continue to change—and change dramatically. But medicine or not, we all still suffer—and we all die. And that, I learned, was our "condemnation" for our chosen slavery to evil. For both Catholics and Protestants, this was an undeniable spiritual fact of our miserable existence.

Now what? I had no idea what I was going to do with how repulsed I felt. Here, already, was *the* answer to my singular question: Why is there such suffering and death? Genesis' answer: "God designed life so that, somehow, someway, we both suffer and die for our choices to engage evil." Somehow . . . and someway.

As a young man, I joined many in wondering whether this drama was written as a parable or as real history. Did Moses make it all up? Or did he write the story as if he had a DVD of that primal scene? I also wondered: Should I really picture God actively punishing us with misery and death? Or maybe I should soften that ancient picture. Maybe, to make it more palatable, I should picture God as more passively standing by—allowing us to make our own bed and then having to lie in it. Staring at the basement wall, I decided that guessing whether the story was actual history or not was just chasing the wind. You could never prove a thing.* I also decided that trying to figure out how to picture God at the dawn of human history was useless as well. After all, what difference would it make? God is still in charge of the universe. He set up the game of life. Whether God is passive or active doesn't matter; we still suffer and die. So for me back then—as well as today—what was important was the story's *meaning*. And that meaning stirred my shocked, jaw-dropping reaction: Do we all really suffer and die . . . did my own family suffer so much and then die because—*because*—we somehow participate in evil?

Kid, as I stared at the basement wall, this epic's meaning stirred such disillusionment, cynicism, and anger in me. Frankly, Hon, it made my skin crawl.

---

*Recently, however, in 2012, an Old Testament scholar who once taught at my alma mater published a book doing an interesting job of chasing that wind, called *The Evolution of Adam*. It's a bit technical but still an easy read.

Who Is This God?

Being one good obsessive among a community of obsessives, I stared at the basement wall rotating this epic's "answer" to the human dilemma 360 degrees in my imagination. I rotated it with some real anxiety. Given that I was driven to find answers, I really wanted to understand this most brief and puzzling depiction of our fall into evil. But just as much, I wanted to resolve how I felt about that depiction. I loved God; God loved me. Yet this ancient story made God look like a monster . . . at least to me he did. I really needed to resolve how I felt about him. Or how I felt about the story. I knew I had to take into account that this epic had been written so long ago, long before modern science. And long before the exponential explosion of information technology. So the author thought about things a lot differently than we do today. But still . . .

As a young seminarian, I did try to put myself in the author's shoes. That's always been my style: to climb into the other person's skin to see and feel what they see and feel. My clients have told me that not only do I know them better than they know themselves but also that I can actually express how they feel better than they can. Besides, as I learned, it is a basic principle of interpreting the Bible to put yourself into the author's place. You have to. You have to get into the author's head if you're going to have a chance at getting the meaning right. You just cannot use Scripture as a springboard for believing what you want to believe. Pastor John as well as my seminary instructors modeled that for me. So in trying to understand Moses, I learned that he may have borrowed an extraordinarily simple but powerful way of picturing life from another nearby culture. He may have used that society's way of thinking to put together his experiences of life and God.

It seems Moses believed that God either "blesses" or "curses" us. In Moses' world, if you obeyed God, you'd be blessed; if you disobeyed, you'd be cursed—and pay a dear price (Deut. 28:15ff). Either blessing or cursing; it was that simple.

266

That's why Moses naturally used the word "curse" in his story of our beginnings. Today, we don't use that word at all like Moses did. Today, the word either means foul language or a witch doctor's pronouncements to hurt someone through an imagined series of incantations that magically manipulate reality. That's not how Moses used the word. Looking at life—at all the suffering and death that surrounded him—he believed we had to have been punished by God. The word "cursed" captured that meaning for him. His story was his way of passing on his belief about why bad things happened to the Jews—and to all people. Interestingly, the friends of Job seemed to think just like Moses. They too thought that life was about being either rewarded or punished. They argued that *he*, Job, must have done something terribly wrong to have suffered so much. Some Christians today still think that way. If you're good, then good things happen to you—the Lord blesses you. If you are bad, then bad things happen to you—the Lord punishes you. In fact, the secular community now has its own simple version of this blessing and cursing: karma. What goes around, comes around. Moses used that simple picture of "blessing and cursing"—that is, rewards and punishments—in setting up his epic. All of life's nonsense was the "cursed" part of life. And that punishment came because we, as a race, did something bad. After all, why else would all of life's nonsense happen to us?

Then I realized: I'd been introduced to this idea of the "curse" growing up. I'd already been singing about it through one of our famous Christmas hymns: "Joy to the World."

> No more let sins and sorrows grow,
> Nor thorns infest the ground;
> He comes to make His blessings flow
> *Far as the curse is found,*
> *Far as the curse is found,*
> *Far as, far as, the curse is found . . .**

The idea of a curse had already been gently indoctrinated into me at Christmastime, year after year. I hadn't realized it. My studies

---

*"Joy to the World! The Lord Is Come," Center for Church Music, SongsandHymns.org, http://songsandhymns.org/hymns/lyrics/joy-to-the-world!-the-lord-is-com.

now stirred it to consciousness. I was intrigued. I really had no idea what that word "curse" meant until I studied the Old Testament. In fact, I don't think I had ever given it any conscious thought as a kid or young adult.

Using *his* way of thinking—not ours—Moses put together this basic picture of the human condition: either rewards or punishment. But in mulling over the Christmas hymn, I wondered: Why would I have joy in the face of such a simple but brutal picture? Don't get me wrong, I wanted that joy. But it didn't make sense to me to have joy about it. Joy that Jesus came and made his blessings flow . . . yes, I get that. But that we were "cursed" in the first place . . . bizarre. Moses' story left me, as well as other seminarians, with many disturbing questions. Here are just a few of mine:

Are you really going to tell me that my own traumatic suffering as a little boy was part of the "punishment" for the race's sin?

Or was I punished for my own sins yet to come?

Or was I punished specifically for my parents' sins?

Did my parents suffer so much because of their own sins? Or was it their parents' sins? Or simply everybody else's sins?

What about other people who sin but who seem to get by in life without much suffering?

I recoiled from all this odd questioning. It really felt strange. I snapped back with exasperation and wondered: Aren't all such questions foolish? Isn't life just a soup mix of evil and suffering ending in death with no rhyme or reason as to how any of it is parceled out? It just is. As Ecclesiastes says, both the fool and the wise die (2:16). Besides, I was just an infant when I was traumatized. What sense does it make that I was "punished" as a member of the human race as an infant?

Indeed, what sense *does* it make?

No one in their right mind would say that any dear, sweet infant is guilty of high crimes against the Almighty. Still, both Catholic and Protestant leaders have agreed for centuries that the Bible makes one thing crystal clear: "Innocent" babies are born gripped by the power of sin. All infants are mysteriously built with the forces of evil; they are born sinners. Hitler, Saddam Hussein, and Stalin were all once cute babies—seemingly innocent babies forever incapable of hor-rific crimes against humanity. But the real forces of sin within them grew into intractable evil. These men were not aliens from another planet. Such men were—and are—us. From your own stories as a parent, I know you have seen the slow emergence of darker motives within your children—embryonic sin that needs parental training to be forged into wisdom and character. So, do infants suffer and die *because* they are born slaves of sin? And do so even though they had no choice but to be born sinners?

It is at least a raw, harsh fact of life that babies do suffer and die—as well as the mothers who attempt to give birth to them. In early America, one to three out of every ten babies died before age five, depending on the health of the environment. Given the number of children women had—typically five to eight—the mother's chances of death during childbirth were at least one in eight. For this reason, one New England poet, actually the first poet to publish in America, Anne Bradstreet, penned her fear of death in childbirth. In her poem "Before the Birth of One of Her Children," Anne penned to her husband:

> How soon, my Dear, death may my steps attend,
> How soon't may be thy lot to lose thy friend.*

On her deathbed, Anne wrote a letter to her children. After experiencing the hardships of life in New England and so many deaths around her, she candidly shared her own draw to atheism:

> Many times hath Satan troubled me concerning the verity
> of the Scriptures, many times by atheism how I could know
> whether there was a God.**

These tough facts of life of infant and maternal mortality are painfully depressing for many of us, if not at times infuriating—facts which make a mother like Anne wonder. And facts which drive all of modern obstetrics. God *could* stop it all. But he doesn't. He stands by. So the more maddening question here is the meaning of it all: Is suffering to babies and mothers—including my suffering

---

*Anne Bradstreet, "Before the Birth of One of Her Children," as quoted in http://www.annebradstreet.com/before_the_birth_of_one_of_her_children.htm.

**Anne Bradstreet to her children, as quoted in Andrew Delbanco and Alan Heimert, ed., *The Puritans in America: A Narrative Anthology*, 3rd ed. (Boston: Harvard University Press, 1985), 140. Citation is to Harvard University Press edition.

as an infant—really a consequence of the race's unfathomable par-ticipation in evil? Of my personal choices to sin? Of my intrinsic slavery to sin?

As if those questions were not enough—though indeed they were—I asked myself even more. I knew Moses didn't think like we do today. I kept telling myself that. I had to. Still, given my idiosyncratic scientific bent, it bothered me that Moses never questioned how it was that all animals—in fact, all living things—came to suffer and die, not just human beings. Given his story of suffering and death—and given that Moses knew all animals suffer and die—it was baffling to me why he hadn't addressed the issue. Obviously, he didn't think that way, but it still bothered me, especially since I was being taught that this story was some divinely inspired account of how we came to suffer and die. If the story was the depiction of how life's nonsense entered our world, then it made sense to me to be wondering about suffering and death among all living creatures. If death came to us humans because we sinned, then did death come to all life forms because all life forms sinned? That seemed blatantly absurd to me. But had Moses even asked himself this question? If he had, you'd never know it from the story he wrote.

What about my dog Tiny? Had Tiny been inadvertently caught in the web of the human dilemma like I had as an infant? Had Tiny earned her arthritis by her own sinful choices? If indeed animals can have a phylogenetically primitive morality, then can they sin? Can animals engage evil?

I have to admit, Kid, right or wrong, the more I stared at this epic, the more Moses' depiction struck me as ridiculous. My questions of this text were honestly an embarrassment. Don't get me wrong. I believed my questions were reasonable questions. But not reasonable to ask of *this* ancient story. God's Word or not, this simple, primitive depiction just could not bear the burden of such questions. Before seminary, I had used high-tech equipment for research and had spent an inordinate amount of time analyzing problems with complex mathematical equations. So sitting there in the basement asking such technical questions of this most brief and cryptic story without a shred of scientific evidence to draw on did actually feel embarrassing. *I was embarrassed.* I was embarrassed in my own presence.

Beyond that, Moses' god struck me as jarringly similar to abusive parents.

ROUND 2
Whose Fault Is It Really?

The God of the Epic

In my early twenties, I didn't have training as a psychologist yet. But I had been traumatized by my parents. So I knew what it felt like to be abused. Moses' god felt abusive.

Here's how.

An abusive father brings a child into the world, then randomly punishes her for no apparent reason. But—this all-powerful father makes his little girl feel like the erratic abuse is all *her* fault. That parent never says, "I'm sorry." That parent never repents of the abuse. The little girl thinks: How can the all-perfect parent be wrong? So she frantically tries to figure out what *she's* doing wrong instead. But she can't. She cannot pin down any one thing she is doing wrong. So it has to be that she is doing most things wrong. That is, she comes to believe that she must be inherently bad. She must be. She must even be worthless. It's the only explanation as to why one day she is loved, but the very next day she is horrifically punished—that is, abused—out of the blue. She then desperately wonders how she can make it all stop.

If the parallel is not obvious, consider this: God is the perfect Father. When good things happen in life, God must be loving us. When we randomly but intensely suffer, we scramble trying to figure things out—thus the book by Rabbi Kushner, *When Bad Things Happen to Good People*. But, like that little girl, we can't nail down any one thing we're doing wrong to earn the suffering. So it must be that we are doing most things wrong; we must be inherently bad. We conclude, just like the little girl, that that's why God hurts us

271

and even destroys us, like he did with the race at the time of Noah and the flood. We must be evil. Perhaps even worthless. And like that little girl, we desperately wonder how we can make it all stop.

That's precisely the picture this epic painted.

I thought I had already fought my way out of abuse. In climbing out, I had both asked and answered the question: Had I personally earned the suffering at the hands of my own mother and father? *No—I had not.* So why in the world would I want to walk right back into that same nonsense with Moses' god? For those of us traumatized, life is horrific enough. But to contemplate that our trauma—that *my* trauma—might actually have flowed from the hand of my own Creator as part of a sweeping condemnation against the race was terrifying. Research shows us that trauma *at the hands of another human being*—like rape—is more damaging to the psyche than impersonal trauma, like a tsunami. Damage done to us by another human being provokes rage and a craving for justice . . . if not revenge. We don't crave getting even with a tsunami, but we do crave getting even with a rapist. So to think the God of the universe might be mysteriously punishing me for my unchosen slavery to sin was just . . . well, unimaginable. But Moses imagined it. In fact, the entire history of the Jews in the Old Testament is the drama of their learning to obey God to prosper . . . or disobey him and be punished severely. Years later, another Christian client who had studied the Bible for decades found herself saying to God, "If I treated my dog like you've treated me, I'd be in prison." I knew the feeling.

As much as I love to sing the hymn "Amazing Grace," it has Moses' view buried within it: "Amazing grace, how sweet the sound, that saved a wretch like me."* A wretch? Really? Am I so morally bankrupt in the eyes of God that it is actually reasonable to him that I suffer multiple traumas in this life? Is all my suffering really part of the payback for my duplicitous enmeshment with evil?

I was disheartened, Kid. I had been so enthusiastic as a Christian in college. I longed to tackle the tough issue of the human condition; that's why I went to seminary. Once there, however, I was hit in the face with an astonishingly simplistic answer to my one key question

---

*"Amazing Grace Lyrics," Constitution Society, http://www.constitution.org/col/amazing_grace.htm.

that put me right back home with my parents. I couldn't stand it. This is exactly why my skin crawled.

This tough picture of an extraordinarily punishing God has made sense to a lot of good people—some theologians and many passionate preachers. In fact, it has been just this kind of punitive, black-and-white thinking that has led many preachers throughout church history to deliver impassioned sermons about an angry God who would send you suffering in this life—and then send you to hell in the next—unless you obeyed him. But for me, as a budding theologian—and, as I later discovered, for innumerable experienced theologians around the world—Moses' dramatic depiction made his god look shamefully cruel, by whatever standard you want to measure it. The fact is, Moses lived in a very tiny world. He wouldn't even have known about the existence of North America, let alone billions of galaxies. So for him, the world was so much smaller and simpler—and the human dilemma pretty straightforward. Life's wide range of exquisitely nuanced suffering culminating in our utter annihilation couldn't be God's fault. *So it had to be ours.* Thus, as our Christmas hymn notes, we were "cursed."

As I sat staring at the basement wall—as my internalized parents sat with me—I asked myself this unnerving question: Just why would I want to embrace such a god? *Why?*

The Royal Robe

I am aware that many may think I was being very reasonable as a twentieth-century young man to question things like I did. Though others may think I was arrogant or even blasphemous. I hope many won't think that. Still, some will wonder: Who was I to doubt, let alone challenge or disagree with, the "Word of God?" But as the Catholic Church had discovered the hard way in its dealings with scientists that the sun, not the earth, was the center of the solar system, we always have to take real life into account in trying to understand the Bible—which is another key thing I learned at seminary. Always ask the tough questions. And always look at the hard evidence. Otherwise, we risk being blind. We risk wrongly interpreting the Bible. The scientist in me could do no other. With Moses' epic, I strained long and hard to ask the tough questions and look at the hard evidence.

Besides, the dirty little secret that is rarely talked about in seminary or our churches is that everybody's personal history strongly affects how we interpret—and how we react to—the Bible. Everybody's, including theologians. One way or another, our personal history affects how we picture God—and even how we picture God in the Bible. Our nonconscious issues give rise to what turns us off and what turns us on to this or that passage. To what verses make sense and what don't. I was no different. I was just trying to be honest with myself about what turned me off about Moses' god—and why.

I was sorely tempted to believe that Moses' depiction of blessing and cursing was a mere projection of his own primitive psyche. Or the collective psyche of his violent culture—a backward culture by today's standards, where stoning to death was used for many violations of its rules. Moses' simplistic story sure didn't smack of some divinely inspired wisdom about the human condition. Although one has to wonder, and as a young man, I did, what should divine wisdom about the human condition look like anyway?

I also wondered how Moses' picture of God fit with Job's protest. After all, arguing against his less than empathic friends, Job vigorously asserted he was innocent of earning his sufferings—*and God agreed*. God agreed Job hadn't earn all his suffering by his own sins. So it seems Job's friends were wrong for their one-dimensional view of sin and suffering. Suffering is not always karma—with what goes around comes around. Nor is suffering always some divine punishment—a "curse"—for some personal sin (Job 42:7–9).

Beyond that, how did Moses' epic, with its emphasis on the violent punishments of suffering and death, fit with my ecstatically loving encounter with the Spirit of Jesus? Or with the Gospels' picture of a compassionate Jesus—a Jesus who absolutely hated both suffering and death and fought for our liberation? I was baffled.

I could feel the powerful magnetic draw back to the enormously less maddening—and easier—belief that suffering and death were just a natural part of the never-ending cycle of life. That that's life. Even in writing this now, I can feel the draw . . . and the relief. It's a whole lot easier. Mother Nature gives life; Mother Nature takes it away. That's it. Suffering and death have no divine meaning. The *Lion King's* portrayal of the cycle of life seems straightforward and true: We live, we sin, we suffer, and then, we die. But we do not suffer and die *because* we sin. While the darkness of the human mind, its built-in propensity for evil, is real—and no thinking person disputes the human capacity for evil—it made incredible sense to me that there just is no moral connection between human evil and death. Yes, we sin. We do perpetrate evil on one another. But we do not suffer and die *because* we sin; we simply suffer and die. We suffer and die like all creatures, including my dog Tiny. That's just the way life is.

It was so tempting for me—both back then as well as now—to utterly disregard this ancient epic's view of the human dilemma. Tempting . . . except for one thing.

It was precisely this meaning of our "original" or first sin and our condemnation to suffering and death that the apostles wrapped around Jesus like a royal robe (Rev. 19:16). Dealing with this inexplicable tie between human evil and suffering—culminating in death—was *the* central purpose of Jesus' ministry and his coming back to life. I was absolutely stunned, Kid.

Boxed In with No Way Out

Like the air we breathe, we now take it for granted that if there is a God, that that God would have to be a God of love. After all, we live in a Western society that has been shaped by Judeo-Christian language and ideas. The idea of God as love is preached from pulpits, stamped on posters, and creatively imprinted onto Hallmark cards. Ask who or what God is, and we think, "God is love." It is in our bone marrow. Besides, like C. S. Lewis, none of us really wants to believe that the Creator of all things is a sadistic tyrant . . . or an abusive parent.

But if, like Moses, we look at life's evidence—the way life "treats" us, with its ups and downs—it's just not obvious that God is love. As I stared at that basement wall, I knew the cosmic processes that make galaxies—and the stars and planets within them—are all physically violent. Nature is violent with her hurricanes, tornados, earthquakes, tsunamis, and droughts—not to mention an occasional asteroid that hits the planet, wiping out most life forms, making way for new ones. As you know, my nephew and his wife were caught in the recent tsunami in Japan. Fortunately, they were unharmed. But so many lost their lives to what turned out to be the most violent earthquake in Japan's recorded history. That tsunami took many lives out to sea as if they were so much rubble to be swept away. The movie *Impossible*, based on the true story of a family in Southeast Asia, powerfully demonstrates just this. Without question, nature is violent; anthropomorphizing nature, some would even say nature is cruel. Human beings suffer in innumerable ways, including being traumatized at the hands of their own families. And every creature is some other creature's lunch; it is indeed a dog-eat-dog world. We live in a universe where suffering and death inevitably bring down every living thing. So, no, it is not obvious that there exists a God who tenderly and compassionately cares about his creations. Not obvious at all.

Nor was it obvious to Moses. That's why life appeared "cursed." And why it appears cursed to all who sing "Joy to the World"—or at least to those who, unlike myself growing up, actually reflect on the song.

Knowing nature's punishing violence, it struck me what the apostle John wrote, "For God so loved the world that he gave his one and only Son, that whoever believes in him may not be lost but have eternal life" (John 3:16, NCV). For the apostles, the clear evidence of God's love for us is Jesus. The evidence isn't how majestic or kind Mother Nature is, for Mother Nature would just as soon wipe us out with a tsunami as she would grace us with the beauty of her ineffable sunsets. The apostle Paul knew that. He knew the crazy flow of life is not—nor could be—the measure of God's love:

> Can anything separate us from the love Christ has for us? Can troubles or problems or sufferings or hunger or nakedness or danger or violent death? (Rom. 8:35, NCV)

The apostle did not create a myth that being a disciple of Jesus would guarantee a certain quality of life. Nor did he assert that God would "bless" this life with many circumstantially good things. Instead, he affirmed that in reality, life hits us with some pretty tough stuff, including famines and poverty and violent death. Consistent with my youthful mission, I found the apostle's ruthless realism encouraging. It is this tough side of life—the very condemnation of suffering and death that stands over and against us—that actually holds the potential for separating us from a keen awareness of God's love for us:

> Yes, I am sure that neither *death*, nor life, nor angels, nor ruling spirits, nothing now, nothing in the future, no powers, nothing above us, nothing below us, *nor anything else in the whole world* will ever be able to separate us from the love of God that is in Christ Jesus our Lord. (Rom. 8:38–39, NCV; italic mine)

The apostle Paul made it clear that life continues to throw all manner of nonsense at us. There is no relief. Yet, regardless of what life throws at us, nothing—absolutely nothing—can separate us from

God's love. But the apostle's guarantee of that divine love is Jesus—not the quality of our lives. Indeed, the quality of our lives reflects our condemnation—the curse of suffering—and that very condemnation offers no hint that we are loved. None. But God loves us in Jesus—and that love is guaranteed no matter what.

So, as I stared at the wall—as my internalized parents who suffered so much stared at the wall with me—I knew that what the apostle said had to be the absolute core of my faith . . . *if I were to continue to have faith at all.* Life was too messed up. It could not be the revelation of God's love. It couldn't. Only Jesus was that revelation. But—when bad things happen to good people, as it did for C. S. Lewis during the painful ups and downs of his wife's battle against cancer, that core truth is easy to forget. Over the decades, like Lewis, I have too often forgotten it.

I also have to keep reminding myself that the bad things that happen to good people—the bad things that have happened to me—aren't just "bad things." If you buy into the Bible's portrayal of the dawn of the human race, all bad things are a result of our fall into evil. So good people aren't just "good people"—at least, not according to Moses. All of us good people are also sinners—sinners to whom bad things happen because of our enmeshment with evil. So, according to Ecclesiastes, it should be no surprise either *that* or *when* we suffer.

Because of my stomach-turning skepticism about Moses' epic, I was utterly dismayed to learn that the apostle Paul stood squarely on his shoulders:

> Sin came into the world because of what one man did, and with sin came death. This is why everyone must die—*because* everyone sinned. (Rom. 5:12, NCV; italics mine)

So there it was, Kid—the same exact meaning of our dilemma as the one Moses gave. I was floored. Paul stated it succinctly with even greater clarity: *We die because we sin.* All of us. That's it. And several paragraphs later in that same letter, the apostle plainly said: "The payment for sin is death . . ." (Rom. 6:23, NCV).

Indoctrinated in his youth with Moses' story, the apostle Paul, now an adult, stood with Moses. It was a united front. The Old Testament and the New were forever inextricably linked. Many

Christians think the New completely set aside the Old. I myself wanted Moses' epic to be set aside. But it wasn't. Instead, the apostle affirmed that this primitive story accurately depicted the human dilemma—and used that depiction to explain Jesus. The meaning of the Jesus story stood squarely on the Moses story.

So Paul simply but unequivocally asserted: Suffering and death come to us *because* we sin. I was now boxed in with no way out. This view of life directly threatened me. It threatened how I wanted to picture reality. I really didn't—and, frankly, still don't—want to believe it. As I stared at my seminary's basement wall, this meaning of our human dilemma just seemed nuts.

Still, there was my answer to my key question—*again*. But like all trauma victims, including Job, everything inside me screamed out that I did not earn my trauma. Not from my parents. Not from life. Not from karma. And not from my God.

But—hadn't God agreed with Job? Hadn't God agreed that Job never earned his suffering? And didn't Jesus fight suffering? I still didn't get it. I just didn't.

ROUND 3
Why Was Jesus Murdered?

Death for Evil . . . Again

In Bill O'Reilly's well-written book *Killing Jesus*, the authors do not discuss the real reason why Jesus had been killed. But the apostle Paul did.

The apostle called the ubiquitous dance among evil, suffering, and death the "law of sin and death" (Rom. 8:2, NIV). It is a law of the universe.

This law of sin and death is like the law of gravity. It just is. When we shot the moon under President Kennedy, we took our sin—and suffering and death—along with us. When we reach for Mars or Europa someday, we'll take them there as well. No matter where we travel in the universe, the law of sin and death will follow—if it's not already there waiting for us.

Repulsion or not, I either had to deal or bail. Though sorely tempted, I wasn't ready to bail. So I looked to Jesus once again to deal.

Many people think Jesus died only as an example of God's love. Not true. If that were the case, Jesus would be useless. Instead, Jesus *had to* die if we were to be set free. He had to die *because* of the way God had set up the universe—because of that law of sin and death. In fact, our Father planned Jesus' murder from the beginning for just that reason (Gen. 3:15b; Acts 2:23). The meaning of his murder had been revealed through the prophet Isaiah. Kristen, you rehearse this prophetic vision when you sing Handel's glorious composition *Messiah*. Here is a very brief portion of this prophesy that plainly reveals Isaiah's meaning—a meaning, however, that inadvertently stirred my relationship with my mother. See if you can guess how as you read it:

He was hated and rejected by people.
He had much pain and suffering.
People would not even look at him.
He was hated, and we didn't even notice him.

But he took our suffering on him
and felt our pain for us.
We saw his suffering
and thought *God was punishing him.*

But he was wounded for the wrong we did;
he was crushed for the evil we did.
The punishment, which made us well, was given to him,
and we are healed because of his wounds.

We all have wandered away like sheep;
each of us has gone his own way.
But the LORD *has put on him the punishment*
for all the evil we have done.

He was beaten down and punished,
but *he didn't say a word.*
He was like a lamb being led to be killed.
He was quiet, as a sheep is quiet while its wool
is being cut; he never opened his mouth.
He was put to death;
he was punished for the sins of my people.

But it was the Lord who decided
to crush him and make him suffer.
The Lord made his life a penalty offering,

After his soul suffers many things,
he will see life and be satisfied.
(Isa. 53:3–11, NCV; abridged; italics mine)

Standing on Moses' dramatic depiction, this inspiring prophet envisioned the Messiah as a lamb led silently to the slaughter for the people's evil. Centuries later, the apostles would call Jesus the

"Lamb of God"—who silently went to the cross to pay for the evil of the world (John 1:29; 1 Cor. 5:7).

Isaiah's portrait of the Messiah stirred what I had witnessed with my mother.

As with the Messiah, life had oppressed my mother and deeply afflicted her with pain. Like the Messiah, she had been a silent sheep in the face of it all. In fact, while I do recall a few of her words, I cannot hear her voice in my head. Like the Messiah, my mother had passively submitted to her pathetic lot in life. Like the Messiah, she had suffered on behalf of others—doing her duty—because it was, as Isaiah said, the Lord's will. Like the Messiah, she had been driven by her unspoken mission.

That mission turned your grandmother into my family's "suffering mother"—imprinting me in a way that made the idea of the messianic "suffering servant" palatable, deep within my psyche. Like the Messiah, your grandmother suffered through her hardships that I might have life. She surely wanted me to graduate high school and leave home successfully before she died. And I did. When your grandmother saw that new life ahead for me, she was "satisfied."

However twisted, however masochistic, my mother had been the family's suffering servant—and effectively primed my psyche for Jesus as humanity's suffering servant. I am not saying she was an accurate portrayal of the Messiah. I am saying her sacrifice for the family set me up to be inexorably drawn to Jesus as the sacrifice for the race. That's why Isaiah made intuitive sense to me; that's what made his prediction "click."

I wasn't the only one conditioned to have Isaiah make sense. Jesus' disciples were as well. The disciples were Jews. Their Jewish system of sacrifices had already imprinted them with the belief in sacrifices for human evil. They had already studied what Isaiah said; his prophesies had been repeatedly read in synagogue. In fact, Jesus himself had studied Isaiah, shaping how he thought of his own identity. When Jesus began his ministry, he read Isaiah out loud in the synagogue, saying that he was now fulfilling this prophesy. That was his salient argument back to John the Baptist when John anxiously questioned whether he was the hoped-for Messiah or not. The apostles had long believed what Isaiah said—and they used that prophet's vision to explain what Jesus had done.

If we put the apostle John's now infamous declaration of John 3:16 together with Isaiah's stirring prophecy, it would look something like this:

For God so loved the world that he gave his one and only Son—to cause him to suffer, to crush him and then kill him, in order to be an offering for our evil—that whoever believes in him shall not perish but have eternal life.

God required death for evil. So he sent Jesus to die. It was either him or us.

The Cosmic Liberation

Like the other apostles—and standing on the great prophet Isaiah—the inimitable Paul clearly affirmed that Jesus was indeed murdered to pay for our collective evil (Gal. 3:10–13). After paying for our evil, Jesus came back to life, thereby crushing our last enemy—death (1 Cor. 15:26).

The learned apostle compared Adam and Jesus side-by-side. It was simple and direct. They were alike but different. On one hand, Adam represented us. Through Adam, we entered the drama of evil, suffering, and death. On the other hand, Jesus represented us too. Paul called him the last Adam. But unlike Adam, Jesus did it right. Doing so, Jesus ultimately set us free from the law of sin and death. So now there wasn't any condemnation. No punishment remaining. As the Christmas hymn "Joy to the World" goes, "He comes to make his blessings flow far as the curse is found."* No more curse—no more nonsense—for anyone who believes in Jesus (Rev. 22:3). *For them, the cosmic ordeal was over.* The entire drama of good versus evil was now done:

> Therefore, there is now *no condemnation for those who are in Christ Jesus*, because through Christ Jesus the law of the Spirit of life set me free from the law of sin and death. (Rom. 8:1–2, NIV; italics mine)

It was over.

This freedom from life's nonsense is central to why all the apostles were so passionately excited about Jesus. For them, humanity's ordeal was done. Suffering and death had been dealt its own death-blow. Jesus had the Spirit of Life. It was the same Spirit I ecstatically

---

*"Joy to the World! The Lord Is Come," SongsandHymns.org, https://songsandhymns.org/hymns/detail/joy-to-the-world!-the-lord-is-come.

experienced a number of years earlier. Jesus coming back from death by the power of that Spirit of Life was God's plan to liberate us from the human dilemma. This is what the apostle John meant when he wrote, "For God so loved the world. . . ." God so loved the world that he sent his Son to liberate it from evil and death.

If I accepted that Jesus had come back to life—if it were really true—then I had to accept the very meaning that so turned my stomach. The resurrection and its meaning were two sides of the same coin. Unless that crazy cosmic dance really exists—unless we really suffer and die *because* we have engaged evil—Jesus' resurrection ends up useless. Trite. One man coming back to life is no doubt an unbelievably interesting event. It would get any person's blood moving. But it would not change the universe. Whether it made any sense to me or not—whether it seemed barbaric or not, abusive or not, tyrannical or not, just plain nuts or not—the Bible's picture of the human dilemma had to be true. Otherwise, Jesus was useless. Useless for me and my children and my grandchildren . . . and my great-grandchildren.

In the strange machinations of my psyche, Marie from my Clarkson days actually sealed into my psyche my acceptance of this bizarre picture. She made intuitive sense of it all. Through my crush on Marie—though her impact went much deeper and was much more profound than some simple infatuation—this young woman had become a new "first woman," so to speak. She imprinted me with a vision for what a woman could be. She was the woman of my future. Marie's imprint, however, also made intuitive sense out of Jesus being the new "first man": Marie offered me a new vision of a new woman freed from my mother's pathology—which made sense of Jesus offering me a new vision of a whole new people freed from humanity's pathology (1 Pet. 2:9). Incredibly, my magnetic draw to Marie not only set up my inexorable draw to your mother but also my irresistible draw to Jesus as the new Adam.

And it still does.

To Believe or Not Believe

Hon, I have marched to the same drumbeat my entire adult life. It's because Jesus came back to life—and *only* because he came back to life—that I have ever been willing to consider that somehow, some-way, evil and death were tied together in some crazy cosmic dance. Otherwise, it would never have even crossed my mind . . . let alone become part of my belief system.

I did "bow the knee" to that dance in my youth. But I did so only with great reluctance. Fast forward to today: Many of our own denominational leaders are still struggling with this same dance. In their disquiet, our own Presbyterian Committee on Congregational Song, authorized by our General Assembly, voted 9–6 to drop the hymn "In Christ Alone" from our new hymnal. They wanted an ear-lier version that moved away from the following words:

'Til on that cross as Jesus died
The wrath of God was satisfied*

Tough words: Our Father's "wrath" is somehow "satisfied" by Jesus' cruel death. Right or wrong, the committee's decision has drawn criticism. I point this out to show how so many of us yet wrestle with this mystery of "death for evil." It is such an uncomfort-able topic. We're just not sure how to talk about it, let alone how to finally picture Jesus' death paying for evil—or if the two, death and evil, are to be pictured as being tied together at all . . . now that we are in the twenty-first century.

Before becoming the new pope, Pope Francis, named after my childhood patron saint, revealed his own concern about how the twenty-first-century Catholic Church is wrestling with this dance:

---

*"In Christ Alone," Wikipedia, http://en.wikipedia.or/wiki/In_Christ_Alone.

It is no use to lament the sufferings of this world if our life goes on as usual. And so the Lord warns us of the danger in which we find ourselves. He shows us both the seriousness of sin and the seriousness of judgment. Can it be that, despite all our expressions of consternation in the face of evil and innocent suffering, we are all too prepared to trivialize the mystery of evil? Have we accepted only the gentleness and love of God and Jesus, and quietly set aside the word of judgment? "How can God be so concerned with our weaknesses?" we say. "We are only human!" Yet as we contemplate the sufferings of the Son, we see more clearly the seriousness of sin, and how it needs to be fully atoned if it is to be overcome. Before the image of the suffering Lord, evil can no longer be trivialized.

The Cross of Jesus is a cosmic event.*

To so many theologians, priests, and ministers across the globe, the pope and the Bible are wrong. Evil and death should not be tied together. That cosmic dance does not exist. It is foolish and naïve to believe it. To the Bishop Spongs of the world, "death for evil" is culturally primitive and outrageously cruel. If it isn't very obvious, I certainly understand. But this pope's meditations offer us a balanced view—a much more careful view—revealing this pope's deep appreciation for Jesus' sweeping impact across the entire universe.

If we go against this pope's wisdom and reject the truth that evil, suffering, and death are linked, then we strip Jesus of his royal robe (Rev. 19:16). If we do that, the whole house of cards called "church" comes tumbling down. And it's already happening. Denominational membership in the United States is going down dramatically. Europe has already become hugely disinterested in Jesus. Protestant or Catholic . . . doesn't matter.

The implication of disregarding the cosmic dance is the same: there is no useful God. So eat and drink, for tomorrow we die. If we strip Jesus of his royal robe, all that is left for those who play the game of "church" is some New Age, quasi-spiritual social work

---

*Cardinal Joseph Ratzinger, *Meditations on the Stations of the Cross* (Libreria Editrice Vaticana, 2005), http://www.vatican.va/news_services/liturgy/2005/documents/ns_lit_doc_20050325_via-crucis_en.html.

ministry. Jesus offers no real vision. He offers nothing to mobilize the passions. There's no muscle left to him anymore. The core problem with our crazy universe remains. So there's no good reason to believe in him. And there's simply no good reason to get out of bed to "go to church."

Instead, I chose as a young man—and have continued to choose over the decades since—to embrace that cosmic dance. I don't like it. It still sounds bizarre to me. But I accept it. And I live with the tension. It is the tension between accepting the cosmic dance while thinking it's barbaric. It is the tension of believing an old, old story while living in the twenty-first century. It is the tension of believing evil and death are linked without any scientific proof except for the resurrection of a single man. I accept all this tension. And it *is* tense—very tense—at least for those like me.

As a young man, I stood on the law of sin and death, whether I liked it or not. Doing so, however, made it possible to stand on the other law: *There is therefore now no condemnation for those in Christ Jesus.* For me, my liberation from humanity's pathology hung in the balance. My eternal freedom from life's nonsense stood on the meaning that Moses and Paul and Isaiah—heck, the entire Bible— gives to the dance. Jesus could only break the back of sin and death if the law of sin and death were true. I didn't understand it then; I don't understand it now. But I accepted it back then. And I daily bow the knee to it now. But I do so for one reason and one reason only: Jesus came back to life.

One Favorite Hymn

When I counsel seniors who are having significant health problems, a typical focus of our work is on their despair—a helpless feeling mixed with anger—about how life (the law of sin and death actually) is systematically destroying them. It's crushing their bodies. And it's robbing them of their minds. They knew it was coming; we all know it is coming. But now, they're living it.

The law of sin and death is slowly but conspicuously bringing them down. Just this week as of this writing, in the Lehigh Valley a prominent man in his early eighties—well respected and a high achiever—killed his wife. Then took his own life. His wife had Alzheimer's. The family has no doubt that their father deeply loved their mother. With his own declining health, he may have felt he would soon no longer be able to fulfill his promise of keeping her out of a nursing home. She had no use for dying there. Like your grandfather, I certainly identify. Whatever this husband's motives, there is little doubt that despair wrapped his psyche real tight. The family reported that, tragically, their dad had not reached out to discuss the inner torment churning within him. Right or wrong, their father chose to have the final word in the face of the law of sin and death.

Many are like this father: unwilling or unable to talk about their tortuously slow demise. While this family came across as willing to have talked with their father, many families are too frightened to talk. They do not want to face their loved one's decline, let alone his or her death. They don't allow themselves to feel the pain of seeing a loved one who was once vibrant and full of life brought down. My uncle Don, a strapping, barrel-chested man, was brought down by cancer. He shriveled up into nothing . . . painful to witness.

Sometimes, family members don't want to face *their own* future demise, so they refuse to face the demise of their loved one. They may even criticize their loved one for complaining all the time about his or her aches and pains—without realizing that complaining is his or her cry into the universe. Seniors who whine and complain are desperate to have someone bear witness to the cold, cruel fact that their very identities are being mercilessly torn down. As best as I can recall, in the 1998 chick flick *Stepmom*, the terminally ill character Jackie says to her children's future stepmother: "We all need at least one person in the universe to bear witness to our lives." Absolutely true; we do. Mysteriously, bearing witness grants some sense of meaning to the ordeal. Unfortunately, wrapped in their own pain and fears, family members often just don't talk to their aging parents.

So I talk with them instead. We talk candidly about the human condition. As our former senior pastor described in a sermon, we blossom for a time, then hunch over and hobble around with a cane, move about in a wheelchair, lie on our backs in a nursing home, and finally, die. That is the panoramic. While such discussion is morbid for depressed seniors, it is nevertheless refreshing. They feel that—finally—someone understands them. Someone is willing to call a spade a spade. Someone is willing to bear witness to their agonizingly slow but obvious deconstruction. They feel relieved to unload their secret fear and desperation about how they are losing the fight to the forces of death now overtaking them. Death is deliberately and inevitably crushing them. They know it—and they hate it.

So do I. Beyond my disabilities, no doubt you notice the signs of the law of sin and death slowly bringing down your mother and me. I sure do.

Our heavenly Father took on that law through Jesus. I had actually been singing about that fact in one of my favorite hymns from Koinonia days, "To God Be the Glory." I loved that hymn then, and, because of its imprint on me as a young college student, I still do. Part of what I've loved about it over the years, even though it has an extraordinary simplicity of both word and melody, is its accuracy. I hadn't grasped the richness of its meaning until I learned about that strange law of sin and death. Though not fully appreciating this hymn, I had already tasted the "wonder" and the "transport" of my ecstatic encounter with the Spirit of Jesus at age eighteen, so I sang that hymn with some eager expectation and real enthusiasm. If I have the privilege of being aware of my own dying someday, I'd love you guys to sing hymns with me as I go—and I want this one to be among them:

To God be the glory, great things He hath done,
So loved He the world that He gave us His Son,
Who yielded His life an atonement for sin,
And opened the life gate that we may go in.

Refrain:
Praise the Lord, praise the Lord, let the earth hear His voice!
Praise the Lord, praise the Lord, let the people rejoice!
O come to the Father, through Jesus the Son,
And give Him the glory, great things He hath done.

O perfect redemption, the purchase of blood,
To every believer the promise of God;
The vilest offender who truly believes,
That moment from Jesus a pardon receives.

Great things He hath taught us, great things He hath done,
And great our rejoicing through Jesus the Son;
But purer, and higher, and greater will be
Our wonder, our transport, when Jesus we see.*

The hymn says it all: Jesus is the revelation of our heavenly Father's love; life is not. Jesus is our Father's "perfect redemption," the perfect rescue from our dilemma. He pulled this off by paying the price of his own death—the "purchase of blood"—and to be crushed in place of us. His death was therefore an "atonement for sin"—the lamb of God killed for our evil.

The hymn then rightly celebrates that our liberation from evil—and the suffering and death that flows from it—belongs to everyone who believes, even the worst among us.

Finally, as all seniors know, death takes no prisoners—except Jesus—whose great escape, as the hymn rightly affirms, opened the eternal "life gate that we may go in."

In these ways, "our Father who art in heaven" reversed the original sin and beat the original condemnation against us.

Maddening mystery or not, I do love that simple hymn.

---

* "To God Be the Glory," HymnSite.com, http://www.hymnsite.com/ lyrics/umh098.sht.

ROUND 4
Caterpillar-Becoming-Butterfly

My Pops

God schemed from the dawn of human history to redeem us from the cosmic dance (Acts 2:23). His vision was to use Jesus to bring us back to himself, the source of life: "Through Christ, God made peace between us and himself . . ." (2 Cor. 5:18b, NCV). The fact is, God longed to have us come back home:

> Because of his love, God had already decided to *make us his own children* through Jesus Christ. That was what he wanted and what pleased him. . . . (Eph. 1:5, NCV; italics mine)

Along with being a member of a new race headed by Jesus, I was now a member of a new family. I was his child.

I got some mere mortal's sense of my heavenly Father's divine desire to have me be part of his family from the prodigal son story. The father—representing God—joyfully runs out to greet the tired and spent wayward son coming back home. Candidly, though, I couldn't identify with the prodigal son. I hadn't felt like a prodigal, because I had been raised "a good Catholic boy." I had been in the fold since my infant baptism like the older brother in the story. Besides, I had made my seminal choice to stay on the straight and narrow in high school. So I've never felt like the wayward one—the prodigal—whom my heavenly Father needed to welcome home.

Talking about home . . . growing up, I never felt my home was actually "home." But this raises the question: *What is home?*

Our newspaper *The Morning Call* included a brief excerpt from a local college president's motivating address during its baccalaureate service. In it, he asks and answers, "What makes a place *home?*"

> It's not just where you sleep at night, but where you feel safe and challenged. A place where you know and are known by others who are close to you—both physically and emotionally. Where a web of mutual obligations and needs bind you and them together. Where you are challenged and supported. It is a place where you can discover who you are and who you were meant to be—a task that can be difficult and uncomfortable and that will continue for your entire life. Home is the only place where you can do this important work.
>
> "Here's something else to remember about 'home.' You can have more than one . . . . In the end, however, when life's inevitable storms come at you, it is home where you will find the comfort, security, support and safety you need."*

True enough. On one hand, home with your grandparents in Dutchtown was indeed a place of mutual obligations and intense needs that bound us together. It was also a place, not so much of discovering who I was, but of actually creating who I've become—those solid core values that make me "me," the same moral values that made your dutiful grandparents and our hard-working neighbors the fine people they were.

Beyond my childhood home, I've had other homes. Koinonia, Dick and Mary's farm, and the Oreland church were all homes where we were not only bound by mutual obligations and needs but where I was safe enough to blossom. The home I created with your mom was all that. It was also the opportunity, as well as the challenge, to create a safe place for you guys.

On the other hand, I neither knew your grandparents nor was known by them. Nor was I safe in their hands. Tragically, these things—not being known, fear, insecurity, and no comfort—were

---

*"Peyton R. Helm: Sometimes it takes an odyssey to find your real home," *Morning Call*, May 18, 2013, http://articles.mcall.com/2013-05-18/opinion/mc-leaving-finding-home-muhlenberg-helm-0519-20130518_1_real-home-rhett-odyssey.

all built *into* me. Day after torturous day, these things were poured into my identity—from infancy into young adulthood. As a result, most of the years of my life I've not been "at home" with myself. My parents' tragic home—the patterns that made my family "home"— was and still is *within* me. While I am wrapped tight with superb values delivered to me by my family, church, and neighborhood, those values were wrapped around trauma. Trauma is at my core. Trauma and home were one.

Growing up, Mother Nature had become my adoptive mother and more "home" than Rugraff Street. Still, look at how cruel my adoptive mother has been to me. My disabled state—courtesy of her, my parents, and the tobacco industry—certainly hasn't made my body safe. So my own body—along with my mind—does not feel like home. Obviously, Mother Nature is not safe. This world is not secure. And this world offers no loyalty to us. As the title of one hymn asserts, "This World is Not My Home."

As a young man, and still today, I take great comfort from the apostles' view of this world. They knew life was not safe, with famines and earthquakes and diseases to bring them down, not to mention being savagely persecuted for their faith. All but one apostle had been murdered. They definitely knew that like the prodigal son, we as a race had left home—with horrific consequences. We had mysteriously left our heavenly Father and lost our way. Like the prodigal son, proclaiming ourselves wise, we became fools. In becoming fools, we lost paradise. It was only *after* Pentecost, however, that the apostles got a real feel for what it meant for paradise to have been lost. When the Spirit came to them and the real meaning of Jesus' mission dawned on them, they knew without a doubt that they were only visitors and strangers in a very strange land—a strange and bizarre land of suffering and death (Heb. 11:13). A land that, like an old dilapidated building, had long been condemned.

This world is not my home, not even close.

During high school and college, I had a good friend who eventually entered the priesthood. He and I shared a lot about our faith journey. He told me he could confidently remain celibate for life because he felt so very close to the Blessed Mother. He talked with Mary daily and felt some infusion of her gentle femininity that kept him "pure." I understood. I felt close to the ineffable Mother Nature. Mother Nature was to me as the Blessed Mother was to him—though, don't get me wrong,

I never prayed to Mother Nature. In our projected fantasies, however, both "women" nurtured us. But now I had a nurturing father:

> The Spirit you received does not make you slaves, so that you live in fear again [like we did under condemnation]; rather, the Spirit you received brought about your adoption to sonship. And by him we cry, "Abba, Father." (Rom. 8:15, NIV; brackets mine)

It mattered to me that I was now a part of the family of God and could boldly talk to God as my Father, or "Abba," which is more intimate, like "Daddy" for a young child, or as your brother Paul calls me, "Pops." No fear. No enigmatic condemnation. And my Father was not far away. Nor was he some impersonal quantum-mechanical energy. He was my Pops.

My Home

Though feeling thrilled that God had liberated me from life's nonsense, I still didn't get it. Hypnotically staring at the basement wall, all I saw was the same old, same old. Nothing looked new . . . nothing. Neither the wall nor life. I still sinned. I still had to suffer. And I'd eventually die. Nothing new.

I found some comfort in the fact that the apostle Paul admitted that nothing was new. Not yet anyway. That's why he declared that our new life is still hidden:

> Set your minds on things above, not on earthly things. For you died, and *your life is now hidden* with Christ in God. When Christ, who is your life, appears, then you also will appear with him in glory. (Col. 3:2–4, NIV; italics mine)

The apostle affirmed that when the universe went down, with us in it, our Father set in motion the "hope that the creation itself will be liberated from its bondage to decay" (Rom. 8:20–21a). That hope—that liberation—was Jesus' singular mission (1 Cor. 15:24). So when he finally fulfills that panoramic hope, the universe, with all its galaxies, planets, and black holes, will be "brought into the freedom and glory of the children of God" (Rom. 8:21, NIV). Our Father will rebuild the universe—and, in so doing, rebuild you and me in it, for we are his children (1 Cor. 15:50–54).

So, while I still sin, suffer, and will indeed die, at that *future* point in cosmic history, the apostle says that what is now hidden with Christ in the heavenlies will be unleashed. Jesus will finally and fully crush the law of sin and death. Then my Father will raise me to new life, just as he had Jesus. The "glory" and power of Jesus' body will become the glory and power of my body. Because I am tied to Jesus *now*, I am tied to that new creation yet to come. Jesus is my down payment on my new identity in that gloriously transformed universe where there will be no decay (1 Cor. 15:42–49).

The apostles' futuristic depiction more than stirred my latent boyhood caterpillar-becoming-butterfly hope. That award-winning drawing unconsciously represented my insatiable craving for a new life with a transformed identity free from my family's sin and psychopathology. And Jesus offered me just that.

The apostle John had his own "caterpillar-becoming-butterfly" vision:

> Then I saw a new heaven and a new earth, for the first heaven and the first earth had passed away. . . . "He will wipe every tear from their eyes. *There will be no more death or mourning or crying or pain, for the old order of things has passed away.*" He who was seated on the throne said, "I am making everything new!" (Rev. 21:1–5, NIV; abridged; italics mine)

No more pain. No more crying. And no more death. This futuristic vision began with Jesus' miracles of liberation. It was paid for by his death. It was guaranteed by his resurrection.

Hon, it felt like the apostles had taken my childhood depiction drawn in crayon and turned it into a grand vista painted with the stars and galaxies of the cosmos. Given how I was built—given my boyhood vision—how could I not be drawn?

Would you please join me in listening to *American Idol* and Grammy Award winner Carrie Underwood on YouTube in her moving rendition of "How Great Thou Art" with guitarist Vince Gill? With her passionate voice, that beautiful rendition of the hymn captures the joyous emotion I feel when I contemplate the grand panorama revealed by Jesus' resurrection: When I die, I will not be going home. I won't. Instead, home will be coming to me. Like the prodigal son's father who comes running out to warmly embrace his spent boy, my Pops will come bounding out to embrace this spent servant by recreating me from the dust—making me into a glorious body with the power of new life to be lived out in our transformed universe where there will be no more nonsense.

Then I'll be home.

 *Pulling It Together*

Father O'Reilly Was Right

In my youthful naïveté, I tried "shooting the moon" by going to seminary. I had hoped to find out just what our heavenly Father actually thought about evil, suffering, and death. You now know some of what I learned. And, between the lines, so much of what I didn't. I did find the answer to my why question. I didn't like the answer then—and I still don't like it now.

Like Job, I did not, however, find the answer to the more specific question "Why me?" or "Why my family?" Why did *my* family have more suffering than my friends' families? Just why was I traumatized? At least I thought I hadn't gotten an answer until many years later, when I became disabled. At that time, I flashed back to something one of my professors candidly put on the table for us students to ponder—something that strongly resonated within me. I found an odd comfort in his words. But I'm getting ahead of myself.

My mad pursuit of Jesus at seminary was one way I worked through my trauma, though I didn't think of it that way at the time. To the victim, many things emerge in trauma's wake. One of them is trying to make sense of one's shattered world. That's one reason why I was at seminary: like Moses, I was trying to make sense of my painful little world. In doing so, I was hoping to make some sense of the entire universe.

One has to be pretty obsessive to pursue these issues like I did. But that's what trauma victims do: We push and push, beating up on the tough issues in a grand effort to integrate our fragmented and contradictory world. If you once thought God protected the

299

little children, trauma teaches you otherwise. If you thought life was about happiness, trauma demands you think again. And so it goes.

After three years of intensive study, I was tired. I was bone tired. And I had many more years ahead for my training as a psychologist. Groan. If I wasn't already neurotic enough going into this venture . . .

Gratefully, by graduation, I had nailed down my core beliefs.

I had chosen to stand on the strong shoulders of our many historic religious leaders, both Catholic and Protestant, who over the millennia worked hard to get—and keep—the story line and its meaning straight. At key moments in church history, our leaders struggled to codify what the apostles witnessed and taught. The beliefs were summarized as creeds. The Apostles' Creed—now my creed—was the earliest one. At the time of its acceptance, there was no "protesting" church—though centuries later, the Protestant movement embraced the same creed.

I did leave seminary with many more questions than when I entered. I do take comfort from the fact that over the centuries, Christians across the globe have wrestled with the story of Jesus and with the very same questions. They too have tried to figure out just who "our Father who art in heaven" is. So I haven't been the only one with loose ends. In fact, in wrestling with their own questions, Christians have had strong and numerous disagreements among themselves. These Christians have been thinking people. They've been good people. But they have also been sinful people who, by degrees, have been blind to their own motives. That's why we now have so many denominations—including the fundamental rift between Catholics and Protestants. Yet it's the same Jesus story.

Perhaps, as I alluded to at the beginning of this long letter, by some people's standards, my beliefs about my Father had become too complex. Yet, in a way, they were still more or less "simple" when compared to crunching quantum mechanical equations. Nevertheless, I give you that my faith has never been simple. But that's because, like it or not, both life and Jesus are complex. After all, Jesus is both a man and God—and that truth certainly is not simple. And his mission has been one of cosmic proportions. And that truth is mind-boggling. Still, simple or complex, I had come to affirm the succinct but gutsy core beliefs that Catholic Church leaders had already nailed down so many centuries ago.

Over hundreds of years, both Catholic and Protestant leaders have believed the same Jesus story—with the very same core meaning. Tear off the institutional husks. Peel back the layers of disagreement and myth. Swallow hard on the fact that both sides executed alleged heretics. And finally, put parentheses on personality differences. Do all that—which, I give you, is one tall order—but do that, and you're left with a core meaning of the Jesus story that Catholics and Protestants alike have agreed on.

It is a huge shame. So many religious leaders, both Catholic and Protestant, have acted so unchristian. Many have even been corrupt, acting no different than some scheming secular politicians. Selling indulgences in the Middle Ages is but one example. Our leaders—both sides—believed it was their moral right to execute people for religious disagreements. The power of the state and the power of the church had been one. It was that way for so long that it made complete sense to them to kill people they judged held wrong beliefs. It was because the state held the power to kill people for their *beliefs*—not only their *actions*—that Thomas Jefferson pleaded for the separation of church and state powers.

Beyond this, Christians have disagreed on a wide range of issues, including infant versus adult baptism; the Communion wafer as symbol versus the actual body of Jesus; the historical versus allegorical meaning of Moses' epic story of human beginnings; purgatory versus no purgatory; and the use of hierarchy in the church. These disagreements led to people creating the many denominations we have today.

Amazingly, in spite of all this, over the centuries Protestants and Catholics have agreed on the basics. They've confessed with one voice that Jesus actually lived; the stories about him were real history. They've agreed that, as a race, we are born into a perverse slavery to evil. Both sides have unequivocally affirmed that Jesus beat suffering and death. Both have agreed he died for our collective evil. Both sides have trusted the eyewitness testimonies that he came back to life in this world. Both sides have asserted that he will recreate the human body into a physical body of immortality. And both sides have hoped in the panoramic that Jesus is just the beginning—"the first fruits"—of a transformed universe.

Father O'Reilly was right. There has been something a whole lot bigger than either the Catholic or the Protestant Church happening.

Before modern theologians gutted the Jesus story to make it palatable, these had been the radical but shared core beliefs of both Catholics and Protestants. In fact, the real definition of the "church" is just that: Those who sign on the dotted line affirming these outrageous core beliefs no matter their church membership. That's why I have no single loyalty to any one denomination—even though I was raised Roman Catholic and have been Presbyterian for decades. Such institutions are, more or less, arbitrary rules of engagement by which Christians live as a faith community. I am a Presbyterian. I have held myself and others accountable to play by our own rules; I am on our Presbytery's Permanent Judicial Commission. Still, my fundamental loyalty is only to Jesus—and to my Pops whom he revealed. Institutions come and go. But our Father is forever.

PART 4

Back to the Future:
Wrapping His Royal Robe around My Past

The Moral Trap

The Dilemma

With seminary behind me and now embarking on my studies to become a psychologist, I had to finally and fully square off with the traumatic damage to my mind. I didn't want to. But I knew I had to.

From the research, the picture of what happens in the wake of someone traumatizing us is clear. Whether a person damages us by a criminal act such as rape or kidnapping, or severely injures our psychic development through horrific parenting failures, several powerful things happen.

We, the traumatized, deeply mourn our injuries and losses—and may grieve at various times and in various ways for a lifetime. Those losses, however, stir intense anger—even rage. Buried in that rage is the often silent but instinctual primal scream crying out that the perpetrator had no moral right to do what he did to us. With every fiber in our being, we demand justice. In the blinding shock of our pain, our hearts long to take that justice into our own hands. We may have momentary fantasies of hurting the perpetrator. We may even have moments when we consider destroying him. Whether we do so for real or only in fantasy, those moments—driven by primitive longings to strike back—declare that vengeance is ours.

We also use our rage to figure out ways to protect ourselves from anyone ever hurting us like that again. In our resolve to protect ourselves, we block our inner agony, keeping it from consciousness. We think that if we allow ourselves to feel the pain, the perpetrator would be victimizing us all over again—and we would be betraying ourselves by doing so. Finally, beyond all the pain, rage, and longing to draw the perpetrator's blood, the traumatized ache for freedom from it all.

And so it was for me. In my continued search for freedom—unlike your grandfather—I've learned to cry. If I've wept once grieving my pain, I've wept literally a hundred times. Male or female, one cannot secure freedom from trauma without the shedding of tears. Whether family trauma, war trauma, or rape, tears heal. Tears unlock the shocked, frozen psyche—like my tears moved me out of shock as a young teen when I got jolted with electricity. Sobbing releases inner pain, making room for good things—for thinking new thoughts and feeling new feelings. I've had to come to terms with that fact of life as a man. As a man, I'd rather keep my anger. It feels stronger, more self-protecting—even more self-respecting . . . and certainly more natural. In that anger, I once longed for vengeance as much as I longed for justice. In fact, at an emotional level, I'm not sure I even knew the difference.

Like so many who are traumatized, I buried my pain deep inside so I wouldn't have to go through it all again. Burying my pain came instinctively; it just happened. I never thought about it. Silencing the pain most likely began as an infant, but certainly as a toddler. It would start in the morning with suppressing the lonely isolation of my mother's disengaged silence throughout the day. And it would continue through the night with managing the sheer terror of that abandonment breaking into consciousness—until I fell asleep from sheer psychic exhaustion. But to gain my freedom, I somehow knew as a young man that I had to stop silencing the pain. I had to stop running. In my profession, I now try to help my clients stop their mad retreat from the pain. One client, a top executive of a local corporation struggling to face her childhood, asserted with great frustration: "Why would I want to deal with the craziness I went through as a kid only to feel that pain all over again? I will never give them the satisfaction of hurting me again! What is the point?" She knew what the point was. We had discussed it repeatedly and at length. But she was terrified to stop running.

Kristen, we all live and die with problems. Our problems, however, are not our pathology. Our pathology is our defense against the truth wrapped in and around the problems. All the defenses we use have two things in common: They are driven by fear, and they blind us to truth. Like this high-performing executive, your grandparents had been driven by fear and blinded themselves to their reality. But fear also gripped me from my infancy on. And I used my own defenses to blind myself to the truth of what was happening to me— the very same defenses my parents used. Because of the intense drive to blind myself, choosing to face what happened has required great discipline. But I somehow knew I had no other choice.

In squaring off with my trauma, I pondered: In what way were your grandparents morally responsible for what they did to me? Buried in that question was the maddening search for their state of mind. I ached to know: In their private moments, just what were they thinking? And what were they feeling about what they were doing to me? In families where horrendous things happen—from the murder of a family member to profound child neglect to outright physical abuse—the community struggles with just those questions. Getting at the perpetrator's state of mind is key to the question: Just what is the perpetrator's responsibility? I discovered that there is no final resting place for this one poignant question. Still, I tried to find one.

I first looked to the legal community.

Guilty or Not Guilty?

When a child tragically kills his own parents, the legal community scrambles trying to figure out why the child did it—and how to respond. It rightly holds the troubled child responsible for his outrageous act while trying to figure out how it was that he could end up in such an awful place. The court wants to get a realistic picture of how the parents treated the child behind closed doors. It desires to show mercy to the child—but only if mercy is called for. Judges, jurors, and attorneys compassionately think through the child's inner turmoil. They struggle to fathom the dark but powerful emotional forces that had driven him to commit such a heinous act: fear, pain, rage, revenge—and the desire for freedom. The court wisely considers the possibility that the violence may have gone both ways: from the child to his parents, obviously—but also from the parents to the child.

In its effort to exercise justice, the legal community developed verdicts integrating state of mind, responsibility, and mercy. The court uses the verdict "guilty and sane," for example, to describe someone who it believes knew right from wrong—yet chose to commit the crime anyway. The court judges that the community should punish the person. No mercy is given.

The description "guilty but insane" combines punishment with mercy. The court holds the person responsible and imposes a sentence; the perpetrator is "guilty." But it also judges that the person does not know right from wrong—or at least didn't at the time of the crime—and should be helped. Thus the verdict, "insane." Along with the punishment, the court requires that the person receive psychological treatment for his or her "insanity." The court shows mercy.

"Not guilty by reason of insanity" is the verdict that the person was not responsible for his behavior due to his mental illness; that he should be helped—not punished. The court believes punishment won't do any good for either the person or society. The court judges that the perpetrator should receive treatment for the mental illness that gave rise to the crime. In such a case, mercy becomes central. This was the verdict in the case of John Hinckley, who attempted the assassination of President Ronald Reagan.

Though these categories exist, applying them can be very difficult. A 2002 court judged Andrea Yates, who drowned her five children in the bathtub, as both "guilty and sane." Shocked and repulsed by the crime, the jury just couldn't wrap its collective mind around the idea that she didn't know right from wrong—even though she said a voice told her that drowning her children was the way to save them from "damnation." The jury adjudicated that she knew what she was doing was wrong. She knew the children would end up dead—and their deaths were murder. The court showed no mercy.

But four years later, upon appeal, another court found her not guilty by reason of insanity and committed her to a low-security state hospital for treatment rather than punishment.

These verdicts are attempts, however wise or unwise, to take the complexity of the human condition into account. They are efforts to integrate culpability and mercy. Still, the legal community has no single, clear answer as how best to understand and judge people's poor choices.

In my effort to understand what your grandparents had done to me, I applied—or tried to apply—these descriptions of responsibility and mercy to them. I wondered: Should I find my parents "guilty and sane"? That is, should I believe that my parents knew what they were doing was wrong—but did it anyway? Should I therefore "punish" them in my heart by forever hating them?

Or should I find my parents "guilty but insane"? That is, should I believe my parents were indeed responsible for their behavior and punish them in my heart—even though they never really knew what they were doing to me? Were they, in a sense, not in their right minds? In holding them responsible, should I continue to harbor anger toward them? But if they never really knew what they were doing to me, how can I hold them responsible? How should I react?

Or should I find my parents "not guilty by reason of insanity"? This verdict would be just like the one the jury had decided for John

Hinckley. Should I relieve my parents of all responsibility because they hadn't a clue what they really were doing to me? If so, what do I do with the rage I feel?

How can I—how ought I—picture their state of mind, and therefore, their responsibility? And what then? What do I do with how I think about them? What in the world do I do with how I feel toward them?

The Trap

The secular community has created various pictures of our moral dilemma. In the entertainment arena, *Star Wars* brought us the New Age idea of the "Force" through the well-worn phrase, "May the Force be with you, Luke." With that universal Force came the ubiquitous struggle with its "dark side," personified in Darth Vader (dark father). In the end, Luke's father turns away from the dark side. He "repents." *Star Trek* pitted logic against emotion—rationality against irrationality—in Spock versus Dr. McCoy, with Captain Kirk as the integration of the two. And my profession has several models of an inherently conflicted psyche. One is the struggle between the animal part of the brain and the cultured part. Society demands we behave in ways that go against our built-in instincts. For example, nature built us as animals to lust. Yet religion tells us not to lust. If we do lust, both religion and society tell us not to betray our spouses doing so. We all know the moral conflict within the human psyche is both universal and very real. That's why we work so hard at picturing it. We at least want to understand it, if not—like Luke and Darth Vader in the *Star Wars* drama—master it.

The Bible also paints us a picture of the human dilemma, where we are all born in sin and find ourselves unwittingly slaves of it. Moses illustrates our slavery in the first murder, where Adam's own son Cain killed his brother Abel. From there the dominos toppled down through human history, affecting all future generations, including your grandparents . . . and then me and you. None of us could escape.

As I looked back on my own family tree, I realized that—cascading down hundreds of generations—the forces of sin had engulfed my parents. I did not know my grandparents' histories. And even though I knew Nanny, I didn't know her or her two husbands' histories. So I didn't know what sin patterns my grandparents passed down to my parents. Nor did I know what critical choices they had made . . . and when. All I knew is that all their sins had converged on my parents. Those sins shaped them from the very beginning. Sin didn't appear suddenly—and magically—like at some arbitrary age of reason. It doesn't work that way; sin doesn't suddenly emerge out of nowhere. The forces of sin were built into my parents right from the beginning. Those forces came through their genetic and family histories. Mother Nature built dark motives within my parents' brains in utero. And once born, their families inadvertently taught them specific ways of expressing that darkness.

From seminary, I knew that Protestants and Catholics both believe that sin is woven into our very being. In that way, no baby is "innocent." All babies are built sinners. And all babies stand under that enigmatic condemnation for which Jesus died. After all, we were all once infants—but we've all sinned and suffered, and eventually, we will die. No one escapes this. That's why Catholic church leaders over the centuries believed that infants needed to be baptized as soon as possible after birth. They feared that without baptism, they would die "in sin" and not be saved. Protestants don't agree with the idea of an urgent need to baptize. Still, Protestants and Catholics alike agree we are born trapped by the forces of our inherent evil.

To innumerable secularists—and many Christians, frankly—when we talk this way about the human condition, we sound stupid. Just plain naïve. They think we're foolish to believe babies are born "sinful." So let me be clear. Most Christians do believe that infants are, in an obvious sense, "innocent." No one would ever accuse a newborn baby of immoral behavior. And, just to make the obvious point so absurdly obvious, no one would ever bring criminal charges against a baby. As newborns, my grandchildren were indeed sweet, cute, dependent, fragile, and totally innocent of wrongdoing.

Yet, beyond any choice of their own, these dear grandchildren of mine were born into the human dilemma. In utero, my grandchildren had been fashioned with the biochemistry of death built into them. As the psalmist declared, they will blossom for a time. But then their flowering identities will slowly wither, and the winds of death will blow them away (Ps. 103:15–16). Sadly, like the rest of us, my grandchildren will suffer in this life—and will then die.

My dear grandchildren also came out of the womb with their brains already built conflicted. You've seen it. One moment, they can be sweet and tender. The next, nasty or jealous. In that way, they are not "innocent." They are already contaminated by merely being human. It's simply the way they're built. The ill motives that drive my grandchildren's sins are universal to the human condition. William Golding portrayed this dark side in his 1954 novel *Lord of the Flies*, where he depicted the evil nature of boys between the ages of six and twelve marooned on an island in the South Pacific—representing Eden—after a plane crash. While fictional, Golding was right about human nature.

But that's not all. We adult sinners will raise my dear grandchildren. So, like it or not, our sins will be passed on through modeling, if not by training. As my Little Man, Miss Leah, and Miss Hannah grow, they will borrow our sins, sometimes giving them their own creative twists. After all, toddlers do covet, lie, take things, hit, become jealous, and perpetrate nastiness to their parents or other kids. You see some of that in your children. We adults don't necessarily have to teach or model those things. They are quite capable of coming up with them on their own.

You and your husband wisely had your children baptized as infants in the Presbyterian church—as did your brother and his wife, baptizing their child in the Byzantine church. Some might think it was "unbiblical" for our families to do so; only adults should be baptized. But right or wrong, those baptisms—like any dedication or christening—were our recognition of your children's slavery to sin. It was also our pledge to equip them to fight the fight against evil—first in their own hearts, and then in the broader community. It was our resolve to teach these precious ones about Jesus dying for their personal sin as well as the collective evil of the race. It was our commitment to tell them about the eyewitness testimonies to Jesus coming back to life. And it was our determination to instill the hope that Jesus would rescue the entire universe from destruction. My dear grandchildren's baptism meant all that.

Incredibly, my parents' moral trap growing up was just like my grandchildren's are now. Whether at age two or forty-two, your grandparents' choices emerged from the bewildering entanglement of good and evil within them. Don't get me wrong. Dylan, Leah, and Hannah have a much better shot at life than my parents. Your mom and I have worked hard over the years to "crucify" our sin and nurture our new identities in Christ. You and your brothers—as well as our dear grandchildren—are the recipients of that hard work. But you guys be the final judge of how well we've done; we're within our own skins. Still, knowing what I came from, I am grateful. I am thankful that I've succeeded in mitigating the impact of my parents' poor choices on you guys to the extent that I have.

Because of such hard work, along with your own hard-fought choices, you are a wonderful woman and mother. The man you chose as your husband is a gentle, compassionate father, deeply invested in you and Dylan and Leah. And your brother Paul made choices to be a great father. Like your husband, he is a gentle and compassionate man who chose a very loving and dedicated wife. And these children have a very hard-working, talented, committed, and caring uncle—and godfather—in your brother Matt. So while the intergenerational patterns of sin continue, they are not as rampant or intense. And certainly not pathogenic like the patterns of your grandparents.

Nevertheless, Leah, Dylan, and Hannah are caught in the same moral dilemma as your grandparents. They are members of the race, in the line of Adam. That's the human condition. That's the trap.

And it is that moral trap that my own parents played out against me.

I Am Not the One Doing Them

Trap or no trap, within our own morally conflicted skins, we all have decisions to make about how we're going to conduct ourselves. We all have to decide whether we are going to deal with the sin built into us . . . or not. And how. My parents were no exception. In my pain and anger, I didn't want to let them off the hook.

One could argue, however, and as a young man I did: How in the world can we do anything but sin since we are sinners? After all, Mother Nature built us this way. And then, beyond any choice of our own, our families raised us this way. The bottom line is that without our choice, we were born cut off from the life of God. So how can God expect us to do anything but sin? How can a shark be anything but a shark? That's how God and nature built us. True enough, I suppose. But, according to the apostles, it is precisely for that built-in sin that Jesus died and for which we must, like Darth Vader, decide to "repent."

For the Bible, repentance is a real choice. But looking at an Andrea Yates or a John Hinckley makes one wonder how much a choice it really is at times. For most of us, however, choices do seem real. I counseled one man who was a latent schizophrenic. At times, he'd have psychotic breaks from reality. A major goal of ours was to prevent breaks from reality that required hospitalization. We've now succeeded for over twenty years. Since stopping therapy, he has kept in touch by snail mail and shares his continued success. Still, his people skills and mental world were—and are—limited. He earned only minimum wage. Yet, time after time, at work and with friends, he courageously chose what was morally right in his eyes—even though he was very frightened to do so. In contrast, I knew a wealthy businesswoman who had great people skills and whose mental world was huge. Nevertheless, she repeatedly chose to manipulate, lie, and deceive others. In her own words, she was a "snake in the grass"—and enjoyed slithering into the snake pit to play the game. Over the years I've learned that mental health is no guarantee of moral wisdom. So, even though we are born and raised sinners, our choices to act morally or immorally are real. While each of us brings varying degrees of freedom to life's table, that freedom, however large or small, makes our choices squarely our responsibility.

I had to face the fact that the Bible holds these two basic truths about the human condition in dramatic tension—without any resolution. On one hand, we are responsible for our choices. Yet, on the other, we are enslaved to the forces of sin that set up those choices. A paradox. That paradox gives rise to the legal community's challenges in discerning culpability. That paradox also makes it challenging as a psychologist to discern the degrees of freedom someone has mentally to make clear-headed choices. Still, the paradox forced me to face that my parents were indeed responsible for their choices while being trapped by real forces of darkness built into them.

The apostle Paul revealed this paradoxical tension between choice and the forces of sin within himself:

> I am not spiritual since sin rules me as if I were its slave. I do not understand the things I do. I do not do what I want to do, and I do the things I hate . . . . I want to do the things that are good, but I do not do them. I do not do the good things I want to do, but I do the bad things I do not want to do. So if I do things I do not want to do, then I am not the one doing them. It is sin living in me that does those things. (Rom. 7:14–20, NCV; abridged)

I deeply appreciated the apostle Paul's candor. He humbly describes his own almost unfathomable frustration with his inner moral conflict. For those of us who are not sociopaths or hardened criminals, we can identify with the apostle. Sin grips us at our core, and the struggle to choose wisely is, at times, exasperating. The secular community recognizes this complex moral dilemma, which is why the courts came up with many nuanced verdicts.

If your grandparents had been self-aware enough, would they not have exclaimed in similar passionate frustration, "I do not do what I want to do," and "I am not the one doing them. It is sin living in me that does those things."

What was a young man supposed to do knowing he had been horrifically damaged by his own parents—but parents trapped within this most mysterious moral paradox?

The Verdict

In the more "normal" range of sinning, most children learn to accept that their parents are both good and bad. A major challenge for a child growing up is to learn to say to herself, "Oh well, that's Mom," or "You know, that's just how Dad is," when putting together Mom's and Dad's sin with their good side. In fact, your brother Paul has said, "Oh, that's Dad," to you guys as a way to poke at me. Joking like that could not happen unless he had already accepted the good, bad, and ugly within me. But, tragically, when the sin is horrendous—and the emotional damage keeps piling up over the years—the child cannot put together the parent's good with the evil.

One client I had the privilege of working with I diagnosed as "multiple personality"—what we now call dissociative identity disorder. As a little boy, he instinctively put his memories into mental boxes. He put the good ones into one compartment of his mind and the painful ones into another. He created different states of consciousness using those memories. Some think of these altered states of consciousness as trance states. He set it up, in a sense, so the right hand didn't know what the left hand was doing. He did this to protect himself from facing that his own father was both physically and sexually abusing him. As a little boy, he did what soldiers do when tortured as prisoners of war. A tortured prisoner will "dissociate" or distance himself from the torment by thinking about his family. The soldier creates a trance state where he can block some of the pain and protect himself.

I will spare you the gruesome details, except one. My client's father would play with him in the bathtub. Then, out of the blue, he'd push his head under water until he'd nearly drown. Only then did he bring him back up. He'd do that repeatedly. Like a prisoner of war, the little boy retreated to a special mental place to remain sane. But the times of terror happened so often—and were so intense—that the special place he used for escape became permanent. Years later,

317

as an adult, that special place named "George" remembered only the good things his father had done with him, like playing ball and reading books. George tenaciously held onto those precious memories. But—where did this little boy put the memories of abuse? He locked them away in another special place, called "Anthony"—a place George never went to. Anthony's consciousness was forged by those unbearable memories. He was filled with rage. And his emotional pain was unspeakable. I did manage to get the two parts of his divided mind—George and Anthony—to "talk" with one another. Anthony looked down on George, thinking he was naïve and blind. Anthony knew his father was despicable, so he couldn't accept George's fond memories. George, however, desperately wanted to protect the good memories of his father, so he was not willing to admit to himself that his own father tortured him. He'd argue with Anthony that he was making stuff up . . . or at least exaggerating. Neither Anthony nor George wanted to embrace the memories held by the other.

Driven by the primal instinct to survive, this little boy inevitably split his mind in the face of his torture. He did this, however, because his reality was split—divided between good and evil. He couldn't put the two together. He couldn't put together his father's contradictory sides. He couldn't understand—let alone, accept—that his own father would be kind to him one moment yet torture him the next. His reality made no sense. It made no logical sense. And it made no emotional sense. He just had no way to get his mind wrapped around it all. But—neither does the legal community. Neither does the psychological community. And neither does the religious community. Back in seminary, that was my challenge with Moses' picture of my heavenly Father. One time he blesses. The next time, he punishes. We all can describe the problem. Good versus evil. God versus Satan. Bad things happen to good people. Good things happen to bad people. But no one can explain it. The fact is that no philosopher, theologian, or scientist understands how it is that good and evil can coexist in a single individual, let alone the universe. If adults can't, how can a child?

One has to wonder: By what yardstick does one measure human suffering? I don't believe I suffered like this dear man did. Yet, like him, I couldn't wrap my mind around what my parents did to me. Still, I tried. I ran my finger along the perimeter of this moral quandary, asking myself a series of tough questions. After some grand wrestling—and working through my own strong emotions—I came up with these answers.

Do I believe your grandparents were born and raised in sin?
Without question.

Did their birth into—and growing up in—sin set in motion powerful forces that ultimately damaged me?
Yes.

Did they choose to have those sinful forces built into them?
Of course not.

As adults, did they have tough choices to make in the face of those powerful forces built into them?
Extraordinarily tough.

Forces or not, did they make poor choices?
Sadly, they made many poor choices in their lives, like drinking and chain-smoking, not facing their losses, not reaching out to one another, and not talking as a family.

Were they responsible for making those choices?
Yes. They made their own choices.

Did those poor choices—not just the forces within them—severely damage me?
Severely.

Did they fully comprehend the impact of their choices?
No.

Did they blind themselves to the damage they did to me?
I have no doubt.

Do I firmly believe enormous fear drove their blindness?
Yes.

Were they also victims of their own ignorance?
No question.

Do I judge that they were responsible for choosing to remain in ignorance?

Yes, I do. They could have chosen to learn.

Were they responsible for their choices—including their ignorance and blindness—even though they were afraid?

Yes. Courage is not the absence of fear, but choosing while afraid.

The answers above were, and are, brief. But getting to them was not. In my struggles to understand your grandparents' state of mind, I have no evidence—none—that their eyes were open to the bigger picture. They had blinded themselves to the massive damage their choices were making to them and to us kids. In their blinding denial, they created no strategic plan. And, for whatever reasons, ignorance and apathy perhaps, our local parish priests and the Veterans Administration staff chose not to help them build one. If I momentarily imagine that my mother had been sober—if her eyes had been, in fact, open to the bigger picture—would she ever have wanted to hurt me like she did? The evidence is clear. She lived out her life as a dutiful mother as well as a disciple of Jesus Christ. If she had been in her "right mind," I have to admit to myself that I don't believe she would have ever hurt me.

If my dad hadn't been so terrified and self-absorbed in his own tragic struggle for survival, would he have used me up like he did? Did he even know what he was doing to me? If I look at how he tried to be a good father when we lived in Dutchtown, I doubt it. Neither of your grandparents was "criminal." Nothing they did to hurt me was cold-blooded. Still, they did damage me. And the damage has been enormous . . . and lifelong. The tough reality to swallow is that their free and foolish choices emerged from minds trapped in ignorance, fear, blindness, difficult circumstances, and powerful inner forces.

Among their foolish choices was the unspoken, hidden decision to never talk about what was happening to us. They never asked the question, "Now what?" after their dreams shattered. *But they could have.* Instead, they both chose the coward's way out. Somewhere in their collective psyche, they had a few degrees of existential and moral freedom to choose. But drowning in ignorance, they *chose* not to learn. Gripped with fear, they *chose* not to deal. And in their blindness, the consequences nearly destroyed me. Their cowardice cost me dearly.

So around and around it all went for them: fear, ignorance, seeing no way out, no one to help, poor choices . . . fear, ignorance, seeing no way out . . .

Your mom has a card with the following words:

> Courage, real courage, is no quick fix. It doesn't come in a bottle or a pill. It comes from discipline. From taking everything life hands you and being your best either because of it or in spite of it.

Your struggling grandparents were too scared to face the truth. More accurately—they *chose* not to face the truth *while* being afraid. Your grandmother foolishly sought courage in the bottle. And your grandfather hung on through mindless exercise and chain-smoking. But both found only more cowardice. They never delivered their best.

In my efforts to understand my parents' moral responsibility toward me, I did get some answers. But I've never been able to collapse those answers into a singular conclusion. I've never come up with some final pithy verdict, like "guilty but insane." The closest I've come has been the apostle Paul's analysis that your grandparents were "slaves of sin," yet, slaves or not, they were responsible for their choices—and could have chosen otherwise. That's it. That's as far as I've gotten. I've never been able to get my mind wrapped around it any better than that—either for myself or anyone else.

Given that, what's been my response? How have I chosen to react to the not-so-satisfying picture of my parents' culpability? The answer came in the heat of battle one day.

The Path to Freedom

Vengeance or Mercy?

I was lying there in the psychologist's recliner with my jittery eyelids once again closed, ready to face the past. The image emerged spontaneously. I saw the spider form from the blackness. This time, I felt ready for it. I gazed at this creature from my bed in the darkened attic as it slowly clambered up the creaky wooden stairs. To my surprise—after all, I was now an adult—sheer terror rose into consciousness. I was taken aback. My heart was pounding and my palms, sweating. But this time, I didn't retreat under my covers. I didn't suck my thumb and roll my head back and forth as I had done as a little guy. As I laid there mustering the courage to take on this creature, the spider spontaneously turned into my mother. Then, in an instant, she transmuted into Frankenstein, a popular monster of the 1950s, haltingly ascending the stairs. These phantasms of my imagination kept switching back and forth between the surreal and the real.

Terror continued to bathe my consciousness. The spider slowly inched its way along the attic floor to the bed. It gently crawled onto it—positioning its many hairy legs around me with its grotesque body hovering over me and its mouth wide open, ready to devour me. The murderous spider then changed into my mother. She stood over me with a knife—poised to plunge it into me. We were now outside in the woods in the Saranacs of New York. It was nighttime, with only the moon as light. I threw my mother off me. We wrestled for a few moments in the leaves—but I got her pinned. I grabbed the knife from her, holding it in both hands over my head. The roles

323

were now reversed. Terror transformed into rage. I was now the one with the power. I felt ready to plunge that long knife into her . . . my own mother. The hatred pulsed through me. I felt such passionate longings for justice to be satisfied; I wanted to punish her. I continued to hold the knife over her. I wanted her to taste the terror I felt as a little boy night after night and year after year in my attic prison cell. For a few brief moments, I debated how I wanted all this to really play out. As I felt the hate course through every inch of my body, I knew that such vengeance would only keep me entangled in this sick woman's web. What I really needed was to be free. I wanted out. I desperately yearned to escape from the pain of her rejection. I ached for freedom from the terror that her ignoring me day after day had created. I knew that my emotional freedom would allow me to be more of my own man. But still—I hungered for the sweet fruit of revenge. I ached for some sense of justice paid. But then I thought: I can't be tied to her forever in a sick dance of pain, rage, and bitterness. Yet, the craving to get even kept sweeping over me in waves. I couldn't take it anymore. With rage surging to a peak and my heart pounding against my ribs, I lifted the knife even higher over my head, and with as much strength as I could muster, I swiftly plunged the knife into the ground next to her—and let her go.

I wept. I had made my decision.

My New Identity

My mom never came at me with a knife . . . not in real life. At least, I have no memory of any such thing happening. Nor do I have any evidence whatsoever of that. But as a little boy, I would sit at the kitchen table watching her cut meat for dinner with a large knife. I yet have a vivid picture of that knife etched in my consciousness—the same knife I used as a symbol of her rejection in that vignette. As the spider changed back into my mother, she held that very knife as if to kill me.

Your grandmother indeed had been "killing" me—but doing so emotionally by an unimaginable wall of terrifying silence and disinterest. As a toddler, I didn't know why she was doing what she was doing to me. No one told me she was an alcoholic. No one told me she was severely depressed. My father never wanted to admit it to himself, let alone his children. If someone had explained it to me when I was little boy, I likely would not have understood it. But at least I would've had the idea planted in my head that just maybe her profound lack of interest in me wasn't *because* of me. All I knew was that she ignored me. Without an adult to tell me what was really happening, I figured she must not have wanted me—and she didn't want me because something was terribly wrong *with me*, not her.

But—why go through what I went through in that psychologist's office? What really is the point in facing the past?

Most people think that the past is the past; you can't change it, so why dredge it up. Let sleeping dogs lie. The problem is—*the dogs aren't asleep.* The brain is an information processing organ—that's what it does. The remembered past is information—what we call "memories"—that continues to be processed behind the scenes, affecting how we think, feel, and behave. While it is true that the past as real history cannot be changed, the past that gets remembered can. And that matters. Or I'd yet be trapped—and so would my clients.

Without memory, we wouldn't have a sense of identity. In the last years of President Ronald Reagan's life, he developed Alzheimer's. As he lost his memory, he lost his sense of who he was. On the *Today* show, Ann Curry asked Maureen, the president's daughter, "Does he remember being president?" She managed to avoid answering that painful question. The fact is, memories create identity. And our memories—and therefore our identity—include our family's sin patterns laced through our remembered experiences that shape us growing up. Those dysfunctional patterns, as well as the healthy ones, have an intergenerational history going all the way back to the dawn of the human race. So our memories—and therefore identity—stand "in Adam."

From my seminary studies, I knew my identity was no longer forged only through the generations before me through Adam. I was no longer a slave to the sin patterns that had passed down through my family's history. My identity was now rooted in Jesus and his coming back to life. Yet, like John the Baptist and all the apostles, I had to come to terms with the fact that we were not going to get all of our new identity now. Like it or not, Jesus had not swept the universe with new life when he came. The apostles assured us that we'll have it all when he comes again, though we have no idea either when or how. Until our Father reveals that new life in glory—until he revamps the universe—we are called to keep a laser-like focus on the fact that we can have a "taste" of that new life now. A taste . . . but we get that only if we work at it:

> You have begun to live the new life, in which you are being made new and are becoming like the One who made you. This new life brings you the true knowledge of God. (Col. 3:10, NCV)

Pastor John had already taught me this. Resurrection life began *now*—so *now* was the time to grow up in character.

As I entered my training as a psychologist, I applied this futuristic vision to my trauma. This vision fit my two-pronged approach in dealing with life. I knew I had been already built in Adam through my parents. But I kept telling myself that I now had a new foundation for my identity—Jesus. I wasn't "in Adam" anymore. I was now "in Jesus." He was my magnetic draw into the future; he was the Omega point of my new identity. Though I had been forged by my past, I was now being "reforged" or recreated by my future—a future already secured in Jesus. I caught the apostle's vision and tucked it deep inside my psyche. It was that vision that fueled my grand effort to fight the fight against trauma. I wanted my new identity . . . and I wanted it bad.

On one hand, I believed therapy could transform my identity. It would set me free from trauma by changing how I thought and felt about my past. More specifically, since I am my remembered past, if I actually changed the memories, I'd change me. That's what I did on that psychologist's recliner. I changed the past in my head. I changed my reactions to the past. So I changed me.

On the other hand, I thought if I played it smart, I could also transform my sin that emerged from that trauma. Through therapy, I could distance myself even more from the sins of my parents. I could liberate myself through the hard work of facing myself:

> From this time on we do not think of anyone as the world does. In the past we thought of Christ as the world thinks, but we no longer think of him in that way. If anyone belongs to Christ, there is a new creation. The old things have gone; everything is made new! (2 Cor. 5:16–17, NCV)

I did work hard not to consider myself from the world's point of view any longer. I kept telling myself that I wasn't *just* a traumatized young man from a pathogenic family. To be sure, I knew I was that. No doubt about it. Still, in Christ, that's not *all* of who I was. Through Jesus, I was also a young man now tied to a whole new future. A new humanity—a new me. Eventually, a new me in a new universe. So when I edited my inner movie on that recliner, permanently altering my relationship to my mother, I believed I was growing something of that new identity. Unconsciously, I was working to yet fulfill my boyhood mission of the caterpillar-becoming-butterfly. With the dogged determination of my dad, I kept a tight grip on my vision. With the spiritual persistence of my mom, I pursued that vision. I figured if I worked long enough and hard enough, the Spirit would work with me to set me free—transforming me from one degree of glory into another into the character of Jesus Christ (2 Cor. 3:17–18).

Mercy and Freedom

Many people think feelings are just feelings. They also think feelings are neither right nor wrong; they just are what they are. Many counselors think this way as well. But, apart from hormonal imbalances, that's not true. For a human being, how we *think* determines how we *feel*. How we interpret our reality—the picture of life that we create in our imaginations—forges how we feel about our reality. If I think you are going to hurt me, I might feel afraid or angry. If I believe you love me, I might feel joy and peace. Thinking and feeling are two sides of the same coin. Sometimes, we can have a certain feeling and have no idea why. But that doesn't mean it's "just" a feeling. It means we are not yet aware of what it is we are really thinking that gives rise to that feeling. So how I feel depends on how I think—and how I think is a matter of how I interpret reality. How I interpret my reality is ultimately a matter of truth and wisdom.

Jesus taught, "But I tell you that anyone who looks at a woman lustfully has already committed adultery with her in his heart" (Matt. 5:28, NIV). Some think Jesus meant that the thought is as evil as the action. Not true. Jesus was not saying that the *thought* of lust has the same outcome—or the same moral gravity—as the *action* of adultery. Similarly, a momentary murderous thought is far different in its outcome and moral gravity than the act of murder. John Wilkes Booth's *thinking* about murdering Abraham Lincoln would have been far different in its outcome from Booth actually having assassinated Lincoln.

What Jesus was saying was that both the action and the thought were made of the same stuff within us. To pretend otherwise would have been hypocrisy. It was just that kind of hypocrisy among the religious leaders of his day that Jesus targeted in that teaching. In confronting those pretentious leaders, Jesus taught us to look inward. He wanted us to look at how we really think and feel in the secret places of our hearts. He called us to face our imaginations—whether having sex with someone else's spouse or killing someone—because the inner workings of the heart mattered. He knew thoughts and feelings give rise to actions. Actions ultimately emerge from thoughts—and evil actions emerge from evil thoughts.

Looking at my own heart: If, in the secrecy of my own imagination, I had chosen to punish my mother by "killing" her instead of showing mercy—if I had chosen to take justice into my own hands—then what would have happened to me? And how would my heavenly Father have judged me? If I had murdered my own mother in fantasy—in the deepest parts of my mind—which of those legal verdicts we discussed earlier would have best described *my* own moral culpability? If I had plunged the knife into my mother—even though it was just a fantasy—would God have judged that I knew exactly what I was doing? Would my Father have held me responsible for that murderous inner drama? Would he have judged me "guilty and sane"?

Or would my Father have judged that, within my own tumultuous imagination, I was understandably out of control with my overwhelming and long-overdue demand for justice? Would he have mercifully found me "not guilty by reason of insanity"? Or would God still have held me responsible—finding me "guilty but insane"?

In that recliner, I certainly felt an almost overwhelming surge of passion. Even though she was my mother—my own mother—I craved justice, if not revenge. Yet, I knew if I played out my passion in my mind, like Jesus said, my heart would be made of the same stuff as the imagined act—and I'd be morally corrupt. My strong sense of moral responsibility had nothing to do with some residual fear of punishment from God. I was beyond that. Rather, it had to do with fearing the here-and-now consequences of remaining trapped by my own rage—a rage that sought vengeance for my pain. I feared that if I indulged in vengeance, I would never stop indulging—and spiral downward into a bottomless pit. I feared for the long-term consequences to my own identity. So, as I held that knife above my own mother, I knew I had a choice. The choice was real. The choice was palpable. And the choice mattered. Fortunately, I had the inner power—and, if I give myself some credit, perhaps it was also courage—to make a wise choice as those passions unleashed. And so I did.

If, over the years, we secretly keep choosing to draw the blood of those who hurt us, then those choices to hate will forge a lifetime of pent-up rage, bitterness, an inability to forgive, depression, and narcissism. That's the bottomless pit. Beyond a miserable existence, such inner imaginings can drive us to act out. Hatred—if repeatedly acted on in our unconscious imaginations—could lead to physical abuse of someone we care about, like that father who pushed his own son under the water in the bathtub. Harboring hatred could also lead to suicide or murder. I personally knew a family man, a former neighbor, actually, who, seemingly out of the blue, shot each one of his children in the head. He did the same to his wife. And then to himself. What fantasies had this man nurtured in the deep recesses of his pained and vengeful heart? With whom was he really trying to get even by destroying his own family? Harboring hatred and vengeance is a dangerous game.

If we make smart choices—strategically moral choices—in the secret places of our minds, then we can forge a purpose-driven life filled with joy and love. Whether any of us like it or not, our secret mental dramas are life altering. Our thought life is like an incubator. Thoughts—even, or perhaps especially, unconscious thoughts—determine our feelings and then our actions. In so doing, they shape our continued identity. They forge our destiny. If I had continued in my hatred; if I had kept a death grip on my desire to get even with my parents; if I had continued to punish my own mother in the depths of my unconscious imagination—would I now be a free man? Absolutely not.

So instead of vengeance, I chose mercy.

Before I chose mercy, however (actually, part of learning to be merciful), I needed to stand up to my mother. I needed to fight back, but I needed to do so wisely. I needed to fight in a way that didn't destroy her, even in my imagination. To destroy her would be to destroy myself. That's why the courts now allow crime victims to confront their perpetrators in court—and say what they need to say. It's a safe way—a legal, physically secure, emotionally healing way—to stand up to the assailant. I had to do the same thing. In the safety of the psychologist's office, I confronted my assailant, my mother. If I had remained powerless in my own imagination—if I had remained a little boy frozen in terror in that attic prison—I would never have been able to choose mercy. But once I fought back—throwing my mom off me and grabbing the knife away from her so she could no longer hurt me—then I could choose to show her mercy. And I knew mercy would set me free.

In showing mercy, I chose to forgive. I forgave your grandparents without lying to myself about what really happened to me. I didn't suppress the truth. I didn't lazily claim, "Oh, yeah, I let it go a long time ago." I actually faced it—and worked very hard to transform it. I forgave them by standing up to them. I forgave them by understanding them. I forgave them by sobbing out the pain that perilously fueled my vengeful passion for justice. And I forgave them by embarking on a mission of liberation to create a purpose-driven life. But—I forgave them *without* relieving them of their responsibility for their choices.

All this I did in my imagination.

Hon, the problem with hatred is not that we hate. We ought to hate evil. The problem with the cravings for justice is not that we crave justice. We ought to long for—and fight for—justice where there is no justice. The problem is whether we fight smart or not. Whether we fight in ways that destroy ourselves—and bring others down doing so—or fight to rebuild ourselves and lift others up in the process. In the civil rights movement, Malcolm X wanted to use violence to change things. Martin Luther King knew better. He fought smart. As former President Clinton noted, Martin Luther King knew that if he was going to advance the civil rights cause in a law-governed society, he had to choose non-violence. We now honor King with a federal holiday; we do not honor Malcolm X.

In struggling to figure out how to fight back—and in finally choosing mercy—I learned to shed tears over what my relationship with my mother should have been but never was. I learned to grieve. In squaring off with the symbolic attic monsters that haunted me nightly—and in allowing myself to sob—my mother became less of a terrifying figure and more of a sincere but pathetic lost soul who hurt me very deeply. Grieving was part of my fighting smart.

This grand effort served many purposes. But one was to set myself free to snuggle with you guys, talk with you, read to you, tuck you in, and kiss you goodnight. Given *my* bedtime routine, I couldn't ever imagine doing otherwise.

Mercy's View

Your mom and I have friends who stood in a long line to shake hands with the president of the United States, William J. Clinton, as he came off Air Force One at our airport. They were thrilled—even though they claimed they had no use for the president's character or even his policies at the time. I understood. In this culture, to say we've shaken hands with the president of these United States is a huge deal. Not many of us get to do that.

Years ago, when you were very young, our family went with Emily and Ralph to take a tour of the United States Capitol in Washington, DC. We were to pick up tickets at the Washington office of the uncle of one of your mom's friends. He was a retired congressional representative who sold his continuing influence in Congress to various corporations. We brought the *Bethlehem Star* as a gift in return for the tickets. When we arrived, he was smartly dressed and graciously accepted our gift. He actually seemed enthused to meet us and was very talkative. He guided us to a small office off the main conference area where he pointed out the many pictures of him posing with other more politically powerful figures. He was obviously proud. In one picture, he was standing with former Speaker of the House, Thomas "Tip" O'Neill, with his arm around his shoulders. In another photo, he was shaking hands with the president of the former Soviet Union, Mikhail Gorbachev.

To our surprise, he then said, "Let's go." We glanced at each other—and at him—a bit puzzled. Then he said, "Well, you came for a tour, didn't you?" And so our tour of the Capitol began. Outside his office building, he hailed down two taxis, threw open all the doors for us, and directed the taxis to enter the Capitol grounds. He picked up the tab. He guided us through the Capitol wherever he wanted, while John Q. Public had to stay between the tour ropes. We got to talk with the Capitol architect, stand where President George H. Bush would be inaugurated, ride the congressional subway, eat lunch together, and discuss the Soviet Union.

By the time we said goodbye, you could see the excitement—and the sense of privilege—in each one of us. This man had spent the entire morning with us. Given our station in life, through his stories, he brought us closer to power than we would ever have gotten otherwise. He himself was a bit giddy in sharing stories about rubbing elbows with power players—and that giddiness was contagious. Like our friends who eagerly stood in line to shake hands with the president of the United States, for whom they had little use, we had developed our own childlike enthusiasm about the vicarious brush with power players whom we had never met.

The fact is, however, as I'm passing too quickly through midlife, I am not impressed with power as the world typically understands "power." Even while we were on that tour as a young family listening to the representative's stories about top world leaders, I was noticing the gap—the huge gap—between what power means to politicians and what power meant to Jesus. I noticed how my own momentary sense of privilege didn't resonate with what I knew about Jesus. Jesus had an entirely different view of power than the political world order around him. For Jesus, power was the ability to love. It was love that valued others as ourselves. What drove his power—what drives divine power—is the vision to liberate those in bondage and forgive those who commit evil when they repent. True power is always servant power that way. In loving others, Jesus invested in those without worldly political power—like prostitutes, lepers, and corrupt tax collectors—in order to help liberate them. He intentionally—and especially—loved them:

> As Jesus went on from there, he saw a man named Matthew sitting at the tax collector's booth. "Follow me," he told him, and Matthew got up and followed him.
>
> While Jesus was having dinner at Matthew's house, many tax collectors and sinners came and ate with him and his disciples. When the Pharisees saw this, they asked his disciples, "Why does your teacher eat with tax collectors and sinners?"
>
> On hearing this, Jesus said, "It is not the healthy who need a doctor, but the sick. But go and learn what this means: 'I desire *mercy*, not sacrifice.' For I have not come to call the righteous, but sinners." (Matt. 9:9–12, NIV; italics mine)

Some think that Jesus' attitude of loving others, serving others, or being a "Good Samaritan" means that others are more important than us. Not true. In fact, that is exactly the attitude Jesus was fighting. Jesus had little use for the religious leaders' politically corrupt exercise of power—using their power for self-aggrandizement with the attitude that they were better than the masses. Instead of serving those whom they led, they used their positions for money and political influence. Jesus had no use for that game. Life was about love and liberation. On the flip side of that, Jesus did not mean that we were to think less of ourselves either. That would be putting ourselves down. It would be co-dependently blind. It would actually rob us of our inner power to love. Loving someone requires we see them as our equal. We must love others . . . *as ourselves* (Matt. 22:38–40). Our equal. When we love, we do so because it is our free choice to love an equal among us. *How* we exercise that love fits our means and our values. Otherwise, loving others becomes a power game with winners and losers: either becoming Pharisees or the co-dependent, politically weak, and blind followers. And you already know, Hon, how I feel about following anyone or anything blindly. God expects mercy to flow among us. But such mercy should not be blind. Being merciful does set people free—but does so without self-promotion or self-deprecation.

My identification with all that—with Jesus' use of power—has its roots in witnessing your grandparents' lot in life. Your grandfather had been terrified. He wondered how he'd ever make ends meet. And he had a lifetime of coping with being quadriplegic. He felt stripped of his sense of identity as a man, leaving him with little motivation to build or create anything in this life. He had no political power, no social status, little economic strength, and only modest education. And your grandmother? A frightened and depressed lost soul with similar powerlessness. While responsible for their choices, your grandparents' struggle to create a meaningful life stood in the context of having little worldly power.

As I looked at your grandparents; as I looked at the power players in Washington; and as I then looked to Jesus, I realized that your grandparents were among those that Jesus thought of as the oppressed (Luke 4:17–19). They were not among the "strong" who had the power of money, position, or influence. The apostle Paul called such disciples the "weak" ones of this world order (1 Cor. 1:27). Without question, your grandparents were among the sick, the oppressed, the weak, and the marginalized. No, they were not oppressed and marginalized to the sidelines of life by political forces. But they were oppressed by innumerable life forces—from intergenerational to physical to intrapsychic. Your grandparents' unrelenting plight became the driving force within me for my identification with the powerless. So, when as a young man I looked to Jesus, I was magnetically drawn to his use of power to love the "weak." Now in midlife, Jesus' power is the only power that impresses me. His was the power to liberate.

Long before Jesus, the prophet Isaiah penned this beautiful image of the Messiah's use of servant power:

The Spirit of the Sovereign LORD is on me,
    because the LORD has anointed me
    to proclaim good news to the poor.
He has sent me to bind up the brokenhearted,
    to proclaim freedom for the captives
    and release from darkness for the prisoners,
to proclaim the year of the LORD's favor
    and the day of vengeance of our God,
to comfort all who mourn,
    and provide for those who grieve in Zion—
to bestow on them a crown of beauty
    instead of ashes,
the oil of joy
    instead of mourning,
and a garment of praise
    instead of a spirit of despair.
They will be called oaks of righteousness,
    a planting of the LORD
    for the display of his splendor.

(Isa. 61:1–3, NIV)

The Messiah proclaimed freedom. But tragically, your grandparents, like John the Baptist and the rest of us, were not finally and fully set free. Not yet. Your grandparents were not comforted. Nor were they released from their darkness. Jesus said, "Come to me, all you who are weary and burdened, and I will give you rest" (Matt. 11:28, NIV). Sadly, I never did see your grandparents rest until their deaths.

So, I look to the future. I look to what is coming but is not yet. I eagerly wait for my parents' "crown of beauty instead of ashes," for their "oil of joy instead of mourning," for my dear parents to be wrapped in a "garment of praise instead of a spirit of despair." In our renovated universe to come, I look forward to your grandparents becoming "oaks of righteousness" who put on display the splendor of the Lord. May it be so for them.

Lord, have *mercy*.

The Road Less Travelled

That dramatic encounter with my mother in my imagination was just the tip of the iceberg. I've forced myself over years, not simply months, to face what happened to me, Kid. I've taken the proverbial deep breath to stare at and then rework the immeasurable damage these two poor souls did to my life—memory by memory by memory. I've stood back in fearful awe studying the dark forces within them—and within myself. Invisible forces that were unconscious but just as real and just as powerful as the invisible forces bound up in a few pounds of uranium in an atomic bomb.

I've done this because I had chosen to walk the road less travelled. It is a road of transforming the nuclear damage to my psyche into character and wisdom. There's a bridge in this country—the Golden Gate Bridge—where engineers performed an unparalleled feat. They propped up that bridge to allow traffic to flow while they reconstructed portions to sustain stronger earthquakes. That's what I had to do. I kept my life going while I deconstructed and reconstructed myself. In doing so, I've found that real forgiveness . . . transformative forgiveness . . . forgiveness that sets one free, comes at a very high cost. The amount of time, energy, and effort has been incalculable. It's been a grand effort to liberate my heart from trauma—and embrace your grandparents as two sincere but lost people.

Many think if they hold onto their anger—their desire for revenge really—they can become free. The revolutionaries of Jesus' time thought that. Opposing the "enemy," or killing off the enemy—even if it's just in fantasy—makes us feel empowered. Especially for men. But to stay angry, forever fighting an internal enemy, uses up our core energy fighting unconscious battles from day to day. In that way, the enemy wins. This is why many who have been traumatized remain depressed for a lifetime. Depression is a sign. It's the mind's signal that so much inner energy is being used up fighting deeply nonconscious battles that there's not enough left over to really live life. If one is going to have a purpose-driven life filled with joy and love, the purpose sure has to be a whole lot bigger than opposing or killing off the enemy.

But the bondage of vengeance goes deeper.

My parents were, and still are, "in me." To continue to get even—to harbor intense resentment—and not reconcile with them would also have been to not reconcile with myself. I'd be divided within myself. I'd be like my multiple-personality client who was abused by his father. You know the expression, "We have met the enemy, and he is us." I and my parents are one. To be sure, I am more than my parents. Still, I *am* my parents. So to hate my parents would be to hate my internalized parents. To hate the parents within me would be to hate myself. To want to destroy my parents would be to want to destroy myself. That's what sometimes happens in suicide. The person kills self, unconsciously trying to kill his internal parent. Or lives a self-sabotaging life getting even. When I chose to "love my enemy-parents," I chose to love myself. In loving myself, I could then be free to love those entrusted to my care. If I hadn't done so, I would've been narcissistically preoccupied with my own inner pain. I would've been lost. Just like your grandparents.

Reconciling with my parents—and therefore with myself—set my talents free as well. It is a strange reality. But when we cast the net of suppression to bury painful memories, that net drags our talents down with it. It's like casting the net for tuna and accidentally trapping dolphins in it, causing them to die because they need to surface to breathe. Facing inner pain, however, lifts that net and sets our talents free. Our thinking becomes more creative. Intelligence increases. Musical and artistic talents emerge. Innate athletic prowess gets stirred. And sexuality once repressed becomes unleashed. I had one midlife client whose sexuality was mobilized in a way where her hormones changed, her face became softer, and she reported that her breast size increased. Believe it or not, stranger things have happened.

Your mom and I have an old friend from college days who was abused as a child. She managed to build a quality life—and is a woman of deep character and wisdom. She loved playing the piano, though her ability was at a very basic level. After several years of therapy in midlife, she discovered her greater talent in music. On a trip heading north into New York, she stayed overnight with your mom and me. She sat at our old spinet piano where her gentle fingers orchestrated a complex piece of music. It sounded magnificent to me. But, more importantly, it sounded wonderful to your mother's trained ear. Our dear friend was playing extraordinary music, though she said she had no idea technically what she was playing. The music simply flowed out her brain, down her arms, and into her fingers—intuitively. Her gift of music had been liberated. She had disentangled it from her deep psychic pain—one of the many rewards for courage in transforming trauma into character and freedom.

Fortunately, she's not alone. People across this country who have faced their inner demons have likewise liberated their talents. The fact is that hiding pain and anger from ourselves—or allowing them to captivate our imaginations—is a death trap. Such blindness to the truth of what lurks deep within us uses up our inner energy and keeps our talents suppressed. It kills our potential . . . like it did for my parents. We end up living pitiable, self-sabotaging lives. Or mediocre, depressing existences wondering why we're even on the planet.

As I've walked this road less travelled playing the hand dealt to me as best as I could, I've asked myself at various points along the way: How much of my potential is yet buried along with the pain? How blind am I still?

The Humility of Fear

By varying degrees, I know I've been blind. And the maddening thing about it is that I didn't know to what extent I was blind *while* I was blind. But of course I didn't know; you don't know until you know. It's that way for everyone.

I take only a sliver of comfort in the fact that we're all blind. We're all blind because, for one reason we are all by degrees naïve—like your grandfather.

Your mom and I were packing up our Sunfish sailboats for the season at Spruce Run when an old salt strolled by with his dog. We said hi and got to talking, for about an hour and a half actually. We found out he was in his midseventies. He noted how when you're talking about life with someone younger, you can tell that they sometimes just don't get it. They don't get it because they're simply not there yet. He shared this knowing we were significantly younger than him, being yet in midlife. But this man had had a talk with another old salt who was his elder by about twelve years. He said he could tell that this man was looking at him with that same knowing look—as if this most senior salt knew things he yet didn't. Together we wondered what it was that that eightysomething senior discerned about life that the three of us still didn't.

We can't have wisdom from life that hasn't been lived yet. If fact, I have this tongue-in-cheek definition of wisdom as that which we learn too late to really use. Overstated, but true enough. But we're also blind because at times we proclaim ourselves wise when we're really fools—not truly interested in the truth (Rom. 1:22ff). We are also like the anorexic looking in the mirror. Nobody sees himself or herself—or God—completely accurately. We distort truth. Not to mention the fact that truth is just plain hard to get. In fact, even with the Spirit of Life within us now, we yet see only a dim reflection of truth in life's mirror (1 Cor. 13:12). We too often live life based on those shadowy reflections without being aware that that's what we're seeing: shadows. Until the consequences catch up with us. Sometimes, those consequences smack us in the face, waking us up in time to change course. Other times, it's too late—the consequences have already destroyed our lives. Hon, I've learned to never underestimate my power to blind myself to truth. Or distort the truth in the service of my darker motives.

To help me keep my eyes open, I have always surrounded myself with men and women of wisdom whom I respect and to whom I could go for advice. I ask them directly if I am "out to lunch"; I neither need nor want "yes" friends who humor me. Sound living and sound leadership require that. I don't always take their advice. Advice has to make sense to me, not just to them. But since life's reflections are dim, even dark at times, I submit my thoughts to them in case my thinking is twisted or I don't see something I should. I do carefully count the cost of my decisions, looking ahead as best I can to the consequences. I have tried very hard not to harm others or myself in the process, though I know I have. Like your grandparents, my own fears, ignorance, blindness, inner dark forces, and poor choices have played out in my relationships with your mom and with you guys. I know that. Like David in the Psalms, my sin is ever before me (Ps. 51:3).

In the struggle with my own dark forces, I have taken the apostle Paul's words as sober counsel:

> Therefore, my dear friends, as you have always obeyed—not only in my presence, but now much more in my absence—continue to work out your salvation with fear and trembling. . . . (Phil. 2:12, NIV)

It, indeed, has been with fear—and, at times, with literal trembling—that I have struggled to work out my own salvation. But it has not been with the fear of punishment that I've done so. After all, as the apostle explained, "there is therefore now no condemnation for those in Christ Jesus" (Rom. 8:1, NRSV). I wasn't concerned about my Father coming to get me for my sins—either purging me in purgatory or punishing me forever in hell. I had been forgiven; Jesus had already taken the eternal consequences.

Instead, my real fear was whether I would have enough discernment to make wise choices in the here and now—because in *this* life, choices still determine consequences. Forgiveness in Christ or not, foolish choices—immoral choices—bring bad consequences.

No doubt, you've seen it. I've had shivers sent up my spine by the price tag many have paid for refusing to enter life's sweat tank. My own dermatologist is now spending years in prison for downloading and trading in child pornography. A minister in our own denomination was defrocked for seducing a parishioner. An alcoholic lawyer alienated his family for life for hitting his wife. A top executive lost the affection of her children for working too long and too hard. A colonel in the army lost his wife to divorce because he shut down emotionally. Tragically, the list could go on.

In one letter, the apostle Peter encouraged certain Christians to stop being blind to how they're playing out their hand in life. He encouraged them to wake up—and prodded them to catch the vision in Christ. He confronted them with the fact that they were living as if they had forgotten they had been set free:

> But anyone who does not have these things cannot see clearly. He is blind and has forgotten that he was made clean from his past sins. (2 Pet. 1:9, NCV)

In that same letter, the apostle Peter scolded Christians who were not only making blind, foolish choices but were then leading others into their foolishness. Quoting from Proverbs, the apostle warned them that people who go back into their old sin patterns after having tasted freedom are like dogs going back to their own vomit. Thinking they are free, they're really slaves—but absolutely blind to their own slavery (2 Pet. 2:19–22). The apostle Peter's repulsive image stayed with me. I've never wanted to lap up my own vomit—not to mention the years of lapping up my parents'. When I have, I couldn't stand it; I was disgusted with myself. The apostle made it clear that we can either remain blind or wake ourselves up—and walk into freedom.

On this road less travelled, I have to admit that I've felt like I've been in life's sweat tank too many times already. Still, I keep choosing to walk this road. It's the only one to freedom. I walk it at times with some real fear and trembling. I believe fearing my own stupidity and blindness is both smart and realistic. Such fear constitutes humility, not self-deprecation. I saw what ignorance and blindness could do. It is only in walking this road with such fear that I have any shot at having enough clarity among life's shadowy reflections to secure more of my new identity hidden with Christ.

PART 5

Clutching His Royal Robe

I Am—But I'm Not—Thomas

Your Grandfather's Demise

Being fully quadriplegic, your grandfather developed awful looking sores on his body. They eventually became badly infected; he had to be hospitalized. Though his legs were essentially paralyzed, he nevertheless could feel pain. With those sores and whatever neuro-muscular damage accrued in his legs over the decades, that pain was now excruciating. Not only could I see the unspoken agony in his face, but also noticed your grandfather's eyes welling up as he was lying in his hospital bed—with a single tear gently falling from the corner of his right eye. I had never seen him tear up in pain like that before. The doctor—a sensitive young man who seemed to lock in on my dad's predicament—gently asked him if he wanted his spinal cord surgically cut to stop the ordeal. Your grandfather refused. I don't think he could bring himself to accept that his fight against MS was ending in defeat—let alone admit that his life was now drawing to a close.

I was twenty-eight. As my mother had envisioned toward the end of her life ten years earlier, I was on my own finding my way—though I was yet pretty insecure: My mom had been gone for a decade; I didn't have much of a relationship with my father; my brothers had moved on with their lives; I was pursuing my advanced studies in psychology and accruing enormous debt doing so; your mother and I had our first child; I had embarked on the mission of squarely facing my trauma; and now, my father was dying. It was a lot. Though my relationship with my father had been weak, from mercy's viewpoint, I felt a great deal of compassion for him in

345

his last days. Besides, he was my father—and there was only one
of him.

Apart from impulsively blurting something out about being a
"cripple" when I was a little guy, your grandfather was not one to
speak much about himself—and his last days were no exception. I did
venture to talk with him briefly about Jesus, and he was willing . . .
at least willing to listen. I noted that Jesus forgave him for his sins
and even prayed with him. He dutifully followed my lead. I also told
him that I looked forward to seeing him again in the resurrection; he
simply nodded in agreement. Nothing else was said.

As I quietly sat with my dad, I did wonder whether he was
saved . . . or not. Whatever your grandfather had done to me, I did
not wish him ill. Within mercy's viewpoint, I felt some compassion for him and would have given a lot for him to be set free . . .
physically and mentally. With seminary behind me, I now understood more what the apostle Paul meant when he used that word
"saved." So I wondered: Was my dad truly tied to Jesus? Tied so that
his sins against me and my brothers were forgiven and that he would
indeed come back to life? Given his psychic blindness, I doubted he
had ever asked Jesus for forgiveness for what he had done to me.
He certainly didn't ask me for forgiveness as he lay there. Then I
thought back to that conversation with one of my seminary peers
who had said Catholics can't be saved. Foolish arrogance. Still, as I
sat there, the question remained: How do I know that my own father
is saved? The question then spun around on myself: How do I know
I'm saved? Or anyone for that matter?

I momentarily thought back to Martin Luther, that protesting
Catholic monk who ended up as one leader among many of the
Protestant movement. I had joined Luther in his reaffirmation of
what the apostle Paul had declared: we were saved by faith in Jesus;
we couldn't "work our way to heaven" (Eph. 2:8). Working my way
into God's heart had become as absurd to me as the idea that I could
recreate myself in the resurrection.

From my vantage point—and I had no other—my father believed
in Jesus. He had received the Eucharist time after time, supported
his children's Catholic education, and kissed the saints' relics in the
hope of salvation from MS. Wrapped around all this was his desperate dialogue with God about why and his brief dialogue with
his boy about practical faith. Whatever mix of motives there might

have been behind this, one motive was that he believed. And without question my dad had Jesus' core values. But my father believed in Jesus and held onto Jesus' core values *while* playing out a disordered life. And he held onto his core values *while* believing his version of having to work his way to heaven—like most good Catholics back then. But some might think that that belief of working one's way to heaven, along with my dad's outrageous treatment of me, just shows he was not a Christian. Some might believe he didn't have, as the title of one book goes, "the marks of the Christian."

Sitting there, I knew that being my father's son, I had his solid core values while yet struggling with my own sin and disordered side—sin and disorder borrowed from him. So in key ways, I was no different. A few years earlier, I also had known seminarians whose character I thought was out to lunch. Since then, over the decades, both in being a psychologist as well as an elder in my church, I've had to deal with some pastors whose behavior has been shameful: from lying, to passive-aggressive hostility, to refusing to deal directly with their own lay leaders, to manipulating congregants, to betraying their spouses in extra-marital affairs. In contrast, I have known atheists who have displayed more "fruits of the Spirit" than those pastors; they certainly had more character. Still, while behaving sinfully, these men and women who donned the pastor's frock sincerely believed in Jesus. They believed *while* sinning. They took Communion . . . while sinning. They prayed . . . while sinning. They led their congregants . . . while sinning. They read their Bibles . . . while sinning. They had core values like my father . . . while sinning. The fact is, they believed—while playing out their disordered selves on the stage of life.

Over the years, I have also known innumerable Christians whose beliefs about the Bible and Jesus struck me as terribly uninformed or twisted. One elder believed the position of his hands during prayer was a factor in the power of his utterances. And I have known innumerable Christians whose lives have been disordered by hugely varying degrees. One dear lady who was deeply conflicted from her childhood would sit on the closed toilet seat in her bathroom rocking back and forth chain-smoking cigarettes, filling the bathroom with thick white smoke while repeatedly uttering in mantra form, "Thank You, Jesus . . . Praise the Lord . . . Lord, help me." She rocked back and forth to keep the deeper intrapsychic forces from breaking into consciousness much as I had done as a little boy rocking my head back and forth in my attic prison to keep my sanity.

So—where do I draw the line? Where and when am I willing to say someone does not belong to the family of God because of this or that sin or disorder?

I wasn't willing to go there as a young man watching my father's last days—and I am not willing to go there today. I am not shy about exercising discernment about others' behaviors; I get paid to do that very thing. And I do judge—that is, make discernments about—my own behaviors. I do hold myself and others accountable for how we treat one another and for what we believe about the Bible. No question. So I am willing to judge whether I or others have the marks of the Christian.

But as I looked at my father's gnarled body in that hospital bed, I neither had the authority nor the discernment to know whether he belonged to Jesus. So, at his bedside, I treated my father as he had lived: a man who believed in Jesus, who had Jesus' core character, but who, like so many on the planet and in our churches, had his own sin and psychopathology. Based on all that, I did tell my dad I'd see him in the resurrection. Whether in the end he is raised to new life or not, I leave up to God.

Back then, hospice was just beginning and was not on anyone's radar screen. But your grandfather refused to stay in the hospital any longer. Though over the decades he had fought his MS blindly, he nevertheless had fought, so the doctor and I had no idea how long he'd linger. So your grandfather went home. I had no choice; I had to go back to school to finish my semester's studies. I waited for a call from his caretakers to let me know when the end was imminent. When that call came, your mom and I rushed from Bethlehem to Rochester, but by the time we got there, your grandfather had already slipped into a coma. I was grateful I had had that time at the hospital with him to talk and pray, but I was upset that I didn't get to say a final good-bye. Instead, I sat by his bed and just talked to him for a while. Then suddenly his body lurched—and with a spontaneous gasp, he passed away.

As I thought back to his badly broken body in the hospital—and his cold, stiff body lying on the bed he had used for years for his innumerable fitful nights' sleep—I once again wondered about the Jesus story. You'd think after all the hammering out of my faith that I did at seminary there'd be nothing left to wonder about. But I discovered that's not the way faith—and therefore trust—in God works.

I've learned that trust takes time and experience . . . trust in anyone, including God. You know how people say, "Time heals all wounds." Not true. Time heals nothing. Time is only the conduit within which things can happen, like the body scrambling to heal itself after getting wounded. The body needs that time to do what it does. People also need time to do what they do. So people build trust with one another over time by actually doing the nuts-'n-bolts things that in fact are trustworthy. It's those practical, day-to-day things that, over time, drive trust into the depths of the psyche. Trust gets built into us layer by layer, not all at once. In that way, trust is earned. For example, spouses earn trust in one another by being kind to one another every day.

But trust can be damaged. Spouses sometimes harm their growing trust during vociferous arguments. They may throw each other's sins or weaknesses up in each other's face. They then walk away feeling that the other can no longer be trusted with their hearts: "Why should I tell you anything? You're just going to throw it back in my face the next time we fight." To reconcile, they not only have to forgive but also treat each other kindly once again to rebuild the broken trust.

This is the way it is for all of us. Trust has to be earned and learned . . . and relearned—one nuts-'n-bolts experience and one layer of the mind at a time. We don't—we can't—simply trust.

All this holds true for building trust with our heavenly Father as well. We can't just jump out of our skins to trust him. So as I thought of my dad, I asked myself: How do I come to emotionally trust my heavenly Father? And trust him *for what* exactly?

No one can trust me to fly a commercial airliner; I have no training. And you can't trust that I will not forget things, especially mundane details, like what you typically order at Frank's Pizza when we go out for lunch. You can, however, trust that I will be sincere.

Similarly, we must ask: For what can we trust our Father? What exactly does he do for us that we can rely on? Which raises the other question: What does he *not* do for us?

Can we trust him for a certain quality of life? C. S. Lewis apparently thought so; he kept getting his hopes up that our Father would rescue his wife Joy. And when he didn't, Lewis became despondent. His depression clearly showed that he clung to the belief that his

Father should have rescued them from cancer. But his Father did not. Lewis never really came to terms with the clear evidence of life: We cannot trust our Father for any particular quality of life. We know that from the flow of life. The evidence before us is clear. Nothing is divvied out fairly, whether health or wealth. We also know the apostle Paul clearly implied that we are not promised a rose garden (Rom. 8:38ff).

So, for what can we trust our Father?

In the face of such a stark and brutal reality as my father's life as a quadriplegic, his agonizing demise, and finally his cold, dead body, could this newly exposed layer of my psyche actually trust that my heavenly Father loved your grandfather and me? Looking back, like both your grandmother and Lewis, I was still naïvely expecting— even secretly demanding—that my Father show his love in the flow of my family's life. I wanted his love on *my* terms—terms which I've never thought were unreasonable. Besides, without the day-to-day, nuts-'n-bolts evidence of my Father's love, how was I to *know* he loved me, let alone *feel* his love?

My heavenly Father's love came across like your grandmother's love: duty without feeling. He did his duty in Jesus. "Jesus loves me— this I know, for the Bible tells me so." That's it. That's how I know he loves me. And nothing more. No guarantee of rescue or protection or good things happening from day to day. No more baptisms in the Spirit. Nothing. My Father was done . . . until the end when Jesus comes again. The apostle Paul told us that explicitly: our life was hidden until the end. So I had to tell myself to forget looking for a certain quality of life from our Father. He never promised it. He's under no obligation to give it. Nor should I be under any illusion that he'll ever deliver it in my lifetime. He didn't for your grandfather.

But—and it is one huge but—how in the world was I supposed to *feel* the truth that he loves me? How? Was I supposed to just look back to Jesus and simply know I'm loved—like looking at my darned socks as a kid and knowing that my mother loved me? Was that it? Or was I supposed to hang onto that ecstatic encounter with the Spirit for the rest of my life? The years passing by makes such an experience wear pretty thin. How could I drive the apostle's truth in and through all the damaged layers of my traumatized psyche to *feel* my Father's love? Frankly, I couldn't get past my inner demand to *feel* the love on at least some of my terms . . . in a way that made some sense to me. Not getting his love on my terms pushed me back to the same question I had while in the Koinonia fellowship: If Jesus came to set us free from suffering and death, then why weren't we free of suffering and death?

Ah, foolish me—a decade old question revisited. It was like mental Whac-A-Mole: Old questions popping up like new ones. But—like it or not, they were old questions emerging from a *new* and as yet untapped deeper layer of my traumatized psyche. So there was no escaping them.

Staring at my dad, now gone, my mind drifted back to when I was a young boy living on Rugraff—when my father acted like a dad. I fondly remembered throwing the ball with him as he sat on the front porch steps and his handing us a cigar box full of baseball cards. I also found myself thinking back to my pet goldfish. As a little boy, I kept three fish in a small bowl. One morning I woke to find all three floating at the top. They were on their sides and their bodies were badly bent—and stiff. I just stared at them. As a little boy, the sight so mesmerized me that my memory of their floating bodies is as vivid today as it was the moment I discovered them dead. Seeing them floating there lifeless brought death close to me as a little guy, much closer than killing ants had. I then thought back to my mother gently holding Tiny in our family's deathwatch for our pet. I never did see Tiny actually die; I just was told she was gone. And I didn't stay at the vet's to see my second Tiny die. But I did witness my own father die.

My mind turned to the apostle John's futuristic vision: "Then death and Hades were thrown into the lake of fire. The lake of fire is the second death" (Rev. 20:14, NIV). Supposedly, Jesus' coming back to life meant that Death itself would someday, somehow, "die." Mysteriously, Death would be destroyed.

I had seen my mother in the casket at the funeral home. But sitting close to my dead father lying in the same bed I had lifted him from for so many years of my troubled youth was different. Palpably different. Stiff and lifeless like my pet goldfish, my dad would never wake up. He'd just decay into mere dust. Nothingness. I took in the power of death. Ants. Goldfish. Dogs. My mother. My father. Death took them all.

Obviously—though not trivially so—I had not seen or touched Jesus myself after he came back to life. Still, the divine expectation was that I'd have to trust the apostles for that. Yet, like I said, trust wavers, and only experience delivered through time can drive trust deeper. So, in the face of life's evidence, I felt just like the apostle Thomas . . . unapologetically so. Squaring off with his own life's evidence, the apostle Thomas refused to trust his friends until he saw the risen Jesus for himself: "Unless I see the nail marks in his hands and put my finger where the nails were, and put my hand into his side, I will not believe" (John 20:25, NIV). I certainly understood that feeling . . . that demand. I had my own.

The apostle Thomas got the privilege of seeing and touching the risen Jesus for himself. That's why he trusted. That's only why he trusted. Touching Jesus drove trust deep into his bone marrow. *His* bone marrow—not mine. I only saw and touched Death. I witnessed my father being put into the ground—and he has never come back out. I did not witness Jesus being put into the tomb, nor have I ever had the opportunity to touch Jesus after he came back out. I could only "touch" Thomas from a distance—a very long distance—and it was only through Thomas that I could ever hope to touch Jesus.

I noticed myself staring at my father's dead body. I closed my meditations; it was time. We had to call the doctor.

I thought, may you finally rest in peace, Dad.

As If Childhood Trauma Were Not Enough

On a Dime

It was just three years later after grandfather passed. Your brother Paul and I were out camping in our little pup tent when I was a young father. He was only four; I was now thirty-one. Now that I think of it, we were the same ages as you and Dylan as of this writing. While we were lying there in our tent playing a game, he pulled out a plum from our backpack, held it up, and declared: "This is the biggest grape I've ever seen." While it is one of those cute moments where you had to be there to appreciate it, we roared. We both remember it to this day.

I woke up at midnight to the wonderful aroma of campfire smoke—a country smell I so thoroughly enjoyed while camping in my youth—but I woke up wheezing a bit. My asthma first developed in college when I was exposed to several kittens in the apartment I shared with three other guys. One of the men brought in these cute little fur balls, and, being in the lower bunk, I'd usually end up with two of them sleeping with me. One typically curled up just under my left knee, and another usually settled in for its night sleep on my chest. But one night I woke gasping for air. The first doctor I went to said my X-ray was clear. Then, making a joke about my symptoms, he dismissed me. Besides arrogance, I have no idea why. But the second doctor was the college physician who immediately diagnosed it as asthma—and told me to get rid of the cats or leave the apartment. A doctor back home confirmed the diagnosis, and so I began injections. With those regular injections, the mild asthma had gone into remission for years. Midnight that night, camping, my wheezing was mild, so I decided to just drink some water and go back to sleep. About seven hours later that morning, however, the asthma came back with a vengeance. My lungs became constricted and red-hot—as if a heated fireplace poker had been surreptitiously embedded into my chest while I was asleep.

Shortly after that campfire exposure, I began injections again. Oddly, though, that poker heat stayed with me for about seven years. Using my medications, however, I could engage in any outdoor activity I wanted—even going on vacation to our church's weeklong Kirk Camp nestled on Lake Swanzey near Keene, New Hampshire, which Mom and I had hoped would become our family tradition. I had gone to two doctors over those seven years, but neither one had any idea why my lungs felt red-hot 24/7.

Those seven years later, once again my lungs suddenly changed. Within a couple days, I went from that red-hot burning sensation in my lungs to no heat at all. None. It was a great relief. At first, I thought the injections had worked and the worst was over. The injections had worked, but the worst wasn't over. It had just begun.

I felt a slight discomfort breathing; I felt myself straining a bit. My Theophylline and inhalers were no longer enough. But the allergist told me that there was nothing else to do. He said I was not severe enough to go to the hospital. He instructed me *not* to take my emergency steroid—saying steroids were too powerful to take unless absolutely necessary—and, in my case, they were not necessary. Nor did he refer me to anyone else. He let me leave his office straining to breathe, saying there was nothing else to do. He was wrong—but he didn't know he was wrong. Neither did I at the time. Tragically for me, he didn't know what he didn't know. As the patient, I thought this was simply the state of medicine at that time—and I was stuck with the challenge. So I sat tight, a decision I would regret the rest of my life. I sat tight because I trusted this doctor. He was sincere and I felt I could talk to him—and given my need to talk, that mattered to me. Like most good patients, I depended on him to know his job. And like most good patients with difficult medical conditions, fear drove that dependency.

Looking back some years later, besides my fear-driven dependency, I had relived my family through this doctor. In fact, such fear and dependency drove that reliving. And that's typical. When someone else has authority in our lives—like a boss or police officer or doctor—there is always a tendency to flash back to our parents' authority. Doing so sets up reliving the family pattern. So I didn't immediately go to another doctor because he unconsciously reminded me of my parents: a relationship of sincerity laced with ignorance and suffering. It was a familiar cocktail mix. He was like Mr. Dattilio at Camp Massawepie: sincere but blind, not knowing he was blind. I stayed under his care too long. Two weeks later, I felt incredible discomfort throughout my abdominal area. That discomfort snapped me out of it. I took the dreaded steroid—*against* this doctor's advice. It was a good thing I did though. Taking that Prednisone immediately stopped whatever was happening to my body.

I was now able to breathe more easily. I also could discern what had actually been going on with my body: the muscles in my abdomen and back had gone into severe spasm. The steroids stopped the spasms immediately. But my decision was too late; the damage had been done.

I left that doctor and found one who had received training at the renowned National Jewish Hospital in Denver, Colorado. After a candid discussion about my body and my now high distrust of allergists, he looked me straight in the eyes and said, "With what I know, if this were my body, I'd do precisely what I'm recommending." His directness persuaded me; I came under his care. That decision I've not regretted. While working his game plan for my lungs, I pursued physical therapy for the muscle damage. I also sought help from a physiatrist—a doctor who specializes in damaged muscles and fascia.

I've made significant progress since. But over twenty years and thousands of dollars in physical therapy later, I still have massive myofascial damage, including symptoms of fibromyalgia. Therapy is always very painful. My abs are yet stiff and tight, including far up under the ribs. The muscles between the ribs intensely hurt with slight pressure. My entire back feels like leather. And I feel like I have a tight jacket wrapped around my upper body. A lot of the damage is permanent. Many of the muscles have taken the twenty years to rehabilitate to about 60 percent of normal. Prior to this fiasco, I had been doing full-body workouts at a sports center to keep in shape. Never again to be. Even using a bicycle or treadmill now creates a great deal of discomfort in my back and abdominal muscles, including nausea, by overstimulating the vagus nerve running up and down the center of the abdomen. That happens often.

Still, I do it. I manage the discomfort with stretching, supplements, an anti-inflammatory, and a muscle relaxant. I also use elastic bands to provide a minimum of muscle toning, though that too aggravates the condition.

At thirty-eight, with three young children ranging in ages from six to eleven, besides the severely damaged muscles, my lungs were now in bad shape. They were hyper-reactive to allergens, but I was still discovering how much. And I was hoping against hope for normalcy. So I headed out to a camping event with Matt and his Scout troop. On the way, I had a spontaneous attack that forced me to go right back home. Matt was crying and my heart was broken—for him and me. I suspected, but didn't know until it played out: Matt and I would never go camping together.

The allergist and I both had to learn how my body was going to react now. He rolled up his sleeves to fight the disease on my behalf. Over the years, he kept me alive, out of the hospital, and in my practice so I could earn a living. After many years of fighting this disease together, I was so grateful that I gave him a plaque honoring his work on behalf of me and our family. In my allergist's judgment—and that of the doctors at National Jewish Hospital where I stayed for a week of testing—your grandparents' chain-smoking was responsible for the extreme state of my asthma. With my father at home all the time, your grandparents created an enormous amount of secondary smoke. The house was constantly filled with it. Uncle Herb has asthma, but it's mild. Being nine years older, he grew up in a period when your grandparents were a bit healthier. My father was still working so it likely spared him the extremely high amount of secondary smoke exposure responsible for the severity of my asthma.

Shortly after my lungs got so bad, we were supposed to go to Kirk Camp. As I found with the aborted camping trip with Matt, there was no way I could go. The exposure to outside air 24/7 would have been too much. In trying to keep some semblance of normalcy—though a part of me has always regretted this—we decided that Mom would take the three of you to camp without me. Doing so, however, tore my heart right out of my rib cage. As I stood in the driveway waving to you guys as Mom drove off, I just couldn't believe that my life had come to this. Mom told me later that you guys cried on and off most of the way there.

When I went back inside after seeing all of you off, I found myself standing at the kitchen sink—in shock. It felt like the shock of that electric jolt I experienced as a young teen; I was dazed. I just stood by the counter. Then I began to sob. I went upstairs and lay on the bed for hours, staring at the ceiling . . . frozen. You know me, Kid; I've lived for family. To be separated from you guys when we were supposed to be on vacation *together* . . .

As I lay there, the reality of what was happening to me was sinking in moment by torturously long moment: *I was now disabled like my father before me.* With surges of terror shooting through me, I knew that life would never be the same; it was imploding right in front of me. Like my parents before me, my dreams were shattering. I was experiencing a creative reenactment of their broken lives. Like my parents, I had few mental and emotional skills to handle this new trauma laid on top of the old. While my dad modeled determination, it was blind. He modeled little in dealing with his suffering— and I had this man inside me. I just couldn't believe it. I sensed the steep mountain ahead of me I had to climb. In my gut, I knew it'd take years . . . if I had a shot at all. I couldn't wrap my head around the fact that I had spent all those years climbing up and out of the trauma my parents perpetrated against me in my childhood, only to have them retraumatize me from the grave during prime time with my budding family. First, they stole my childhood. Then, they stole my adulthood—robbing me of my dreams for my own family.

Lying in bed with my psyche ripped wide open and gripped by raw fear, like C. S. Lewis, I secretly wondered again: Where the heck was Jesus?

Here We Go

I don't know if or what you recall; you were pretty young. After the huge loss of Kirk Camp, that steep mountain I knew I had to climb appeared over the hazy horizon. I now couldn't go outside any longer than forty-five minutes without a heavy mask on to filter my air.

I became a late-phase reactor, meaning I could be accidentally exposed to an allergen like mold one day but have the scary life-threatening asthma attack the next. Strange. At the time, I didn't know such a thing could happen. So imagine the surprise when I'd be driving around the Valley and out of the blue I'd have such an attack. Back then, we didn't have cell phones, but Mom got me a mobile phone that was hard-wired into the van. When I'd have a surprise attack, I'd call the doctor immediately and he'd prescribe a dose of the Prednisone to halt it. And it always did. For months, it made driving by myself one unnerving enterprise. But the doctor was always on target with his dose, so I never had to go to the hospital. Talking about trust earlier: His expert judgment time after time helped to drive trust in him deep into my psyche—and helped me relax a bit knowing I would not die this way.

As we caught on to the pattern of my disease, the doctor then put me on a daily regimen of Prednisone to preempt such spontaneous attacks. Like the previous inept allergist, this doctor knew steroids had many powerful side effects, so he too was reluctant to use them on a daily basis unless he absolutely had to. But he had to—and *unlike* the previous doctor, he knew he had to. Doing so kept me alive and brought some stability. But my body and mind eventually paid a dear price . . . a very dear price. I do not blame the doctor for it; it was the price tag for using the only medicine that would keep me alive at that time.

Over the months and years ahead, I gained forty-five pounds: steroid-induced Cushing's syndrome. On top of the severe muscle damage, I felt and looked terrible. Beyond that, Mom said, a bit tongue-in-cheek, I became the only man she knew who actually understood a woman's PMS. I was, as some women say, "hormonal." If I didn't already have enough underlying depression from my trauma growing up, and now this disability, I had even more from the steroids. I had impulse-control problems with my anger; we called it "'roid rage." It was as if someone had implanted an electrode in my brain and would just juice me on whim. So I asked Mom to coach me. When I couldn't manage my emotions well enough—which happened often—she'd tell me to walk away, especially in handling matters with you guys. My mind and my steroid-induced urges were constantly butting heads. And I knew it. I did my best to manage myself, but I often failed. It was like having a brain tumor. I just couldn't stop the steroid-induced emotions flooding my consciousness. I did my best, but my best was no doubt disrespectful and hurtful. At times, I was ashamed . . . very ashamed. Playing off the apostle Paul's frustration with sin, I want to say, "It was not me, but the steroids within me."

I had become a physical mess. In those first few years, I feared I'd die soon from the disease. Many others had. When in downtown Bethlehem, I'd leave my car in the parking garage, only to be so winded after a number of steps that I'd lean against a concrete pillar for a respite—and a brief moment of morbid reflection. With my possible demise in mind, I decided to throw a big party for your mom's fortieth birthday. I flew in her high school friend from upper New York State; invited old friends from Philadelphia; arranged for her to be driven around town in a limousine to places where friends were waiting to greet her; faked a family portrait to get updated photos of her to create a collage; and invited our pastor and friend who came in costume as a tomato to read her humorous poetry. I thoroughly loved surprising her with that modest celebration.

I parked the car in downtown Bethlehem because I had to rent another office for my practice. At my original office, I had a professional service come in to steam clean my carpet. They foolishly saturated the carpet, which quickly grew musty. My hypersensitive lungs couldn't tolerate it. On an urgent basis, I rented a second office to buy time to install a new floor, including a subfloor that was necessary, in my office. In my ignorance, I tried installing sheet vinyl. The new odor from the vinyl and its urethane coating so irritated my lungs that I began to cough up blood. The carpet at my second office, however, also provoked the asthma; I had to leave. Our senior pastor graciously offered his office for a time. Then I used a small room off the church's hallway. I finally ended up at home—using our own living room for my consultations. I thought for sure that playing roulette with our meeting place like that would so destabilize my clients that I'd lose the entire practice and not be able to support the family. Like your grandfather when he lost his job, I had become frightened, confused, and desperate.

Throughout that crazy period of extraordinary professional instability, believe it or not, I lost only one client. A few years later, that client went out of his way to apologize to me. He said he just couldn't handle my instability given his own. I understood completely. Others saw me as the compassionate wounded healer who knew suffering firsthand; several wanted to rescue their psychologist. One client offered me his home for my practice until I found a way to make my office safe—which I finally did by installing ceramic tile. Professional boundaries would never permit me to accept his generous offer. Still, I was grateful for his genuine and gracious concern. Deep gratitude for my patients' care toward me notwithstanding, however, the whole thing just felt bizarrely surreal.

Shortly after Mom's fortieth surprise celebration, my morbid self-reflections revealed themselves again in my asking her to show you guys pictures of me as you grew up should I die soon. I didn't want you to forget that you had a father who loved you very much. And, given your age, Kristen, I was especially concerned that you'd not remember me. Mom understood.

Steroids kept me alive. In the meantime, injections with allergens were our major weapon in rebuilding my immunity—and ascending that steep mountain to health. After the first five years, as I got some traction, we tried cutting back the steroid. I couldn't; my body severely reacted to the withdrawal. My adrenals were now too weak and steroid dependent to stand on their own. In fact, I nearly had Addison's disease, which is the final destruction of the adrenals. President Kennedy had to use steroids because he had Addison's, which gave him the slight bronze coloration to his face. As you know, when I'd cut back the steroid—even a tiny bit—and I'd sit or lie down for a while, I was so weak and unable to "connect" with my own limbs that I couldn't get up on my own. Mom and one of you would have to pull me up and walk me for five to ten minutes to get my adrenals working enough to stand and walk on my own. When these odd symptoms first appeared, I consulted an endocrinologist.

At our first meeting, the specialist was taking my blood pressure when, out of the blue, he asked me, "Are you Mormon?"

"What? No, I'm Presbyterian."

"Oh, I thought you were Mormon," he said. "Do you believe in God?"

I had no idea where he got the idea I was Mormon, let alone why he was even asking me these questions. I found out later. I answered him, though: "Yes, I believe in God. And actually, I believe Jesus came back to life."

He immediately threw up his hands, and in an exasperated and almost pleading tone, asked, "How can an intelligent man like yourself, a psychologist no less, ever believe that a God would exist who'd care about tiny creatures on a little speck of dust in a virtually infinite universe?"

With a gracious smile, I retorted, "It is outrageous, isn't it?" I sat down with him and Mom in front of his modest-size desk in a small room to discuss what we were going to do about my body's profound dependency on the steroids.

He began, "My son went to seminary and became a pastor. I told him he was wasting his life—and needed a real job that made some real contribution to society. And I advised him that I was only joking when we said grace at meals."

Apparently, his son was on his mind when I crossed his path that afternoon. I never did mention that I had gone to seminary.

Then, with one arm outstretched pointing to my chest, he declared, "Look at you. You're a physical mess. And you think God cares about you?"

While his bedside manner left something to be desired—in his midseventies, he was a bit eccentric, but had likely been so his entire life—I nevertheless appreciated his ruthless candor and keen mind. As I got to know him, I actually liked the man, strongly valued our discussions because they were based on research, and highly respected his expertise. I was saddened when he passed away. At this first meeting, I asked him why I couldn't be hospitalized, strapped to a bed, and suffer through withdrawal. He said it didn't work that way. My body wouldn't be able to handle the shock; I'd die. I had to come off slowly . . . very slowly. It took an unbelievable five more years to safely come off Prednisone. During those five years, my body became weak every time I cut back. Through modest aerobic exercise—modest is all my damaged muscles could ever tolerate—I managed to strengthen my adrenal glands. But they'll never be the same, especially since I can't push exercise because of the massive muscle damage.

As the asthma played itself out, I not only couldn't go outside longer than forty-five minutes, but I couldn't go outside longer than forty-five minutes for ten years—*ten years* in prime time with my young family. Five of those years were coming off the steroid. For a decade, I had become a prisoner in my own home. After growing up with what I grew up with, I desperately wanted "normal"—but the doctors and I just couldn't make it happen. The tradition of Kirk Camp was never more to be. Besides camp, I wanted to make hiking and camping a tradition with you guys. We even bought a pop-up camper in preparation for that . . . but, as you know, got to use it only one time. Twenty-seven years later, it's now yours. And, to answer again the question you asked me as you and your husband stood in the driveway one night evaluating the camper, it is indeed very meaningful to me to pass that camper onto to you and Ryan and my grandchildren to experience the joys of camping outdoors. But camper or no camper, the love of camping has already passed on to you. I guess it's like what happened with my father and my love of football. I never did see him play—but his love of the game became mine. And so it is for us. For that, I am grateful.

Though keeping me alive, steroids damaged my body in other significant ways. They softened the corneas of my eyes so that I recently needed surgery in an attempt to salvage them—and we're not out of the woods yet with that. Prednisone sucked the calcium out of my bones, inducing osteopenia. It also permanently destroyed my male hormonal glands, adding to my feeling weak and tired. I have to take a male hormonal supplement that my damaged muscles do not tolerate well at all. As a result, I cannot take as much of that hormone as I really need, and what I do take irritates my damaged muscles a great deal, which then irritate the vagus nerve, making me slightly nauseous. Last but not least, I have steroid-induced diabetes.

Still, after a decade of "house arrest" and struggling to come off the steroids, I felt I was climbing the mountain. I was reaching for the summit, hoping for a few degrees of freedom to spend several hours outside without a mask.

But then . . . it happened again.

Again

I went with your brother Matt and some of our youth from the church to a *Batman* movie in a local theatre. Going to loud action adventure movies was one of the things I really enjoyed and could do with my severe asthma. When Matt and I watched *Jurassic Park* at home, I hooked the speakers from our stereo to the TV and placed them behind the couch—and torqued up the bass. Felt like we were there. Matt and I thought it was pretty cool to feel the throbbing through the sofa as the Tyrannosaurus pounded its way through the Park.

This *Batman* movie was no exception to loud. As much as I loved loud, this movie struck me as especially loud, so loud that I thought I'd end up with a headache. I momentarily considered leaving the theatre, but I didn't want to disrupt others' viewing and have Matt and the other youth leader raise questions right in the middle of the action. So I decided to stay—another decision I'd regret the rest of my life. I took pieces of tissue I happened to have in my pants pocket and, rolling them up, stuffed them in my ears to soften the sound. I sat back and watched the rest of the mindless flick.

When I walked out the theatre doors into the lobby area, I was stunned. My ears were ringing like crazy. Beyond that, they were extremely sensitive to sound—all manner of sound, and all ranges of volume. Driving back home, my ears hurt, like I had two earaches. Back home, clinking a glass with a spoon hurt. The sound of the refrigerator bothered me. I couldn't turn up the television without it hurting. I was spinning: *What the heck just happened to me?*

I went to a friend and fellow member of our church who is an ear, nose, and throat specialist. He said I had tinnitus and hyperacusis—ringing in my ears and hypersensitivity to sound induced by exposure to loud noise. The damage was likely permanent; nothing could be done. He only offered me Xanax, which I tersely declined.

I scrambled.

I consulted with another ear specialist in the Valley who also had nothing to offer. Then I talked with the director of the Tinnitus Center at the University of Maryland, who graciously gave me about twenty minutes on the phone free. He prescribed medication through my endocrinologist—which unfortunately did not help. My endocrinologist thought the steroids likely damaged my ears long before the movie theatre, setting them up for the hyperacusis. We'll never know for sure . . . not that that matters now. I then consulted with two other doctors in Philadelphia—one at the University of Pennsylvania—who offered no hope. And finally, I consulted with a surgeon at Johns Hopkins University School of Medicine by phone after I filled out about an hour and a half worth of questions regarding my history to see if I qualified for surgery. He said there was nothing that could be done. I told him I had a couple of questions for which I'd like forthright answers.

I asked, "Has any surgeon gone into the ear to identify the structures responsible for such a problem?"

He said, "No."

"So no one has surgically opened an ear of a patient disabled with hyperacusis—whether live or posthumously—to identify the injured structures?"

"No."

"Regarding hyperacusis, you're operating almost completely in the blind?"

"Yes."

That was that.

If I thought my world had become small with severe asthma, incredibly, it now shrank down to a tiny stubble. My world became as small physically as your grandparents' world had been mentally. I could no longer go to our church for worship. The crowd noise, the organ, the electronic amplification of the pastor's voice . . . all of it hurt. I couldn't walk outside without ear plugs and Bose electronic quieting headphones because of traffic noise. Or go to your concerts or plays. Or turn up the TV. Or fly in a plane. Or go to a restaurant with other people around. I've lost some high-frequency hearing in both ears, more so the right. Interestingly, that's the same ear I had the painful earache in as an infant. When talking around the table as a family, I am unable to pull out my conversation from the others. The sounds of certain letters easily get blurred in my hearing and words are therefore easily lost. Even if there are no other conversations, I cannot hear the sounds of the letters *s, c, z,* or *ch* or *sh* well enough in the flow of a fast conversation to lock in on various words. I have to use context clues to guess . . . or just ask someone to repeat. I cannot hear the dialogue in television programs or movies well, especially with background music or noise. When I can, I use captions to follow the dialogue.

Beyond all that, both ears were now in intense chronic pain 24/7. Having such pain inside one's head like that—versus more distant like the foot—was maddening. The full intensity of the ordeal lasted for over five years, softening just a bit over the next five. Some years later I learned from attending my mother-in-law's funeral that I could no longer travel in the car more than a couple hours at any one time because the road vibration would redamage my ears. My ears hurt for over seven months after that funeral.

As if that were not enough, I could no longer go to the shore with Mom, her favorite place to go.

The loud ringing in the ears, the loss of hearing, losing the ability to pick out my conversation from background noise, the hypersensitivity to sound, the strong reactivity to vibration in the car, the ease of redamaging the ears—all of it was permanent.

Time after time after time, in the maddened places of my mind, I asked myself: *How in the world did I get here?*

The physical pain in my ears just about drove me nuts. It piled on top of the emotional pain of my losses. I felt emasculated. I didn't want to cry—doing so just made me feel more neutered. But, once again, I had no choice.

Still, crying or no crying, I became very depressed—and found myself tempted to lose my way.

I recall one moment of self-pity sitting in bed with Mom. Choked up, I turned to her and asked, "Do I have a sign on my forehead that says: 'Go ahead, abuse me'?" The fact is, behind that sarcastic self-pitying comment, I doubted my worth. I flashed to Jesus and the Roman soldier, thinking, "You healed his servant. Why not me? What am I . . . chopped liver?"

I had to face it: My parents' poor choices set me up for trauma on top of trauma on top of trauma. It is a tough fact of life that suffering too often begets more suffering—much like poverty begets poverty. But internalizing that reality was both humiliating and infuriating.

There was no resting place for it in my head; there was no Sabbath rest.

Hon, I had felt knocked down for almost the full count with the onset of severe asthma. I struggled with every fiber in my being to get up off the mat, and I did—after all, I am a survivor. I recall a poignant moment in the car driving back home after church one Sunday when, as a teenager, you told me that I was the kind of man who always got up after having been knocked down. I don't recall how that topic came up, but I will forever remember your kind words.

Kind words or not, however, this new trauma tore open more layers of my already traumatized mind. So, among other things, I was back again to pondering about my heavenly Father: For exactly what was I supposed to trust him? What could I expect him to do in my life? Just like C. S. Lewis, I still hadn't fully come to terms with the reality of who my Father was—and how he conducted himself. Nevertheless, to my credit, I worked very hard at trusting my Father—trusting him on *his* terms, not mine. Trusting that he actually cared about me even though it didn't feel that way—and it didn't feel that way precisely because it didn't look that way. Life's evidence was piling up. I kept going back to the Bible trying to drive that trust in my Father deeper into the exposed layers of my psyche.

But now . . . Now, on top of my long-standing confinement from asthma, I had innumerable permanent restrictions from this ear damage, not to mention the maddening pain in my ears. Candidly, Kid, I was a broken man. Like your grandmother before me, I was spent—exhaustion wrapped in utter despair. I was tired and disillusioned beyond words. My spirit had been crushed. There was no more fight left in me. This soldier in life had been traumatized one too many times—and it broke me. I just wanted to go home.

Enough Is Enough

Going Home

I've shared a lot with you so far, but what follows is the most difficult to tell you guys. I debated and debated about putting this in this letter. Here's why.

I don't want to hurt any of you, and I feared that telling you these struggles might somehow do harm. I also don't want to disappoint any of you . . . but I just might. Beyond that, narcissistically, I don't want to be thought less of. I don't want to be secretly disrespected. Or worse, be thought of dishonorably. For me, along with a lot of men, to be respected is to be loved. Still, I said at the beginning of this letter that I wanted you guys to get to know me—and to get to know me specifically regarding my faith journey. What I am about to share was certainly relevant to that journey. So, after having talked at some length with your mom, we decided to include this tough transition in my life . . . in our lives. Your mom and I also thought that talking candidly about such a difficult and even taboo topic just might be of some use to someone along the way. While your mom fully supports my sharing this with you guys, the final decision is mine alone.

I had once thought if I fought smart enough, hard enough, and long enough I could grasp onto some small portion, a taste—the Bible's "first fruits"—of my new identity in Jesus. But, as I now stared at my life—at all my losses laced with intense ear pain 24/7—for the hundredth time, nothing looked new. Either to my endocrinologist or to me.

Consequently, I was drawn to death. For a brief time, I craved it. Death would either bring me closer to the apostle John's new universe or take me into Stephen Hawking's eternal nothingness, and with it, eternal peace. Either way, I'd win. I desperately wanted out of this life.

This craving was not a sober judgment call. It was not a calculation. It was an involuntary desire—a desire that came along with thoughts that were likewise not consciously chosen. Actually the "thoughts" were more images than thoughts. The draw to death and the imagined scenes that materialized with it were intruders into my consciousness. I hadn't invited them in. They came spontaneously, like momentary feelings of attraction when we notice someone who is stunning. Such reactions emerge instinctively and spontaneously with no forethought.

One moment, I'd picture hanging myself from a tree limb in our backyard. As I stared at my unsettling morbid fantasy, I sensed that the thick rope around my throat represented the choking off of communication between me and my heavenly Pops. I just couldn't talk to him anymore. What was the point? He had long stopped listening to me. And he didn't "talk" to me either . . . not to mention doing something to help me. I have wondered what specifically Robin Williams or Pastor Rick Warren's son wrestled with prior to their suicides. Among other things, I know I felt as abandoned by "my Father who art in heaven" as I had by my own mother growing up.

Then I'd imagine your mother coming home to find me hanging there.

Another moment, I pictured running a tube from the exhaust pipe into the car's window as I was parked near the woods at Mount Ampersand in my old stomping grounds of the gently rolling Adirondacks—symbolic of my precious losses. I imagined quietly reflecting on my demise as I slowly, and perhaps peacefully, fell asleep. I also pictured writing to you guys. I'd want you to know how much I loved you . . . though I just couldn't take it anymore. And then I'd imagine your mom finding me slumped over at the wheel.

Still another moment, I imagined buying a gun. I pictured standing at the store's counter, nervously knowing the real reason why I was there. One scene I painted in my depressive imagination was pulling the gun out at the dinner table with all of you there and shooting myself. In melodramatic fashion, I wanted to put my pain on display. After all, I had wanted my heavenly Father to bear witness to my pain. *But he wasn't even listening.* I desperately wanted to wake him up to the misery he was allowing me . . . as if he wasn't already awake. Still, since *he* wasn't listening, I wanted you guys to listen instead—and bear witness to my pain. Such a horrific scene would not only make you guys bear witness as a substitute for my Father, but it would put on vivid display the violence life had dealt me—violence my heavenly Father was willing to stand by and let happen. But—I'd picture the horrific impact on all of you. I couldn't do that to you guys. And then I'd picture the three of you having to clean up the mess. So I played the scenario out again—this time, in the privacy and confinement of the bathtub. But then I'd picture Mom having to clean it up. All symbolic of you guys having to clean up the emotional mess I'd leave behind.

I was livid, Kid. I was disillusioned with all of them—my parents, my heavenly Pops, Jesus . . . life itself. I felt powerless. And that powerlessness just fueled my despair—with nowhere to go with my humiliation and fury except at myself. So my psyche spontaneously and beyond conscious control crafted self-destructive fantasies.

I said these vignettes were intruders . . . and they were. But I didn't chase them away. I had learned a long time ago to listen to my spontaneous feelings and fantasies; they taught me a great deal about myself and the human condition. So I listened.

The danger in listening, however—the danger in dialogue—is that we become persuaded by who or what we are listening to. As noted before, that's why so many people refuse to dialogue with others or the evidence or their own hearts. They refuse to dialogue with life. They're scared. So they choose not to listen. But I chose to take that risk. In taking the risk to "dialogue" with my own fantasies of death, I was almost irresistibly drawn to them. Death was a seductress. She offered peace. Blissfully blind, quiet, mindless, painless peace. I momentarily indulged in her dark but enticing beauty. Her peace was quite a lure. It was another moment in my life when I was like the moth drawn to the beguiling brilliance of the all-consuming flame. Death's peace was the counterpoint to God's peace—both of which, for many, surpass human understanding (Phil. 4:7).

I knew my psyche had intuitively but artistically designed these morbid scenarios for the purpose of giving dramatic expression to my deeper thoughts and feelings. It was the artist in me creating a rich though tragic Broadway play by which to express what felt so complexly inexpressible. It was the same artist who would dream dreams at night. Over the years, I have been in awe at how the dreamer in me could create such original plays in my imagination while the thinking "I" was asleep. He never consulted with me; night after night, the dreamer in me just went ahead and dreamed. There's no way on my own that I could ever paint, draw, write, or direct a play or movie like my dreamer could. I don't have his talent. Maybe a Steven Spielberg . . . but not me. If there is no "ghost in the machine," then it was I myself who created these wondrous works of art while asleep. But how? I have no idea. And so it was with my suicidal fantasies.

I'd hypnotically indulge in my daydreams. Like a Greek tragedy, it was actually cathartic to watch it all play out in my imagination. But I knew if I listened, my fantasies would reveal how I was really feeling and thinking behind the curtain of the play. But only if I really listened. And only if I listened smart. If I hadn't, the hidden thoughts and feelings would have continued to fuel those seemingly unstoppable cravings for death—with the risk of the dreamer acting out creatively on the stage of life. It's at that moment of a suicide that the dreamer and "I" become one . . . as it had for Williams and Warren. This is very much like someone who hypnotically indulges in daydreaming of a romantic affair with a coworker. Unless she listens carefully and listens smart to her daydream to figure out why she is so disillusioned with her husband, she runs the risk of acting the imagined affair out on life's stage. So too with my suicidal daydreaming. Though I felt my heavenly Father wasn't listening to me, *I* decided to listen to me—and worked at figuring out what was really going on behind the curtain.

The morbidly seductive fantasies were involuntary. But what I did with them was not. In fearfully listening to my imagined tragic play, I discovered that I didn't really want to be *dead* dead. I only wanted to be dead to the pain. I really wanted to be alive. I wanted to stay alive—but with a different life . . . with a different body. Though I didn't want to be dead—and most who attempt suicide don't either—I was near my breaking point. Everyone has a breaking point; the only question is: Where? My suicidal daydreams indicated I was near that point—and I wasn't yet mentally skilled enough to deal with all that life was throwing at me, including dealing with my heavenly Father's abandonment. Like your grandmother and Mother Theresa, if feelings were a measure of the presence of God, then my Father didn't even exist. The fact is, trauma upon trauma upon trauma created my dark night of the soul— where the mental skills I had busted my butt to develop over the years had been maxed out. My pain and losses had outrun my skills. I was walking around the house, playing with you guys, talking with your mom, and going to work—all the while in deep psychic shock. Just like your grandparents.

Your mom recently shared with me the sermon Rear Admiral Margaret Grun Kibben, the chaplain of the US Marine Corps and Deputy Chief of Navy Chaplains, delivered to our church. The admiral noted that the worst moment for a "wounded warrior" was when he or she woke up in the hospital, only to discover both arms and both legs gone. Like your grandfather with his loss of legs and arms, such wounded warriors find themselves in shock, frozen in sheer terror. I noted earlier that it is challenging if not impossible to compare human suffering. We each have our own interpretation of our personal suffering. And we each have our own journey in dealing with it. Still, like many wounded warriors who are suicidal, my self-destructive fantasies were wrapped in shock driven by fear and pain. I hadn't yet fully come to terms with my losses. Doing so was a skill still in the making.

In further listening to my fantasies, I discovered that to die at my own hands would be a protest. It would be a passive-aggressive shaking of my fist at my heavenly Father—not unlike the Tibetan monks who, in recent years, have poured gasoline on themselves and lit it as a protest against the Chinese government. Nearly a hundred men have done so. I could intuitively feel that my self-murderous fantasies were symbolic protests against my Father's mismanagement of his universe . . . for his mismanagement of *my* universe.

In listening some more, I discovered that my longings to be gone from the planet were my mother's longings to be gone—longings built into me over the years growing up. Instead of a quick suicide, however, she had committed a slow suicide through alcoholism. But it was still a suicide—a self-destructive form of bailing from life that eventually led to her early demise. She had died at forty-eight. She had long given up on the game of life, though she had kept doing her duty, even toward the end to see me off. I could feel her self-sabotaging choice inside me. I could viscerally sense it driving my inner cravings for death. My mother's choice to bail from life was now the wellspring of my own dark desire to bail from my own life.

I noted earlier that harboring angry, depressive thoughts and feelings is a dangerous game. And so it is. The quiet depth of the human psyche is an incubator. I knew that. So, as I unpacked my inner drama, revealing even more of my secret thoughts and feelings, I worked at giving voice to them. In doing that hard work, my psyche spontaneously began to turn its anger away from me and toward my heavenly Father. Another skill in the making. I didn't just put "God on the witness stand"; I grabbed him by his tunic and shook him. I yelled at Jesus about how useless he was while beating him with my fists. As I beat him, I swung from anger to tears. As my tears rose up through my anger, I felt something of the inscription on the wall of a concentration camp in Hitler's Germany: "If there is a God, he will have to beg my forgiveness."

In giving voice to how I really felt, my craving for death actually began to soften. I didn't have to turn my anger in on myself anymore. Like Job long before me, I knew my Father was a big boy and could handle my rage. After all, he knew long before I did how I really felt about him. As the psalmist alluded to, my thoughts were no secret to him, only to me. And as the apostle Paul noted, I *am* saved by grace.

Along with being direct with my heavenly Father about how I both loved and hated him, I was determined to weep out the pain of his abandonment as well as my serial losses, purging the inconsolable feelings that would have continued to feed my irrepressible cravings to be dead.

Figuring out the meaning of my morose fantasies kept me from nurturing them into blinding impulses. And from blinding impulses into well-thought-out plans for self-destruction. So, Hon, what I've shared with you were brief daydreams. They were never plans. However, they were never plans precisely because I consciously chose to work my imagined scenarios to force them to cough up their secrets. Perhaps it was my father's determination in me that drove me to fight for those secrets. Whatever the reason, I chose to deal with those deeper parts of me one by one—all the while knowing I was doing the hard work my parents should have done while I was growing up . . . but hadn't. It was a bitter pill.

Beyond all this, I had four good reasons to fight to live.

Trumping Meaninglessness

You might wonder, Hon: Why wasn't family enough? Why didn't I love Mom and you guys enough so that those dark scenarios never spontaneously formed in the first place . . . let alone intrude into my consciousness, knocking me on my butt?

The fact is, life induces urges and fantasies beyond immediate conscious control about all kinds of things—if we're honest with ourselves—from the spontaneous urge to throw the middle finger in the face of someone driving unsafely to momentary daydreams about having an affair with a best friend's spouse to flights of fancy about beating the crap out of a politician who obviously just lied to us. Then we have the challenge of what we're going to do with those spontaneously induced fantasies. Life's tough times induced spontaneous daydreams in me. Those daydreams were diagnostic of life, my family growing up, and my lack of mental and emotional skills to handle what was happening to me. They were not diagnostic of a lack of love for my family. However—and it's one huge however—what I did with those intrusive daydreams *did* indicate my love for you guys.

I love your mom and each of you. I didn't want to hurt or betray Mom or you guys. *And I didn't.* Your mom needed a husband and you still needed a father, however limited that husband and father might have been. As a boy, I knew I needed my father, but never had him after age eight. Beyond that, out of some residual self-respect that I was able to muster in the wake of this trauma, I wanted to see you guys grow up, become the fine men and woman you have become, and be friends. I wanted to meet my as yet unborn grandchildren and love them and grow with them. I sure am glad that I have met my "D" man, Miss Hannah, and little Miss Leah. My love for the four of you gave meaning to my life. So, regardless of how desperate I felt or how much physical pain I was in, I somehow wanted that meaning to trump the meaninglessness of my losses.

Meaninglessness . . . Unpacking my depressive fantasies, I flashed to a number of things. Among them was what the apostle Paul said in his letter to the church at Rome: ". . . in all things God works for the good of those who love him, who have been called according to his purpose" (Rom. 8:28, NIV). I thought about how so many Christians—desperate for comfort—believe this means that one's individual suffering has some inexplicable divine purpose that benefits that person . . . or others. But the verse doesn't mean that.

I already knew that suffering and death were part of our dance with evil. And I knew all too well that suffering had not been divvied up fairly. Still, the apostle asserts that it is in the midst of this universal mess that our Father uses "all things," including suffering and death, to move us to a transformed universe. As noted earlier, our Father planned it that way from the beginning—and the apostle encouraged us that nothing is going to stop him from pulling it off. That's the panoramic. That's what the apostle assures us of in this verse. The tough reality, though, is that he'd pull it off on *his* terms, not mine or C. S. Lewis' or anyone else's . . . including John the Baptist's. He'd do it in the long run, not the short run. That was Jesus' message back to John the Baptist—and that's why John got beheaded instead of being rescued. Jesus and his Father were not going to rescue John on his terms. Nor have they rescued any of us on our terms. So John wasn't alone that way. In fact, all but one apostle were murdered. So, like it or not, that's the apostle Paul's message here in this verse: God will rescue the universe—he will work all things to that ultimate good for those who love him, who are called according to his purpose—but he'll do so on his terms, not ours. Consequently, the apostle Paul himself was likely murdered by beheading.

I knew what the apostle did *not* mean to say. He didn't mean that my Father allowed me to suffer trauma after trauma in order to build my character. Or to call me to be a psychologist who'd become street smart about suffering. That would be like God saying, "Let's abuse the psychic crap out of little Frankie, and then beat him some more later in life, to make him into the godly man we want." That's absurdly cruel. But that's just the kind of logic some people reach for in order to feel that they're not suffering for nothing. They're willing to believe that their heavenly Father is tormenting them in life's fiery furnace in order to forge more character in them—a kind of Protestant purgatory on earth.

What the apostle did say was that, given the fact of life that we do suffer—*given* that fact—we can *use* suffering to build our character, ". . . knowing that suffering produces endurance, and endurance produces character, and character produces hope" (Rom. 5:3–4, NRSV). I already knew that and lived it. But, honestly, Kid, I was fed up with building character out of my suffering. Enough is enough. Still, in the middle of my momentary cravings for death, the choice was crystal clear: either keep on keeping on with building character . . . or go ahead and die. Die by suicide. Die by drinking like your grandmother. Die by pretending. Die in anger, bitterness, and depression. But die. It was either live or die. I chose to live. I chose to keep busting my butt to build character. My Father didn't send me lemons to see if I was smart enough, loyal enough, or determined enough to make lemonade. But given that life handed me lemons—given that I was at that breaking point— the Spirit of my Father was calling me to develop more skills to continue squeezing those lemons into lemonade.

In squeezing whatever I could from life's lemons, I flashed back to a seminary professor. He was a professor of apologetics—which is the study of defending the faith against contrary arguments— who had been trained in both philosophy and theology. He thought deeply about faith. Only five of us took his class; I do not know why only five except that his work was known to be complex. He was a careful teacher, closely following his notes and speaking with a slow, even dry, rhythm in order to deliver his best. Perhaps he was too dry for many. I found out later he had lost his son at twelve. I share that because what this man said one day was no doubt informed by that reality. What he said was not merely academic.

One day in class, we were talking about the search for meaning from an atheist's as well as a Christian's point of view. I actually recall the moment vividly. After describing how existential philosophers had been searching for "the nonmetaphysical ground of meaning and being"—is it any wonder why only five took his course?—he looked up and off to the side to momentarily deviate from his notes, gather his thoughts, and perhaps even decide whether to say it this way or not. He then shifted his gaze, looking directly at us. I sat to his right. He first looked at me and then at the other four one by one and said, "Men, maybe part of what makes evil 'evil' is that it is just nuts."

Having this man who deliberated on complex matters say this in plain English, with such quiet passion, determination, and candor, became a striking imprint in my young psyche—one with which I immediately resonated. And still do.

I pondered: Indeed, maybe part of what makes the evil of my suffering so maddening is that there is no divinely hidden good to it. To be sure, our Father has a plan to rescue me from it; I just won't see it on this side of the grave. But maybe part of the price tag for moving away from our heavenly Pops—the divine source of meaning—was the terrifying loss of meaning in and through our suffering. Just perhaps part of what makes our suffering so insufferable is that there is no core meaning buried deep in its belly. Don't get me wrong. Like most people, I'd love for there to be some divinely specified purpose for all my suffering. If there is a purpose meant just for me, it beats the heck out of me what it is—and in that way, such a purpose is useless to me. Instead, perhaps suffering is simply what it is: devastating, maddening, anti-life, anti-meaning, and ultimately anti-God. After all, it is our condemnation. Maybe that's why Jesus himself couldn't stand it—and wept. And if Jesus is God, then our Father wept in the face of our condemnation. He wept for our suffering. "Our Father who art in heaven" cried for us.

I admit, I did crave death for a brief time. And I admit I entertained my fantasies. But I had asked and answered the question posed by a short book I read while in college entitled *Despair: A Moment or a Way of Life?* I chose a moment. I didn't want to make a choice that horrifically imprinted you guys or created a damaging model for my future grandchildren or great-grandchildren. I didn't want to hurt any of you. Besides, life with you was meaningful, my suffering notwithstanding. So I did what I needed to do. On one hand, I sought counsel. I worked at sobbing in my wife's arms to release the unbearable pain. And I told my Father exactly how I felt about his standing by. On the other hand, as I climbed out of my abject darkness, I refocused on what I did have. I clung to my core vision. Picking myself up off the mat again, I reaffirmed that my life was indeed worth living. As the navy chaplain noted, the turning point comes when the wounded warrior decides to create a life from what she does have and stops focusing on what she doesn't have. All wounded warriors in life have to ask and answer the very question your grandparents refused to: "Now what?" That's what I had to do;

I asked and answered that question. Meaninglessness notwithstanding, I chose to continue creating meaning through building my little empire of family and practice. Since grammar school, I had worked hard to wrap purpose around life's craziness—and I wasn't going to stop now.

All that—all of it—is what has made my life an adventure. If it isn't obvious, I don't mean that in some trite way. For life to be an adventure, we have to embrace fear. We have to accept and then release the maddening pain of the meaninglessness buried in the belly of our suffering lest we turn despair and cynicism into a way of life—into the informed atheism of a Bertrand Russell or the tactless cynicism of a Bill Maher. To live the adventure with some optimism and courage, we have to internalize that our Father himself hated life's nonsense—and sent his one and only Son to deal with it. We have to mourn our lost dreams . . . and then dream new dreams. As our former senior pastor noted one time, we may have to replace track A with track B or C, or even track D. We sometimes have to claw our way to those new dreams. That's the way it is. It isn't fun a lot of the time, at least not for those of us traumatized. But it *is* an adventure.

I wasn't ready to go home.

How Should I Then Live?

Carpe Diem

I was sitting on a folding chair in the soft sand with my brimmed hat on, long-sleeved sweatshirt over my arms, pants covering my legs, and a light blanket draped over me to protect my hands and sandaled feet. The doctor told me I shouldn't be exposed to the sun. Besides, it was a bit breezy and chilly that day at Beltsville Lake. Lost in thought, I was just staring out at the water.

Ending a long decade of house arrest with my idiosyncratic asthma and coming off the steroids at a torturously slow snail's pace, I could actually enjoy the outdoors for a few hours. With the ear damage, I had to be careful where I went, but with only a few quiet people at the beach that day, I could sit without my ear plugs. I was a shell of a man. Still, I pondered: What could I now do outside for fun? I gazed at a few people out on the lake, letting them stir my imagination. I could feel my desperation. It was a bit like feeling seventeen again, when I felt so anxious to leave home for college.

My mind drifted to my at-home hobby that had helped keep my sanity over the decade. As a kid, I had had a ten-gallon freshwater tank for tropical fish, so when I became disabled, I reached back to that hobby and gave it a twist. Saltwater fish are much more difficult to care for than freshwater but are unparalleled in their beauty. Like the praying mantis that captivated me as a little boy, these gorgeous creatures fascinated me, giving me a whole other way to connect to my dear Mother Nature. I set up three marine tanks: a 125-, a 75-, and a 30-gallon tank. In the 30-gallon tank I had a small fish, about two inches long, called the Flame Angel. It was a pygmy coral angelfish. This little guy was a gorgeous red-orange with black vertical stripes. It acted a bit like a pet. Since I couldn't have a dog because of the asthma, he'd have to do. When I'd approach the tank, it would scurry to hide behind an ornamental bridge. Then it would coyly peer out from behind it to look at me. Eventually it would come out to swim around and follow my hand as I moved it slowly across the glass. While nowhere near as intelligent or engaging, it sure was cute, momentarily reminding me of my dog Tiny.

Now, both my body and my mind were aching to do something more than my homebound hobby. It was time. A passing motorboat entered my reflections. I momentarily fantasized about being in that powerboat, which would be foolish, of course, because my ears would be crushed by the motor's noise. I then pictured hiking the Adirondacks with Uncle Herb, but, regrettably, hiking now was out of the question. Even though it would be refreshingly quiet, my asthma could never tolerate being out in the woods; I only had a few hours outside as it was. Besides, I couldn't travel far in a car. Then I spontaneously flashed to my good friends twisting my arm to go sailing on the little Sunfish. I recalled how we flipped that boat over and over—and the blast I had. The light bulb went on: *I could do that.* I could sail. Didn't matter to me that I was weak and out of shape. I'd be able to breathe OK and there was no motor. It was doable. With an upbeat tone, I put the idea on the table with your mom. She thought it was a great idea—though saying so a bit pensively because she had never sailed before.

Sitting there feeling like a decrepit old man, I kept mulling the idea over and over in my imagination. It got my blood moving. Sailing would tie together so many pieces of me: I'd be outdoors with nature. Like with my marine hobby, it would be an opportunity to learn. As I found out later, all things considered, unlike golf, it's easy to sail—though it is very challenging to sail well. So I'd have a lifetime of learning. I'd be using my body; like I said, I love to sweat. So pushing and pulling things on the boat would be just what the doctor ordered—if I could rebuild my body enough to do that. Your mom and I would be doing something enjoyable—outside— together. I would be with good friends. And I dreamed that maybe you guys would sail with me. Hon, I could hardly contain myself.

Your mom and I went down to Nockamixon State Park to check out the sailboats. As you know, they have hundreds moored there. We discovered that the park had fleets and a sailing club, and the park's management was very supportive of the sport. As we were walking around mentally trying on the various boats for size, the secretary of the Flying Scot fleet introduced himself and gave us a tour. Perhaps it's needless to say, but he was especially excited about the Flying Scot—though so excited he talked it up with the passionate enthusiasm of an evangelist trying to convert us. And he did.

Coincidentally, Mom had a friend at church who told her that she and her husband were thinking of getting into sailing. We had them over for dinner and decided to partner together. It wasn't easy finding a used Scot in good condition that we could afford. We got ourselves informed about what to look for, including tapping on the deck and hull listening for the "thud" of a soft spot—a sign of rot. We found a boat in North Carolina, and your mom and her friend decided to venture out to see if the boat was worth driving back. The owner and I talked by phone beforehand, of course. He knew these two women would be traveling quite a distance, so we talked candidly about the condition of the boat. When they met, Mom said he was very gracious and had given me a spot-on description. The boat was in very good shape, and Mom said there were no thuds. They negotiated the deal. Mom had never driven with a boat behind her before, but you know Mom. They had fun—though she made sure on the trip back that they never pulled in anywhere where they'd have to back up.

Blood moving or not, for someone almost completely green to sailing, the Scot was intimidating. Nineteen feet long and nearly a thousand pounds, and my not knowing how to sail a two-sail boat combined with virtually no skill working the tiller, made for one interesting challenge. This wasn't unprecedented, however. Decades before, we had bought a little bright-yellow manual transmission subcompact Mazda when I didn't know how to drive a stick shift. Mom taught me after we bought the car. This time, however, neither of us knew what we were doing. Still, we were up for the challenge of learning to sail together—she the jib, and I the mainsail and tiller.

Unfortunately, as I soon discovered, besides the challenge of learning to sail, every time I sat in the boat, I relived the fear—at moments, even terror—of what had happened to my body over the past decade.

At a conscious level, it did work on me that I couldn't swim. I was intimidated by the water. I was also aware that I feared capsizing because there was a lot of metal and fiberglass between me and the water—and my body was broken enough. Like the Sunfish, the Scot had a centerboard, not a weighted keel, so it could flip over. Still, it couldn't capsize until we were in higher air, above fourteen knots. So it wasn't just that. It took a bit of self-reflection to figure out that the natural side-to-side bobbing motion of the boat in the water provoked my fear. I found out later that that swaying motion provokes fear in many non-traumatized people, like one of our pastors . . . and you, to my surprise. That pastor graciously declined to join us because of that fear, though another loved it. But I could feel that my fear came from a different place. It mimicked the insecure emotional "bobbing" of a decade of traumatic turmoil. In my enthusiasm, I hadn't anticipated that.

But given my profession, I knew if I stuck with it, I'd come out the other side OK. I would "desensitize" to the fear. Eventually, my emotions would get retrained. Still, it was frustrating, and required a great deal of patience from both of us. Once, after who knows how many times going back and forth in the cove, Mom and I were eating a picnic lunch together looking out over the lake. As I stared into the distance, I shared how far away my healing from the traumatic fear yet felt—and wondered if I could really do this. It was my one moment of doubt. Mom reassured me—and we kept on with the game plan.

It took several seasons, but I made it. I did have one friend along the way who said she would never go through what I was willing to put myself through for only the hope of eventually having fun. I told her that, while having a moment of doubt, I knew I'd enjoy the sport; I just had to do what I needed to do for as long as I needed to do it to get there. It kind of paralleled my faith journey, though it certainly was my style with most of life. Besides, I didn't have any other bright ideas that captivated my imagination like sailing. I told her I had only sailed once as a kid, but I knew I had fallen in love with it—and knew I'd love it again once my emotions calmed down. And they did, though I still never want to capsize. There really is a lot of boat between me and the water—not to mention the same for your mom and our guests. Still, Mom and I love to sail, and so do our friends. We especially love the higher air now—fifteen to twenty knots—when we get to "ride the rail" in sitting on the side deck to stabilize the boat. In air above twenty knots—and I've been there several times—I find it is just too much work and too hard on my body. It's survival mode then. I also discovered that going upwind, the wind off the sails and the water off the bow are loud enough that sometimes I have to use my Bose headphones. I will often head downwind to take them off to talk with Mom and our friends, as well as give my arms and back a break from working the mainsheet. Still—we all do love to ride the rail upwind.

Sailing made it feel like I was back in the game, Kid. I found myself saying to Mom that it makes me—and us—feel normal again. And because I am my father's son, I felt more like a man—able to sweat a bit exerting myself to work the boat in Mother Nature's air. Your mom and I have so grown to love sailing our Scot—and the friendships we've nurtured around it—that we finally named her the well-worn phrase *Carpe Diem*. While perhaps overly used, that phrase nevertheless does capture how Mom and I do love *seizing our days.*

Seizing My Days with Joy

Sailing or not, all things considered, it perhaps does not appear that I have had much joy in my life. And not much "joy of the Lord"—given my multiple, long-standing traumas beginning at birth and the spiritual maelstrom I had been unwittingly drawn into since childhood.

Or does it?

It really depends, doesn't it, Hon? It depends on what one means by "joy." And what one means by "the joy of the Lord" or to ". . . be full of the joy in the Lord always" (Phil. 4:4, NCV). Joy—and the joy of my faith in Jesus—is laced throughout this letter. And has been throughout my life, if one has eyes with which to see it. But such eyes have to see through a strange lens. It is a lens different from this culture—not only the secular culture but even contemporary Christian culture. Knowing you, I have no doubt you have that lens.

Over the years, I've wrestled with a key question for myself and my clients: How can those who suffer have joy? Really—how? Aren't the two contradictory? Aren't the attitudes and feelings forged under suffering the opposite of joy? So with that . . . How can soldiers with posttraumatic stress disorder ever have joy? How can anyone on the planet who has been traumatized by life, including me, ever have joy? How can those who endure severe depression? How can my friend from seminary in chronic, intense back pain? How can those who are quadriplegic like your grandfather had been? How can those who are flat on their backs in nursing homes? How can a family living in a dump outside of Cairo, Egypt? How could those in concentrations camps? How could those in the Russian gulag? How can those in Third World countries who walk hours a day for water? How can those in poverty in these United States? How can any of them, and millions upon millions like them across the globe, ever have joy . . . or the joy of the Lord? If we use our contemporary culture's view—secular or Christian—they can't.

384

I've noticed that among other words like "honor" and "obey," the word "joy" is not often used in our culture. "Happiness" is. Going full circle to the beginning of this letter, I noted that social psychologists have studied how so many in our culture focus on stringing together moments of happiness—and securing the money that can buy those moments. In counseling, people often start with the goal *I just want to be happy*. Sometimes they blurt it out months later in the middle of a tough session. If I sense that I can trust the client to accept my tongue-in-cheek comment while making the serious point, I sometimes say: "You've come to the wrong place if you want happy. I don't do happy." They nervously laugh. But they get something of the point.

And they do get the point. Deep in their bones they know it already. Life *is* difficult. There is no guarantee of life circumstances, whether in Christ or not. None. The apostle Paul himself presumed that. We all know it. Life—trauma and hunger and concentration camps—prove it. And I'm just a little guy. I'm a limited human being who's had to scratch and claw my way to a small place in the sun like everyone else. I have some skills to offer, but I can't *make* them happy. They know that . . . deeper down. But they have a hard time admitting it to themselves.

Still—they stay with me. They know what I am saying is true. So they trust me—and bargain with me . . . and bargain with life through me. They cut a deal to work hard to transform their lives, and, as the Serenity Prayer challenges, to discern what they can change about life—and what they can't. They decide to use me to train them to make that discrimination—to create a more meaningful life with what they can change and then wrap that around what they cannot. In that way, they have a shot at joy. Later and deeper into therapy, they often exclaim with great exasperation, "This is so hard." Once again, if I trust the client to hear me right, I assert, "We don't do easy here." And, once again, the client nervously laughs.

I'm just the messenger. I am in no preferred position. I have to live all this stuff too. When I advise them, I sometimes say in my idiosyncratic way, "Beggar to beggar, this is what I'd recommend." It helps make their medicine go down. They sense I've had to swallow my own. It helps.

The game of life is just too complicated and too hard to boil down this little but sacred word "joy" to the simple accrual of happiness moments. Given that, let me feel my way in sharing how I've come to understand how I could have—and have had—joy.

Because joy is not happiness, creating joy—the process by which we get joy—goes contrary to our culture. It even goes contrary to some in my own profession because, contrary to how they think, joy is not the opposite of depression. Joy and depression are not incompatible. They really aren't opposites, though it seems that way. Nor is joy incompatible with pain. Joy doesn't magically stop our inner recoiling to physical pain. It didn't stop my seminary friend's pain. He had fallen out of a helicopter onto a battle ship carrier below and broken his back. He was the consummate host and very engaging while in enormous pain and peering through eyes made glassy from narcotic drugs. He had joy while in pain. Nor did joy stop my unrelenting ear pain. Joy doesn't stop our sobbing in the face of losses; it didn't stop mine. The fact is, whatever joy is, we can have it *while being miserable*. Misery and joy are not opposites. The apostle Paul states so in his letter to the church at Rome:

> We also have *joy with our troubles*, because we know that these troubles produce patience. And patience produces character, and character produces hope. And this hope will never disappoint us. . . . (Rom.5:3–5a, NCV; italics mine)

It is worth another moment to note how the apostle James puts it:

> My brothers and sisters, whenever you face trials of any kind, consider it nothing but joy, because you know that the testing of your faith produces endurance; and let endurance have its full effect, so that you may be mature and complete, lacking in nothing. (James 1:2–4, NRSV)

"Joy with our troubles" and consider trials "nothing but joy," they say. How is that possible? Are they nuts?

It's taken me years to learn the skills the apostles so briefly outlined in those paragraphs, Kid—skills I've had to develop through various "troubles" because I had never learned them growing up. Rooted in the apostles' vision, I've learned from my troubles that joy is really a posture toward life. It is a way of coming at life—all of life, whether good times or bad. It is forged in making the most of our circumstances—whether happy or troubled. It is created as we strategically play the hand that's been dealt to us in order to grow up into maturity, as the apostle James says. It emerges when we fight for the spine to deal with the tough stuff of life; when we allow ourselves to grieve when we lose and celebrate when we win; when we struggle to crucify our sin, learn to love, and celebrate one another. In those ways, joy is an attitude toward life that arises from character. And in building character, we create meaning that becomes the backbone for joy. Thus, joy . . . and character . . . and meaning are all tied together. The full depth and breadth of joy— joy as a way of dealing—is forged in life's sweat tank, not just the fun stuff. Given that life is difficult, the primary goal in troubled times, besides survival, has to be the task of building character. So we get our joy of the Lord from building character—from being transformed from one degree of glory into another into the image of Jesus Christ. We get such joy because we create character. We learn joy as we learn character. In this way, joy cannot be—and the joy of the Lord certainly is not—a desperate retreat from trouble in the search for some elusive happiness. Happiness is circumstantial and therefore comes and goes. Character lasts. And, according to the apostle, joy and character are two sides of the same coin.

Besides being an attitude or posture toward life, joy can and often does have a feeling side to it. From the science of the mind, we know that how we choose to think—and how we choose to behave— creates emotions within us. But in our culture, we tend to do the opposite: We operate on the idea that how we feel should create how we behave, as if feelings were more the core of us than our judgments. If I feel angry, I should be angry. If I feel depressed, I should act depressed. But that's foolish. If I act depressed, I will end up feeling depressed, like many productive people whom I've counseled who retired without much to do. They got depressed. So we know that how we choose to behave creates how we feel. There are limits to this to be sure. Medications—like my steroids—can create their own emotions. And for some, major depressive episodes can be fueled by a genetically determined chemical imbalance which affects how they feel. And life's onslaughts can and do induce feelings and fantasies that are morbid. Still, we can have an intuitive, feeling sense of joy while troubled. But that kind of joy is the byproduct of character—character learned only through tough times. There's no way around that. If joy is a feeling, it is a feeling to be learned. Over the years, I've learned joy.

Steroids or not, depressed or not—as a feeling state, joy is the deep satisfaction that arises out of a set of goals that excites our passions and mobilizes our skills on behalf of a vision. Like flowers emerging from the soil reaching for the light of day, joy emerges from the soil of a purpose-driven life reaching for the light of truth—whether in good times or bad. It flows naturally from the content of character that we build and the richness of meaning that arises from that character. That hard work of building character and imputing meaning—and all the skills we learn to do that work—induces a feeling of fulfillment that is our joy. It's similar to gratitude that way. The apostle wrote, "In everything give thanks . . ." (1 Thess. 5:18, NAS). We don't give thanks for everything, but *in* everything. The same thing for joy. Joy springs neither from happy times nor troubled waters, neither from winning the lottery nor being raped. It's what we do with those experiences that creates joy. The fact is, one can be happy without having joy. And one can have joy without being happy. While joy can be wrapped around happy moments, it is bigger, deeper, and wider than happy. Happiness is like the bubbles in a glass of champagne: delightful to the palate for the moment. But joy is like the air we breathe, giving and sustaining life itself.

Joy through the Dark Night of the Soul

I've been fortunate to have had innumerable moments of circumstantial happiness in my life. And don't get me wrong, I'm all for feeling happy. I'd be an idiot and a masochist to think otherwise. I have fun sailing with Mom and my friends. And one would hope, as the apostle John did, that in our new universe to come, life's troubled times will be destroyed. In that unimaginable renovation, happiness and joy become one. That's because character and meaning and happy times become integrated. The universe will no longer be split into good versus evil or happy versus troubled.

I've had a lot of fun and many moments of happiness both as a child and with Mom and you guys: discovering the sweet smile of a little girl at age four on my first day in kindergarten; throwing the ball with my dad; going to Frontier Town as a little guy with my parents; hiking and camping with Uncle Herb; playing the guitar; sharing Mass with dear friends before school; snowshoeing in the Adirondacks; encountering a beautiful young woman of impeccable character as soon as I got to college; working on campus projects with my fraternity brothers; driving my Tank; bowling, skiing, and driving fast with my good buddy; the many fireside chats out on the farm; leg wrestling with your mom when we were once young and strong; playing Ping-Pong; sledding with you guys at night by flashlight down the hill at Illicks Mill Park when you were little; and chasing my grandchildren around the house acting nutty as the "Grampy Monster." Incredibly, the list could go on and on at great length. But this letter was not intended to be a catalog of those fun moments; it was to put on display my journey of faith. But that goes to the point. We think of fun and happy moments as joy. But I'm not writing about fun and being happy. I am writing about having joy in my faith journey. And the fact is, my joy is not the same as fun and happy.

I said I enjoyed the sweet smile of a little girl at age four in kindergarten, and I did. That moment was what it was: a four-year-old little boy discovering girls. It was happy. But it was more than that.

It was the sweet smile from a very young "woman"—a smile I never got from my mother. The meaning of that little girl's smile stirred a rich depth of feeling that would not have been there except for my traumatizing relationship with my mother. The meaning of that moment went far beyond discovering girls to discovering that a woman, however young, could be warm. And that sweet little lady became an imprint. That imprint set up my draw to that young woman Marie in college; she too was warm. And that set me up for marrying your mom; and she is warm. Incredible, isn't it? The content of my character in relationship to women, the fullness of meaning in my relationship to your mom, and the very contours of my family life were set in motion by that little girl at age four. That full depth of meaning with that little woman, and with it, the intuitive feeling of joy, emerged precisely because of the depth of loss with my mother. I have never forgotten that little girl's warm, innocent smile. And I am forever grateful because that smile forged a depth of meaning that became the platform for my choice of, and my life with, your mom. In that way, one little girl's smile was transformative and has been my lifelong joy. Unbelievable. So joy can—and, for me, did—emerge from trauma. In doing so, joy is so much deeper and wider than happy, wrapping itself in and around the more "normal" moments of happiness—like discovering girls.

I would submit that I also discovered joy—and the joy of the Lord—through the despairing moments of my own suicidal fantasies. Obviously, that struggle was neither fun nor happy. However, through it, I was liberated further from life's nonsense. Here's how.

As I already noted, I learned where my emotional breaking point was—and honed my skills to master that breaking point and then go beyond it. In doing so, I learned more about myself and the human condition. But far beyond that, I came to grips with my inner demand to put life—and my heavenly Father's behavior—on my terms. I let that demand go. I didn't want to. I didn't like my Father's behavior. And still don't, frankly. I don't like my Pops' emotional ability to stand by while all hell breaks loose on planet Earth. It doesn't resonate with me or most people I've met. I know—my Father didn't stand by: He sent his one and only Son. But that's never been satisfying enough. A two-thousand-year-old story didn't relieve me of my misery. But—like Job, I've matured. I've learned to accept my place in the universe more. I am neither God nor God's judge. So I let my demand go. That is my joy.

But how? How in the world can that be thought of as joy? Isn't that just biting the bullet? Isn't that an unconditional surrender to life's nonsense? Isn't that like someone coming to understand, accept, and having sympathy for an abuser's point of view—in this case God—while the abuser holds the person hostage to the fear of more abuse? In my profession, we call that "identification with the aggressor." Isn't calling all that "joy" just a foolish reframe on a most pathetic and desperate situation?

I could be fooling myself, Kid, but I don't think I am. While I did bite the bullet, in doing so I also chose to do what Jesus had done. If sweating blood before his crucifixion and then crying out to his Father during it "My God, my God, why have you abandoned me?" is any indication, Jesus had joined all of us in questioning our Father's game plan.

Jesus wanted out of his "troubles" in the Garden of Gethsemane:

> He said to them, "My heart is full of sorrow, to the point of death. Stay here and watch with me."
>
> After walking a little farther away from them, Jesus fell to the ground and prayed, "My Father, if it is possible, do not give me this cup of suffering. But do what you want, not what I want." (Matt. 26:38–39, NCV)

In that garden, Jesus was terrified . . . and, if we don't downplay his reaction, wanted out. Later, on the cross, he cried out in agony—citing one of the psalms he had so deeply internalized—passionately and desperately wondering why his own Father was abandoning him. If we don't trivialize his humanity, in the horrific pain of the moments sliding toward his demise, Jesus was genuinely in deep emotional and spiritual anguish wondering where the heck his own Pops was. I could identify; I wasn't the only one to wonder.

But Jesus ultimately bowed his knee to his Father's plan. I had to do the same.

Let me be clear. When I say I learned my place in the universe, I am not saying I was ashamed of questioning my heavenly Father. I frankly wasn't. Keeping such questions buried would just have fed my depression—and, with it, my suicidal craving. The fact is, Job had the wisdom to put all his questions out on the table. I followed his lead. So, instead, what I am saying is that I have learned to let go of my inner demand to have life—and my Father—on my terms. I let go of quietly expecting the flow of life to go where I thought it should. And I let go of expecting my Father to intervene on my behalf in ways that I thought any reasonable God should. I do consider that growth. And it is growth precisely because neither of my parents ever got there. Both of them secretly demanded life on their terms—and they never gave that demand up. They froze. So they could not move on and create a meaningful life for themselves. Built into any alcoholic's unspoken attitude is the refusal to obey nature, the refusal to deal with life on life's terms—and the refusal to deal with life on our Father's terms. Any twelve-step program, including Alcoholics Anonymous, stands on that core truth. The same thing with my father's chain-smoking and mindless obsession with exercise while neglecting me. To Job's credit, he asked "our Father who art in heaven" the tough questions. Then he dealt with the tough answers back. So did I. Doing so was my liberation from my parents' disillusionment and bitterness. It was my freedom from my own understandable demand to have the fullness of resurrection life now . . . in my lifetime . . . on my terms. Unlike my parents, letting go of my demand to have life on my terms set me free to move on. If I hadn't, my suicide would have been, among other things, my psyche frozen in my demand. I'd go down shaking my fist. Just like your grandmother. And just like your grandfather. But I wasn't going to repeat my parents' mistake. I followed Jesus instead: not my will, but my Pops'. That was my maturing—my further liberation—and it was precisely that kind of growth in Christ that was my joy.

Surely, one has to have eyes looking through a very different lens from this culture's in order to see all this—especially to see this in the middle of one's own dark night of the soul . . . much like using infrared night goggles by which to navigate in the pitch blackness of the night.

Joy—And Feeling God

Unlike my parents, I chose not to freeze in my demand. I moved on.

I moved on to keep on learning to love. And if joy and love are intimately tied together—as they were for the apostle Paul (Phil. 4:1)—then I've also felt the joy of the Lord through community. If we succeed enough in getting our collective acts together, then we have a shot at feeling God's love through one another. Gratefully, those around me have succeeded enough; I have tasted God's love. My friendships in the Koinonia church, Inter-Varsity Christian Fellowship, the daughter church in Philadelphia, its mother church in Oreland, and our present church of over thirty-five years have all been sources of love and joy. And whatever the challenges, my friendships with Mom and you guys have filled me with love—and therefore, joy.

Beyond feeling human love, I have had that inimitable encounter with the Spirit of Jesus where ecstatic feelings of joy cascaded through my psyche for hours. But—I hate to say—beyond that one time in my youth, I join Mother Theresa. I have since never felt God's love one-on-one, God-to-man, heavenly Pops-to-earthly son. Never. Like your grandmother, like Mother Theresa, like so many others on this planet, I just never did. Whether any of us like it or not—and I sure don't—that's the way it has been. The fact is, my most powerful feelings since my youthful encounter with the Spirit of Jesus have been the mind-bending hormonal cascades of a decade of steroid use for my life-threatening asthma. Not God. Steroids. And steroids made me feel lousy. Just lousy. I felt so bad, so down, and so agitated, day after day I could have chewed bullets for lunch.

Many contemporary Christians might think something's wrong with my spirituality. Both leaders and laity tend to focus on feeling God. Folks come out of worship services saying they felt the Lord and therefore—therefore—it was a good worship service. If the aesthetics of worship feel good to them—whether traditional organ hymns or ear-ringing contemporary music—then the Lord

was present. If not, then he wasn't there. At least not enough, as if
he were a quantity of feelings to be experienced. If I borrow that
logic, then I still "feel the Lord" in ornate, Gothic architecture and
old Latin hymns. But that's not true; all I'm feeling are the aesthetics. God is not especially present in ornate architecture or in
the Latin language. Besides, the universe in now his temple—not
some architecture made with human hands. Unfortunately, with its
strong emphasis on feelings, contemporary Christianity is danger-
ously misleading—and I see the results behind closed doors. Instead
of chasing the winds of secular pleasures to make themselves feel
happy, many Christians chase the spiritual winds of trying to feel
Jesus. But, as one seminary professor suggested, maybe Jesus isn't to
be felt. Maybe he is to be lived (Rom. 12:1; 1 Pet. 2:5).

Have you ever wondered what the "joy of the Lord" meant for
the Lord himself? Just what was the Lord's joy? That is, what meaning did the word "joy" have for him? What was Jesus' feeling of joy?
And when he wept over Jerusalem; when he raged against corrupt
religious leaders; when he was rejected and despised; when he sweat
blood in terror of his own coming crucifixion; when he suffocated
to death on the cross—what did he specifically feel? Have you ever
noticed: There isn't even one reference to Jesus laughing in the gospels? Not that he didn't. But we'd never know it from the story. We
have: "Jesus wept." But we don't have: "Jesus laughed." Still, would
anyone dare say that the Lord was morbidly preoccupied with the
tough side of life? Would anyone say he was feeling too maudlin?
Would anyone say he felt too depressed or too melancholic—and
needed medication? Would anyone challenge Jesus that he somehow missed out on feeling the joy of his own Father in his own
"troubled" times?

So, joy—the kind the Lord had—can permeate a life that is circumstantially, and even emotionally, miserable. But for me, such
joy required a big vision and an incredible amount of practice. It
required a set of skills I didn't get growing up. Though it was and
continues to be tough work, the good news is that I and anyone else
can have such joy while being depressed, or suffering flashbacks
from PTSD, or going through the dark night of the soul. If anyone
had divine joy, it had to be Jesus. But our own Lord had the joy of
his Father while he bowed the knee to his Father's plan—bowing
his knee to his own crucifixion . . . bowing his knee to his own dark

night of the soul. But in our culture, that is simply an oxymoron. It's stupid. Nevertheless, like Jesus, we can learn joy in and through any variation—any—of the dark night of the soul. That's precisely because joy is ultimately a way of life. In everything, the apostle Paul noted, give thanks. By extension, in everything, learn joy—for this is the will of God in Christ Jesus concerning you (1 Thess. 5:18). This posture—this way of life—is really so odd in our culture, both secular and Christian. But it is a way of living that stirs the deep hope within us that just maybe, in the end, we will not be disappointed by our Father . . . just as Jesus wasn't disappointed on the third day after he cried out on the cross, "My God, my God, why have you abandoned me?" (Rom. 5:5; 12:12; 15:13).

Seizing My Days in Hope

The tagline from the *Astronaut Farmer* "If we don't have our dreams, we have nothing,"* is accurate—except when dreams are done being dreams because they've come true. If I were to die tonight, I will have died a rich man. One key dream, among others, has been fulfilled. I have loved and been loved. The apostle Paul noted, "So these three things continue forever: faith, hope, and love. And the greatest of these is love" (1 Cor. 13:13, NCV). And so it is. I love your mom, you guys, my grandchildren, my dear friends, and my heavenly Father. In ways that mattered, but different from loving you, I have also loved my parents; I think you know what I mean. I've loved my brothers, with special gratitude to your Uncle Herb. I thank you guys—and my dear friends—for loving me. Love is indeed the greatest . . . and certainly the most powerful dynamic on the planet.

But what do we do when dreams remain unfulfilled?

At the heart of as yet unfulfilled dreams is hope. While joy is the engine that drives seizing our days, hope is the engine that drives our dreams that shape those days. I've been driven by hope since reading the indulgences on the last page of my Baltimore Catechism as a boy—the hope of finding the truth. That hope fueled my newfound faith. And it drove my passion to love. I've strongly identified with the Colossian Christians that way:

> You have this faith and love *because of your hope*, and what you hope for is kept safe for you in heaven. You learned about this hope when you heard the message about the truth, the Good News . . . (Col. 1:5, NCV; italics mine)

You have this faith and love because—*because*—of your hope.

---

* "The Astronaut Farmer."

Like the Colossian Christians, after I heard the message about the truth—the Good News that Jesus had come back to life—my hopes, big and small, were radically mobilized. The big cosmic hope hidden and kept safe for me in Jesus magnetically drew me forward through all my smaller hopes of living a life of faith and love from day to day, month to month, and year to year.

As the apostle Paul noted in his letter to the church at Rome, a way to keep that hope in Jesus growing is through the hard work of building character. You read what he wrote already, but here it is again:

We also have joy with our troubles, because we know that these troubles produce patience. And patience produces character, and *character produces hope*. And this hope will never disappoint us. . . . (Rom. 5:3–5a, NCV; italics mine)

We're back to that theme: building character. For the apostles, character fuels not only faith, joy, and love, but also hope. I find that truth not only strange but somewhat mysterious. How is it that character builds these qualities in us, including hope? The apostle James does say that without growth in character, faith becomes hollow, even "dead" (James 2:17). Without character, joy is indeed reduced to happiness. Without character, love becomes a fickle feeling; it loses both spine and perspective. And, incredibly, without character we also lose the hope of where we are going in life . . . and of where this universe is going.

Maybe I'm wrong, Kid, but I think hope without that hard work of building character makes one simply a dreamer—anchorless and lazy and irrelevant to the real flow of life's vicissitudes. And hard work without hope makes one lost, blind, tired, depressed, and anxious—all wrapped in utter despair. Just like your grandparents. Your grandparents did work hard at life. But they worked blind. Yes, your grandfather did have the hope of getting better. But his hope wasn't realistic. Besides, he and my mom both blinded themselves to the actual hard work at hand: to create new dreams with new meaning centered on learning new ways to love one another and their children. That failure to love—that failure to build more character in the face of tough circumstances—fueled their despair.

In a concentration camp during World War II, Victor Frankl, a psychiatrist and prisoner of the camp, gave himself meaning by observing others. He noticed that those who loved—those who shared their meager bread and broth with others—tended to live longer than those who stole bread. Their love for others forged hope. That hope kept many of them alive long enough to see freedom. (Based on what he saw, Frankl launched a therapy focusing on meaning and hope, called Logotherapy.) So, unlike your grandfather, I do *not* get my hope from some vision to conquer my auditory disability. I do not envision that my ears will ever allow me to be free of my chains. I have accepted the fact that medical science isn't there yet, and my heavenly Father has chosen not to get me there. Instead, unlike my parents, my vision for the future remains the same as that of my youth: to build character so I may love. I choose to continue to learn to love you guys, your mom, my friends, and my clients—to share my bread and broth with all of you—and letting that love fuel my hope in Jesus. Sadly, my parents never did that.

Though I am in the last big phase of my life—and the law of sin and death threatens to undo me further—I continue to dream dreams. I hope I have enough health remaining for enough years ahead to bring my golf game into the low eighties. How's that for dreaming! My friends would no doubt confirm that that is indeed a dream—a pipe dream. I want more years with your mom, sailing our Flying Scot together. I want time with you guys and my precious grandchildren—time to teach my grandchildren how to sail, build model rockets, share my love of science and discovery, and talk about who Jesus is to me. I want to see your families prosper and my grandchildren grow up to age fifteen or twenty. Heck, I'll take as many years as I can get . . . as long as I'm not flat on my back in some nursing home. I'd also like to write more; I have several books in my head. I love to teach, so I hope I can do more of that. And I have my practice—where I absolutely love what I do—which I plan on continuing until I am unable to do so.

I'd also like to raise enough money to build a motor home that is acoustically safe for people with hyperacusis. I am looking to start a fund for this purpose, so keep in touch with my website for developments on that. A motor home would likely have to have a double suspension system that would isolate vibration enough to make it safe traveling. We think of Bose as being in the business of making sound equipment, like my noise-cancelling headphones. However, Bose has also designed a sophisticated electromagnetic suspension system for cars that could offer a lot of hope for those of us with hyperacusis. But, for whatever reasons, the company has delayed bringing it to market. Still, such a motor home would take big bucks.

Then there's my big hope.

I have this ritual: As I shower in the morning, I remind myself what the game of life is about from my Father's point of view. Flowing from that, I ponder how I can best love those entrusted to my care. However well or however poorly I perform, I do set my day that way. Admittedly, the scientist in me is forever frustrated that I will never have any new information to throw into the mix for my daydreaming about Jesus and his coming back from the dead. Still, however odd it may seem and however obsessive it is, after all these decades, I note the resurrection to myself daily in that shower. I often flash to what the apostle Paul said in passing in his letter to the church at Corinth: that many in the hearing of his letter would appreciate what he was saying because the risen Jesus had appeared to over five hundred of them. Over five hundred . . . incredible. Such an offhanded comment anchors my days and draws me forward. Don't get me wrong. I still wonder at times if I am the village idiot for trusting such a comment. A dear friend of mine who is an ardent atheist has clearly and unequivocally told me that I am. He believes that my belief in Jesus is irrational. And the content of my belief is utter nonsense. I understand . . . and have told him so. I have also told him that his belief—standing on Ayn Rand and the objectivist philosophy she founded—is *not* nonsense. It's not. But I've made clear that his belief about the human condition is too short-sighted and simplistic. Still, I wonder. And, along with that, I wonder if, like so many other Christians on the planet, I am a transitional person in the history of our global culture: going from ancient religious beliefs to a full secularization of the mind. That's happening already in Europe—and happening fast. And it is happening to mainline denominations in our own country. But, as you already know, that's me . . . eccentric, scientific, always-willing-to-talk, always-wondering me. I'll die this way.

Some Christians would perhaps want to rescue me from my divided psyche; I may be too double-minded for them. My faith isn't clean enough or singularly uncomplicated enough. But I really don't need rescue from it. My split mind is not only "diagnostic" of me but also of life. My mind is split because life is split: good versus evil; God versus Satan; the good side of my parents versus the disordered side of my parents; the beauty of nature versus the violence of nature; life as celebration versus life as a struggle for survival; living while dying; "God is love" yet "you'd never know it by the way life treats you." As I noted at the beginning of this long letter, I never bargained for this journey. Long before I had a choice, I was thrown into this spiritual maelstrom—and this letter has been about that storm and what I've done with it. Like so many, I've done the best I could with what I've had. And I have used my unchosen split psyche as a tool—hopefully to my and others' advantage.

The doubting Thomas in me has always anchored me in the evidence. Yet—the believer in me has always challenged the doubting Thomas in me with the possibility of the unbelievable.* Ever since my encounter with that last page of the Baltimore Catechism, I have challenged myself to think outside the box. But to think outside my tiny world—while demanding evidence to climb out—creates tension. Enormous tension. It just does; all paradigms open to new evidence do. I have and will always live with tension.

The fact is, the whole universe is in tension . . . waiting for its freedom.

This tension—along with the threats and insecurities and fears that such tension brings—makes life an adventure. It is life's dynamic edge. It keeps pushing one to explore. To discover. To fight for truth. In that context, then, how can a vibrant relationship with Jesus Christ not be tense? Here I am, standing on a two-thousand-year-old story . . . of a single man . . . on a single pale blue dot . . . in a virtually infinite universe . . . who a handful of people say came back to life to transform that universe. And in that transformation, I will be completely recreated from nothing. Wow! Talk about tense. That is one large dream driven by one large hope grounded in one outrageous story. So, I must join the apostle Paul; I have to. Either I am indeed an idiot as my dear atheist friend fondly thinks—and my faith is in vain—or my heavenly Pops really pulled off the unthinkable in defeating evil and death, making Jesus, as inscribed on his royal robe, the King of kings and Lord of lords! (Rev. 19:16).

---

*For my further commentary on "Believing the Unbelievable," go to my website www.peakperformancediscipleship.com.

So this is my final dream: When Jesus as Lord brings this universe back to my Father, I wake from death to see my Pops running to greet me with open arms. As he gives me one big bear hug, he kisses me on my cheek and whispers, "Welcome home, my good and faithful son. Welcome home . . . at last."

Well, there it is, Kid.

On Easter, I love to listen to the "Hallelujah Chorus" on my iPad or from a church service on television. It so movingly captures the singular reality of Jesus as Lord. I get a little choked up every time I listen to it. Would you please join me in worship by listening to the rendition sung by the choir of King's College (November 10, 2009, is especially moving)? May the grand perspective of that "Hallelujah" chorus pour the prophet Isaiah's "oil of joy" over both you and me, stirring within us the most outrageous hope on the planet—the hope of the resurrection . . . and with it, the death of Death.

Love you, Hon,
Dad

My Mom and Dad

He has sent me to bestow on them a crown of beauty
instead of ashes, the oil of joy instead of mourning, and
a garment of praise instead of a spirit of despair.
They will be called oaks of righteousness. . . .

(Isa. 61:1–3)

Carpe Diem

ABOUT THE AUTHOR

Frank Barbehenn is a licensed psychologist in Bethlehem, Pennsylvania, and has been in practice for thirty-five years, from 1980 to the present. Before his training as a psychologist, Frank was theologically trained for three years at Westminster Theological Seminary in Philadelphia, Pennsylvania, from 1974 to 1977. He did not go to seminary to enter the pastorate but to sort out his personal faith and ultimately integrate the Bible with psychology. Prior to seminary, he had been trained in his first love, physics, for four years at Clarkson University, formerly the Clarkson College of Technology, from 1969 to 1973.

Frank is a Clinical Fellow with the American Association for Marriage and Family Therapy and a Fellow with the American Psychotherapy Association. While he has a general practice, he specializes in relationship and trauma therapy, as well as the integration of faith and the Bible with the tough issues he faces clinically.

He is an elder at First Presbyterian Church of Bethlehem, Pennsylvania, and serves on the Permanent Judicial Committee of the Presbytery. He has been a middle school and high school teacher, as well as adjunct faculty in psychology at the college level. He has led seminars, year-long discipleship programs, and church committees and has also taught adult education.

Frank is a father of three—Paul, Matt, and Kristen—and the proud grandfather of three (as of this writing): Dylan, Hannah, and Leah. He loves to sail and play golf, along with launching model rockets with his grandchildren and chasing them around the house as the "Grampy Monster."

Finally, Frank is the survivor of multiple traumas, including emotional trauma at the hands of his own parents, beginning in infancy.